A SHORT HISTORY OF SPANISH MUSIC

A
SHORT
HISTORY
OF
SPANISH
MUSIC

Ann Livermore

DUCKWORTH

First published in 1972 by
Gerald Duckworth & Company Limited
The Old Piano Factory
43 Gloucester Crescent, London NW1

© 1972 by Ann Livermore

ISBN 0 7156 0634 4

Printed in Great Britain by
Western Printing Services Ltd, Bristol

CONTENTS

LIST OF ILLUSTRATIONS vii

PREFACE ix

I   Early Spanish Music 1

II Music of Muslim Spain and the Northern Kingdoms 24

III Music of the Restoration and Hapsburg Expansion 48

IV Music and the Spanish Drama 92

V   Music under Bourbon Rule 109

VI Spanish Popular Music 141

VII 'Spanish Music with vistas towards Europe' 179

VIII Spanish Music in Latin America 219

GLOSSARY 245

BIBLIOGRAPHY 254

INDEX 256

LIST OF ILLUSTRATIONS

I*a* Statue of Mercury with ten-string lyre, from the Temple
   of Mithras at Mérida   *facing page* 54

 b Detail from above   54

II The Shahrud, from the Kitāb-al-mūsīqī of Al-Fārābī
   (d. 950)   55

III Musicians, from the Beato de Liébana (786), copied in 1047   55

IV Orchestra of Angels: Morisco decorative art of the
   Aragonese School (1390)   86

V Alfonso X dictating the first *Cantiga de Santa María*   87

VI *Cantigas de Santa María*. Five groups of Musicians, redrawn from the Escorial MS. for J. F. Riaño: *Early
   Spanish Music*   182

VII Home of the Zarzuela   183

VIII A Family Concert: sketch by Casanovas (late 18th century) 183

IX Francisco Guerrero   214

X Fernando Contreras   214

XI Cristóbal Morales   214

XII Isaac Albéniz, aged 17   215

XIII Enrique Granados   215

XIV Manuel de Falla   215

XV Joaquín Rodrigo   215

PREFACE

The direction of my steps to the study of Spanish music was so singularly guided by kindness that I must both in justice and gratitude record the names of those who helped me. To the Spanish ambassador in London, Merry del Val, who gave me my first introductions to musicians in his own country; to Pablo Casals who drew the attention of Granados's friends to my first article on the composer's music, thus opening many doors to me and first of all, his own home at San Salvador; to Manuel de Falla and his sister, doña Maria del Carmen, for courtesies of the rarest nature; to Joaquín Rodrigo and his wife, doña Victoria, who generously offered me the joy of performing with them in Spain; to Arturo Saco del Valle, master of the royal chapel; to Fernández Arbós, genial conductor of the Orquesta Sinfónica; to Mgr Higinio Anglés who, unasked, brought to my student's desk in Barcelona manuscript treasures from his Catalan archives; to Eduardo Toldrá who volunteered to accompany a programme of Catalan lyrics; to Baltasar Samper whose keen intelligence focused my awareness on Mallorcan influences; to Miguel Llobet, who showed me all his programmes and then played me the items from those I wanted; to Ignacio Tabuyo, singing-master to the royal palace of Madrid and professor of the Real Conservatorio, who taught me that there still remains a strongly entrenched conservative musical taste in Spain which is not to be despised by youth in a hurry to join the progressives; to Conchita Badía, purely dedicated to the higher expression of Spanish song and to that unaltered transmission of every detail of Granados' art, not always preserved in the printing of his scores to all these and to many other musicians in various parts of Spain who enlarged my understanding of their arts and music, I remain incalculably indebted. It was Manuel de Falla's introductory note to Igor Stravinsky in Paris that led me there to study Latin American music with the Brazilian interpreter of Stravinsky's scores, Vera Janacopoulos, and to some familiarity with the effervescing aesthetics of students who made up a Latin American quartier of their own, and enabled me to renew those early contacts with South American life first met in my own family, which, as I now

Preface

perceive, stirred my imaginative longing even in kindergarten days to enter this unique and fascinatingly wide world of Spanish music.

ANN LIVERMORE

Vancouver
November 1971

CHAPTER I

Early Spanish Music

Those who go to Spain in search of *alegría* and the musical expression of its joy will find expectancy confirmed throughout a millennium and a half of history and in more ways than may have been supposed. In the time of Visigothic rule the climax of musical creativity centred on those jubilatory alleluias whose lengthy fervour and exuberant expression of early Christian joy surprise more sober minds today. Muslim Spain's insistence on lively rhythms, emphasised with every device of instrumental punctuation, passed into peninsular lore and remained when Muslims disappeared from view. Alfonso X's *Cantigas de Santa María* stress that it is with alegría that our praises to the Virgin 'Rose of beauty and semblance, flower of joy and pleasure' should be created. The pilgrimage to Santiago de Compostela—one of Europe's most genial inspirations—reached its climax when pilgrims passed beneath the Pórtico de Gloria sculptured with a crowded scene of players whose symphony of welcome anticipates the choirs and consorts tuning up within.

The Spanish Restoration was not a dream of aesthetic beauty reflected in renaissance polished minds, but a century of thanksgiving, of psalms, Te Deums thundered on the organ, old romances sung in victorious celebrations of covenants and vows upheld through centuries of frontier war, and ballads shortly to be tuned to new songs in a strange land, as Psalm 137 had promised. The 16th century was not complete until its higher task had been recorded in the works of Cabezón, Morales, Guerrero and Victoria as these finally dispersed the excessive Muslim mourning over death—which Christian Spain had long disapproved—and left in its place the musical testament of a spiritual world that Spaniards recreated, lived and breathed in, and inhabit positively still.

This restoration now assured, musicians found a welcome waiting from writers in the theatre, especially for their interludes and alegría of dance and song, and when the high tide of drama receded, musicians showed the liveliness of miniature form, through fragmentations of that golden period to which composers still return to drink its springs of happy natural inspiration. It was a racial determination to be cheerful in its own way that ensured the emergence and survival of the national *zarzuela* and its spoken dialogue wedded to music, for a public impatient of alien operatic formulas whose inevitable slowing of the action was intolerable to Madrid audiences notoriously impatient of impediments to the excitement of unchecked movement.

Spinoza, purifying those mingled philosophic strains he had inherited from Spanish and Portuguese medieval thought, finally told men to seek felicity. Falla's last message in a major work, the *Concerto*, leaves in what he calls 'a beautiful social utility' the assurance that *alegría* is always with us on the way of life, offering the springtime song of birds in token of perennial revival, as in the popular air 'De los álamos vengo, madre' he shares among the group of chamber players. Carlos Chávez, brilliantly exemplifying the harmonising strands of Mexican and Spanish nature, sums up his thoughts in *El Pensamiento Musical* by insisting that the joy of life is in this creation of alegría. 'There are many things that may be simulated, but not true joy. The miracle of art is in the proportioning of joy and felicity that nothing can destroy, and which raise and edify life perpetually.'

The traditional forms of Spanish musical expression remain few and clearly delineated, a sign of constant communal participation, from the dance as celebrated in Roman times to the song which is communally preserved, as from the time of Isidore's hymns of praise created first in Seville. The shortest form of song practised in Spain is the *alegría* of alternating five- and ten-syllable lines.

Spaniards have remained uniquely faithful to Augustine's advice in *De Musica* that men may most profitably exercise this art in the lesser forms of dance and song, and it is because they have cultivated these forms that their vital sense of joy has been preserved intact. Proof of this may be heard in those translations of its elements through Spanish-speaking spheres in America, where their unaltered transference remains a miracle of instinctive art. Latin Americans, like their peninsular ancestors, still practise that musical art defined in *De Musica*: 'knowing how to make controlled variations of sound correctly . . . and especially those movements which are an end in themselves, and exist for their own beauty or for the pleasure which they cause, not for some end external to themselves. Movements of long duration, for example of an hour or more, are not adjusted to our immediate sensibility. Music, making her way forth from some most intimate core of being, has left her footprints, both on our senses and on the objects of our sensations. We should follow these footprints to arrive at that most intimate core,

for that is the only way; and to do so, we must neglect the longer intervals of time, and confine ourselves to those which are shorter, of
lengths that occur in performances of song and dance.' Like the so-
called 'colonial' architecture, Spanish American music has inherited
some deeply-rooted concepts from the world of classical antiquity.

The appearance of hunters and scenes of dancing depicted on cave
walls through the Spanish Levant suggests to some archaeologists that
the bow played a part in music-making here as it did among those
Rhodesian Africans who were related by culture to primitive peoples
in the peninsula. These archers are to be seen at Terelló (Tarragona), in
Morella la Vieja, in the Barranco de los Gascones near Teruel, in the
cave of los Caballos, at Valltorta, Albocácer, Castellón de la Plana and
in a war scene at Les Dogues. There are scenes presumably of dancers
in the cave of la Saltadora and in a fresco at Cogul, near Lérida, though
here there are signs which show that these drawings are not all of the
same epoch. Musically, such evidence is barely circumstantial, however.

More concrete evidence that palaeolithic man blew and whistled is
provided by the examination in the cave of Aigues Vives near Solsona,
of perforated objects such as shells, which by their size may have been
strung as collars. Another shell, in the cave of Zajara, near Almería,
belongs to the Aurignacian period in the early stages of the upper
palaeolithic period and may have been perforated for use in pairs as a
primitive kind of castanet. Long horns with stylised ornamentation,
such as those in the Cuento de la Mina in Asturias, could have been
calling-horns when perforated or used as a castanet when struck with
bone or stick. Perforated amulets were also capable of yielding sound,
suggesting an association of supernatural powers with primitive music.
An example, possibly of the calling-horn, from the cave of Rasines,
Santander, is now in the Hispanic Society of America's museum.

The isolation of prehistoric Spain was ended only in neolithic times
when the early civilisations of the Near East spread westwards by way
of the Mediterranean islands or North Africa, founding the primitive
cities of Almería. The copper and bronze cultures of Almería spread
westwards into the valleys of the Guadalquivir and Tagus and northwards up the eastern coast. In this way influences from Syria and Egypt
were felt, and after 1000 B.C. the Phoenicians at Cádiz were in direct
contact with the native state of Tartessos, near the mouth of the
Guadalquivir. Rather later, Celtic peoples began to enter the peninsula
by crossing the Pyrenees. Some of these Celts settled in the region of
the Ebro and intermingled with the native Iberians to form the Celtiberian federation. Of these people Strabo mentions that they worshipped the moon, celebrating the full moon by dancing until dawn

outside the doors of their houses. Celtic dances, songs and instruments were probably in use throughout the north.

In the south, the influence of Phoenicia was followed by that of Carthage, which for a long period blocked the Straits of Gibraltar to all intruders. The Greeks, however, reached eastern Spain and planted several colonies such as that of Ampurias, where their city adjoined a native town. There is much evidence of Celtic or mingled musical interests. At Osuna reliefs show men blowing large straight trumpets: the trumpets found at Numantia in Celtiberia are probably of the 2nd century B.C. A more southern, Turdetanian, specimen of the 3rd century is circular and widens towards the bell. Iberian vases found at San Miguel de Liria display male and female dancers holding hands in an open carola preceded by a man playing a single aulos while a woman plays the double. In another ceramic fragment a young woman with floating hair, trousered, plays the double aulos with curved tubes, while a man plays either a horn or trompa, but possibly the single aulos. This fragmentary evidence is enough to suggest that a fertility ceremony is represented.

Ionic writing, important in Greek musical notation, was known in hellenistic Spain and Phocaean colonisers brought their decorative styles with scenes of war, hunting and the dance. Of Phoenician influence fewer traces are found; however, their religious rites are commemorated by inscriptions, as to Melkart (Hercules) in Cádiz. The Phrygian cult of Cybele and Attis extended the length of the levantine coast as far as Mahón and west to Mérida; both had temples in Barcelona, Gerona, Tarragona, Lisbon, Medellín, Cáceres, while in Córdoba and Italica the mysteries honoured Sabazius, their substitute for Jupiter; the Greek plaints therefore were very likely to be heard. Mithras had his Mithraeum in Mérida and was venerated as far away as Málaga. Serapis was also celebrated at Mérida, Valencia, Astorga and Ampurias. Isis held sway on the coasts, and these oriental cults extended even further than Astorga, to Lugo. Evidently music played a very varied part in attuning these many peoples to harmony divine, and it may seem accidentally symbolic that Mercury's great lyre at Mérida marks the culmination of this heterogeneous way of life. Placed in the temple dedicated to eastern divinities, it has, like the more ancient Greek lyres, a large resonating body to which are joined two twisting horns terminating in the *transtillum*.

The Carthaginians, who intervened in the 5th century B.C., left traces in Ibiza of a faun with mask and tail and in dancing posture. However, the Greeks maintained their supremacy aesthetically, as witness the decorated ceramics at Ampurias where dancing girls and instrumentalists rehearse familiar scenes; nevertheless, it was the Carthaginians who brought about the intrusion of Rome and the alteration to these mediterranean comminglings which faded away at the sound of the legions' heavy tread.

To the Roman Empire Spain contributed magnificently with its emperors, Trajan, Hadrian and Theodosius; with its Andalusian writers, Columella, Lucan and the Senecas, and more especially the Aragonese Martial, a Celtiberian from Calatayud, and Quintilian, a Basque from Calahorra. Both the latter were critical observers and it is to them that we owe those lively accounts of contemporary musical scenes that do not stale with time.

Martial describes in his epigrams the dancing girls of Cádiz whose sinuous movements graced the Roman banquets.

In contrast, he recalls the serious sounds of the *choros Rixamarum* heard along the banks of his native Ebro (IV, lv, 16).

Quintilian's *Institutio Oratoria* details the musical life of Rome, its mimes, citarists, singers and dancers whose counterparts were also to be seen in Roman Spain, such as the faun at Córdoba playing the pipes provided with a *forbeia* so as to reinforce the air; the mosaic of the sacrifice of Iphigenia at Ampurias; other faunesque dances and theatrical scenes in mosaic at Mérida and in Navarre; and the silver disc commemorating Trajan's rule, of about 388, with little cupids carrying miniature lyres, in a style whose decoration already suggests the Byzantine.

Though Christianity spread quickly, the priests did not find it easy to cut the people off from their deeply rooted pre-Christian customs. Pacian, bishop of Barcelona, who lived during most of the 4th century, found it particularly difficult to curtail the carnival festivities opening the new year, in which the dancers disguised themselves as animals like their ancestors of earlier times. His complaint was to be echoed through the centuries.

In the northern fastnesses tribal customs were less sophisticated. Strabo describes the mountaineering folk here who danced to the pipes and trumpet as leaping into the air, then crouching low (*Geography* III, iii. 7) and Silius Italicus depicts the noisy Galicians as finding enjoyment in howling the rude songs of their native tongue 'stamping the ground and clashing their shields to the beat of the music' (*Punica* III. 346–349). Still today these northerners preserve this kind of dance, to the call of the great conch or horn's notes of do, do, re flat, re flat, do,

in a 6/8 rhythm which urges them to prolong this feat of endurance till they reach exhaustion, though clashing their sticks (*palos*) till they can stand no more. However, the 'howling' is no longer heard, only the hard breathing growing louder and louder as the common will to continue holds them in its grip. Quintilian's comparisons of musical forms include those indigenous songs which even the most barbarous folk enjoy for as he points out this art is ruled by numbers (*musica ratio numerorum* IX. iv. 139), whether applied to leaps in dancing or the size of melodic intervals. Even such a primitive dance as this, with its rhythmic leaping and deliberately monotonous pattern of tonic and flattened second which is rigorously controlled and unchanging, proves that his fear for the degeneration of music does not apply to the land of his birth.

It was a Cordobese bishop, Osius, who defined the Nicene creed and it was at this time that St Leo began the organising of singing schools with the object of unifying the liturgical monody. It was at this time also that the synagogal psalm-singing and a kind of chanting were used. Spanish translations mention these canticos, psalm-hymns and spiritual songs. The aleluyas, melismas and the amen were accepted formulas of the ritual. Such melismatic traditions may have passed into folk-lore from this pre-Islamic period and are thus probably semitic in origin. Spaniards link them to those cantos aleluyaticos of which St Paul speaks.

Even the extreme west and north of the Spanish peninsula were linked at this time to the eastern practices when Orosius in the first years of the 5th century visited St Augustine, becoming his pupil, and then travelled on to Bethlehem to consult with St Jerome.

A few years earlier the Galician abbess Etheria travelled between 385 and 388[1] from this region, troubled with religious uncertainties such as Priscillianism, to make her way to Jerusalem enquiring and comparing as she went, making it her business to acquire exact knowledge of the primitive oriental liturgy and the approved organisation of monastic life. St Damasus, a Spaniard, busied himself in the ordering of the liturgy to conform with the practice of Jerusalem including the manner in which the hymns were to intervene in the service, this at the time when St Ambrose was also intent on the composition of hymns in the ritual. A little earlier Gregorius of Iliberis wrote five homilies on the Song of Songs, a source for Christian writing which was to survive and enter the main stream of Spain's literary and musical tradition. Against this background the hymns of Prudentius addressed to the Virgin Mary proved to be the most decisive influence in establishing her cult, with musical overtones that were to grow and expand through

1 *Peregrinatio Etheriae.*

6

the centuries; his example was followed by Sedulius, so that the practice became a rooted tradition.

The western frontiers of the Roman empire were overrun in the first years of the 5th century A.D., and Germanic tribes, the Sueves and Vandals, were settled in northern Portugal and Galicia. Another Germanic people, the Visigoths, entered Italy, sacked Rome and were settled around Toulouse where they intervened in the affairs of Spain. A century later, the expansion of the Franks drove them out of Toulouse and most of the tribe settled in north-central Spain, the present Castile. The Goths had their tribal heroes whom they commemorated in epics or ballads. Their singing was thought harsh and frightening to Roman ears. They amplified their war-songs by holding shields in front of their mouths. But they had been converted to Arian Christianity, and in 589 they adopted orthodox Catholicism, after which Latinised music gradually prevailed among them. Their cousins, the Ostrogoths, had occupied Italy, and the court of Theodoric the Ostrogoth at Ravenna maintained the Roman tradition; there Boethius wrote a lost treatise on music as well as his great classic, *De Consolatione Philosophiae*, and Theodoric chose a suitable musical instrument to send to the Frankish king, Clovis. In Spain, the Visigothic court at Toledo responded to Byzantine influences, but the tribal mass of homestead settlers pursued their quarrels with their neighbours and among themselves for generations.

It is to the sons of the king's functionary in the province of Cartagena that the history of Spanish music owes not only a knowledge of the past but also the laying down of guide-lines that were to determine the most decisive course of its future. The mother of Leander and Isidore was of Gothic ancestry and of the Arian faith; their father had emigrated to Baetica to escape the Byzantine seizure of Cartagena. Thus Isidore, born in 556, had evidence about him in infancy of the conflicting, unharmonised strands in the Spanish way of life, and it was not unnatural for so studiously analytical a character to set himself to the task of codifying the inheritance of the past into a universal encyclopedia as a guide and enlightenment for generations to come.

The inheritance of knowledge was already vast even in the field of music which much concerned St Isidore. Complete conformity of ritual was not established in the Roman church before the 6th century and this lack of coordination preoccupied the council of Gerona in 517, as a result of which the unification of liturgical music was ordered throughout the province of Tarragona. Except for the psalmodic melodies it is not possible to assume that the church's singing was clearly defined before the 7th century, though Gevaert believes there may be direct traces of Greek music in the Christian antiphons since the 4th. To this century possibly may be traced the *Pater noster*, traditionally said to have been sung in Visigothic Spain; in it the congregation punctuated the priest's chanting with a simple Amen, murmured on two notes.

All this musical activity called for re-assessment of the past, and St Isidore's labours, culminating in the *Etymologies*, include accounts of music's place in the classical world which since his Visigothic era have been handed down as basic principles to be consulted by every educated musician. His own position with regard to the conflicting viewpoints among classical authorities is nearer to that older tradition which drawing on Plato considered music as an adjunct to poetry; thus it was linked to grammar—that is, grammar in the wide sense meant in the schools. The Pythagorean theory of number and its application to music placed the latter in the sphere of mathematical sciences. Among the older Romans, Cicero, Varro, Seneca, Quintilian—note that two of these are from Spain—the association of music with grammar was the natural one; in the second, third and fourth centuries both traditions appear, from which time the mathematical theory was increasingly favoured, maintaining its ascendancy till the end of the middle ages. Despite his occasional definitions of music as pertaining to mathematical science, Isidore treats of the art in non-mathematical style, and various attempts have been made to find the origins of his mixed considerations. Boethius', Augustine's and Cassiodorus' music treatises have been compared with his accounts but the solution is not yet clear. Boethius' position at Theodoric's Ostrogothic court gives him a peculiar prestige in relation to Visigothic Spain and his great classic *De Consolatione Philosophiae* moved men of Isidore's days deeply, so that his work endured throughout the Dark Ages and in the early days of printing emerged into new fame on its appearance with St Thomas Aquinas' *Commentaries*, thus taking its place as a bridge between classical and Christian life. It is here that he gives his final account of music as one of those muses to turn to for consolation of the purest kind and here, in Book II, at the passage beginning 'But now tis time to take refreshment . . .' he explicitly refers to music as 'a younger daughter of our house' in relation to rhetoric, or poesy. This picture remained in men's memory when theories broke up and diminished into fragments.

It may be suggested now that this is paralleled by St Augustine's writing in the *Confessions* on music's place in the Christian world, again as handmaiden to the Word; he insists on this despite his deep love of music, and as with Boethius' pages, such personal confessions have stirred the imaginations of countless searchers after truth in many forms when arguments in treatises lie gathering cobwebs in the organ-loft.

Another Isidorean observation pertaining to music—*nisi enim ab homine memoria teneantur soni, pereunt, quia scribi non possunt*—'for unless sounds are held in men's memory they perish since they cannot be written down'—has been a cause of conjecture from Ramón de Pareja in 1482 to Mgr Higinio Anglés in our own day, some attempting to relate it to the conundrum of the uncoded Visigothic pneums of notation. Again, light may be shed on its apparent ambiguity if it is compared to Augustine's authority, and again, not to his treatises, but to that portion of his *Confessions* where he breaks off his personal narrative to enter into argument on the means to secure the Church's foundation on earth, going on from the enumeration of all those forms of created life placed here by divine will to that consideration of time's relation to eternity in which his chosen illustration becomes that of music and the part played by memory in the recollection of song. Augustine's theory of time and eternity has not yet been superseded and it is not perhaps surprising that Abbot Suger, in reconstructing the abbey church of St Denis from which the Gothic image throughout Europe was to take shape, drew on its strenuous argument and superb textual illustration of biblical commentary for inspiration in his novel construction. Possibly it should be considered now among those influences which formed Isidore's conceptual views in the musical world and even in the masterminding of the *Etymologies'* accounting for universal human activities, adapted from classical collections of information to the Christian world.

It is in Book XII of the *Confessions* that this relation of time in eternity, as time past present, time present present, and time present future is concerned with the example of sound and the function of memory, as 'For each sound so soon as made, passeth away, nor canst thou find ought to recall and by art to compose'; this is so close to Isidore's enigmatic observation that all this passage should be considered in relation to his musical ideas, beginning with: 'And who, again, is of so sharp-sighted understanding, as to be able without great pains to discern, how the sound is therefore before the tune; because a tune is a formed sound; and a thing not formed may exist; whereas that which existeth not, cannot be formed. Thus is the matter before the thing made; not because it maketh it, seeing itself is rather made; nor is it before by interval of time; for we do not first in time utter formless sounds without singing, and subsequently adapt or fashion them into the form of a chant, as wood or silver, whereof a chest or vessel is fashioned. For such materials do by time also precede the forms of the things made of them, but in singing it is not so; for when it is sung, its sound is heard; for there is not first a formless sound, which is afterwards formed into a chant.' Here follows the parallel to Isidore already quoted, and this is then followed by 'So then the chant is concentrated in its sound, which sound of his is his matter. And this indeed is formed, that it may be a tune; and therefore (as I said) the matter of the sound is before the form of the tune; not before, through any power it hath to make it tune; for a sound is no way the workmaster of the tune; but is something corporeal, subjected to the soul which singeth, whereof to make a tune. Nor is it first in time; for it is given forth together with the tune; nor first in choice, for a sound is not better than a tune, a tune being not only a sound, but a beautiful sound. But it is first in original, because a tune receives not form to become a sound, but a sound receives a form to become a tune. By this example, let him that is able understand how the matter of things was first made, and called heaven and earth, because heaven and earth were made out of it . . .'

Great importance was given to chanting and hymn singing in the Visigothic church and these were documented with remarkable care. Leander, Isidore's brother, companion to the future Pope Gregory during their stay in Byzantium (579–582), composed much music for Office and Mass, with great skill and taste according to Isidore. At the various centres, Toledo, Seville, Saragossa, Braga, there were clusters of composers at work. Eugenius II (d. 657), Ildephonsus (d. 667), and Julian (d. 690) at Toledo were associated with these and the brothers John and Braulio were in charge at Saragossa; Braulio also completed Isidore's last labours at the *Etymologies*. Conantius (d. 639), bishop of Palencia, newly recast many old tunes. Music by Rogatus of Baeza is included in the *Antiphoner* of León, which contains chants attributed to Isidore, Ildephonsus, and to Julian of Toledo. This century saw Visigothic coordination and organising power at its height.

In the light of the close connections between Visigothic Spain and the Augustinian sphere of influence the context of Isidore's definition of music is significant. 'Music is the practical knowledge of melody, consisting of sound and song . . . ' 'Since sound is a thing of sense it passes along into past time and it is impressed on the memory. From this it was pretended by the poets that the Muses were the daughters of Jupiter and Memory. For unless sounds are held in the memory by man they perish, because they cannot be written . . . Without music there can be no perfect knowledge, for there is nothing without it. For even the universe itself is said to have been put together with a certain harmony of sounds, and the very heavens revolve under the guidance of harmony.' A further association with Augustine's comparison of the creation of heaven and earth out of matter to tune taking shape from sound is thus apparent here. The analysis of music's parts—*harmonica, rhythmica, metrica*—contains an echo of the earlier Augustinian general

10

Early Spanish Music

definition in Isidore's 'Song is the modulation of the voice, for sound is unmodulated, and sound precedes song'.

In addition to the 6th century Visigothic view of classical precedent we are given precious descriptions of contemporary musical taste. 'In North Africa it is not the custom to sing alleluias every day of the year, but only on Sundays and on weekdays from Easter to Pentecost, to signify joy in the thought of a future resurrection; but on the other hand here in Spain we follow a long-established local tradition when we sing alleluias every day of the year, except fast days and during lent. For it is written: His praise shall continually be in my mouth.' (*De ecclesiasticis officiis*, I, xiii, 3.) In this same passage Isidore draws an analogy between Spanish usage and the ancient Jewish custom of singing alleluias at the ends of psalms. If the Hebrew psalmist could sing alleluias because of his joy in contemplating the church to come, should not we now rejoice in being members of it? he asks.

Isidore's opinions on war and amusements are couched in Augustinian tones of disapproval when analysing spectacles and games. 'Comedians are they who represent by song and gesture the doings of men in private life, and in their plays set forth the defilement of maidens and the love affairs of harlots. Tragedians are they who sang in mournful verse the ancient deeds and crimes of guilty kings, while the people looked on.' There is a Gothic note, too, in this: 'In battles, too, the music of the trumpet fires the warriors, and the more impetuous its loud sound the braver is the spirit of the fight. Also, song cheers the rowers. For the enduring of labours, too, music comforts the mind, and singing lightens weariness in solitary tasks.'

Here we have early pronouncements on aspects of musical life that were to continue, as were the episcopal fulminations against the spiritually defiling spectacles, and that uncontaminated singing of labourers in the fields, lightening weariness and giving renewed rhythmic vitality to their solitary tasks.

Compared with this intensive organising of Christian music into a conformable unity, our knowledge of secular performance is meagre, though not negligible in significance, for the evidence shows that desecularisation in everyday life did not proceed so fast nor so zealously. Choristers were admonished for their levity, though choirmasters spent seven years learning by heart the liturgical melodies to be taught in cathedral schools (see the *Antiphoner* of León). In the third Council of Toledo, Canon 23, it was thought necessary to prohibit profane songs and dances within the churches. Likewise those labourers who in the course of their work within ecclesiastical precincts broke into love songs were to be reprobated.

Isidore writes of those songs which students sang for newly wedded

11

couples. One was called *De Nubentibus*. Citing those instruments which stimulate the dance and those which sweetly accompany the songs he describes 'the exulting citara', and two Jewish instruments, the cinara, a small harp for cheerful songs, and the nablum, or psaltery, proper for dances. With this, the clash of the drums is heard, while soft pipe, lyre and bone pipe accompany the singers. Funereal laments were performed in public processions, but at the third Council in 587, it seemed expedient to curb these popular expressions, though plaints ('plantos') were officially organised for the deaths of royal persons. King Chindaswinth (d. 652) is commemorated by a hymn in the Azagra codex, where Recceswinth's wife, Reciberga (d. 657), is also commemorated. From the Huelgas Codex we learn of the planto for Sancho III (d. 1158), Berenguer IV (d. 1162 Barcelona), Fernando II of Leon (d. 1188), Alfonso VIII of Castile (d. 1214), so that the custom was not only venerable but became widespread among the growing number of ruling houses.

Wedding festivities were recorded, though sometimes retrospectively; at those of Fernán González of Castile in the 10th century juglars played 'muchas cítulas e muchos violeros', and in the 11th juglars played at the marriages of the Cid's daughters. Alfonso VI of Castile's three daughters were married on the same day (c. 1095) and juglars played both wind and string instruments 'así de boca commo de péñolas'. The marriage bed of the Emperor Alfonso VII's daughter Urraca on her wedding to king García de Navarra in Leon (July 1144) was surrounded by actors and women and children singing or playing flutes, and other instruments. These women and children may have been juglars.

Of peculiar interest is the wedding hymn marking the marriage of Princess Leodegundia daughter of the king of Galicia, afterwards Ordoño II, king of León. The Roda codex of the late 10th or early 11th century tells that various instrumentalists played various pieces 'during the banquet presided over by Christ', whose name resounds at the concluding of the panegyric as in the liturgical doxology, but, as elsewhere, the music is set down in Mozarabic neums. Among such events, it seems, are the antecedents of those dynastic wedding musical traditions that were to produce rich and elaborate compositions in Spain and Portugal after the reconquest era as associated with the evolution of operatic spectacles. The plantos become requiems in the course of time. In connection with the church's curb on excessive musical mourning in public for burials, it is worth noting that with the Renaissance revival of the classical *epithalamia* as applied to royal wedding musical celebrations in which Spain and Portugal joined other European courts as dynastic exchanges developed, Spanish composers did not quickly follow that

Italian revival and development of the planto, under its classical name of *epicedia*, which emerged into the elegaic pastorale and evolved with Cavalli, Peri, Caccini and Monteverdi into operatic tragedy.

Above such events set down in the *Chronicles* the nightingale's song should be heard, but alas! the *Disticon Filomelaicum*, recorded in the Azagra codex, like those royal plantos and nearly all else of these centuries of Visigothic and Mozarabic rule, is imprisoned in the still undeciphered neums. A 19th-century musical transcription of this work is not now passed as satisfactory.

We have the testimony of St Valerus that in the second half of the 7th century there appeared the figure of a clerical juglar, Justus, who enlivened festivities by singing lascivious ditties accompanying himself on the citara; his successors were to contribute many lively interludes to the history of the country's music; it is assumed that in this case the juglaresque tradition was already taking shape in the region of León, and more especially Bierzo. Menéndez Pidal is of opinion that already in the 9th to 10th centuries the epic of the *Infantes de Salas* was known and within a century or so that of the *Infante García*.

St Isidore's list of instruments included the following: acitabulum= cup-shaped percussion; barbitos=rabel, lyre; buccina=trompeta; calamus=reed-pipe; cithara=lyre; classicum=signaling trumpet; cornu =bugle; cymbala=cymbals; fides=classical lyre; fidicula=small stringed lyre; fistula=soft pipe; indica=Indian zither; lyra=originally a hollow tortoise-shell over which strings were stretched; organum= general name for a blowing wind instrument; pandura=syrinx; pecten =harp of 20 or more strings; phoenice=Phoenician zither; psalterium =psaltery whose strings are struck, not plucked; sambuca=pipe; sistrum=bronze tambourine of Egyptian origin; symphonia=hollow piece of wood beaten with small sticks; tibia=bone pipe; tintinnabulum =small bell; tuba=straight trumpet as distinct from curved trumpets such as cornua ending in a flaring bell; tympanum=drum.

St Isidore's authority for the singular importance of singing hymns was upheld for centuries, in obedience to the agreement reached at the Fourth Council of Toledo, over which he presided, that hymns must never be omitted from church services. The Eighth Council prohibited the ordination for the priesthood of anyone not knowing the liturgical chants. A Council held in Santiago de Compostela in 1031, in the reign of Bermudo III, ordered that all priests should be well versed in the psaltery, the chants, the hymns and the office of the martyrs; furthermore, it was directed that the singing of hymns should never be omitted on any Sunday of the year.

It is important to note that Augustine, when writing the latter part of the *Confessions*, was concerned with the refutation of heresy, opposing

the Manichees in his doctrine of the formation of the Church's substance, as Isidore was concerned to refute Arianism, so that the comparisons with Augustine's pages on music are especially relevant to
church worship in Spain during the Visigothic centuries.[1]

The earliest Visigothic liturgical manuscript extant is a *Libellus ora-*
tionum, containing prayers and collects for use at Toledo with variants
appropriate for the diocese of Tarragona. Copied about the year 710, it
was eventually deposited at Verona; it does not contain music, but is
otherwise comparable to the León *Antiphoner* the music of which
therefore may be presumed to embody traditions prior to the Islamic
conquest.

There are thirty-eight Mozarabic liturgical manuscripts extant today,
though not all contain music. The term Mozarabic—'made Arab'—
was given to Spaniards living under Muslim rule from 711, date of the
invasion. The precious Codex of Liébana (786) is not a Mozarabic production since it was composed in the Christian stronghold maintained
north of Muslim rule. In this the Byzantine influence is colourful and the
profusion of musical instruments is divided into groups of wind and
strings as in some heavenly orchestra; the wind instruments remain
stylistically archaic but the three-stringed citharas are sufficiently detailed to suggest an evolutionary process.

The Mozarabic manuscripts probably date from before 1100, since
it was not until that year that this rite was superseded by the Roman,
during Alfonso VI's reign. But though through preceding years the
Spanish tradition was tenaciously upheld in their Christian communities under Muslim rule and their sacred books copied and stored, their
notation remains mysterious since the neums have not yet been de-
ciphered in spite of intensive studies during this century. The variety of
forms is such that it cannot yet be said with certainty whether they indicate pitch or rhythmic differentiations. There are regional distinctions, too, and the neum types, *scandicus*, *punctus*, *podatus*, *clivis* and
torculus are written in 9, 10, 13, 17 and 28 ways respectively. Even the
comparison made possible in the San Millán de la Cogolla *Liber*
Ordinum by the fact that the Mozarabic neums for 21 melodies—18 for
burial ceremonies and 3 for Maundy Thursday feet-washing services—
were scratched out and staffless Aquitanian neums substituted, has left
many basic problems unresolved, and this despite the fact that about
half of these tunes apparently are to be found in the neums of the León
Antiphoner and the *Liber Ordinum* of Silos. Nevertheless a good deal of
light has been thrown on less impenetrable ciphers, as is shown by the
translation into modern terminology of 16 antiphons, and counterparts
to preces composed by Julian of Toledo (d. 690) and Vicente of

[1] The Augustinian Origins of Gothic. *Downside Review* April–July 1964.

Córdoba (fl. 820), are discoverable in an 11th-century French MS. of Albi, now in the Bibliothèque Nationale of Paris.

Of the 18 burial pieces in the San Millán MS. Rojo and Prado classify ten as in Mode II and Mode III. They transcribe the Maundy Thursday antiphons in Phrygian or Hypomixolydian modes, concluding that none of these melodies were written in either Lydian or Hypolydian.

The León *Antiphoner*, whose preface and many of whose chants are ascribed to Eugenius III of Toledo, deplores the loss of contact with the original significance given to the old custom of placing three choirs in the nave, by the pulpit and at the altar. If, in fact, this was written *c.* 950, it is not out of place to recall that when Abbot Suger organised the three choirs—for the reconstructed St Denis over the tomb of the gothic king Dagobert in Paris in honour of the Trinity—he was no less anxious to gain information about the exact significance and order of their participation, and like this Spanish prelate, to establish the spiritual meaning of their musical symbolism in this the first of Gothic churches to be consecrated. In fact, the tradition to which the León *Antiphoner* conforms may date back to the time of King Wamba (662), since this ruler's antiphon book is cited as the Leonese book's exemplar.

It covers the entire year's celebration, with additional material for dedicating a basilica, consecration of kings and bishops, marriages, ministering to the sick, burials, chants for the Office and Mass. Of the Mozarabic chant-types—*prolegendum* (introit), *psallendum* (gradual), *sacrificium* (offertory), *trenos* (tract), *laudes* (alleluias)—it is the last which claim most attention for their abundance and astonishing exuberance. The care shown in the illustration of the text is significant in Augustinian terms of music's service to the Word; the jubilus flowering on the second syllable rather than on the initial a, in contrast to the Office laudes where it is marked on the final a; though the word alleluia came after the verse in Office laudes, it preceded the verse of the Mass laudes. Melismata in the León MS. reach as many as 300 notes. Brou states, in comparing Spanish melismata with Gregorian, which were rather short, that Mozarabic liturgical manuscripts show a very considerable number of extended melismas—whether for the alleluia or any other word—and that these melismas were an integral part of the liturgy; they cannot be cut out without denaturing the whole. Moreover, we have every right to believe that they belong to the most primitive stratum of the ancient Spanish liturgy.

The manner of performance was important to Visigothic Spain, as directions in the León MS. detail. Deacons instructing catechumens were required to sing in a loud town-crier's voice. The arch-deacon is advised to sing a Palm Sunday antiphon in a clear voice. The bishop chanting the Passion Antiphon 'Behold the hour cometh, yea is now

A.) Copy (1069) by Arias of the Leóh *Antiphoner* (6th cent.)

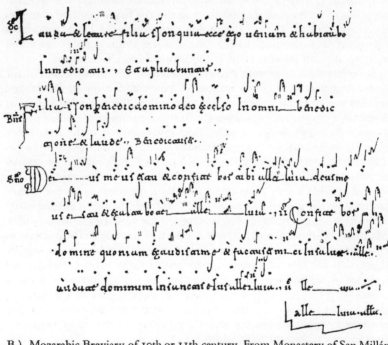

B.) Mozarabic Breviary of 10th or 11th century. From Monastery of San Millán at La Rioja.

come, that ye shall be scattered, every man to his own, and shall leave me alone' is ordered to sing this text sotto-voce. The bishop who sings 'O my people, what have I done unto thee; and wherein have I wearied thee?' is told to begin the Improperia with a tremolo in his voice.

The melisma of Spanish folk-singing, with its apparently instinctive obedience to certain rules for its flourishing on certain degrees of the scale, and that withdrawn, almost hieratic, ejaculatory manner of intoning the text, may be older than that Muslim tradition to which it is often ascribed; such dramatic emphasis in the primitive Church is comparable to the realism of popular carvings of images dating from romanesque times.

The weight of its prestigious authority upheld during the Muslim occupation made many reluctant to dispense with the Mozarabic tradition. Aragon continued the rite until 1071, Valencia till 1238, Murcia till 1266. Among the Catalans, Vich, Urgel, Gerona were linked to Narbonne when Tarragona fell to the Moors; Ripoll also and San Juan de la Peña similarly passed over to the Benedictine rule. The venerable San Cugat possessed music with Aquitanian notation. Nevertheless, the Mozarabic service survived within Catalonia till the end of the 12th century. It is worth noting in this period of gradual change that from the 11th century the sequence or prosa and the tropus were introduced in order to add a convenient text to the lengthy melismata whose many notes were not always now easily remembered, and thus the words enabled choirs to proceed confidently through passages of climax and jubilation.

It was Juan Facundo Riaño's *Critical and Bibliographical Notes on Early Spanish Music*, published by Quaritch, London, 1887, which first made historians aware that there existed a store of Visigothic evidence for the fact that Spain possessed some of the oldest music notation in existence. Since then, the tasks of elucidating its neums have become a major preoccupation to many scholars, such as Fathers Sunyol, Rojo and Prado, Dom J. M. Pinell, Millares Carló, Dom F. Cabrol, Mgr M. H. Anglés and many others in Spain, to Dom Anscari Mundo who suggests now that some Visigothic liturgical scripts of Toledo should be dated as late as the 13th and 14th centuries. Among foreign historians Peter Wagner and Dom Louis Brou have contributed decisively to vital issues, as have Dom M. Férotin in Le *Liber Mozarabicus Sacramentorum*, 1912, Paris, and Dr Egon Wellesz, in 'Early Byzantine Neumes'.[1] Dom Louis Brou in 'Notes de Paléographie Musicale Mozarabe'[2] treats of three problems: Mozarabic manuscripts in Intermittent notation; Toledan manuscripts noted in neums of the north of Spain and the Mozarabic neums without musical significance. These pages are essential to any study of the Visigothic musical codices.

It has long been accepted that Mozarabic neums are concerned with

[1] *Musical Quarterly*, Jan. 1952.   [2] *Anuario Musical X*, 1955.

more than pitch; hence their baffling elements of association. Again, it may not be amiss to recall the attitude of St Augustine in writing *De Musica*, 387 to 389 A.D. His theme is metre, which in classical ages was a branch of music, and he is concerned with *rhythmo*; though he meant to write another treatise, on melody, *de melo*, he was 'too busy'. The treatise thus deals mainly with metrical feet, long and short syllables, numbers, combinations, distribution of syllables, the legitimate length of verses, their divisions, the distinctions between rhythm and metre, the points of silence, rest, or syncope, *silentium*, the caesura's place, the classification of verse forms, the principles of verse groups and stanzas. He concludes with a discussion of rhythm's aesthetic nature and a classification of six rhythm modes, referring all rhythm ultimately to the principles of morality, psychology and Divine Dispensation. We may be fairly certain that the makers of Visigothic musical notation were familiar with this dialogue expounding music in Christian terms. They would approve his definition of music as *ars bene modulandi*, that is, how to make controlled variations of sound in the right way, as stated in Book I's opening, and its conclusion, extended now to *scientia bene modulandi* 'knowing how to make controlled variations of sound correctly . . .' 'Music, making her way forth from some most intimate core of being (*procedens quodam modo de secretissimis penetralibus musica*) has left her footprints (*vestigia*) both on our senses and on the objects of our sensation. We should follow these footprints to arrive at that intimate core, for that is the only way; and to do so we must neglect the longer intervals of time, and confine ourselves to those which are shorter, of lengths that occur in performances of song and dance.' Augustine considers that 'movements of long duration, for example of an hour or more, are not adjusted to our immediate sensibility'. He explains, in finishing the work, that it was written 'because I had observed pious men of the Church, men concerned with education, writing on such subjects in order to confute heretics'. This was the situation of Isidore and his circle.

The Passions and hymns commemorating saints and martyrs in the Visigothic calendar are remarkably documented and prove that from very early times the Spanish church lavished great devotion on the Vigils of oriental, eastern European and African saints besides those more commonly venerated in western Europe; thus these manuscripts enable us to appreciate the rich variety of cults from which Spanish music has taken its colour and sense of drama, for this veneration was the root from which the liturgical representations and their musical accompaniments grew and spread.

The cult of the Virgin Mary was adopted early in this period, perhaps because of Ildefonso's predeliction, though later than in the east where there were Arabian communities celebrating her name in the 4th century. It is thought that her cult came into Spain from the east. However a theory that the feast of the Assumption which was later to assume great importance came also from the east into Spain is not upheld by some writers. The Marian celebration was concentrated in Visigothic times on the Christmas season and was one of the year's most splendid occasions. The feasts of the nativity, however, were established later than those of the martyrs, since it was the latter who were associated with the Crucifixion in times of the persecutions. Though exact accounts of her feasts are not extant before the 7th century, the cult was firmly organised by this time and a solemn festival was inaugurated in order to unify the varying dates upheld by the many churches dedicated to her. Prudentius refers to her in the *Cathemerinon* verses. Her churches, attributed to the 6th century, were in Jerez de los Caballeros, Mondoñedo, in the north; Porcuna, Guarrázar, 'Sorbaces', Guadix, Cabra, where a chapel was dedicated to her in 660, Mérida, of about the same date, 661. She was venerated in Toledo's cathedral dedicated to her and founded by Recared in 586 or 587 and in Mérida's, as titulary also. Tarrasa was possibly dedicated to her in Visigothic times.

It was in 656 that the tenth Council of Toledo decided upon the unification of the various feasts and chose December 18 as one of the most solemn events of the liturgical calendar. Ildefonso was probably the chief proponent of this and it was he who possibly wrote the liturgical texts for the service. The Annunciation and Incarnation are included, and the antiphons also. These Visigothic intensifications are important in view of the evolution of music in her honour which gathered about her festivals all through the middle ages and beyond into the Renaissance. The feast of the Assumption does not appear before 711 and it is partly because this does not appear in Rome until the 7th century that some authorities suppose it was introduced into Visigothic Spain through Byzantine influence there. In Jerusalem there was a 15th of August celebration of the Mother of God as early as the 5th century.

Naturally, Spanish martyrs were pre-eminent in the calendar. St Vincent and St Eulalia are commemorated in mosaics at San Apollinario at Ravenna and at Palermo, their fame extending to Constantinople. William of Malmesbury noted his importance in Oporto and he became more widely known in France than in Italy.

In Africa Augustine preached the sermon after the St Vincent passion was given. This native series of martyrdom commemorations has been given the title of 'epic passions', and the dramatic contrasts given to the confrontation of the saintly Vincent with the persecuting Dacian show more than incipient portents of the latent liturgical representations.

St Eulalia's life at Mérida is commemorated by Prudentius in two hymns. Hydatius and Isidore tell of her protection over this great city of the western peninsula.

The relation of Office and the Mass to the Passion and hymn varied; sometimes the creation of the hymn preceded that of the service; sometimes the Passion was conceived first and the hymn emerged last in the process of composing the whole celebration in the saint's honour. It should be remembered that most Mozarabic MSS. proceed from Toledan models 'which reveal a certain unity of organisational skill', as has been observed of those services in honour of St Leocadia drawn from Toledo's sources. Toledan models set the style for lesser centres and Toledo's authority established the ritual through the peninsula. It was Toledo's third Council in 592 which implanted the reciting of the Creed on Sundays and determined the organisation of chief festivals in the calendar.

St John the Baptist was the most popular saint of the Visigoths: his hymns, office and mass are now confidently attributed to Ildefonso, by Pérez de Urbel. Emphasis on June 24th for his midsummer celebration was early decided upon in Spain, though elsewhere he was also commemorated at Christmas time and in September; his midsummer festival remains the most popular.

The cult of St Cecilia, whose feast appears in the *Oracional Tarraconense*, was not on account of her patronage of music but because of her virginity; for this virtue St Eugenia at this time was most fervently venerated, possibly partly because she was the legendary heroine of a pious novel popularised in the west in the 6th century; the hymns praise her chastity; the legends tell of her life hidden away in a monastery in masculine clothing, falsely accused of crime and proved innocent in the end. Though there is no literary testimony of this tale in Spain, her popularity is shown in this liturgical singing. She is hymned thus in Tarragona, Silos, in the *Antiphoner* of León and San Millán, and in the sacramentarios of Toledo. Prototype of other female saints suffering under a cloud of false witnesses, her Spanish popularity foreshadows some favourite heroines of the Spanish theatre.

Although there was an absence of Pannonian cults, oriental martyrs are more prominent than French or African in the Visigothic calendar. That of St Lucian of Antioch is said to be of great antiquity. St George's cult dates possibly from the 7th century only. St Adrian of Nicomedia figures in Mozarabic calendars on the 16th June and his feast figures in the León *Antiphoner*, the Tarragona *Oracional*, and at Silos and San Millán. Here Natalia is included, according to the legend. The long 7th-century hymn *Hierusalem gloriosa* refers to the Last Judgment in:

Early Spanish Music

Quo tremenda iudicantis
festa quorum predicamus
et quibus non est corona
cum dies illuxerit,
misceamur gaudiis
sit fides ad gloriam.

This passion's incidents, the amputated hand of the saint preserved by Natalia, her aiding the prisoners while disguised in men's clothes and the apparition of Adrian to her as she journeys to Byzantium by ship, contain elements that were to be the seeds of liturgical drama. It is thought that St Adrian's cult came to Spain by way of monastic influence and that this was because these two saints were patrons of a Toledan monastery. The cult of St Babilas of Antioch was upheld in Guadix, where his relics may have been brought by a pilgrim from the holy places since other relics here were brought from Jerusalem. His name also figures in the León *Antiphoner* and his festival probably dates from the 7th century. For the same reason it is supposed that St Christopher was also commemorated in Guadix and he is associated with St Cristóbal of Córdoba. The hymn, evidently drawn from the Passion, appears to support the attribute of antiquity, for there is an absence of allusions to the Arab yoke, which when found in other hymns refers to Mozarabic and not Visigothic years. The feasts of Sts Cosmas and Damian were celebrated early in Rome; St Isidore includes them in his *pharmace* of doctors.

The predominance of Byzantine festivals in Visigothic calendars gives some authorities to suppose that this may have come, not by way of Constantinople, but in very early times from Palestine across Syria; Baumstark also affirms that the cult of St Julian did not enter Spain by way of Byzantium, but through Egyptian monasteries; he believes the monastery of Agali to be of oriental foundation. Associated with St Basilisa, another heroine of chastity, the Toledan *Hymnary* and the San Millán *Antiphoner* give these saints a very long hymn divided in two. According to Salmon, the cult of Egyptian saints passed through Spain to Septimania, and it is indeed possible that the foundation of many churches devoted to them there dates to the time when Septimania was part of the Visigothic kingdom. St Tirso was thought until recently to have had a relatively late cult in Spain, introduced after 711, and centred in the Toledan province; but the discovery of an inscription in Santa María de Mérida shows that this may be attributed to Visigothic years; his festal day is 28th January, thus coming after that associated with St Babilas. The Greeks held his day on the 20th. Since he was a celebrated martyr among the Greeks it may be that his presence in Mérida was

21

due to a colony of Greeks there, including bishops Paul and Fidelis, their influence dating from the 6th century. The inscription at Santa María in Mérida is ascribed to the beginning of the 7th.

Here it may be explained that antiphonal psalm-singing by alternate choirs of men and women first began at about 350 in Antioch; at the end of each psalm the people joined in a doxology. Antiphons as we know them grew out of this early antiphonal singing. By the 7th century the Offertory became an integration of antiphon and psalm verses, the first by the choir, the latter much ornamented by soloists.

Not so many African saints were included in the calendar as might have been expected considering the close relations between the churches of Spain and its African neighbours. St Speratus, however, is honoured in a hymn *Sperati sancti martyris*; the Passion, too, celebrates his martyrdom with his companions:

> *Hunc urbs praepollens Africae*
> *amplectitque occiduus*
> > *Carthago servat martyrem*
> > *Christo dicatus populus.*

The MS. of this Office is preserved in the Silos *Sacramentario*.

It is supposed that this cult may have entered Spain through the monastery of Servitanus which was of African origin.

St Cyprian was commemorated in Spain from Roman days; the churches of Astorga and Mérida resorted to his arbitration in the case concerning the bishops Basilides and Marcial. Prudentius dedicated hymn XII to him and mentions him elsewhere in the poem on the martyrs of Saragossa. His services are widely preserved as in the León, Sílo and Toledan MSS. and there are close connections between mass, prayers and hymn, for all allude to the double preaching of Cyprian 'por su sangre y por su doctrina—by his blood and by his doctrine'. The hymn, like the Passion, refers to the gift which the saint ordered to be given to his executioner. Probably these services and hymns date from the 7th century, the cult having been introduced towards the end of the 4th.

The cult of St Saturninus of Toulouse is very ancient in Spain; Toulouse was the capital of the Visigothic world. His services are included in all the liturgical books, from the time of the *Oracional Tarraconense*. Notable in this aspect are those similarities between the Visigothic and Gallican mass to be found in the *Missale gothicum*, 'Deus qui inmortales', whose *Collectio post nomina* coincides literally to a large extent with the introduction of the Visigothic. St Saturninus' feast was given renewed fervour in the 10th and 11th centuries, due to the arrival in Spain of monks from southern France and pilgrims on their way to

Compostela, and in the region of Navarre it has been maintained to this day.

As has been said, Pannonian cults are absent from Visigothic Spain; oriental martyrs, however, are prominent compared to French and African in general. St Lucian of Smyrna, St George, Marina, Eufemia, Dorotea, had their Spanish festivals. Marina was so popular in the north that she was made a local saint also; and she was heroine of a novel like that of Eugenia. Etheria visited Eufemia's tomb when in Constantinople.

The celebration of saints' Vigils was a long-lasting and deeply-rooted popular observance in Spain. Though in 1322 a Valladolid Council censured the custom of bringing in Moorish instrumentalists to add colour to the music, their instruments could not be held as alien to the origins of some saints venerated here, whatever the creed of their players.

CHAPTER II

Music of Muslim Spain and the Northern Kingdoms

When the Arabs set foot in the Spanish peninsula in 711 the schools of music in Mecca and Medina, which were to become famous centres of poets, players and singers, had not yet been created. The Arabs arrived with the zeal of a new faith that disqualified musicians from normal participation in social life; they were considered immoral and dishonest, fit only to be placed among slaves and infamous creatures. In law, no singer or player could testify as witness; the sale of music-books was prohibited; the sale of any slaves was held invalid if the document in any way suggested they might be singers and the renting of any house for the performance of music was forbidden.

The Arab occupation of Spain extended through three periods: from 711 to 756 their ruler was an emir subject to the eastern capital: from 756 to 1031 this emirate became independent of the east and became the caliphate of Córdoba: from 1031 onwards small kingdoms enjoyed a relative freedom as control from Córdoba lessened and the Taifa kings expressed their common rivalries with cultural displays in which music distinctively flourished in the palaces of Toledo, Córdoba, Seville, Málaga, Jaén, Murcia, Almería, Granada.

Like the Spaniards, however, the conquerors had an ingrained love of music, especially of singing. When we listen nowadays to the fieldworkers' airs based on the old Arab-Andalusian scales, we echo the desire expressed by 8th-century B.C. Assyrians who were so pleased by the songs of toil sung by their Arab prisoners that they asked for more, and we recall St Isidore's lines on the comfort of music to those labouring on solitary tasks. This thread of song is one of the longest in the world. The Christians were allowed to keep their form of worship within the precincts of their churches; only in times of fanaticism were their altars desecrated. It is a curious fact that the Christian church as erected by Charles V within the centre of the great Cordobese mosque represents the situation of the enclaved Mozarabic church in Muslim Spain.

When 'Abdu'l-Raḥman I, first of the Ummayyad rulers in Córdoba, wished to make his western court like that of his Damascan ancestors, he received from the east the slave singer 'Afza, who, like the best singers of this civilisation, was an accomplished instrumentalist, accompanying her songs with the 'ūd (*laúd*). Al-Ḥakam I improved on this record, by lavishing rewards on two oriental singers, 'Alūn and Zarqūn, whose music established a vogue among Spaniards who heard them. 'Abdu'l-Raḥman II was the caliph who founded a school in the west whose musicians might be said to rival those of Medina, and the palace apartments where the singers studied their art were known as the Medinese; the chief singers were now three, Fáḍl, 'Alam and Qalam.

Fáḍl had been slave to one of Harūn al-Rashid's daughters and had learnt her art in Baghdad and then Medina. 'Alam was her companion bought at the same time by the Cordobese monarch. Qalam, however, was a Basque girl who had been sent very young to study in the orient, and especially at Medina; to her musical gifts she added literary study and having a good memory became eminent as a reciter of Arab poetry and of other works and schools. There was also a brilliant young Egyptian, Abu'l-Walid the Alexandrian, another singer, at court; the Caliph's chancellor, however, advised him to give up singing as it might be an obstacle to his political career.

All these musicians were destined to be precursors of the great Ziryāb whose fame as singer and consummate ability to enchant a court was even greater than Farinelli's; over Farinelli, moreover, he had the advantage of being able to establish his own school of succession by the numerous family he raised. He was known as 'the Black Bird' because of his very dark skin, fluent tongue and sweet nature. His meeting with Harūn recalls partly the ascendancy Farinelli held over the Spanish Philip V, for he would only sing for this great potentate songs which, he said, no human ear had ever before heard and which he would sing only for the greatest of kings. It was due to the jealousy aroused by this success that the Black Bird found himself obliged to travel far from his musicianly rivals in the east and so came to Córdoba. Here his place in history became assured for he is credited with the addition of a fifth string to the *laúd*. He also invented a plectrum of an eagle's wing to replace the old wooden instrument; this, and the fifth string, placed between the second and third and coloured red, shows the symbolism of his power over his hearer's ears and emotions. His method of teaching singing still interests students of the art and his knowledge spread through Seville and afterwards to Africa and the Magrib, where it is said that as late as the 14th century traces of his influence were to be noted 'in spite of the decadence in the African empires'. Even in Granada's last years the poets remembered his name in their verse. Thus to the tradition of Medina was added the classical school of Mosulí, whose pupil Ziryāb had been in Baghdad, and both these took root in Spain where the same songs as those heard in the east were performed, even with the same instruments, in the 9th century A.D.

The theorists at the Cordobese court taught the Pythagorean and Greek systems as well as their own and in time the Greek modified the Arab-Persian. By the 10th century, at the height of the Arabic-Hispanic culture, Al-Fārābī so strongly advocated the Greek that the old Arab theory was practically abandoned. Its place was taken by a system which was basically Greek though retaining the old designation and this is the musical system which has since remained in use among the Arabs and Moors of Mauretania. In its earlier less complex form, the Arab-Persian system was introduced into the music schools of Muslim Spain in the 9th century by Ziryāb.

It is said that the Greek system came naturally to the Mauretanians. The Eastern Arabs however appear to have been uninfluenced by the new theory accepted in Spain and held to their own tradition. The treatise *Risala fi'l-mūsīqī*—The Book about Music—by Ibn al-Munajjim (d. 912), a pupil of Isḥaq al-Mauṣālī of Baghdad (767–850) as was Ziryāb, shows that the Arabic classical scale was identical with the Greek Pythagorean except that its intervals read upwards from the bass and not downwards as among the Greeks. This inversion continued in use down to the fifteenth century. It is worth noting here that many field songs in southern Spain emphasise the downward-moving scale by chromatic adornment in the manner of arabesque procedure, thus showing agreement with the Mauretanians' taste.

It is interesting, too, that the eight 'finger modes' (aṣābi') for the lute, in use till the 11th century among the Muslims are, with one exception, identical with Greek and church modes. Thus the music of the Mozarabic enclaves would not sound very foreign to the newcomers. The lute-song they brought was closely derived from the verse and then varied profusely with all manner of differences conceivable. The style of the variation became the favourite form of Spanish musicians whose greatest masters gave it pre-eminence in the European world.

During the reigns of 'Abdu'l-Raḥman III and Al-Ḥakam II Ummayad power reached its height, but these two rulers, like their ancestor 'Abdallah, observed austere laws and so the hey-day of slave singers and salaried musicians was temporarily eclipsed, though Al-Ḥakam II acquired the autograph example of Isfahani's *Book of Songs*. With the rise of Almanzor, the scourge of Spanish Christians, old ways of entertaining prevailed once more though historians record some palace scenes in which the music's sound was drowned in the shouting of drunken revellers. But with the restoration of the dynastic line civilised culture improved to the stage where orchestras of a hundred *laúds* and another hundred flutes performed in the palace of al-Mahdī, and royal princesses vied as performers with the best-known professionals.

Córdoba's most splendid years were graced by the philosopher-musicians Al-Fārābī and Averroës, followed by Avempace of Saragossa. Al-Fārābī (d. 950) wrote the *Kitāb al-mūsīqī al-kabir*—The Grand Book on Music—which later authors never excelled. Averroes (1120–1198) condemned all melodies which led men away from that moral edification which ought to rule society. He excluded the lyre and the *laúd* from his strictures on instrumental music and wind instruments in particular, because to his ear only the stringed forms could produce commendable harmonies. Avempace, however, so loved music that he would run after the cattle-drover taking his beasts down to the watering-place so as not to lose the last threads of the song he was singing; there were critics, however, who thought that he wasted his time in music-making and would have been a better philosopher had he not so passed the hours. Avempace's book was said to rival Al-Fārābī's, but it is lost, though he is thought by some to have composed melodies which passed into the common treasury of anonymous songs in the Muslim world of Spain. Such a reputation and this kind of nameless immortality should be glory enough for the truly philosophic musical nature.

It is to Al-Fārābī that we owe the more precise definitions of rhythms as these were introduced into Spain; he limits the traditional series of these to seven groups:

Ribera draws chiefly on the *Mafātiḥ* by Khwārizmī for descriptions of the four basic rhythmic schemes: hazaj, ramal, first and second thaqīl, each of these having a slow and quick movement. But there was also an exceptional style, the makhurī, which some described as similar to the first thaqīl, while others associated it with the second thaqīl; it was much used and was faster or more allegretto than the thaqīl. His transcription of the *Mafātih*'s description is as follows:

Both Al-Fārābī and Ibn Sīnā—Avicenna—extend these basic schemes to more complex derivative patternings in sevens, tens, and elevens in various combinations of threes and fours. These rhythms were generally strongly marked, as the percussive and pizzicato instruments in common use prove, and with the modal melodies and their ornate florid embellishments constitute the essential style of Muslim music.

After Al-Ḥakam II (961–976) filled the library with some 600,000 volumes procured in Cairo, Baghdad, Damascus and elsewhere, the power of Córdoba passed into other hands as it had in the east and a type of praetorian guard became masters under whose control puppet caliphs tumbled like ninepins; of these the first was that Muḥammad II al-Mahdī whose palace rang to the sound of a hundred *laúds* and an equal number of flutes. After the last of these puppets, Hisham III (1027–1031) fell, the house of Ummaya fell too and in a year or so the state became a republic. Petty states developed their own courts and the Taifa kings vied with each other as patrons of learning and the arts. Málaga, Algeciras, Seville, Granada, Toledo, Valencia, Saragossa, Denia and others became lavish and ostentatious cultivators of music which flourished even more intensely than under the caliphs. Seville, however, outshone the rest. The 'Abbadids here, who ruled Córdoba for a time, were the most important of the Taifa kings and the last of them, Al-Mu'tamid (1068–1091), who made his court 'the resort of poets and literary men' was a singer and played the 'ud, as did his son, though his great passion for this art offended his people. The songs of the court poet, 'Abdu'l-Jabbār ibn Ḥamdīs, a Sicilian Arab, were the rage of Seville. One of the 'Abbadids carried a copy of the great *Kitāb- al-aghānī* with him on his journeys. According to Al-Shaqandī, the city was famed for its manufacture of musical instruments, in which it had an export trade, and Ibn Rushd (d. 1198) testifies that it was a major centre of this industry. Averroes wrote that when a learned man died in Seville, his books were sent to Córdoba to be sold; on the other hand, when a musician died in Córdoba, his instruments were sent for sale to Seville. It may be noted, however, that the writer of these lines was himself a Cordobese who despised the vice and vanities of those who sang sensual airs.

Toledo boasted of its famous musician Abū'l-Ḥusain. Travellers found Málaga inordinately fond of music and a certain Aḥmad ibn Muḥammad al-Yamanī heard the lute, the pandore, the reed-pipe on every side in Málaga where it was impossible to sleep at nights for the sounds which filled the air as music-lovers sat under the orange-trees in their gardens and gave themselves over to the languorous melodic styles for which the place was famous. Ubeda near Jaén excelled in the reputation of its dancing-girls; Saragossa boasted its illustrious theorist and mathematician Abū'l-Fadl Ḥasdāy. It must be noted that in Andalusia music and poetry belonged not to a special class, but to the people. In his *Athār al-bilād*, Zakariyya al-Qazwīnī (d. 1283) tells that in Shilb (Silves) in southern Portugal almost every inhabitant was interested in literature and one could find ploughmen capable of improvising in verse.

In the second half of the 11th century, however, the Christians in the north began seriously to challenge the Muslim states. When Toledo fell in 1085, the Andalusians appealed to their North African co-religionists for aid and as a result of their arrival in 1086 and defeat of the

Christians at Zallaqa, the whole land became part of the Moroccan empire and the petty kingdoms were broken up. The new rulers were fanatics and during this time less is heard of lavish gatherings, though the great Ibn Bajja (Avempace) pursued his taste for the popular song.

By 1230 the Christians had regained most of Andalusia and many Muslims returned to Africa. This, however, was not the end of the Arabian affair in Spain. Granada drew the surviving Muslims who sought its shelter into the fortress state and here the Naṣrid dynasty (1232–1492) held together a kingdom against the Christians.

After the period covered by the great *Kitāb al-aghānī*, that is in the opening of the 10th century, there is little information about the type of verse used in the vocal music of these days, the works of writers of the class of Isfahānī having been lost. Of those 11th to 13th century poets whose words were set to music there is a Sevillian, Ibn Ḥamdīs (d. 1132). Of this period the British Museum possesses a 13th-century MS. with words of songs, each superscribed with the name of the mode in which it was sung.

It was in Andalusia that the popular verse-forms, *zéjel* and *muwashshah*, developed and became general vehicles for songs. Their popularity spread through northern Africa and even to Bagdad, after a significant appearance was made by a blind poet, Muqaddam of Cabra, an Andalusian town situated in the Muslim south. He produced verses whose estribillo he ventured to create in the popular romance tongue, and this zéjel evoked response from versifiers all over the country, in Andalusia, Valencia, Aragon, making a particular appeal in Seville. He was voicing the needs of a changing population, and when the zéjel was set to music it was sung by everyone.

From Andalusia and North Africa the words of the classical *nauba* have survived, though the authenticity of its music is open to doubt. In the former, the nauba received special attention, every mode being employed by the composers. According to modern writers it had five distinct movements as well as a vocal prelude, an instrumental prelude and a *tūshiya* or overture. These five movements, each of which was preceded by an introductory *karsi*, were called the *maṣdar, baṭaih, darj, inṣirāf* and *khalāṣ* (or *mukhlaṣ*). With the rise of petty kingdoms a clamour was set up for the granting of musical privileges such as the ṭabl-khānāh and the nauba—which was a periodic musical performance hitherto reserved as an honour belonging to the caliph alone. In 966 Al-Mutī gave leave for a general to have kettledrums played at prayer-time during a campaign, though this privilege was not always granted, and it seems that this particular general was allowed to keep this privilege on his return.

When the nauba was granted in 979, it was the three-fold nauba which was allowed, not the five-fold which was still a jealously guarded prerogative of the caliph. Yet in 1000, under Al-Qadir, a minister was allowed to beat a ṭabl (drum) for the five-fold honour, as was another in 1017. The Muslim rulers extended these privileges in succeeding generations, but with specific distinctions as to the class of nauba, and the kind and number of instruments to be used. The last Shah of Khwārizm (d. 1231), who boasted of playing the nauba of Alexander the Great, had it performed on 27 drums of gold encrusted with pearls, the players at its inception being the sons of subject monarchs. The Fātimid caliphs also dispensed musical privileges to subject rulers when granting patents or regality—*marātib*.

The Muslim rulers in Spain showed their sense of this importance of musical royal privileges in the organisation of their military bands. Al-Ḥakam II possessed gold-mounted trumpets—*būqāt*; the Almohads reserved drums for royalty alone and the band formed a separate company with the standard-bearers and was called the *sāqa*.

In the *Kitāb al-aghānī*—Book of Songs—by Al-Isfahānī (d. 967) there are several references to a company of musicians being called a nauba. Farmer suggests that the name probably originated from the circumstances that these musicians played at certain specified periods of the day, or that these performers took turns in playing. The word signifies *vez* or turn. In time the term nauba was transferred from the performers to the performance, the periodic playing of the caliph's military band at the five hours of prayer being called the nauba. The *Kitāb* describes the current type of vocal music as the lighter sort—*qiṭa'* —more in keeping with the tastes of the period, but also gives place to the more serious pieces from the *qaṣā'id*, or classical tradition. There were thus these two different kinds of music forms—light and classical —when these privileged musical performances became known as the nauba. Ribera says that the word means typical, the style, the character which gives an unmistakable colour to the music, as to the product of a region, or an author; this was the meaning given to the word by the Hispano-muslims. In *La música hispano-musulmana en Marruecos* (Madrid, 1950), the nauba's place in Tunis is fully described and here it is stated that the Tunisian naubas were brought by émigrés from Valencia, those of Algiers from Córdoba, those of Fez from Seville, and lastly those of Tetuan from Granada. 50,000 emigrated to the Magrib after the reconquest of Córdoba in 1236; 200,000 went to Granada and Tunisia from Valencia after 1238. In the reign of Ferdinand III a new wave of emigration took place from Seville in 1248.

After the fall of Granada in 1492 there was a considerable period during which the Moriscos were allowed to continue their customs and even after the rising in the Alpujarras the population was distributed through central Spain. In Valencia, where their work in the silk industry had made this region a prosperous zone, there were villages where only the priest and notary were Old Christians; and when the final expulsion was decreed in 1609–1610, some landowners escorted their peasants to the ports and even to Oran, so closely had their joint interests been tied. The last order of 1610, issued for Murcia and Andalusia, was less strictly enforced and Castilian Moriscos were allowed to stay.

Musically, the Moriscos were appreciated by their conquerors during much of the course of the reconquest. The Latin chronicle of Alfonso VII, referring to his entry into Toledo in 1137, tells that Saracens, Jews and Christians sallied out to greet him, each in his own tongue, with cymbals, citharas and psalteries; similarly, on the royal entry into Seville after the battle of Salado the Moors made great entertainments for his train. Sancho IV of Castile, son of Alfonso the Learned, had Morisco musicians in his palace, a juglaresa, wife to Zate, Yuzaf, Muza, Abdala Xatibí, Hamet, Mohamet el del Añafil and Rexit el de la Axabeba—these last two referred to by their instruments—a male piper and a Moorish trumpeter. In 1329 Alfonso of Aragon asked the Castilian king to send him two minstrels who played the *xabeba*—and the *meo canón*—which were Arabic instruments; Pedro IV of Aragon in 1337 asked to be sent a Moorish juglar from Játiva called Halezigua, a fine player of the *rabel*; John II, in 1389 asked for an entire family of Moorish juglars to be sent from Valencia, whose chief, Mazot, took his wife and mother together with other female performers and players; they entertained the king for many days and then were returned to their homes well rewarded.

The Portuguese court also had Morisco musicians on its official rolls; the inventory of King Manoel gives five pages to listing effects belonging to the Moorish dances. To celebrate the reception for the royal princes, the son of John II and Ferdinand and Isabella's heiress, all the Moorish communities throughout the country were invited to send men and women who could sing, play and dance, to perform folías.

Morisco weddings were ebullient affairs and drew the curious to listen and watch; the musical interludes may be compared with old Christian weddings in Spain—in both, the reception for the bride was by women performers within and men's salutations without the house. Moriscos were still allowed to hold their *zambras* and *leilas*—their nocturnal fiestas and dances—and lovers serenaded with the lute as Christians with the old guitar. Their burial committals were not so easily approved; as in Visigothic times authorities sought to check what were considered to be excessive expressions of mourning in a Christian state which believed in resurrection; the singing in the streets of dirges and lamentations included endechas and plañidos; it was the excesses of such public displays which were disapproved. The *romerías*, however, seem to have passed as customs from Moorish to Christian communities and are still to be seen gathered about hillside fountains and springs reputed for their pure waters which have been given names of saints or holy men commemorated by wayside chapels; Federico García Lorca's romería scene, like Goya's, both of which illustrate the musical part, takes dramatic licence with what is a country folk's picnicking outing.

The Archpriest of Hita, who wrote songs for Moorish and Jewish women, shows in verse his awareness that Arabic song does not marry well with instruments such as the bowed fiddle—which compete with it in legato melody, but requires those which mark the rhythm and harmony with the plucking plectrum and accented *staccato*. This author of the genial *Libro de buen amor* (*c.* 1343) was one of those Spanish poets who most frequently used the strophic zéjel for his songs, to be performed by students and music-lovers, Christian, Jew and Moor alike, that same metric system which sprang from Muqaddam of Cabra in the 10th century. This form continued its lively rhythm through Cancioneros, such as that of Gómez Manrique, whose number LXII even gives a cradle song in the zéjel movement, too. Gil Vicente, founder of the Portuguese theatre and incomparable exponent of the rustic rhythms, gives it to Cassandra's famous song,

> Dicen que me case yo;
> No quiero marido, no . . .

in his *Auto da Sibila Cassandra*, proving the unexhausted freshness of its perennial springs. Crisóstomo's zéjel in Don Quixote, however, is in a a a b form.

Accounts of Muslim performers are veiled in hyperbole and panegyric so thickly as to obscure the music's features almost entirely and it is from the more caustic comments of composers and authors themselves that the real musical activity is more often learned. Descanting in his book *al-Mukhaṣṣaṣ* on the accommodating nature of the *tonada* to express most human moods, the perspicacious Murcian ibn Sida goes on to tell of the other aspect of musical invention: 'There are musical thieves, the same as in poetry, and of these there are a certain number of varieties. Some rob the entire melody, giving new words to it; others make themselves the masters of a phrase or some ritornello or other; while some disfigure that which they have stolen by introducing rhythmic modifications; others construct their own works by assembling fragments of three or four preceding ones, which produces a motley piece of composition.'

33

The individual artist seems always to have been sensitive to plagiarism, regarding the borrower as thief, though he may return the goods in recognisable form. The anonymous musician, however, and particularly the folk-singer and instrumentalist still revivifies his local stock from generation to generation with these same processes set out by ibn Sida and this is especially true in Spain. The art of grafting was exhorted by St Paul in words that have been familiar in the peninsula since early times and among rural workers it can never be far from their thoughts. In the mixed populations which had to live side by side during the Muslim occupation of seven hundred years, exchange was vital to communication as both zéjel and muwashahas reveal in their mixture of Arabic tradition and local Latin evolving into the romance tongue of the people—in which the Jewish element had its part too. Discoveries like the collection of *kharjas* found in 1948 in a Cairo synagogue are still extending our comparative knowledge of this interchange. Probably composed in the 11th century these Mozarabic songs, of two and four short lines, are written in Castilian romance but with Hebrew or Arabic characters as additions to the muwashaha to which the kharja served as conclusion and also as principal motive. The favourite theme is a woman's love-lament for her beloved in his absence and the pain caused by his forgetfulness or her own jealous fear. Thus, these kharjas of Andalusia thematically resemble the *cantigas de amigo* which very soon after were cultivated in Galicia and Portugal.

The five homilies on the Song of Songs written by Gregorius of Iliberis in early years of Spain's Christianisation are reminders that this theme was familiar to Mozarabic writers and their congregations. The kharja 'Como rayo de sol' complains that the loved one has departed; 'Ya, Rab, si se me tornarad?' It then speaks of feeling weakness— 'Cuando sanarad!' The reference to the younger sisters—'Garid vos, ay ermanelas'; the question asked of her mother—'Qué faré, mamma?': all this follows the verse-text of the Song of Songs, which poets adapted usually in mystical terms but sometimes exceeding these limitations, as churchmen were quick to condemn. With the Visigothic precedents preserved in the Mozarabic enclaves this theme was at hand and natural to Christian and Jewish settings of music alike, the parallelistic patterning being a habit of both peoples. Jewish writers were held in high esteem; Isaac-ben-Simeon of Córdoba, composer, singer and player, and Avempace were close friends and Maimonides's wisdom was as proverbial then as it is world-wide now.

Two instruments of this Hispano-Arabic world have passed into the European stock—the lute, coming from the Arabic *al-'ud*, tuned in the Pythagorean scale, and the *rebec*, foremost of the stringed family before the consort of viols emerged, evolved from the Arabic *rabāb*; but instrument-makers busied themselves with many variants of these two and a considerable quantity of wind pieces for which there was much *afición*. Seville became the chief centre of this industry and it is to Al-Shaqandi (d. 1231) who lived there that we are indebted for the following list of those in use there as transcribed by Ribera: the jayal, el carrizo, el laúd, la rota, el rabel, el canún—and medio canón it may be assumed—el munis, la quenira (kind of cithara), la guitarra, el zolamí (oboe), la xocra y la nura (two flutes, the first of baritone range, the second of treble tone) and el albogue. He adds that these instruments were to be found in other regions but nowhere in such abundance as in Seville itself. 'If these instruments are in use in North Africa it is because they bring them from Spain.'

The violeros—makers of the stringed instruments—constructed various kinds of laúds, baritone, treble, with various number of strings, as well as those which were plucked with the fingers or with a plectrum. Among the wind instruments were the albogue, the añafil, the chirimía, the dulzaina and the gaita, or bagpipe; the first two kept their Arabic names, but the dulzaina was once the surnāy and the chirimía the zulamí. The percussion in use included the adufe, pandero, nacāra, atambor, castañuelas, sonajas de azófar, and so on. It is worth notice that words signifying noisy manifestations often derive from Arabic as; algazara, alarido, alboroto, albórbola, algarabía, rifirafe, zalagarda or zaragata, zambra, leila and so forth; others express types or kinds of songs or dances, as anexir, fandango, zorongo, zarabanda. Salinas, writing in his *De musica libri septem* of five-part rhythm, gives as an example a dance with song used by Spaniards and very frequently by the Moors, quoting 'Arabic' words Calvi vi calvi calvi orabi, and adding its melody, to which the Christians adapted the words 'Rey don Alfonso, Rey mi señor' and which was also incorporated by Gil Vicente into his famous piece *Dom Duardos* which contains an entire scene given over to music and its allusions to the situation and emotions of the chief characters. (In addition to the simple pattern of 6/8 in two groups of three, the Arabs had an asymmetrical bar of 10/9 made up of $3+2+3 \mid 2$ quaver beats where the last beat of each of these four groups is a quaver rest and this was known as the Khafíf thaqīl.)

The twenty-four melody modes (*tubu*) are linked by this name in 13th-century Spain to the four elements which the modes were supposed to reflect. The resonances of the lute-strings were also reflections of natural elements and human reactions to them; thus their correspondences to pantheistic mysticism gave music a pervasive significance which links it to the neo-platonic adaptations of the Cordobese philosophic school.

The reputation of Hispano-Mauresque musicians spread beyond North Africa and through the eastern confines of the Arab world. Al-Maqqarī in describing 'Abd-al-Waḥḥāb al-Ḥusain ibn Ja'far al-Ḥajīb calls this virtuoso of Andalusia 'the unique one of his generation in pleasant music (*ghinā*), delightful learning, fine poetry, beautiful expression, the most capable of mankind in playing the 'ud and in the different modes (*tarā'iq*) played on it, and in composing melodies'. No musician came from the east without seeking to make his acquaintance. A Granadine, Abū'l-Husain 'Alī ibn al-Ḥamāra, surpassed all others in composing melodies (*alḥān*) and was a skilful player on the 'ud. He is credited with having invented a special kind of lute. The Jew of Córdoba Isḥāq ibn Sim'ān, friend of Ibn Bājja (Avempace), was more eclectic and famed as a composer of melodies in all styles. Hind, a singing girl, excelled on the 'ud and Abū 'Amir ibn Yannaq (d. 1152) wrote verses to her expressing his longing to hear the notes of her 'ud in the thaqīl awwal rhythm. Bishāra al-Zāmir was one of the cleverest pipers to come from the East.

An example of one who made his way to the Orient and prospered there was Abū'l-Ḥakam al-Bahilī (1093–1155) born in Almería, who opened a school at Bagdad, then became physician to a camp hospital and finally settled in Damascus where he was highly esteemed as doctor, mathematician and musician. He played the 'ud and his work on music is well known, says Al-Maqqarī, who also praises his dīwān of excellent poetry. A Murcian musician, Ibn Sab'īn, who died at Mecca, wrote a *Kitāb al- adwār al-mansūb* (Book of the related musical modes) and became famous for his *Kitāb al-ajwiba 'an al-as'ula* written at the command of the Almohad sultan in reply to certain philosophical questions sent by the Emperor Frederick II of Hohenstaufen.

The incessant interest in instrument-making is exemplified by Abū Zakariyyā who made many instruments of a composite nature which he derived from engineering (*handasa*). He was an excellent player on the 'ud and built an organ (*urghan*) and 'sought by artful contrivance the playing of it', we are told.

When the Christians took Murcia in the 13th century the king retained a savant there distinguished in medicine, mathematics and music, Abu Bakr, to teach in the schools the monarch then founded. Abu Bakr died in Granada. Excellence in the three Ms was a distinguishing mark of a cultured member of society in Muslim Spain.

This evolution of instruments continued in most of the generic types and produced many variants; the classical lute of four strings, the *'ūd qadīm*, was still used alongside the *'ud kāmil*, or perfect lute of 5 strings fretted according to the 'Systematist' scale: the lute was made in various sizes, some of considerable dimensions. The *shahrūd* was an arch-lute or zither, described as being twice the length of the normal lute. The *qītāra*, presumably flat-chested, and probably quadrangular, was much used; the pandore family held its place and the psaltery and harp (*jank*) were also widespread. The rabāb, or rebec group, was used as a term to cover several kinds of bowed instruments. Wood-wind number about a dozen main types: *zamar, surnāy, nāy, shabbāba, saffāra, yarā, shāhīn, zummāra, zulāmī, qaṣaba*, and *mausūl*. The brass included the *būq* and *nafīr*: and the organ and pan-pipes (*armūnīqī*), were other wind instruments.

Drums may be listed as *kūs*, great kettledrum; *naqqāra, dabdāb* or *ṭabl, al-markab*, ordinary kettledrum; the *qaṣa'* or shallow kettledrum, the *ṭabl tawīl*, ordinary long drum and the *kūba*, hour-glass-shaped drum. Tambourines were the *duff, ghirbāl, bandair, ṭār, mazhar, tiryāl* and *shaq f.* Cymbals, castanets, etc. were *ṣunūj, kāsāt, muṣafiqāt* and *qaḍib*.

After the reconquest of the venerable Toledo by Alfonso VI in 1085, it became the centre from which the Muslim and Jewish culture of Andalusia spread through Spain and into Europe. During the reign of Alfonso VII (1126–1157) it became a refuge from the Almohad persecutions in the south and many Jews settled there. Under Archbishop don Raimundo and with the help of many scholars there began that translation of the Greek classics together with the commentaries of the celebrated Arab writers preserved in Spain which were to transform European thinking in many aspects, including its views on music.

The basis of the Christian forms of music in northern Spain was decisively established when the Roman liturgy replaced the Hispanic rite. The liturgical books came chiefly from France, from Aquitaine, Tours and Cluny. The Cluniac order dominated the scene first with the Aquitanian notation, and their influence in Portugal was decisive also. In the second part of the 12th century the influence of the Chanoines Réguliers de Saint-Ruf spread in their wake to be followed by the Cistercians. By the 13th century the local liturgical customs were organised and fixed within the Roman order.

Catalonia, having been freed very early from Muslim rule and leaning from the end of the 8th century towards France, received the Roman rite as early as the 10th, although certain liturgical codices of the 11th preserve reminiscences of the Mozarabic. The reform naturally extended as the Muslims were gradually driven out of the province. Thus it was that the Aragonese church maintained the Mozarabic rite until 1071, Valencia until 1238, when it was won back by Jaime, el Conquistador, and Murcia until 1266 when it was entered by Alfonso X's and Jaime's troops.

In the Catalan monasteries by this time musical activity reached a high degree of skill. Vich, which was made metropolitan during the temporary recovery of Tarragona by the Muslims, preserved venerable MSS., such as a Sacramentarium of bishop Oliva with Catalan neumic notation of the beginning of the 12th century, and a Troparium-Prosarium, from the second half of that century, with Aquitanian notation. Ripoll, founded 888, evolved its own neumic notation which revealed Carolingian and Visigothic influences, and this was adopted by the monastery of San Cugat. As at St Gall, Ripoll devised its own tropes and liturgical representations. Its prestige in Catalonia paralleled that of Moïssac for France. Oliva of Ripoll (d. 1065), was one of its most distinguished musicians and wrote a treatise called *Breviarium de musica*. San Cugat's codices contain examples in Aquitanian notation.[1]

The Mozarabic rite's decline was only assured by what was called the judgment of God. On 9th April 1077 two knights fought as champions of the national and Roman ritual and the national won; unconvinced, the king, Alfonso VI, tested the volumes of each by fire; again the Mozarabic rite triumphed. It is said that his French queen exerted pressure in favour of the French monks entrusted with the Roman cause by Gregory VI, and so another proverb was added to the Spanish popular store: 'Allá van leyes do quieren reyes'. The suppression was almost absolute, six Toledan churches being allowed to practise the old ritual and thus preserve it from extinction.

Three collections cover the main musical history of Spain from the Middle Ages to the Renaissance; the *Cantigas de Santa María*, the *Codex de las Huelgas* and the *Cancionero Musical de Palacio* represent the national course, the *Codex Calixtinus* adding testimony of activities surrounding the shrine of Santiago de Compostela about the 12th century and the *Llibre Vermell* of Montserrat yielding examples of the early 14th-century hymns and round dances performed by pilgrims in honour of their dark Virgin found miraculously in the Catalan mountains.

The juglar descended from a noble line. According to Menéndez Pidal the *cantares de gesta* were already making themselves heard in late Visigothic times and played a significant role during the grim early days of the struggle to reconquer Spain for Christendom. Alfonso X in *Las siete Partidas* singled the good juglar from the infamous entertainer as being admitted to the table of kings and nobles, so that during their

---

[1] According to Marius Schneider in *El origen musical de los animales símbolos en la mitología y la escultura antigua* (Barcelona, 1946), San Cugat's cloister illustrates an Indian tradition which attributes a particular animal to the different sounds of a scale organised in the cycle of fifths, since a series of animals carved on the columns conforms in general—though not entirely since substitute creatures appear to have been carved, as for instance, a lion in place of a tiger—to the cyclic scale and when approached solar-wise, yield in this way the notes of the melody traditionally associated with the hymn to San Cugat.

meal none other than cantares de gesta and the tale of arms should be heard in order that the king's recreation should be taken with the sound of songs and instruments, listening to the histories and romances of great heroes and their trials and all those things from which men receive both cheer and pleasure. The 11th century *Chronica Gothorum*, presumably by a Toledan Mozarab, gives the first written signs of this tradition whose subjects are widely drawn as from the Cantar de mio Cid, Los siete infantes de Lara, Sancho II of Castile, Roncesvalles, the life of Santa María Egipciaca, the siege of Zamora and go back at length to the betrayal of Spain to the Muslims in the legend of Rodrigo.

Descending to the market-place and other public sites the epic exemplars were tuned to other themes when juglars accorded their instruments to the recital of *romances*: to don Pedro the Cruel, Alvaro de Luna, the Moorish Abenámar, in which King John tells Granada he wishes to wed her; another romance mourns the loss of Alhama, which when first sung in Arabic stirred up such tumult in Granada that its

performance was prohibited. French themes were more fancifully treated as in the romance of Charlemagne and the retreat from Spain, Balduinos, don Gaiferos, taken over by Cervantes and then by Falla in the *Retablo de Maese Pedro*. It may be supposed that the romances sung as variations on the long-desired recapture of Granada, adventures of escaped prisoners, challenges, revenges and combats between Muslim and Christian heroes stimulated the public will when new offensives were about to be started. When heartening news from the frontier reached King Henry in 1462 it caused such jubilation that he ordered a romance about it to be written forthwith and directed that the singers of his chapel should perform it.

The romance was sung either as a solo or, as in this case, by a group, accompanied by *vihuela* in fine company and by *vihuela de rueda* or *sanfoña* by wandering minstrels. To the basic instruments the Ajuda Cancioneiro adds castanets, psaltery, pandero, adufe and so on, distinguishing between the vihuela de arco and vihuela de mano, that is the bowed and plucked vihuela. Since the melodies were relatively short and thus had to be repeated incessantly, the device of difference or variation was gradually resorted to by the accompanists, so that on both sides of the frontier this musical differentiation stimulated the instrumentalist's ingenuity.

These secular heroes and heroines had religious counterparts in the endurance of saints, in scenes of miracles and the exchange of divine charity for courtly loves. Of these the supreme exaltation centred on the Virgin Mary. When Alfonso X (1252–1284) compiled the 417 melodies of the *Cantigas de Santa María* he evoked an early Spanish tradition. This collection contains two kinds, one, narrative, whose songs describe her miracles; the second, songs in her honour, *loores* or hymns, recurring as a jewelled tenth between the *miragres*, like a rosary of sound. The mood was now changed from the durable epic to the softer praise of Our Lady and the gentler Portuguese-Galician speech of poets was set in the more lyrical triple rhythm. The melodies are assembled from many types, from the tunes and sequences of Provençal troubadours, from old romances and popular religious airs sung by pilgrims in romerías and processions, dances which were accompanied instrumentally, and melodies composed by Alfonso and his expert minstrels and clerical authorities. There are rondels from Paris and the virolais or virelai. Though the metrical patternings vary greatly from short to long, and the rhyming includes assonances, the structure is generally consistent, the *estrofa* (strophe) being alternated with an *estribillo* (refrain) which opens and closes the song. Within the form of the virolai there are occasional distinctive developments as in the rondel in which the refrain may momentarily cut into the strophe's second part in a phrase or line. The more complex rondel is much less frequently used than the simpler virolai, however. The melody seldom reaches beyond an octave, and half the examples are within it; in proportion to this, intervals are commonly of thirds and seconds. The melodies are characterised by ingenuous simplicity and are usually cheerful, as Alfonso X said such songs in praise of Mary should be; their modes are preponderately in D, then G and F.

Juglars provided contrasts to *loores* and love-songs generally with those *cantos de maldizer* in which they ridiculed fools and knaves and cuttingly satirised their fellows; this aspect of the tradition may be seen working to the surface of those miracles which describe the corruption and trickery of evil-doers who repent or receive punishment.

Alfonso's court attracted witty poets and skilled musicians as well as some notorious performers. Pero de Ponte, though deformed, composed love-songs as well as satire, historical eulogy and plaints; he was censured by the king for not writing in the stylish Provençal but in the popular occidental vein. Aires Nunes, however, was distinguished for his ease in both; he wrote a romería of a royal pilgrimage to Santiago de Compostela, poems of maldizer, satire again, and an Himno de Primavera, thus fulfilling his dual function as court ecclesiastic and juglar; it is supposed that he collaborated in the composition of the Cantigas de Santa María. Pedro de Ambroa, a Galician from Coruña, was a subject for jest among other juglars for having told of two pilgrimages he had made overseas though they insinuated that he had been no further than Montpellier, and when he affirmed that he had been to Santa María de Rocamador, Juan Baveca, who doubted his first boast, insisted that he had turned back at Roncesvalles. It was Baveca—the name means fool—who wrote one of the many songs which by allusive innuendo secured the lasting fame of María Pérez la Balteira. Though she had the reputation of plucking all the young soldiers whose first enquiry when they reached the frontier was for the whereabouts of this notorious singer, her power to entice men by her arts even when an old woman was celebrated in verse which still conjures up a woman of extraordinary resource and vitality. She also followed the vogue for going on pilgrimage, and like the gadding Wife of Bath survived many men who had spent their substance in yielding to her glamour. The last legend tells of her going to confession when being told to say her piece she could think of only one enormity to recount; 'Soo velha, capellao! I am old, chaplain!'

At his courts in Seville, Alfonso was attended by local artists and Portuguese, such as the juglar Lourenço, who from being a citola player aspired to the rank of troubadour. João García's songs prove him to be in the true passionate line of Galician-Portuguese writers of cantigas de amigo, as in 'Senhor, veedes-me morrer', and another in praise of two green eyes in 'Amigos, non poss' eu negar'. Special interest attaches to Nicolas de los Romances, as he was called, who wrote songs which were sung in church for the feast-days of St Leander and St Clement. In the *Repartimiento de Sevilla* he is cited thus: 'A Nicolas de los Romances, treinta arancadas, seis yugadas en Pilas.' No less would be paid to the writer of hymns for the feast of Isidore, Leander's brother, we may suppose.

Instrumental evolution since Visigothic times is to be seen in the fascinating illustrations in the miniatures portraying musicians and players in action; many of the instruments characterised in the Archpriest Juan Ruiz de Hita's *Libro de buen amor* are seen here, the broad-sweeping strings of canon and medio-canon or triangular psaltery, lute, bowed viol, two-stringed fiddle, the two guitars, morisca and latina, harps, sets of bells, the traverse flute, trumpets, straight and curved, flageolet, tabor, horn, castanets, albogues, shawms or chirimias, the Moorish

41

clashing cymbals, shakers, these are minutely drawn and the performers' faces and movements express 'joy in the making' as they commune in duo.

The types of music, French, Castilian, Galician, Portuguese, Morisco, cover realms and peoples with whom Alfonso X had links in actuality or by dynastic relationship, or in his claims to secure the imperial crown, that prize for which he schemed and dreamed—dreams which were not realised and schemes which eventually brought about his ruin.

He showed special interest in the Visigothic volumes preserved in Toledo and other places, busying himself about St Isidore's own activities which his own encyclopedic efforts came to resemble. His father, Ferdinand III, had recovered Seville, the city of Isidore's etymological labours. In this context, the miniature which heads the first cantiga—in the Escorial MS. B. 1+2—showing him dictating to a scribe with laymen and clerics assembled in council may be compared with the medieval picture of St Isidore at work on his encyclopedic compilations. Since Isidore and his colleagues wrote hymns, there seems reason to suppose that Alfonso the Learned may have done so, also, as he claimed, for his collection.

To these Cantigas de Santa María may now be added the recovery of a fine set of six songs by a juglar of Vigo, Martin Codax, first known examples of the *cantigas de amigo*, a tradition of verse in this region in which a girl mourns her lover's absence. These were transcribed by Eduardo Torner who made a lifetime's study of this northwestern music.

In a passage of his famous *Libro de buen amor*, Juan Ruiz, Archpriest of Hita, not only cites instruments in use in the 14th century, but usefully and acutely characterises their quality. As priests and laybrothers, monks and nuns, duennas and juglars sally forth to receive don Amor, the instruments, string, wind, percussion burst out in a paean of variegated acclamation like the birds of springtime newly discovering their potency of song. In exchange for this personification of the instruments, it is worth noting that in many records the juglar was only identified by the name of the instrument he played.

> *Recíbenlo los árboles con ramos e con flores*
> *de diviersas maneras de fermosas colores,*

> recíbenlo los omnes e dueñas con amores,
> con muchos instrumentos salen los atambores;
> allí sale gritando la guitarra morisca,
> de las vozes agudas e de los puntos arisca;
> el corpudo laud que tiene punto a la trista,
> la guitarra latina con estos se aprisca;
> el rabé gritador con la su alta nota,
> cab el el orabin taniendo la su rota
> el salterio con ellos más alto que La Mota,
> la viuela de péñola con estos aí sota;
> medio canón e harpa con el rabé morisco,
> entre ellos alegrança el galipe francisco,
> la flauta diz con ellos mas alta que un risco,
> con ella el tanborete, sin el non vale un prisco;
> la viuela de arco faz dulçes devailadas,
> adormiendo a las vezes, muy alto a las vegadas,
> bozes dulces, sabrosas, claras e bien puntadas
> a las gentes alegra, todas las tiene pagadas;
> dulce canón entero sal con el panderete
> con sonajas de azofar faze dulçe sonete,
> los órganos i dizen chançones e motete,
> la hadedura albardana entre ellos se entremete;
> dulcema e axabeba, el finchado albogón,
> sinfonía e baldosa en este fiesta son,
> el francés odreçillo con estos se conpón,
> la reçiancha bandurria aqui pone su son;
> tronpas e añafiles salen con atabales;
> non fueron tienpo ha plazenterías tales
> tan grandes alegrías nin atan comunales;
> de juglares van llenas cuestas e eriales.

atambor=drum. *guitarra morisca*=guitar. *laúd*=lute. *guitarra latina*=guitarlike lyre. *rabé*=rebeck. *órgano*=portable organ. *rota*=rote. *salterio*=psaltery. *vihuela de pendola*=stringed instrument plucked with plectrum. *medio canón*=small canon. *harpa*=harp. *rabé morisco*=moorish rebeck. *galipe francisco*=small French recorder. *flauta*=recorder. *tamborete*=side drum. *vihuela de arco*=bowed fiddle. *canón entero*=large canon. *panderete*=small tambourine. *sonajas de azofar*=metal clappers. *dulcema*=shawm. *axabeba*=transverse flute. *albogue*=pastoral recorder. *albogón*=large ditto. *sinfonía*=symphony. *odreçillo*=bagpipe. *bandurria*=bandore. *trompas*=trumpets. *añafil*=Moorish trumpet. *atabales*=kettledrums. *baldosa*=plucked zither.

The *Liber Sancti Jacobi, Codex Calixtinus* belonging to the cathedral of Santiago de Compostela, a 12th-century manuscript collection, is significant for its polyphonic examples rather than the monodic forms, which exceed the former by nine tenths. The most famous polyphonic piece is a *Congaudeant catholíci* by 'Master Albert of Paris', and being a three-part example, rare for the time, its appearance here indicates probably the decisively authoritative change of liturgical direction. Only one of the 15 chants stated as having been composed by pilgrims was by a Spaniard, a Galician; the rest came chiefly from notable French centres, such as Chartres and Bourges. The plainsong antiphons represent the eight church modes. Taken together, these twenty-one two-part descants, and the one in three, the extra-liturgical songs, as the Canto de Ultreja with rhythmic latin strophes, the two refrains, one in Latin, one in Flemish, these latter probably intended for the use of pilgrims, constitute a guide to the music heard in this new shrine to St James. The service for his feast-day is colourful and dramatic; the expansive jubilation of the Alleluia, the deeper tones of 'quod est filii tonitrui' following after the name of Boanerges, the insistent emphasis on each repetition of 'die ista' in the Benedicamus Domino with the sense of rising to a climax in the fifth and final trope, commemorate the apostle's martyrdom with immediacy of participation. Whether it was sung with any traces of the old traditions of the vocal dramatising effects recommended in Visigothic documents cannot be ascertained. Church architecture in the region was strikingly conservative, as in the chapel of Samos, the Leonese Mozarabic church of San Miguel de Celanova and in the structure of San Antolín de Toques, whose monastery was founded in 1060 or 1066 and received donations from Galician royal persons. Mozarabic recollections were doubtless strengthened by the translation of St Isidore's remains from Seville to León and their deposition in the royal pantheon named in the saint's honour, in 1063. It was at this time that Don Diego Peláez was planning the cathedral of St James which was itself archaic in style, though this basic structure is almost entirely hidden by the great additions and adornments bestowed by later patrons. The Codex Calixtinus, however, gives primacy to the new liturgical forms from France; its title, suggesting the authoritative interest of the French Pope Calixtus in this new centre of pilgrimage, links the shrine's cult with the royal family, since Calixtus II was brother to Count Raimund of Galicia and uncle to Alfonso VII the Emperor.

The *Codex de las Huelgas*, belonging to the royal convent for Cistercian nuns across the Duero below the site of Burgos cathedral, contains 186 items, including 59 motets, 32 conductus, 31 Benedicamus, 31 proses, 30 organa, a Creed. 87 compositions are two-part, 48 in three parts, one in four, and there are 49 monodies. Like the Codex Calixtinus, the contents are mainly foreign, especially French, only one Spanish composer being specifically named, Johan Rodrigues, composer of four Benedicamus and an Ave Maria—though Anglés doubts this last attribution. The laments for Sancho III of Castile (d. 1158) Ferdinand II of León (d. 1188) and Alfonso of Castile (d. 1214) are preserved here, in contemporary French monodic style and one for abbess María González (fl. 1325). Since Las Huelgas was founded by Alfonso VIII for his wife, Eleanor, daughter of Henry II of England, it is not surprising that among the French motets there are several now attributed to English musicians, possibly of the Worcester school. Thus, the Codex illustrates this dynastic event of Anglo-Spanish union the interest of which is historically strengthened by the later fact that the music master of Ferdinand and Isabella's royal household, Juan de Anchieta, used a theme from this collection in his own court composition in honour of Catherine of Aragon, their daughter who was married into England, with Henry VIII.[1]

A two-part Ave Maria—a conductus—may be singled out for the resemblance of its Agnus Dei to a famous Catalan nativity song around which many Christmas airs have gradually evolved. This is the *Que li darém*, theme of choral elaborations and motif woven into popular song throughout the province. The final cadence of the Agnus Dei is a motif on the words *dona nobis pacem*, and previously given to *miserere nobis* of the preceding strophes. It is extended, moreover, to the octave range of the sequence which develops similarly on the appearance of the word *nobis* in the phrase, *Tu, qui es nobis omnia nos tua pascat gracia*, on the higher notes. The ternary rocking movement of the Agnus Dei motif is like that of the sequence, and rhythmically identical with the Catalan nativity cradle song. The Catalan song's estribillo, or refrain, is within the lesser range of the motif in the Agnus Dei; its extended strophe, expands to the octave range of the sequence's development of the motif. Since this motif is heard three times in the Agnus Dei and emphasised in the last cadential fall, it is easily memorised and might well have been carried into Catalonia, suitably used as a nativity theme, since this Ave is in honour of the Virgin. The melody of *Que li darém* is also known as a *gaita* tune in Galicia and Portugal but whether it was transported thither from the same Conductus preserved at Las Huelgas would be more difficult to trace, since it lacks the link of Catalan nativity-time with the Ave Maria. However, the gaita is associated with church services, as with the Great Mass of Santiago on

[1] This suggestion of a musical reference to dynastic contemporary patterning in the royal alliances, already suggested in relation to Alfonso X's sources for the music of the Cantigas de Santa María, thus using music as a record of the line of royal descent through the generations, becomes clearer as Spanish history develops.

25th July when the gaitero precedes the hieratic pair of dancers to the altar at the conclusion of the morning's service. The figure of the gaitero with his bagpipe appears frequently in medieval church sculpture. The three-fold likeness might have its root in the Cistercian Marian sequences some of which are old enough to be written in the mensural notation of Alfonso X's time and yet were circulated in the Misales Hispanienses down to the early 16th century. Some of these appear to echo the lyrical ease of popular song. Thus, this example of the Marian Agnus Dei may offer a solution to the linked Catalan and Galician melodic chain which has puzzled many writers.

The *Llibre Vermell*, or Red Book, of Montserrat's monastery—so-called because of the red velvet in which it was bound in the 19th century—contains ten 14th-century compositions, songs and dances for the use and edification of pilgrims to this mountain shrine. It opens with an antiphon, *O Virgo Splendens*, the earliest known canon written in the peninsula and Anglés thinks that on account of its difficulty it was sung by members of the monastery to prepare pilgrims for those services in which they were to take part. It is a three-part canon in periods of 16 notes recalling isorhythmic motets of the early 14th century: the royal house of Aragon at this time closely followed the musical practices of the papal court at Avignon. The second composition, *Stella Splendens*, is a dance melody in French virolai form with a single-line instrumental accompaniment. Number 3, *Laudemus virginem*, is a circular canon simple enough for the most untutored pilgrims to follow, as is number 4, *Splendens ceptigera*. The first stanzas of each extol the Virgin, the second express penitential thoughts. Number 5, *Ballada dels goyts de nostre Dona en vulgar cathalan a ball redon: Los set goyts recomptarem* is a round dance whose verses are sung in Catalan, with a Latin refrain of *Ave Maria, gratia plena*. Its first four phrases are followed by the refrain and after this come the seven coplas, one for each 'goyt' or joy of Mary, each copla having six octosyllabic lines, usually a b, a b, a b. Number 6, *Cuncti simus*, is also headed *a ball redon* and so is number 7, *Polorum regina*. Rhythmic variety is given to these dances by the binary pattern of *Los set goyts* contrasting the ternary of *Cuncti simus* and *Polorum regina*: the two simple canons are paired by their similar ternary rhythm. Number 8, *Mariam matrem*, in contrast to the dance monodies, is a polyphonic virolai, the cantus being vocal and the two lower parts instrumental. Anglés suggests that it may be the first Spanish composition in form of the polyphonic villancico, later to be practised in the royal house at Naples and in the court of Ferdinand and Isabella. Number 9, *Inperayritz de la ciutat iojosa* is a two-part song, whose phrases extending, except to two in four, to five bars, suggest that the contemplation of Our Lady, exalted now in paradise, is an angelic joy to linger on, as the prolonged phrase-ends allow. The Montserrat copyist also dwells on the text of this song by adorning the first letter of each line, a luxury not often seen in music manuscripts of this time.

Both these last examples were probably sung by singers of the famous choir school—the escolans—offering foretaste of those celestial pleasures promised to these 'fizels' praying to her for grace eternal. Thus assured they could turn to the dance of death of the final number 10, *Ad mortem festinamus* and express with some conviction its words *De contemptu mundano* and with that briskness its rhythm rouses in the dancers. Heard in context of this whole experience of musical communion, this Dance of death is experienced as a brief passage only, since Christians are given the vision of paradise *first* and of the Virgin's eternal intercession in that 'musical jewel' as Anglés calls *Inperayritz de la ciutat iojosa*.

These ten compositions are carefully organised to give pilgrims the reward of spiritual contemplation and to send them away with enhanced faith in the Christian religion; it was this power of music that moved Morales' and Victoria's most mystical works when their texts expressed the consolations of faith in eternity at the sharp moment when death approaches. Whatever significance the *Dance of Death* took on in medieval secular spheres, here at Montserrat, it was transcended, as the words De contemptu mundano clearly indicate.

CHAPTER III

Music of the Restoration and the Hapsburg Expansion

Our knowledge of Spanish music in the 15th century, before the union of Castile and Aragon through the marriage of Ferdinand and Isabella in 1469, is enriched by records of the means used by various rulers to demonstrate their prestige with cultural flourish. Accounts of music-making at courts other than Castile fill in some gaps with interesting matter; Navarre, Aragon, Portugal, busily exchanged musicians, instruments and manuscripts across the several states and though in some periods documentary proof of Castile's participation in such affairs is lacking, even at such times her centripetal attraction is influential. The general scene is one in which a substantial foundation is gradually laid so that when Spain became a unified state in 1492 the arts, and especially music, were in a situation to express this new peninsular identity with vigorous independence.

It was in Seville, in whose royal Alcázar many of Alfonso X's Cantigas were composed, that the first musical treatise written in Castilian appeared, in 1410. This work, *Reglas de Canto Plano è de Contrapunto è de Canto de Organo fechas para informacion* by Fernando Esteban, summed up musical knowledge from Vitry to Murino, and praised Ramón de Caçio and Albertus de Rosa, two Spanish theorists of the end of the 14th century: it has been preserved in the Biblioteca Provincial of Toledo. The Escorial Library possesses the 1480 MS. of the Treatise *Ars Mensurabilis et inmensurabilis cantus* whose anonymous author praises the great evolution of music between 1440 and 1480, listing Dunstable first in his examples of notable pioneers.

By this time Bartolomé Ramos de Pareja of Baeza had completed his *Musica practica* (Bologna, 1472) and left his chair at Salamanca for Italy, where he made it known that Spain, too, had its pioneers. Alfonso X's founding of this Chair of Music in 1254 for the study of musical science, that is, of *canto figurado* or polyphony 'que aya un maestro en órgano', undoubtedly played a decisive part in centralising Spanish theoretical study in the period following his death and preceding the reign of the Catholic kings. Pareja's master, Juan de Monte, served in the papal chapel *c.* 1447, and Pareja's references to native theorists before his time, who would otherwise be unknown to us, include a maestro of Osma who was criticised by the English Carmelite, Hothby, an enemy of Pareja's ideas. However, it is through Pareja's expounding of them that the advance of polyphonic invention in Spain is recorded, as for instance, that the canon was practised, including the *canon enigmático*. He may have laid aside some Pythagorean principles, but he retained Boethius' views in mind.

The Latin learning of Spanish theorists, however, seldom obscures the native realism on which their practical musical experiments are based, and Pareja, like Bermudo after him, is no exception to this traditional character of the peninsular schools: it is, in fact, this practical resort to aural experience which has produced much original musical thought in the country.

Spanish music had continued to take nourishment from French churchmen and troubadors as in the 12th century when Limoges and Santiago de Compostela maintained contacts. The Notre Dame evolution in Paris of 13th-century clausulae, motets, organa and conductus owed its following in the peninsula partly to the family ties of St Louis with his cousin San Fernando, king of Castile and León, whose son was Alfonso the Learned. Guillaume de Machaut was in service for a time in 1345 to Charles II of Navarre and this contact with France was kept up by Charles III with an exchange of musicians. The houses of Berry, Foix, de Bar de Borgoña, Anjou, were closely allied to Spanish nobility. Aragon was in contact with the Avignon popes and Franco-Flemish musicians came into this kingdom during the reign of John I of Aragon, 1385–1396, whose chapel, like his father's before him, was filled for the most part by French singers; he had three French wives. All this time the music of Avignon maintained an ascendancy here and secular music, the ballade and virolai, followed this up. In all this the influence of Foix was probably very effective and these contacts continued in the 15th century.

The court of Burgundy's ties were closer with Portugal through their dynastic marriages, though naturally its music filtered into Castile through the network of noble families joining both, ánd it was through this court that Flemish musicians found an open door to peninsular patronage as did their painters.

In the time of the Spanish popes Calixtus III and Alexander VI of the 15th century Spanish musicians went to serve in the papal court, and it was during Nicholas V's period, which saw a great reconstruction in

Rome, that Juan de Monte, Pareja's old teacher, was there. The list of Spaniards in Rome's service lengthens with the century and as it affected their tradition so they influenced its style. The Sforzas of Milan were in touch with Spain and Portugal in the latter part of the 15th century and here the songs of Naples and Verona mingled with the amorous villancicos of Spain, as the *Cancionero Musical de Palacio* shows.

With the succession of the Aragonese kings to Naples and Sicily, the Italian connection was greatly and consistently enlarged and it was with the marriage of Ferdinand to Isabella that this rich stream entered fully into Spanish life. King Alfonso the Magnanimous, uncle of Ferdinand, greatly desired to establish a chapel à la Romana in Barcelona and first sent his cantor Pedro Sabater to Rome in search of the best singers, especially tenors; his demand for organ builders from Valencia in 1420 shows that instruments were already used in Aragonese religious polyphony, and this is also corroborated by various documents. He first visited Naples in 1420–1423, taking musicians from Barcelona with him. His second, but unlucky, expedition in 1432 included ten musicians, trumpeters, an organist, a guitarist and three players of the *xeramies* —shawms.

Proclaimed king of Naples in 1443, Alfonso kept up Spanish customs with Catalan and Castilian nobles about him and the court became known for its splendour and culture, which included moresche danze among other Spanish attractions, there being pantomimes mixed with dancing. When the German Emperor, on his marriage to Alfonso's niece Eleanor of Portugal, passed Holy Week in Capua, Alfonso the Magnanimous entertained him in grand style. Though he died in 1458, the music he fostered continued to flourish in Naples. Johannes Tinctoris (1445–1511) was in service to the court of Ferdinand I (1458–1494), Alfonso's son, who appreciated him highly. This theorist acquired a close knowledge of Catalan-Aragonese music and dedicated a work in 1477 to the king of Sicily, Ferdinand V of Aragon. Among the traditionalist theorists he discusses Dunstable. It is in this context that the *Cancionero de Montecassino* holds special interest since it contains—as does the Madrid *Cancionero Musical de Palacio*—works by Fray Johannes Cornago (3 or 4 parts) who played a fundamental part in the promotion of the canción amorosa at the court of the Catholic kings, Ferdinand and Isabella.

Katherine of Lancaster was wife to 'the Ailing' Henry III of Castile who reigned 1390–1406. Little is known of musical life at their court, though there is much evidence of Aragonese activity in those years: however, celebrations of the birth of the Constable's son retail the customary dances and music performed at entertainments of the time. The *Crónica de don Pero Niño* (c. 1448) shows the prevalence of

French chansons, ballades and virolai; and these were heard in Seville also.

Through the correspondence of Alfonso V 'the Magnanimous' with John II of Castile, whose wife was Alfonso's sister Maria, more is known of musical activity during this reign, 1406–1454. There were exchanges of musicians at this time as well as of instruments such as those small organs Queen Maria wished her brother to let her have. The *Crónica* says that John II was a musician. 'He played, versified and danced very well.' He also reorganised his chapel. The *Cancionero de Baena* was collected for him in 1445 and contained works by poets of the reigns of Pedro I, Henry II, John I, Henry III, and his own. Many of the poems of his own reign contain musical indications such as 'En esta cantiga . . . la cual fizo cantar', showing that it was set for juglars to sing; these verses were by Alfonso Alvarez de Villandino.

In the reign of John II lived the cultured Marqués de Santillana (1398–1458). In his famous letter to Pedro of Portugal, 1441, he explains his preference for Italian poets over French by writing that though the French are masters of a complicated artificial art, the Italians have more lofty imagination, knowing how to adorn their verses with beautiful sounds and to sing them in sweet and diverse manners so that it seems that the great philosophers Orpheus, Pythagoras and Empedocles were born among them. He approves of Machaut for having composed his own music for the great book of his 'balades, canciones, rondeles, lays, virolays'; 'asonó mucho dellos'.

Henry IV (1454–1474) is described as playing and singing 'with graceful style; his voice was sweet in tone and sad songs delighted him'. Isabella's half-brother, nonetheless, is not attractive to moralistic historians, though he had faithful adherents such as the Constable don Miguel Lucas de Iranzo whose *Crónica* details musical celebrations of his troubled reign. This high official was greeted by music wherever he went, as on his journeys to León and Guadalupe, with songs, drummings, and 'many other instruments'. His loyalty is commemorated in a four-part song of 1466—'Verses composed in praise of the Constable'—*Lealtat, o lealtat*—preserved in the *Cancionero Musical de Palacio*.

In Jaén the Christmas festivities included danzas and bailes, tilting, minstrels with shawms, and buffoons. The Auto de los tres Reyes here was also attended with bailes and danzas and in 1462 the Constable himself played the Mago—Wise Man. His wedding was attended by a great multitude and drums, trumpets, shawms, tambourines, timbrels and also three flageolet minstrels played most sweetly and tunefully together. These wedding celebrations continued twenty-three days, generally with the same diversions, though further on there is mention of string players—*tañedores de cuerda*. Soft music was a special provision

51

at marriages both popular and in the grand manner. When a child was born to him, however, the instruments made so much noise that 'it seemed as if the world were falling down'; they now included bagpipes. The alborada was played softly, nevertheless, to waken the people pleasantly. On Shrove Tuesday a great bonfire was lit and the Condestable and his lady went up into the palace tower after supper and the shawms played 'in the said tower' for them all. We are not told whether they ascended the tower on Mayday morning to sing madrigals, but learn that at the spring festival the musicians came to play at his door, he having been betimes to 'Maytines' and returned to bed to sleep. In the procession of Espíritu Santo the bagpipers went in front, accompanied by all the boys and girls of the city. St John's Day was celebrated by tilting, but on Mary's feast, the Assumption, 'se facian todas las cosas'—all manner of things were performed. St Luke's feast was commemorated with a procession, all carrying white tapers while the Te Deum was sung. The organs played one verse, the next was sung in procession, and so on. On royal occasions, when the Te Deum was sung, the organs played one verse and the clerics sang the next, and in processions instrumentalists played one verse, the people singing the next; when the instruments played the procession walked but when the people sang, all stood still. Between dances in the palace of an evening, cossantes and rondels were usually sung by the company.

When Pedro the Constable of Portugal was in Barcelona in 1466 and wrote to his treasurer in June from Granollers to send him all the fruit available as soon as possible as there was a shortage where he was, he added: 'Y mandadnos el clavicimbol del cual os habemos ya antes escrito—and send us the clavicembolo about which we wrote before.' He then also bids him send the manocort of master Gaspar's son. A document of 1420 cites 'Un instrument de cant d'orga, de fusta, appellat manacort' thus showing that this instrument accompanied the polyphony and was classified as a polyphonic instrument.

Portugal's reconquest had been completed in 1250 and her contacts with foreign courts emphasised her independence of Castile since her sovereignty was assured through marriage with the Count of Burgundy; she developed close exchanges with the Flemish also. The Cluniacs and Cistercians had played a large part in determining events in Portugal in the early years of this stabilisation so that through them Franco-Flemish and Burgundian music had also become familiar. The contact was reinforced by the marriage of John I of Aviz to Philippa of Lancaster, John of Gaunt's daughter, for in his time (1385–1433) French was spoken at court. In his book on hunting, *Livro da Montaria*, however, this monarch refers to Guillaume de Machaut, showing that music and hunting, which were to be twin passions of Portuguese royal families till the close of the 18th century, were already associated, though not with that same equality of favour of later generations, since he observes of the music of his hounds: 'podemos dizer mui bem que Guilherme de Machado nom fez fermosa concordança de melodia, nem que tam bem pareça, como a fazem os caaes quando bem correm'. 'We could very well say that Guilherme de Machado does not make so beautiful a concorde of melody, however well it might seem, as the hounds do when running well.'

John II (1481–1495) intensified exchanges with Spain and as the dynastic ties grew closer so did musical understanding, and thus Portuguese musicians served notably in the court of the Catholic kings. Patronage reached its height when John III (1521–1557) received the dedication of Luis Milán's *Libro de Música de vihuela de mano, intitulado el Maestro* (Valencia, 1535), which included the words: 'La mar donde he echado este libro es propiamente el reyno de Portugal, que es la mar dela música; pues en el tanto la estiman; y tambien la entienden.' 'The sea wherein I have launched this book is none other than the kingdom of Portugal, which is the sea of music; for it is there that it is so much esteemed; and also there it is understood.' Fray Bermudo, the great theorist, also dedicated a work to John III.

The Aragonese royal house kept systematic records of musicians and church singers, though it withheld details and Barcelona followed this methodical practice in its episcopal archives. In his father's lifetime, Ferdinand of Aragon—consort to Isabella—already had a chapel of 12 singers and a chapel master, 4 minstrels and 7 trumpets. In spite of the constant lists of names, however, little has been preserved of instrumental chamber music of the late 15th and early 16th centuries, though there were minstrels and vihuelistas at court.

It was sacred music which was always emphasised among the Catholic kings' records. This is made abundantly clear in contemporary lists as well as in accounts of the service for the royal chapel: it was also a tradition previously observed by Henry III, John II and Henry IV of Castile and by Alfonso V and John II of Aragon. Instrumentalists do not figure in accounts of chapel personnel, though official trumpeters assisted at services: Alfonso V wrote to Valencia in 1420 directing that the organs should be in tune with the minstrels' instruments.

It was after the two crowns were joined that native religious polyphony began to be preserved and the composers personally identified—such names as Johannes de Anchieta, Pedro de Escobar, Alonso de Alva, Quixada, Francisco de Peñalosa, Alonso de Mondéjar, Alfonso, and Fernando de Tordesillas. The oldest composer at court was Juan de Cornago of the Neapolitan court, who was in Ferdinand's service in 1475. The music of these composers is chiefly three and four part masses, motets, psalms and so forth, but though the repertory is very often Netherlandish in form it is evident that while some Spaniards of the late 15th century experimented in this Franco-Flemish technique, this was only while they settled to the task of creating a national school of their own. The more florid counterpoint of the north was used in the Kyrie, Sanctus and Agnus: the Gloria and Credo are already treated in what became recognised as the characteristic native style; the Gloria and Credo have archaic roots in Spain. Too much has been lost and too little as yet made known of the music of this time for a just estimate to be formed of its total achievement; however, the extant works of the group named above definitely show that native temperament and sound technique were already at hand when they began to create in a national manner.

Two outstanding leaders were Juan Anchieta and Peñalosa, the first attached to Isabella's household, the second to Ferdinand's They also represent the differences of outlook musically between Castile and Aragon. Anchieta, born a Basque at Azpeitia, related through his mother to Ignatius Loyola, has the directness and a sense of unity of a dramatic concentration upon his texts; he has a Basque rhythmic keenness and like Cabezón later, works his details proportionately into the overall structure. Anglés gives a complete Mass and the Kyrie, Gloria and Credo of a *Missa de beata Virgine* in his 1941 volume *La música en la corte de los Reyes Católicos*. Two motets and a Salve Regina open the 1933 *Antología musical* by Elústiza and Castrillo Hernández. Four secular songs are preserved in the *Cancionero Musical de Palacio*. Charles V pensioned Anchieta in 1519 and he died in 1523. His MSS. are widely distributed in the peninsula, including Coimbra.

Francisco de Peñalosa (*c.* 1470–1528) shows the advantage of Italian contacts in the more expansive style and confidence of his writing. Attached to Ferdinand V as singer in his household, he enjoyed early success at Pope Leo X's court. Six masses, six magnificats, some thirty motets and a set of lamentations are extant and ten songs in the palace song-book rank among the most finely expressive in this collection. He held a canonry in Seville cathedral and is buried in the nave of San Pablo in this city. Anglés believes he was born in Talavera de la Reina. The pope defended his right in absentia at Rome to his cathedral post though the local council disapproved. His singing moved Leo X extremely when he sang the Good Friday passion *more hispano* alone in the papal chapel, where before three singers had intoned the Johannine narration.

Though Spaniards did not use secular themes in their masses and motets so commonly as the northerners, turning generally to the Gregorian for basic material, their exceptions are noteworthy even at

I (a) Statue of Mercury with ten-string lyre, from the Temple of Mithras at Mérida

(b) Detail from above

II. Musicians, from the Beato de Liébana (786), copied in 1047

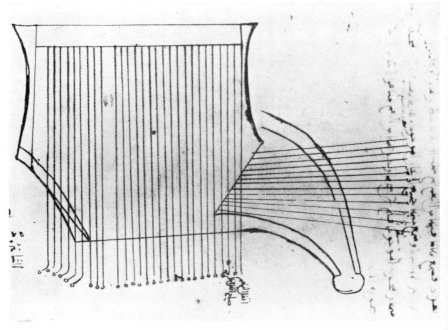

III. The Shahrud, from the Kitab-al-musiqi of Al-Farabi (d. 950)

this time. Anchieta used the famous *L'Homme armé*—a favourite of Charles V—in the Agnus of his *Missa quarti toni*: Peñalosa adopts the same and *Nunca fué pena mayor* as well as *Por la mar* in three masses preserved in Tarazona. Pedro de Escobar drew on yet another popular song *Adiu mes amours*, known to church composers.

The monarch's chapel personnel was large by European standards. The Queen had 16 to 20 singers, one to three organists and up to 25 *moços de capilla*, who sang the plain chant; these were Castilians. Ferdinand's chapel numbered 41 in 1515, without counting the boy singers; his family's musicians had been drawn from France, Avignon and Burgundy, but when the courts were merged, he adopted Isabella's custom of selecting Castilians who now performed native music before their two rulers. The capellanes, entrusted with the Gregorian chanting, rose to 50. Great care was shown in the founding of the royal chapel in Granada's new cathedral and in the celebration of polyphonic music, and this Charles V continued. It was not until after the queen's death that the two royal chapels became one when Ferdinand united them as la capilla de la Corte Real de España. Ceremonial trumpetings on solemn occasions were a feature of Sunday and feast-day services and a memorandum on this tradition was passed on to Charles V. The pay of these minstrels equalled that of the chief singers and their instruments were richly inlaid.

Juan Anchieta was music master from 1489 to the heir, Prince Juan, who had his own suite of musicians. His moços de capilla were Spanish youths and his tañedor e cantor—player and singer—was Iohan Vernal. Instrumentally he was served by a tañedor de rabé, menestril de dulçayna, horganista and tamborino. 'He was naturally inclined to music and well versed in it and because his voice was not as he wished and he was persistent in desiring to sing, in the siesta hours, and especially in summer, Johannes de Anchieta his music master and four or five boy singers of the chapel who had fine voices and of whom one, Corral, had a beautiful treble, went to the palace and the Prince would sing with them a couple of hours or so long as it pleased him, performing the tenor part and he was very dexterous in this art. In his chamber he had a claviorgano and other organs, clavecimbanos and clavicordio and the vihuelas de mano and vihuelas de arco and flautas; and all these instruments he knew how to play. Among his instruments he also had a very fine rrabelico which was played by one Madrid, native of Caramanchel, from which place better works than musicians come forth,[1] but this one was very good . . .' Thus this luckless young prince's love of music is described by Gonzalo Fernández de Oviedo in the *Libro de*

---

[1] Anglés disagrees with Barbieri's suggestion that this was the composer Juan Fernández de Madrid whose graceful songs figure in the *Cancionero Musical de Palacio*.

la Cámara real del principe Don Juan, 1548. He died, six months after marriage in 1497.

The princesses, too, were thoroughly trained in music and carried their tastes and players into those lands to which dynastic marriages led them—to Portugal, to the Low Countries, to England where Shakespeare's Katherine of Aragon, her soul grown 'sad with troubles', bids her lute-player 'sing and disperse 'em, if thou canst.'

The transition from the medieval spirit to renaissance humanism is exemplified in the life and works of Juan del Encina (1469–1529), musician and dramatist. At Salamanca he studied with Nebrija and then served as musician in the palace of the Duke of Alba. Later, in Rome he became active in the pontifical circle and familiarised himself with the Italian secularisation of the arts. Nevertheless, he remained faithful to his Spanish antecedents. Becoming a priest he went on a pilgrimage in 1519 to Jerusalem where he celebrated his first mass. His early works, such as the nativity eclogues, are in medieval tradition, though it is from the comic scenes of the shepherds and their rustic company that his exploration of the pastorale developed in a natural sequence; his music for these interludes also conformed to tradition. Influenced by Virgil—again in a natural transition since Virgil was regarded as a precursor to Christian belief—the later eclogues endorse the Italian duality. His *Farsa de Placidia e Vittoriano* was recited in Spanish before the Pope (1513) though the Inquisition judged the appearance of Jupiter in the office for the dead as irreverent and forbade the work in 1559. His villancicos and songs are markedly Spanish in their unassuming spontaneity. 68 of these are preserved in the *Cancionero Musical de Palacio.* The *Egloga de Cristino y Febea*'s theme of a hermit leaving his solitude for love of a woman and the pleasures of pastoral existence was developed by dramatists of the golden age. Though a gifted musician, Encina was not appointed cantor at Salamanca cathedral as he had hoped and was given only a minor post here in 1502; nor did he stay long at Málaga after being made archdeacon, for he returned to Rome soon after. It was only in 1519 that he was made prior to León cathedral.

The *Cancionero Musical de Palacio* is a collection of songs of the 15th and 16th centuries, mostly composed by musicians of Ferdinand and Isabella's courts and amounting to 458 pieces. Its transcription and publication in 1890 by Francisco Barbieri quickened that revival of national interest in its musical past which distinguishes Spanish musical activity today. It contains about 400 villancicos, more than 40 romances, about a dozen estrambotes, the Spanish term for the Italian frottola, and other polyphonic examples; among the villancicos there are only 30 religious items; 92 other compositions are now missing. Essentially a collection of vocal works, it includes one exception, a *Danza alta* for three instruments specially written by the Andalusian Francisco de la Torre to be performed in the royal household; this is the only known piece of such a kind from the 15th century, it is said.[1]

As a musical testament of the Catholic Kings' reign it extends from before her birth until after his death. It is fully representative of their domains, including the Aragonese lands in Italy which the frottola, added later, may signify; the name of Juan Cornago among the composers probably indicates his importance among creators of the polyphonic love-song. All the important Spanish musicians are included and the finest poets, Jorge Manrique, Juan de Mena, Lucas Fernández, the Marqués de Santillana and so on. The musicians include Anchieta, Alonso de Alva, Almorox, Baena, Encina, Escobar, Gabriel, Madrid, Medina, Millán, Mondéjar, Peñalosa, Ponce, Torre, Triana, and the identities of 53 have now been established. Juan del Encina is represented by 68 songs, settings of his own verse; Millán by 23 songs; Gabriel 19; Escobar 18; Torre 15; Ponce 12; Alonso 11; Mondéjar 11; Peñalosa 10; Baena 7.

Lope de Baena was first attached to Ferdinand's court of Aragon in 1478 and then as vihuelist and singer to Isabella in 1493. Pedro Escobar was chapel master at Seville cathedral from 1507 to 1514, possibly to the year of his death. Francisco de Peñalosa (born *c.* 1470) was cantor to Ferdinand in 1498 until 1516, and also cantor to Pope Leo X. Francisco Millán was cantor in Isabella's chapel, *c.* 1501–1502. Juan Ponce was cantor to Ferdinand; Gabriel Mena was also the king's cantor and Mondéjar succeeded to his service after the queen's death; Alonso de Alva was queen's singer in her chapel service from 1491. Francisco de la Torre, one of the elders of this group, is listed on Ferdinand's rolls on 1st July 1483.

The quality of the Spanish contributions is of the finest, based in the senior composers' music on that old tradition beloved by the royal family; continually the songs echo the strains of past musical experiences, giving deep emotive power to that evocation of the romances to which Spanish spirits still vibrate. The *Cancionero* includes cossantes, also, that type of parallelistic song with which an evening's dances were often interspersed; these, too, stirred dormant memories.

It is possible that this collection, which excels other song-books in every way, was partly intended to continue the precedent of Alfonso X's *Cantigas de Santa María*, which covered Spanish dynastic relations during his reign. Both contain over 400 items. The joint royal houses

---

[1] There are various overlappings in attempts to classify these forms dating from the 16th century. The first index classifies 396 songs as villancicos, 29 as sacred villancicos and 44 as romances.

of Aragon and Castile cover not only Italy, but have close dynastic ties with Portugal: there are Portuguese examples in the *Cancionero*, as in Badajoz' and Pedro de Escobar's music, since both served in that sister state. There is a song by Robert Morton to represent the English alliance, number 27, 'Pues servicio vos desplase'. There is Josquin des Près to represent the marriage alliance in the Low Countries with his frottola, In te Domine speravi, number 84, written whilst he was in the Cardinal Sforza's service.

Francisco de la Torre, composer of the unique *alta danza a 3*, the only piece of its kind included in the *Cancionero Musical de Palacio*, is himself unique since he wrote nothing that was inserted into the collection after its first selection was made. The tenor of this unique three-part dance for the instruments is the basse-dance melody of *La Spagna*, used as a cantus firmus by composers, particularly by Heinrich Isaac (1450–1517), who served in the imperial court of Maximilian, and later by Cabezón. This dynastic connection offers a clue to Torre's choice of his tenor theme for this unique contribution, which he was directed to compose. As one of Ferdinand's musicians from 1483, his Damos gracias a ti Dios (CMP 32) is a thanksgiving for the king's triumph over the Muslims and his motet Libera me has been reserved for archbishops' funerals in Toledo down to the present century; altogether he represents senior authority among Ferdinand and Isabella's musicians. It was through the marriage of their daughter Joanna to Maximilian's son, Philip the Fair, that Spain acquired the imperial crown, coveted by Alfonso X, and worn by Charles V their grandson, so that dynastic interest attaches to this Spanish dance—called *Alta* in the CMP—used by Isaac, musician to Maximilian, as cantus firmus. Moreover, at an earlier wedding also of signal importance to Aragon, that of the Count of Barcelona Ramon Berenguer IV to Princess Petronila daughter of Ramiro of Aragon, in 1150, it was recorded that a dance, linked to weddings as it was also to seed-sowing activities in Aragon, including Alto Aragon, was performed at the festivities. Known as the *danza de paloteo*—dance of the sticks—this included leaps in most instances; though now not so widespread as formerly, it was performed within living memory in San Cugat del Valles. Torres' example of the *Alta* uses skips of a fourth much more frequently than his other pieces, giving the treble no less than 15 upward leaps of this interval.

One domain seems not to be represented, that new found land—America. Here the longest piece in the Song Book may be involved. This number 154, Una montaña pasando, was composed by Garci-muñoz and written as an autobiographical tale of a traveller experiencing strange encounters afar off, in manner of the *romance*. At the end of this lengthy account in Spanish, it shifts to Latin and the four-part fabordón intones '*How shall we sing a new song in a strange land?*' from Psalm 137, verse 4. Psalm 136 was constantly to be heard in celebration of the fall of Granada and the discovery of the New World; thus to include reference to adventures in the new domains in the form of the old *romance* seems very apt, if this allusion were meant.

The single example by Vilches, *Ya cantan los gallos*, no. 155, is textually parallel to Galician songs such as Canta o gallo, ven o dia, on this same theme of the man being urged to get up since the cocks are already crowing, another Galician instance of a girl's song—the opposite theme to the cantigas de amigo which lament the lover's absence. This song furthermore is also included in the Portuguese *Cancioneiro Musical Hortênsia* of Elvas. It may be intended to mark a link with Alfonso X's Cantigas from the Galician-Portuguese tradition. The popular 6/8 melody of Canta o gallo is of the gaita (bagpipe) type.

The sense of continuity which these songs of the Palace song collection show was built into the Catholic Kings' Royal Chapel foundation; its Constitutions give accounts purporting to go back to King Reccared of Visigothic times.

From this period onwards secular music is preserved in quantity, as evidenced by those cancioneros collected in the royal palaces of Seville, Valladolid, Medina del Campo, Toledo, Segovia, Barcelona, Saragossa and Valencia. Nevertheless little of this secular music was printed. Juan Vásquez' publication is exceptional, but whether this was connected with his concentration on 15th-century polyphonic song in which he took as his material the traditional songs of Castile and Andalusia, adopting new poets like Boscan and Garcilaso while maintaining the tradition of romances viejos, remains undetermined; it is fairly clear that in this way his tastes coincided with the royal predilection for old songs and ways.

Juan Vásquez was born in Badajoz about 1500 or earlier and becoming early attached to Seville's musical orbit went to Plasencia cathedral as cantor and then to Palencia in 1541. He was in Madrid ten years later, 1551. In that year his collection of *Villancicos y Canciones* was printed by Osuna University and in 1560 a *Recopilación de Sonetos y Villancicos a cuatro y a cinco* appeared in Seville. This was edited by Mgr Anglés (Instituto Español de Musicología, 1946). His pieces were already in circulation, since both Valderrábano and Mudarra included some of his villancicos in their books. His two collections contain twenty-six and forty-five examples respectively, and as their titles suggest, villancicos predominate in both. Bermudo advised that his villancicos should be taken as models beside those of well-known foreigners, and other Spaniards and vihuelists transcribed them for their own use. Pedrell also singled him out and printed seven of the villancicos in modern notation. The madrigals of the *Recopilación* show the villancico in process of transformation into a kind of Castilian Italianised song, and the villancico amoroso is set beside the traditional native form; but although court tastes were now veering towards the Spanish interests in their Italian courts, Vásquez' love of his native music ensured that this was the base on which he constructed such novelties from over the Mediterranean waters. He shares the gift of those other Sevillians—Badajoz had long been part of this Andalusian region aesthetically—Morales and Guerrero, for his close concentration on his text, so that there is a continual strengthening of one art by the other and indissoluble bonds are forged between them by considerable emotional fire. His service for the dead, *Agenda defunctorum*, was published in Seville in 1556. His choice of texts was followed by discerning successors: 'De los álamos', 'Con que la lavaré', 'Vos me mataste', 'Si me llaman, a mi llama', 'De donde venis, amore' and 'Quando, Quando' continue to delight generation after generation. It is known that he moved in palace circles as a privileged musically-gifted priest and it is to be hoped that more will yet be brought to light about this poetically creative composer associated with the lines:

> *O dulce contemplación!*
> *O preciosa fantasia!*
> *Que me muestras cada dia*
> *Una tal clara visión*
> *Que es salud del alma.*

It was the *romance* which emerged from the slow collapse of medieval forms as the most serviceable to renaissance expression. The 46 examples in the CMP show its more primitive form of four short phrases; there were no repetitions either of words or music and the same music served all strophes. In the 16th century the first stirrings of expansion are seen in the repetition of the last line to give finality to the whole. The vihuelists enlarged this by sections in which they glossed the theme and ventured on instrumental introductions. Then in line with 17th century demand for dynamic movement, estribillos or refrains were inserted, not so much for their own sakes, but in contrast with the familiar binary rhythm which their ternary lightness quickened. It thus became flexible enough to take to the stage, not only in the opening cuatro de empezar—a set introductory piece sung by four— but also as a willing instrument in the dramatist's hands, influencing the choice of theme, deepening the mood of a confrontation, lightening an over-complicated situation by its sudden exuberant joyousness. Some of the theatre's *jácaras* are true *romances*, in spite of their picaresque overtones, and, in fact, many airs, and even dances, are adapted from this form. It even found a way into the churches, disguised as the villancico, which was also experiencing a kind of second and less inhibited youth, and was to be heard intoned on solemn occasions. These alterations there was no valid reason musically to criticise, considering the high official tradition from which the romance had emerged as a younger scion with its way to make in the world. But though it shed much of its old character, the romance remained recognisably of Spanish castizo stock. The estribillo counterpart was not necessarily of the same proven quality, but it was lively, flexible and capable of adopting the irregularly wayward seguidilla and aided by this new dimension it could compete with the villancico.[1]

Isabella was especially fond of the vihuela and kept three or four vihuelists about her. The tañedor de vihuela held a privileged post because although he played the laúd on occasion—the musicians were expected to be proficient on two or three of the same instrumental group—his official title was always given as 'vihuela player'. It was the vihuela music which thrust Spain into the forefront of European keyboard composition and its influence in the evolution of diferencia and variation is shown by developments which followed the appearances of Spanish players in other countries—England, the Low Countries, Italy. The use of the organ—the church of Tona in Catalonia had one as early as 888—had steadily expanded as Pedrell's *Organografía musical antigua española* relates, including the construction of the great Toledo organ in the days of Charles V, begun in 1543 by Gonzalo Hernández of Córdoba, and completed by the Toledan master, Juan Gaytán in 1549. Padre José Antonio de Donastia, the composer, has published a study of Basque organs, including that of Tolosa of 1686, showing that even modest towns thought it suitable to their dignity to possess finely equipped instruments (*Música y Músicos en el País Vasco*, 1951). Already in mid-16th century there were organs yielding an extraordinary range of sound, from the stridently militant—recalling Alfonso V's request for the organs at Valencia to be tuned according to the trumpets—and baroque brilliance to the mellifluous contemplative nature of the registers usually reserved for the Offertory and Agnus.

---

[1] Collections of this period are rich in evidence of these evolutions, as in the Madrid Biblioteca Nacional's *Romances y Letras de a tres vozes*, containing 74. The *Cancionero de Turin* contains 12 for 3 or 4 voices. The *Cancionero de Sablonera* yields 42. The *Cancionero de Upsala* has 54 (see the studies by Leopoldo Querol and Isabel Pope). The *Cancionero Medinaceli*, Madrid, also known as *Tonos castellanos*, yields 15, and possibly more romances. The *Cancionero español de la Biblioteca Casanatense*, Rome, yields 8 (see Charles V, Aubrun's edited texts, *Bulletin Hispanique*, 1949-1950). The *Libro de Tonos humanos*, Madrid, Bib. Nac. triumphs numerically with 215. *Los romances del P. Juan Cererols* (1618-1676), 21 in number, show the estribillo outgrowing its parent stock: see also *Romances de la Bib. Central Barcelona*). To the romances of the *Cancionero español*, Coimbra, must now be added the recently found *Cancioneiro Hortênsia of Elvas*.

The vihuela in Spain was as much a popular as it was a nobleman's instrument; in both spheres the practical advantage of being heard equally well in and out of doors and of being portable ensured its ubiquity, while its association with song both old and new made it an indispensable accompanist. By the 16th century it had become the instrument by which the higher musical skills were tested. Fray Bermudo, for example, advised beginners to practise on the manochord before proceeding to the vihuelas's more complex art; yet the manochord was capable of evoking a considerable range of expressive quality and the high standard of instrument-making in Spain is proved by the survival of such members of the keyboard family. One owned by Queen Joanna, mother to Charles V, still responds to fingers recalling themes and diferencias known to her family, as the present writer can testify.

The distinguishing terms given by these vihuela players to the search for a desired quality of timbre may relate to this native use of the word *diferencia* more frequently than variation. The use of the word 'herir' meaning to touch and strike and also to penetrate, puncture the strings —as for instance in Espinel's *Vida del Escudero Marcos de Obregón* where he praises a vihuelist *'que en la verdad de herir la cuerda con aire y ciencia . . . llegó al extremo que se puede llegar'*. This suggests an artist bent on extracting the maximum differentiation of timbre from his notes, for in truth in 'striking the string with grace and skill he reached the furthest point that can be attained'. Thus the word *diferencia* may have meant to Spanish musicians something more intensively dramatic than *variation*, which was still associated with vocal polyphony and so more diffuse and ornamental by precedent, diversifying, but not necessarily disconcerting with passing disagreements as the vihuela diferencias subtly allow, for these players were more terse, even concise in their dramatically conceived search for expression, and the vocalised variation later evidently learned some lessons from this *castizo* Spanish character. In contrast, the organists used the word 'tentear'—tentear el instrumento—again to express the idea of searching out, but in this case, implying the organist's need to find a way of touching his instrument in a more legato manner, thus producing the title *Tiento*, to specify the music resulting from experiments to evolve a less exterior brilliance of effect than the Toccata as introduced to Spain. The concept is parallel, the vihuelist and the organ player each in his own field searching for the kind of touch by which the special nature of his instrument might be most intimately interpreted. These two instruments also demonstrate their keyboard relationship by this persistence of composers in writing diferencias on the traditional romance themes for them.

Though Luis de Milán was exposed to renaissance influences in Valencia, at the court of Ferdinand V's widow, Germaine de Foix, now married there, and perhaps to the Netherlands styles flourishing in Portugal, his *Libro de Música de vihuela de mano* (Valencia, 1535), characterises the vihuela as an accompanying instrument, still partly influenced by the villancico style, but asserting its own character. This was quickly followed in 1538 by the *Seys libros del Delphín de Música de cifras para tañer vihuela* by Luis Narváez, printed in Valladolid, evidently based on the same foundation as Milán's and expanding that exploration of the vihuela's potential in the melodic, polyphonic, melodic-harmonic and dance forms treated through the differentiation. The industriousness of this school and the material extracted from old themes is to be appreciated by the case of the romance 'Conde Claros' for-which Narváez wrote 22 diferencias, Valderrábano, 120, Pisador 37, Mudarra, 12 and Venegas 5. Milán called his pieces *fantasías* because he claimed they proceeded from his own industry and invention. Narváez, born in Granada, taught the young Prince Philip, Philip II to be. One of his poems contains the following concept of music which is worth pondering in connection with the diferencia:

> *Lo criado*
> *por música está fundado,*
> *y por ser tan diferente*
> *tanto más es excelente*
> *porque está proporcionado.*

(Created things are based on music, and being so different are the more excellent because they are so in proportion.)

Narváez extends his transcriptions to examples from Josquin, Gombert and other polyphonic masters in addition to the type of villancicos, romances and dances of Milán's volume, but the diferencia obviously absorbs his creative powers.

Alfonso Mudarra's *Tres libros de música en cifra para la vihuela* were printed in Seville, 1546 and these expand the instrument's thematic range further, including Flemish, Italian church music and psalms in Latin, renaissance and traditional Spanish verse, all with music adapted or newly composed for vihuela.

Enríquez de Valderrábano's *Libro de Música de vihuela intitulado Silva de Sirenas* (Valladolid, 1547), approved by Philip, the royal heir, also includes sacred and profane songs, dances, fugues, counterpoints and pieces written for vihuelas in duet. This classics-conscious musician claims that the instrument evokes the most perfect and profound music of all.

Diego Pisador's *Libro de Música para vihuela* (Salamanca, 1552) claims to supersede all others so far composed and adds examples by Morales and Basurto, villanescas in three and four parts, and pasos remedados and fantasias in addition to the ubiquitous romance and villancico. Philip is again invoked as patron.

Most widely appreciated perhaps of all was and remains the *Libro de Música para vihuela intitulado Orphénica lyra* by the blind composer Miguel de Fuenllana, printed in Seville, 1554, dedicated to 'don Felipe, príncipe de España y rey de Inglaterra y de Nápoles'. Here fellow Spaniards are given full place and chosen from the very best of Fuenllana's contemporaries: Cristóbal Morales, Francisco Guerrero, Flecha, Juan Vásquez and Rabaneda. In his own fantasias Fuenllana's purity of taste and intense concentration shine, in spite of that corporeal cloudiness which as he explains in his dedication obscures his labours by day and keeps him wakeful by night. He transcribes three of Flecha's Ensaladas, sets romances from Vásquez's collection, three of which deal with the Moors in Spain, as De Antequera sale el moro; A las armas, moriscote and Ay de mi, Alhama, and transcriptions of Morales' church motets and other church forms. One of his own *diferencias* is a setting of Ave Maria Stella, a poignantly suitable theme for this blind genius.

So the stream grew. Esteban Daza's *Libro de Música en cifras para vihuela intitulado El Parnaso*, printed in Valladolid, his native city, 1576, also gives Spanish airs by Vásquez and Guerrero, four and five part motets, French songs, villanescas and includes numerous fantasias of his own.

Linked to these exponents of the vihuela who in such quick succession revealed the abundant riches awaiting the arrival of printing in Spain—in which Seville came first as befitted the city which had been the centre of instrument-making for centuries before—are the publications which extend the vihuela's experience to sister instruments: Luis Venegas de Henestrosa, a member of the famous Cardinal Tavera's suite, published in Alcalá de Henares, 1557, his *Libro de cifra nueva para tecla, harpa y vihuela, en el cual se enseña brevemente cantar canto llano y canto de órgano, y algunos avisos para contrapunto*; Fray Thomas de Santa Maria's volume *Libro llamado Arte de tañer fantasia, assi para tecla como para vihuela* (Valladolid, 1565) and *Obras para música de tecla, arpa y vihuela de Antonio de Cabezón . . . recopiladas y puestas en cifra por Hernando de Cabezón su hijo* (Madrid, 1578).

Cardinal Tavera's chapel at Toledo was splendidly equipped with many players and their instruments; his chapel master was that García de Basurto featured in Pisador's book, and his organist was Francisco Torres. Venegas' anthology includes 138 works by known composers as well as anonymous; tientos on French songs besides romances and fantasias for the vihuela are featured; Antonio de Cabezón's music is outstandingly represented and so marks the apogee of this brilliant and idiosyncratic Spanish creative line. Daza's work was the last devoted exclusively to the vihuela to appear. In ten years' time, the first treatise on the guitar appeared in Barcelona, in 1586, and this was written by a lively doctor, Juan Carlos Amat, who blames the choleric impatience of Spaniards for the appearance of his little work since their music masters become exhausted with trying to teach them this art of guitar-playing in the three days the pupils demand. The little treatise is short though its title is long. *Guitarra y vandola en dos maneras de Guitarra Castellana y Catalana de cinco ordenes, la cual enseña de templar y tañer rasgando todos los puntos naturales y bemolados con estilo maravilloso. Y se hace mención también de la guitarra de cuatro órdenes.* Emilio Pujol believes that the vandola here named is probably related to the Catalan *Llaut guitarrenc*; its relation to the words mandola and mandora suggests a family root for all these smaller instruments frequently associated with guitar ensembles. The harp appears in association with other keyboards throughout this century, but solo music for it does not appear until 1702 when Diego Fernández de Huete's music was printed in Madrid. It was taken to the New World in company with the guitar and violin and took part in many South American balls and other festivities where even to this day it is prominently heard, especially in more remote towns, as in Chile, Argentina and Venezuela.

It was an organist who raised Spanish keyboard music to its most sustained heights in the first half of the 16th century. Antonio de Cabezón, born about 1500 in Castillo de Matajudíos, Castrojeriz, in the province of Burgos, and named the Spanish Bach by Felipe Pedrell, who published his organ music in the monumental *Hispaniae Schola Musica Sacra*, blind and concentrated within a world of contemplative sound-weaving, was already in service to the imperial court as organist to the Portuguese wife of Charles V at the age of eighteen, continuing this attachment to the Emperor until this monarch's retirement to Yuste and then transferred to Philip II in a close attendance which despite his disability made him one of Europe's most travelled musicians. He was with Philip on his extended progress of 1548 through the Low Countries to the Flemish and Brabant towns, Namur and Luxemburg and then into Germany for the Diet of Augsburg and southwards into Italy from Geneva, to Milan and Mantua, then Trent, Innsbruck and Brussels in a tour which lasted a year and a half. Copies of Cabezón's works deposited in libraries such as the Wolfenbüttel and the Saint-Geneviève of Paris suggest that his successes were more than temporary and that his music was studied by musicians in other countries. He was by this time at the height of his powers as a composer of European stature and experience.

Thus when Philip took him to England—with his brother Juan, also a keyboard composer and player—for his marriage to Mary Tudor in 1554–1555 Cabezón possessed an unparalleled knowledge of contemporary music-making across the imperial domains. His only known comment on this stay in England shows him concerned merely to document the royal gift of a thousand ducats from Philip in recognition of his services there and the use of it in the marrying and setting up in household of his daughter Maria.

Many arguments have risen about whether English or Spanish musicians profited most from this Spanish sojourn at the English court. Historically, for the Spanish viewpoint, it should be emphasised that Katherine of Aragon, Queen Mary's mother, had arrived in England as long before as 1497, accompanied by a large suite which included her chapel singers for her wedding to Prince Arthur, and then to Henry VIII, his brother. The Venetian ambassador Sebastian Giustiniani's reports and the diaries of his secretary, Nicolo Sagudino, show that Katherine took part in the musical activity at court; we have seen that the musical education of these children of the Catholic kings was thorough and complete. Shakespeare surrounds her with music in his late play *King Henry the Eighth*. In contrast, the Italian Sagudino reported on the general weakness of the English players: 'Hanno cattiva mensura et debil mano et non troppo bono ajere.' As regards comparisons made between English writing and Cabezón's, it may suffice to say here that Cabezón wrote for the manochord and organ, not for the virginals, which require more profusion of ornament and a technique approaching the sfumato of the harpsichord, thus involving distinct modes of musical thinking on the composer's part.

The digitation in the 1578 publication of Cabezón's works, *Obras de música para tecla, arpa y vihuela*, edited by his son Hernando, shows that Antonio used the thumb and his other fingers with freedom, and that this was common practice in Spain is confirmed in Bermudo's *Declaración de Instrumentos* (1555) where the player is advised to exercise all his fingers so as to be ready for any difficult passage which may confront him. Venegas de Henestrosa in his *Libro de cifra nueva para tecla, harpa y vihuela* (1557) bids the player begin his practice of ascending and descending upon the keyboard with the thumb 'which is the first finger' in ascending exercise; one reason he gives for this is that by so doing the hand is better placed on the keyboard; he also instances the useful practice of crossing the third finger over the thumb.

Proof of Philip's regard for Cabezón was the portrait painted by Sánchez Coello at the king's command to be hung in the palace. Though it was lost in a fire, there remains its description in the palace inventory of 1636: Cabezón was seated on a bench upon a golden cushion, crowned with laurel and playing an organ, and a boy with some flutes in his belt was blowing the instrument. This oil painting is described as 'five feet wide, more or less'; it was inventoried in 1666, 1686 and 1700.

Antonio's son, Hernando, had also entered closely into Philip II's way of life, as is confirmed by such incidents as his being summoned to Lisbon in 1581 because the king found the organists there lacking his own musician's ability, according to a royal letter sent to his daughters on 10th July. The volume of his father's works printed by Hernando in Madrid, 1578, includes music for organ, harp and vihuela, hymn descants, four part tientos, two and three part exercises and instrumental transcriptions of Flemish motets. Best known today are examples of his fine contrapuntal skill in diferencias on romances such as the Canto del Caballero and the villancico Si te enoje, Isabel and La Dama le demanda. In such secular pieces and tientos as Ave Maria stella and Pange Lingua, the Spanish fusion of religious and popular idioms is unmistakable and his polished skill weaves the same tradition effortlessly through the Pavana Italiana and the ever-popular theme 'O guárdame las Vacas'. It is unassumingly achieved with concise equilibrium and though the spiritual temper is fervent it is soberly expressed. His fertile mind extracted more from well-known themes than other musicians of his day; to the two series of Diferencias on Las Vacas, for instance, he added a third in free, improvisatory style which was entitled *Duuinsela*, meaning probably D'oû vient cela? His *ingenio*—the hall-mark of acute Spanish genius—is inexhaustible. He died in Madrid, the 26th of March, 1566.

In his accompaniment to the hours of meditative devotion which later retirement to the austere Jeronymite monasteries of Yuste and the Escorial proved a necessity to both natures, Charles V and Philip II found continuous support: Cabezón's music, concerting every detail down to the most minute part, as Zapata observes in his *Miscelánea*, served them in the hours of unbroken spirituality they sought with a counterpoint from which extraneous matter was excluded, and a faithful weaving of sound that was never interrupted.

Charles V (b. 1500) studied music with the Flemish organist Henri Bredemers who accompanied him on his first visit to Spain in 1517. From 1518 the Spanish organist Martin de Salcedo served Charles' Spanish court until 1525 when he was replaced on his retirement by Cabezón. The Spanish chapel musicians sang the offices with *canto llano*—gregorian chant—while the famous Flemish chapel which Charles had inherited from his father performed polyphony, in which they excelled. Charles maintained and supported those who had served his parents and grandparents, including Anchieta, and when he took on new musicians these were now Spaniards, who accompanied him on his journeys as did the Flemish singers. On retirement to Yuste in idyllic surroundings which he was not long to enjoy with the remnants of health left to him, he took Nicolas Payen as chapel master with seventeen selected Jeronymites to chant the offices; his musical suite also included ten boy singers, some ministriles and Antonio de Avila as organist. Charles was a well-trained keyboard player and had a keen ear, quick to detect faults in performance and plagiarism among composers. Noticing a double example of this, though his performers had not, he is said to have exclaimed 'Oh, what a subtle thief is Guerrero to steal this passage from one musician and those lines from yet another!' His words 'sotil ladrón' express admiration for this skill in grafting, nonetheless. Philip II inherited his Flemish chapel.

The religious music of Andalusia reached such heights in the early 16th century that the schooling from which it emerged merits recognition. It was the Venerable Fernando de Contreras (*c.* 1470–1548) who founded the first school in Seville to train boys in Religion, Letters and Music, and it was on this model that the Colegio de San Isidoro was founded later. When Contreras was a grown man there were still Muslim rulers in the kingdom of Granada. His studies were at Alcalá and in Seville. His school was attached to the archbishop's palace and here the boys entered cathedral service prepared by training in 'lecciones de canto, de arte, y de doctrina' which occupied the day after early morning duties in the cathedral choir and assistance at the altars. Contreras wrote the words and music for many of the hymns they sang and his verses show that he had a poetic vein. He composed chanzonetas for Christmas night which were sung in the great choir of the cathedral, antiphons and many songs in praise of the Virgin. His most important work was for the Feast of the Holy Baptism, the manuscript for this being in his own hand, 'en letra antigua que semejaba en su forma la que se suele escribir en los libros de canto'—'in the ancient writing which resembles that usually written in the song books'. His Latin hymns have an archaic flavour and the Office, antiphons, responses, verses are followed by six homilies of the Venerable Bede. The ms. of his Baptismal Office survives.

Not content with music teaching, he made seven or more expeditions to Morocco to redeem Christians enslaved there, especially seeking out children to bring back to Spain. During these journeys he suffered many hardships, shipwreck and imprisonment, but wrought miracles and knew spiritual satisfaction when living in retreat like the desert hermits of old. His persuading Barbarroja to release captives to him and even to protect his efforts, suggests that Contreras had the gift of a Christian Orpheus. Both Charles V and Philip II esteemed him highly, Philip giving one of his relics, a staff, to the princess of Eboli;

but though efforts to establish his sanctity continued at intervals until 1872, the final step still lacks conclusion, despite the fact that additional evidence was put forward in 1624 by an Augustinian who testified that in addition to his fame as a man of extreme virtue, he himself like other children of his age had heard the venerable Contreras referred to in very popular coplas whose refrain declared:

Sépase que fue Contreras
un buen cristiano de veras.

With this fame on the lips of Sevillian children we may suppose that the music master would have been well content. His likeness was well painted by Luis de Vargas (1502–1568), who was also a musician, and a copy of this was made by Murillo for the sacristy in 1673.

Engravings survive showing him at various ages. One of him, illustrated as Plate X, also depicts captive Christian children. 'He was by nature inclined to a modest and saintly cheerfulness rather than to melancholy devotion and the voice given to him by God was so sonorous and tuneful that it was a pleasure to hear him when he was officiating in the choir. In the hour of his departing this life the cathedral bells tolled mysteriously of their own accord.'

The reputation of Pedro Fernández de Castilleja is aureoled by Guerrero's generous praise of him as 'master of masters of Spain'. He was chapel master to Seville cathedral 1514–1549.

Cristóbal de Morales (*c.* 1500–1553), began as a choirboy in Seville and after being cantor to the Duke of Medina Sidonia, went in 1526 to direct the chapel at the cathedral of Ávila, so that possibly St Teresa may have heard him; her impressionable nature was very early stirred by music. From 1529 to 1533 he was chapel master at Plasencia. He then went to Rome, entering the Pontifical Chapel as cantor in 1535. Four Spaniards were already installed here when he entered, Pedro Pérez, Blas Núñez, Juan Sánchez and Antonio Calasanz; they were joined in 1536 by Bartolomé de Escobedo, the notable composer of Zamora, and three years later by the celebrated Pedro Ordóñez of Palencia.

Within three years Morales' reputation was so high that he was chosen to write the commemorative cantata for the meeting at Nice in 1536 between Pope Paul III, Charles V, the emperor, and Francis I of France. Returning to Spain in 1545 he was appointed chapel master to Toledo cathedral and held this post till 1547. In 1551 he occupied the same post at Málaga, having served the Duke of Arcos at Marchena briefly between these two appointments. He died two years later during a summer absence, the place of his death not being known. Increasing illness had shadowed his life for some years, and was probably a cause of his several changes of work. At Toledo, for instance, he had been allowed to wear a cloak while on duty in the choir.

The character of the man and the nature of his music is suggested by Morales' dedication to Paul III of his *Segundo Libro de Misas*: 'All music which does not serve to honour God or to exalt the thoughts and feelings of men fails completely in its true end.' Though three of his masses are based, not on sacred but on secular melodies, such as were used by other composers of the time, his *L'homme armé; Mille regretz* and the villancico *Tristezas me matan, triste de mi* mark him as having dramatic instinct and it is this emotion which activates the sublime moments of his creation. His dramatic expression of hidden mysteries, however, does not obscure his consciousness that his art lies in their expression purely through musical science and that immediacy of impression in which music excels the other arts. Although he manipulates with unrivalled skills the imitative style of the Franco-Dutch school of which the music texture of the day was commonly fabricated, he never relaxes a watchful concentration on the words he is setting, seizing on their inward sense to impose their significance on what to him is a backcloth to the Christian mystery of death, penitence and divine misericordia.

His Cantata for the Reconciliation at Nice gives the text to five voices, above which the sixth, a tenor, repeats—at irregular intervals—during the two parts of the work the word *Gaudeamus*—key to these festivities—on the basic plainsong around which the counterpoint circles in various combinations. When in 1539 Hippolito de Este asked him to write a work celebrating his elevation to the cardinalate, Morales again employed five voices for the complicated polyphonic texture and gave the solo—significantly, the treble now—the words Magnificate nomen tuum in aeternum to repeat—but here regularly and continually—upon the plainchant. Perhaps this basic difference points the essential distinction to be made between earthly celebrations and eternal rejoicings on sacred events of this kind, when the son of Alfonso I of Ferrara and Lucretia Borgia joined the church élite, if not the elect.

He wrote more masses than any other composer among his contemporaries, at least twenty-one, of which sixteen were published under his own supervision at Rome (1544). His other works appeared without the dedications he wrote for the masses. Twelve of his masses—four of them unpublished ones—are for four voices; seven for five, and two for six, both these last being published by him. Only ten movements of his fourteen published duple-metre masses have triple metre, but he works numerous passing triple passages into the duple-metre movements. He also employs opposing rhythms, three minims against two and occasionally three breves against eight minims, and for specific texts, significantly in the mass on Spanish words *Tristezas me matan*. On the other hand, the Spanish recourse to sharpened notes, frequent at the time, is not common in Morales' work, certainly not as compared with Victoria's. Dr Robert Stevenson has conclusively shown that his modes were chosen according to their emotional fitness to his themes, and according to Bermudo's teaching. The two musicians were loyal colleagues, commending each other's work fervently.

In the collection entitled *Magnificat cum quatuor vocibus* (Venice, H. Scotus, 1542), Morales' examples are outstanding masterworks and their advanced style brought him prompt and wide recognition; particularly Spanish in character are those liturgical *entonaciones* which alternate with psalmodic choral passages; again attention to textual potential is paramount in the whole design. The Magnificat in the mode VIII evokes profound contrasts as in Fecit potentiam in brachio suo, from whose swelling parts the voices later decline into the pained murmurs of Esurientes, where melancholy is deepened with the drawn Amen which finally establishes the spiritual longing for eternal peace after yet another climax of tutti on Implevit bonis. The workmanship with which the text is expanded is constantly varied by Morales' skill. His progress was constant as the 16 Magnificats prove.

The *Missarum Liber I* contains eight works, six on liturgical and two on secular themes. It is supposed that these last two, on *L'homme armé* and *Mille regretz*, were written to exercise himself in current Flemish-Roman practice; the first was set at least twenty-four times by French and Flemish composers and he may have taken it as a challenge to his ability; he wrote two masses on its theme, the second being included in the *Missarum Liber II*. It was in the dedication of his second book of masses that their creator wrote: 'We musicians ourselves are aware that the spirit of the times constantly demands something new from us.'

The Mass for the Dead places the inexorable fate of men in that context of eternity which softens the end by the recollection of God's peace, and here he combines the Spanish qualities of realism and charity in unique fashion. Similar expressiveness is given in the Lenten motet Emendemus in melius where grandeur and pathos, operating through the music's unremitting penetration of the climactic words, as peccavimus, ignoranter, Memento homo, lead through prayer for forgiveness to confidence in divine mercy.

The dedications of his masses show traces of the aims set forth in *De Musica*. This treatise's advice, furthermore, is actively practised by Morales in significant ways. His constant pursuit of unity may be compared with Augustine's final pages on this principle as 'the base of rhythm' which leads to the last emphasis on rhythm's service to the

Lord of all things. These lines, contrasting the lack of rhythm in 'carnal perception' with that 'vital movement, agile with temporal intervals' of universal rhythm, may have prompted Morales to that distinction between irregularity in textual illustrations and the regular movements in those two cantatas composed for Nice and Ferrara, respectively.

His impressive use of silence in the *Missa pro defunctis* and elsewhere may be compared with the discussion on silence in *De Musica*, Books IV and V. Here the effect of a sudden cessation after a sound has struck the air, to be followed after the pause by another sound, is described as evoking a peculiarly intent response of attention 'because the psyche is now intent on response to another sound' and therefore loses the memory of that earlier sound. This is the effect of Morales' music as he leads his listeners' spiritual experience of In memoria aeterna—pause—to the consoling In memoria dormit. He always follows that injunction of Book VI 'We must experiment with our own individual opinion.' The freedom with which his rhythmic evolution expands is that of the craftsman (*faber*) who 'operates rationally with rhythm in his art, using Perceptive Rhythm in the artistic tradition' and with this, Progressive Rhythm, in strict regard for that 'co-rationality' through length 'to breadth and height', Augustine adds. There seems little reason to doubt that Morales' own strenuous experiments in 'comparative movements of different durations' were also stimulated by following the study of *De Musica*'s pages.

The Lamentations of Jacob—called a marvel of art by Adami da Bolsena—and then of Jeremiah remain outstanding achievements of controlled pathos. The latter work again uses the prepared effects of silence and in Rome brought the work an enduring place in the memory of men. His motets, printed in three volumes (Venice, 1543–1546) show this range of dramatic pathos in its most original forms; among these the *Sancte Anthoni, pater monachorum* has been continually singled out for his cadential illustrations of the words 'faciem creatoris' and 'gemma confessorum'. To this may be contrasted the three-part *Puer natus est nobis* which recreates the Spanish joyous celebration of the nativity. Fray Bermudo placed the Hymn to the Holy Spirit among the elect works of music, and Spanish composers recognised Morales' supremacy and responded to his native genius by glossing his works above all others.

Works like the Lamentations of Jeremiah show him as a forerunner of the Spanish painters to come in Andalusia. The chiaroscuro of these, the distances of perspective achieved by the placing of the voices announce the renascent and plateresque generation as already born. But perhaps only Alejo Fernández, leader of those late primitives in the south who included Pedro Fernández de Guadalupe, may compare with Morales. The *Piedad* of 1527 in Seville cathedral, once ascribed alternately to both these Fernández', has the depths and distances of Morales' conception of dark desolation in sound. From this recollection of Metsys, Alejo Fernández proceeds gradually towards a grandeur of architectural background which, if not yet wholly romanised, portends the echoing vistas of centralising power to come, though against this his human figures still retain a gothic purity. Morales' sonorities, archaic in mood but bold in experiment, find their points and arches of corresponding resonating climax here. His artist namesake, Cristóbal de Morales—son of the painter Luis de Morales, el Divino—whose *Burial of Christ* is in the Seville Museum (Museo Hispalense), moved also in Alejo Fernández' orbit.

Francisco Guerrero (1528–1599), also a master of this Sevillian school, was already chapel master at Jaén at the age of eighteen, became cantor at Seville cathedral in 1550, and four years later moved to Málaga, in the wake of Morales, but remained there only a year on his succession as director of the metropolitan chapel, a post he held till his death. A prolific composer, largely in the religious sphere, his works were reprinted widely in his lifetime. The dedication of his *Liber Vesperorum* (Rome, 1584) to Philip II repeats Morales' uncompromising ideas though in softer words, saying that he had never sought to charm the ears of the pious with his music but that above all it was needful to arouse devout meditation on the sacred mysteries.

His veneration of Morales was affirmed in letters to the Sevillian chapter and he followed this master's steps throughout his own works. Like Morales, he published two books of Masses, one in Paris (1566) containing nine, and the other in Rome (1582) containing eight. He wrote 18 in all. Like Morales, he wrote a cycle of Magnificats in every tone. His motets, totalling about 115 (Seville, 1555; Venice, 1570; Venice, 1589; Venice, 1597) follow Morales in closest expression of the text, singling out the more poignant phrases for his own interpretation, although he differs from him in a more frequent use of formal canon here. The best known of these is still the Ave Virgo sanctissima a 5. It is in the Masses where he delights in discoursing musically on Morales' motives, showing them in every possible light that can enhance their fundamental truth, and in the two Requiems (1566 and 1582) which he composes basically with short monodic sections alternating with polyphony as had Morales in his development of this Spanish taste.

His own individuality shows clearly in the sixty-one spiritual part-songs, *Canciones y villanescas espirituales* (Venice, 1589). Though he used the Italian word *villanesca*, his songs are consistently Spanish, and this discrepancy still causes discussion. It is possible that the word was used

73

deliberately to show in Italy that this secular song was capable of sharing the *villancico's* capacity to transform itself to the spiritual translucence of the divine from the human. The author of the prologue to the 1589 edition, Mosquera de Figueroa, auditor general of the Armada which had sailed against England in the previous year, adds these words to his more general praise of Guerrero's work: 'Among his merits that deserve applause is his pioneering success in fitting music to Spanish verse so that the very life and rhythm of the poetry are preserved.'

Unlike Morales and Victoria, between whom he served as a spiritual link, Guerrero never took office in Italy but went there to supervise publication of his works, taking the opportunity of visiting Venice in 1588 on such business and to sail for the Holy Land on 14th August, returning to Venice on 9th January 1589. His published account of this pilgrimage brought him wide fame, though not of that miraculous kind attributed to Contreras, whose ordeals when rescuing captive children in north Africa grew into legend.

Guerrero's ties with Seville cathedral were lifelong, for he studied with its music director Pedro Fernández de Castilleja, as well as with his own brother Pedro. His advice for instrumental playing was followed by the chapter, so that care was taken that the players should not get in the way of one another's glossing, particularly in improvisation, and his memorial shows how full a part shawms, cornets, sackbuts, bassoons and recorders were now taking, vying with the singers in their art of the variation. The tradition of church celebration with instruments dating from before the unions of the royal chapels of Aragon and Castile was continuously enriched.

Rabelais and Father Martini praised Guerrero's music; Cerone, not always generous, includes him among the few Spaniards he admired; Morales, Lobo, Victoria, Tapia and Salinas. Born 4th October 1523 in Seville, he died there 8th September 1599, considered by all as 'el genio más dulce y amable' of the Sevillian school, an example of that mild, sweet nature to which this region has often given birth, as some of its finest artists show, including Murillo in the next century and Turina in our own.

Signs of Guerrero's application of *De Musica* to his own composition may be seen in the following. In his parody of Morales' motet 'Sancta et immaculata virginitas', his own first mass, he leaves his elder at that point where Morales passes on to the next motive without looking back to the previous ones, and returns in 'Et in terra pax' after composing I to III, to I. In the 'Qui tollis' he develops vI and vII, and then returns to I and v. This returning upon his pattern continues through the mass. The principle involved may be found in *De Musica* Book I,

where the power of numbers to return upon themselves and so to create series is discussed, thus proving the superiority of measurement and limitation over indefiniteness. It was to be taken up theoretically as a basic element of music's essential unity in Mexico within the next hundred years, and then re-worked in 20th-century music.

Proof of Guerrero's deep meditation is shown by Dr Stevenson's close analysis of the two settings of 'O Domine Jesu Christe', a motet appearing in the 1570 and 1589 collections. His text reads: O Lord Jesus Christ, I adore thee, wounded on the cross, drinking gall and vinegar. I entreat Thee that thy wounds be the remedy of my soul. The analysis shows that the various changes made in the second setting are in general to result in doubling the clause treating the words 'drinking gall and vinegar', enlarging the clause melismatically on the word drinking so as to place it in spiritual relief. Dr Stevenson suggests a parallel here with the Ignatian Spiritual Exercises with their emphasis on the physical details of the Crucifixion and this is not to be disputed, given the relationship of contemporary sensibilities. However, given the context of the lasting influence of *De Musica* on musical thinking in Spain, its origin may be sought in Book VI's relation of the soul's sickness as it feels the body's suffering in decay to the restoration of its health 'after the Resurrection of the Body, in which, before we understand it fully, it is good for us to believe by faith'. The soul is keyed up intensely by the body's changes, and this is twice referred to tastes impinging on our palate and the capacity through sight, hearing, tasting and touching, to assimilate the agreeable and resist the disagreeable. These pages draw on the text from Romans: 'I am an unhappy man; who will free me from the body of this death?' This follows the description of the soul becoming weaker by a divine law, after sinning. Thus, Guerrero's music seeks 'the remedy of my soul'.

With this, an inspiration for Guerrero's youthful but individually conceived transmutations of secular songs to the divine may be sought in Book VI's opening where the purpose of the treatise 'to lead young people of ability . . . with Reason for our guide, from the things of sense to God . . . and through human concern with music, as in grammar and poetry, to the spiritual. 'It is easy to love colours, musical sounds, voices, cakes, roses and the body's soft, smooth surface . . . In all of them the soul is in quest of nothing except equality and similitude . . . Why, then does the soul slip from the truest citadel of equality, and then, with the mere debris which it drags from it, erect terrestial structures instead? . . . Consider what kind of man he is, who finds a better method with which to meet these occurrences.' There follows the description of the power of music and its rhythms rightly ordered to attach other souls to its influences which thus possibly influenced the Spanish habit of translating songs human to songs divine—*a lo divino*, as the practice is called. Its great creators, Guerrero and Juan Vásquez, carried over into these lesser, shorter forms the age-long memory of the saint's counsel that music must always follow the text. Vásquez' praise of Guerrero calls this art 'the secret'.

The second half of the century produced a composer equal to Morales in the first. Tomás Luis de Victoria, born at Ávila about 1548, ranks with Palestrina and Orlando de Lasso in the a capella music of the age. In Spain, he brought this polyphonic church style to a perfected equilibrium as Cabezón had crowned the instrumental evolution of his compatriots, and with the same close dedication. He began as a choir-boy in Ávila cathedral, *c.* 1558, where Bernardino de Ribera was chapel master 1559–1563, to be succeeded by Juan Navarro and then by the unsympathetic Hernando de Yssasi 1567–1587. Cabezón played here, in 1552 and 1556; Bartolomé de Escobar returned from Rome in 1554 to a benefice at Segovia, whence Victoria's mother had come. Receiving a grant of 45,000 maravedis from Philip II in 1565, he went to Rome the next year, entering the Jesuit Colegio Germánico seminary as an invited student and in 1569 was appointed 'cantor y sonador del órgano' to the San Apolinar chapel. For five years he was attached to the Oratory of San Felipe Neri.

In 1587, however, he resigned these duties to take service with the dowager empress María, widow of Maximilian and daughter of Charles V, becoming her chaplain at the Descalzas Reales convent when she and her daughter Doña Margarita retired there in Madrid. This post he held until the empress's death in 1603. From 1604 he was given one of the three chaplaincies founded by her and assumed the office of organist until his own death on 7th August 1611. Those who visit this recently restored convent and admire the fine memorial sculpture of the Infanta Juana, its founder, by Pompeo Leoni close to the chapel's altar may pause to recall that Victoria wrote the organ settings of his works here during this, the longest settled period of his life.

Dedications of his printed music suggest self-revealed characteristics, less energetically vigorous than Morales, less uncompromising outwardly, yet equally tireless in his labours, and seeking close personal harmony in that retirement to which he withdrew. It is not surprising that the composer of the motet *O Doctor optime beate Augustine* should himself write in self-deprecatory words and almost confidential manner of his own works, for these were years in which St Teresa's autobiographical style was familiar and she had read St Augustine's *Confessions* closely before writing her own. On presenting his *Libro de Misas* (1583) to Philip II, Victoria explains: 'Since that epoch in which having left Spain for Italy I arrived in Rome, not only did I dedicate

myself during some time to other noble studies, but also employed much labour and care in the art of music. And already from the beginning I proposed not to attach myself to the delight of the ears and mind alone, nor yet to content myself with this knowledge; but rather, looking beyond this, I resolved to be useful, so far as possible, to those alive now and those to come. Desiring that the fruits of my talent might achieve greater diffusion, I learned the task of putting to music, above all else, that part which with every step is celebrated in the catholic Church. For to what better end should music serve than to the sacred praises of that God from whom proceed rhythm and measure, and whose works are disposed in such portentous form that they show admirable song and certain harmony? By this it may be judged that they err very gravely and merit censure without pity who, practising a most honest art and one apt to alleviate sorrows and recreate the spirits with joy almost indispensable, give themselves over to singing dishonest songs and other unworthy matters.'

'I had previously composed and published many works, which, according to what I heard, have been received with pleasure; and tired since of this labour in composing, I have decided to make an end of it . . . adding this last birth of my spirit. The hour of return to my own country having arrived after long absence, I ought to bring with me some offering which at the same time may be conformable to my profession and agreeable to Your Majesty . . . I do not judge my offering unworthy of the Royal Chapel, above all on finding itself honoured by the name and protection of Your Majesty.'

The dedication to the Prince Cardinal Alberto of another collection of *Misas* and other examples of religious pieces published in Rome in 1592 explains that he had been 'moved to write this opusculo by the reiterated pleas of many persons insisting with great earnestness that in the time left to me from my continuous occupations I should occupy myself with this production, to the end that it would be possible to celebrate every festive day of the year with the varied harmony of voices . . .' The more ornate dedication to Philip III of the *Misas* published in Madrid, 1600, suggests that the times had passed when men devoted to religious objectives could, as in Philip II's days, speak their minds in simple words to their royal protector.

The dedication to Pope Gregory XIII of the volume *Himnos para todo el año a cuatro voces* (Rome, 1581), however, recalls Teresa's manner of writing to great churchmen and princes of this world alike. 'In music, principally sacred and ecclesiastical, to which I feel myself inclined by a certain natural instinct, I have occupied myself and worked for many years, and to speak truly, not without fruits, according as I deduce by the judgment of others. Recognising that this is due to the grace and beneficence of God, I should not be altogether ungrateful to Him, from whom all good things proceed, abandoning myself to a lazy and shameful inertia and defrauding the Lord of that just and expected fruit, if I were to bury that talent with which he had endowed me.'

He was only twenty-four years old when his *Motets*, dedicated to Cardinal Otto Truchses, were first printed in Venice (1572); these were for four, five, six and eight voices. His book of masses, psalms, magnificats and other pieces appeared in 1576. In 1581 the collection of hymns to the Virgin 'for all the year' followed. In 1583 the *Motets* were reprinted in Rome, and amounting now to 33 pieces, again for 4, 5, 6 and 8 parts and a new one for 12, a 'Laetatus sum'. These were quickly reprinted. The famous and exceptional *Office for Holy Week* was printed in Rome, 1585, the year which saw the reappearance of the Motets with which were included works by Guerrero. Reprints continued until the last in Venice (1603) where, it is interesting to note, Victoria omitted revisions of earlier editions and presented the volume as an *editio princeps*. It was in this year that his patron lady, the empress dowager, died and he wrote a six-part requiem mass in memory of her. His works include 20 masses, 2 requiems, 44 motets, the Office for Holy Week, 18 magnificats, 34 hymns, psalms, antiphons, sequences, and a Litany. None of his masses—with one glorious exception— depart from church themes. The chromaticisms to be found in his early music and again in his later works may derive from Spanish reminiscences, as likewise that steadfast glow of humanity which suffuses his nativity themes and some portions of the mass.

It is not surprising to find allusions to Augustine's thoughts on music in the lines to the 1583 edition at Rome of the *Missarum Libri Duo* written to Philip II. To find Victoria's development of style involved consistently in illustrating *De Musica* and thus depending on its directions, however, is a matter of unusual interest. He was neither the first nor the last composer to follow its injunction that music should serve the text; though his adherence to it grows in apt illustrations, it is always mindful of the place, proportion and circumstance of its performance, as the treatise also advises.

He observes other fundamental considerations; first of all, in the dimensions of his major pieces, which are notably smaller than Palestrina's; for instance, his masses are reduced by as much as a third in length, and even a half, as his evolution proceeds. This, too, he observes when revising and editing his works for the press, cutting, condensing wherever possible. So the admonition that 'movements of long duration, for example of an hour or more, are not adjusted to our immediate sensibility' and that we must 'confine ourselves to those which are shorter' is a measuring rod for restraint that Victoria kept beside him until the end.

He never loses hold of the other principle that music should keep its own beauty and power to cause pleasure, rounding and bringing his parts into continually progressive harmony. He tends towards the expression of joy and praise culminating in Hosannas and Alleluias, again developing this concept in maturity as he turns to the use of major tonality with increasing confidence, adding to this a higher tessitura and the brighter keys to express *De Musica*'s advice in ways

Missa
pro Victoria
(Ex editione anni 1600)

that the modes were not so free to follow. In his burial service he leaves
the sombre sections to the plainchant and works consolatory passages
into those parts that the text allows, though Morales built the whole
structure of such movements upon the chant. His frequent sharpening,
an early native trait to which he resorted with increasing insistence on

returning to Spain, may also corroborate the treatise's principles on pleasure and bright joy's potential in sound. The growing flexibility of his rhythmic use of triple beside duple metre agrees with *De Musica's* many pages on metre's potential variety. His many hymns agree with Isidore's injunction as also with Augustine's joy in them; his Office for Holy Week, an exceptional series, agrees with Visigothic ritualistic emphasis on this season as with Augustine's experience that it was the culminating music season of faith.

One late work, nevertheless, exceeds these self-imposed dimensions, and it is one which still rouses conjecture. This is the *Missa pro Victoria* which Victoria called his Battle Mass, the one exception to his rule never to write on a secular theme. Janequin's *La bataille de Marignan* drew forth Victoria's most picturesque sound-painting and some commentators suggest that he had a specific battle or campaign in mind, though this remains unidentified. It did not refer to any warfare in Philip III's reign, for the volume containing this mass was in the printer's hands awaiting a costing when Philip II was still alive; he died on 13th September 1598, and the contract was not signed until 1st October.

It is worth remembering that Philip II had ordered a painting al fresco in the Escorial's Great Gallery of the victorious battle of St Quintin over the French in 1557 when Philip's forces routed them and he himself visited the battlefield, though he let slip the chance to occupy the panic-stricken Paris. This triumph was dear to his heart, comparable to the religious glory of Lepanto, where his fleets routed the Turks, an event celebrated with an emotion that wells up in Sigüenza's pages describing the sudden arrival of Don Juan of Austria the victor at the Escorial's gates riding ahead of his men who were still battling against one of those wild storms which not infrequently battered the Guadarrama sierra.

The battle of St Quintin had religious purport for Spain too, for the success there led on to Gravelines, in which English and Flemings fought beside Spaniards and forced the French Henry II to sue Philip for peace—after Charles V's death in April 1559—and by this the suppression of heresy throughout France, viewed by the Spaniards as a serious danger to themselves, was achieved. Thus, even this exception, given its religious importance, scarcely broke the rule of a lifetime, and if Victoria had this scene in mind even enhanced the meaning of the mass. The choice of this Frenchman's chanson—subject for one of Janequin's own masses, too—was an apt one. In his imitation of Janequin's deployment of gunfire the diffident Victoria, more given to diplomacy than war, turned the enemy's guns back upon their own emplacements with a vivacity of joy that fittingly crowned the king's reign and illustrates Sigüenza's account of the painting—'fire on every side; in the artillery, in the infantry, from those afoot and those on horse, with so many differences of cannon, great and small' and where death pressed on all with such cruel haste that a man might die in an instant without so much as a moment to cross himself. Such words would also justify the music's simultaneous firing and the plea 'dona nobis pacem'.

De Musica Book VI allows for such a martial subject thus: 'So earthly things are subject to heavenly things, seeming to associate the cycles of their own durations in rhythmic succession with the song of the great whole. In this array there are many things which to us appear out of order and confused, because we have been attached to their order, their station in existence . . . not knowing the glorious plan which Divine Providence has in operation concerning us . . . A soldier on the battlefield cannot see the dispositions of the whole army.' Since these pages discuss the relative use of long and short syllables, Victoria's exceptional contrasts of quick staccato notes with unusually slow harmonic rhythms are worth noting, as his firing of shots during Dona nobis pacem 'appears out of order and confused, because we have been attached to their order, their station in existence'. It was the victory of St Quintin on San Lorenzo's Day which led to the founding of the Escorial in this saint's honour. It was the most signal mark of divine providence in Philip II's life, and thus he commemorated it.

Victoria's *O doctor optime beate Augustine* was not printed in any of his collections so the existence of this MS. motet a 4 has roused particular interest. Several likenesses to Victoria's other works leave little doubt that it is from his hand. To these may be added the following; his single-part motets are divided into two parts of approximately equal length separated by a general pause in all voice parts, coming immediately before an epithet of adoration. Dr Stevenson writes that it is 'for the purpose of emphasising these ejaculations that he precedes them with silence in all voices'. The motet *O doctor optime*, though not printed with the rest, conforms to this same principle, he adds. To this may now be added the interesting fact that Augustine treats of this principle in an original penetration of psychology's relation to physiological experience in those pages of *De Musica* of which, apparently, Morales had already taken note.

This Barcelona MS. was given to Narciso Puig about 1597 by Jerónimo Romague, who served as chapel master in an Augustinian church or convent. Six motets, among a total of sixty-six items in the manuscript—now in the Biblioteca Musical de la Diputació de Barcelona, Vol. I, pp. 244–246—are in Augustine's honour. Book VI gives a further direction for these motets. 'Nothing can be proportionate or

rhythmic without equality, with pairs of equivalent members responding to each other. All that is single must have some central place, so
that equality may be preserved in the intervals extending to the central
individual parts, from either side.'

Underlying Victoria's evolution is a tendency towards a vertical
view of harmonic organisation: this is strengthened by developments
in his polychoral masses and antiphonal structures which pull the whole
design into a central unity, aided by tonal integration made closer by
the introduction of major and minor pervasiveness. In all this the organ
plays a supporting part, a guide in more elaborate dimensions. In *De
Musica* Book VI, after the several kinds of rhythmic structure have been
evaluated, Augustine moves to trace the ascent from rhythm in sense to
the immortal rhythm which is in truth. Here time is discussed as an
imitation of eternity and we are warned not to place our joy in what
merely imitates equality and to remember that the higher things are
those in which equality resides, supreme, unchangeable, unshaken. The
discussion of equality is related to unity and the harmonious inter-
connection of its parts. 'We must not deny to rhythm which is concerned with our penal mortality its inclusion within the works of the
Divine fabrication, for such rhythm is within its own kind beautiful.
But we must not love such rhythm as if it could make us blessed. We
must treat it as we would a plank amid the waves of the sea, not
casting it away as a burden, but not embracing it and clinging to it as if
we imagined it firmly fixed. We must use such rhythm well, so that
eventually we may dispense with it.' Encouragement to those who
follow this advice is given: 'In all that we perceive and in all that we
make, we gradually get used to what at first we rejected. It is by order
that we weave our pleasure into one. We only like what has a beginning harmoniously woven on to the middle part, and a middle part
harmoniously woven on to the end.'

The pursuit of unity through the integration of parts into simul-
taneousness and equality according to *De Musica*'s precepts may be
heard, and seen, in Victoria's number of parts which exceed those of
his time in Italy as in Spain and in his preoccupation with the movements of harmonic blocs, sequences and massive repetitions. He heeds
the warning not to cast away the plank of rhythm but to use such
rhythm well, leaving it to those who came after to dispense with it
eventually; he heeds, too, the warning 'to divert our joy away from
what merely imitates equality', while not denying 'beauty, within its
own class and comparatively, to something which at least imitates
equality, in so far as it does so'. Such observations, coming towards the
treatise's conclusion, draw the mind from horizontally conceived
musical practice towards the vertical as the consequences become less

84

obscure. Perceptible rhythm only contains a shadowing of fixed and enduring equality while it passes us by, we are reminded, and the soul thus loves the sequence of truth more than the pleasure of rhythm striking the ear. *De Musica*'s last analogies begin from all growing things in the vegetable world, the roots of a tree and its reproductive dispositions, showing that even earth has its equality of parts, length, breadth and height in a regular progression. Above this base, the other elements rise in progressive unity until the sky consummates the whole. 'Here, beyond even the rational and intellectual rhythm of blessed and saintly souls, here is the very law of God.'

It is in Fray José de Sigüenza's *Historia de la Orden de San Jerónimo*, written while he was organising the Escorial library under Philip II's direction, that we learn some significant facts about musical life at the monastery and the care taken to ensure that its music acquisitions were equal in quality to its sculpture, painting, tapestry, bejewelled reliquaries, emblems of imperial power and the king's personal connoisseurship. The most intimate hours of Philip's later years were spent in the library and the chapel. Though he experienced rare satisfaction in poring over newly acquired manuscripts, it was the singing in the chapel which brought tears to his eyes which he did not attempt to hide.

Even such a detail of the choir's sculpture as the prominence given to an angel blowing a trumpet into the ear of St Jerome, the monastery's patron, is explained by Fray Sigüenza as signifying the continuous memory the saint had of the last judgment while writing his books. This was linked to Augustine's theory of time in eternity from which his association of music is never absent. In fact, when guiding us meticulously round the chapel, Fray Sigüenza stops before every item to give the inner meaning of its placing here and in this sanctuary draws on Augustine's principles of architecture and music to explain the mystery of each and glory of the whole. Since Augustine had drawn on Plato's theories for his own interpretation of the arts, as Sigüenza reminds us, the synthesis here established between Christian and classical principles proved as satisfying as we know it to have been to Philip as it was found useful to check those critics who were astonished to find a Jeronymite monastery so adorned with mundane riches. Philip, we read, like Augustine, reminded people that the proportion of beautiful arts and music found their echoes in men's souls. The equilibrium of the purest composers of his reign, Cabezón and Victoria, expressed this concept with absolute equanimity.

Philip saw to it that each member of the choir had his own book. Like his father he was critically aware of wrong notes, though not so unspoken about them as Charles V is said to have been at Yuste. The sound of the first chime of bells brought him quickly from his bed.

85

Hearing of the arrival of the first plainchant volume—of which the chapel service was at first solely composed—and wishing to be the first to see it, he entered privily through a window before matins lit only by a candle held by his aide Santoyo, and blushed to find himself so caught by the Prior who having heard movement came that way on making his night rounds to be certain that all the monks were in their cells. In describing the method by which the novices in the choir were taught, Sigüenza explains that Augustine's caution was kept in mind, as was also St Bernard's expression of it, that they should proceed by strict attention to the text and not wander into emotional states alien to the words they sing, 'Que lo que no es escrito que se cante, no se cante.' 'That which is not written as to be sung, should not be sung.'

Philip's love of music and of church bells is shown in that tireless care with which he sought out old Franco-Flemish carillons which he installed at the Escorial though this foreign invention did not please everyone who came to wonder at the monastery. Sigüenza ends his account of how the keyboards of these chimes sound together in concert like an organ and produce music that might be played on any other instrument, by adding that this is an invention of the Flemings and Germans 'who have patience and ingenuity for such things, though here it does not sound so well to us as it does to them'. Describing the bell-towers, he counts nineteen bells which accompany divine service, of different sizes, large, middling and small. In the other tower there are 'if I have not counted ill, forty. Some of the campanas are upwards of two and three hundred years old' and these resemble one, which 'if the lettering beneath does not lie, was founded in 1189, on January the third, which makes a little less than four hundred'.

The last music to sound in Philip II's ears was not from the bell-towers above, but the chanting of the choristers rising up from the chapel below where they were singing in the early dawn. 'So fell asleep in the Lord that great Philip the Second, son of the Emperor Charles the Fifth, in the same house and temple of St Lawrence which he had built and almost above his own sepulchre, at five in the morning and when the boys of the Seminary were singing mass at dawn.'

Though other instruments were permitted from time to time in the monastery chapel, Philip authorised only the organ, and to replace those sounds of minstrelsy which were making their way with increasing volume into the churches, he finally endowed the Escorial with eight organs, four of which were large and four small, one of the latter silvered and thus very costly, having belonged to Charles V. The rest were made by the best organist of the time, by name Maese Brevost. One of the Escorial's first organists was Fray Jerónimo of Saragossa (d. 1573) who had been one of Antonio Cabezón's finest

IV. Orchestra of Angels: Morisco decorative art of the Aragonese School (1390)

V. Alfonso X dictating the first *Cantiga de Santa Maria*

pupils, 'and one of those most dear to him'. The keyboard instruments were in service to guide the boys' voices.

In the introduction to his collection of his father's works in 1578, Antonio Cabezón's son Hernando called the organ 'a divine instrument', and as such it features with the heavenly choirs in countless paintings of the 16th century in the Escorial as elsewhere, accurately detailed amidst a fantasia of clouds and angelic beings.

Born in Córdoba in 1534, the composer Fernando de las Infantas, an intimate of Victoria and Soto de Langa, became a priest at fifty and though relinquishing musical activities was nonetheless persuaded by Philip II to dissuade Pope Gregory XIII from a plan to reform the Graduale Romanum which he had entrusted to Palestrina. Since this scheme entailed the putting aside of traditional liturgical melodies, it is not surprising that Philip with his family affection for the old ways intervened in this characteristic roundabout manner, and that Infantas, who enjoyed Charles V's friendship as well as Philip's, and moreover had printed several music-books in Venice, succeeded in averting this error of judgment. Córdoba had its school of musicians as it had a school of painters; Juan de Risco, praised by Góngora, directed the cathedral chapel; Rodrigo Ceballos (d. *c.* 1572) possibly preceded him there. Espinel eulogised him in the same breath with Morales and Guerrero, but this was in a poem. In Aragon, Melchor Robledo (d. 1587), first chapel master to the cathedral of Pilar was so highly esteemed in Saragossa that his was the only music allowed performance there beside the polyphony of Josquin, Palestrina and Victoria.

Two families, each represented by uncle and nephew, were outstanding among Catalans. Mateo Flecha, the elder (*c.* 1481–1553), was chapel master at Lérida, then taught the princes, and finally became a monk at Poblet's venerable monastery. He is known for the secular part-songs collected by his nephew under the title of *Las Ensaladas*, because of their mixed texts, as in vogue at the time, and published in Prague, 1581, where his nephew, also Mateo, was in service to Charles V's daughter Maria, wife of the emperor Maximilian II. This royal service brought exotic contacts, for he became abbot in Tyhan, Hungary, in 1568; in 1569 he was confessor to Isabel of Hungary, widow of the French king Charles IX; twenty years later Philip III appointed him abbot of Portella monastery and there he died. His music, and he wrote in both kinds like his uncle before him, was printed in Venice and Prague, though not all of his work survives.

The line of Catalan organists was strengthened by Pedro Alberch Vila and continued through his nephew Luis Ferran y Vila (1565–1631). The elder emerged from the ancient diocese of Vich, early free from primitive influences by its ties with the French church, and in

Barcelona's cathedral he formed a school of organ-playing and instrument-builders. He left polyphonic scores in manuscript, printed a book of *Madrigals*, and a *Libro de Tientos*, the loss of which is deplorable, judging by the quality of two pieces by this contemporary of Cabezón published in the *Libro de cifra nueva para tecla, harpa y vihuela* by Luys Venegas de Henestrosa, Alcalá, 1557, and reprinted by Santiago Kastner in his *Antología de antiguos maestros españoles y portugueses* (Schott).

His nephew succeeded him as organist, but no music of his is now known.

The growing secularisation of Spanish life did not halt the consolidation of organ music based on the tradition of Morales, Victoria, Guerrero. In the royal chapel Bernardo de Clavijo, his son Francisco and Martínez Verdugo maintained the old tradition dating back to Cabezón's school. Bernardo Clavijo del Castillo was chapel master and organist at the Neapolitan court about 1588; from 1594 he was professor at Salamanca and then organist to Philip III; he died in Madrid in 1626. A fine tiento preserved in the Escorial proves his adherence to the masters of the variation and diferencia. It is possible that he was succeeded at Naples by Giovanni Maria Trabici, and it is supposed that Clavijo may have had contacts with the blind Antonio Valenti there whose work shows some similarities with the Spanish keyboard tradition.

Francisco Correa de Araujo, organist in the San Salvador church of Seville, and of Portuguese stock, is the author of *Libro de tientos y discursos de música práctica y teórica de órgano intitulado Facultad Orgánica*, 'with which, and with moderate study and perseverance, any average player may go forth advantaged thereby' (1626, Alcalá de Henares). The *tiento* results from the efforts of Spanish composers of religious keyboard music to adapt the lively and worldly Toccata to a more legato style through the expansion of the well-tried Fantasia of the peninsula. In the process of adaptation its various potentials were explored; for instance Milán's lean more towards the virtuoso elements of the Fantasia, but Cabezón, though beginning with this emphasis went more deeply into the matter and soon adapted the form to his own natural expression of austere sobriety and concentration and thus established a norm whose fluidity nevertheless allowed for different emphases, as in the tientos of Tomás Santa María, Soto, Francisco Pereza and the relation of its form to the older diferencia evolved by Correa de Araujo. The fact that the Fantasia's development section was relatively short also presented a problem to be considered as the more extensive potential of the tiento began to emerge. Araujo's modern editor, Santiago Kastner, describes his tientos as fusing the ancient

Spanish tradition of Cabezón, Soto, Vila and the Portuguese João Leite Pereira and Padre Manuel Rodriguez Coelho with contemporary developments. He was, at the same time, an extraordinary and daring innovator whose creative thought incessantly produced rich variations in what he called 'otro nuevo orden' and as his introduction tells the player 'you will find many observations and indications set out in the discourses of this book, a new thing and a practice never before exercised'. Such practices included contrary sonorities and sudden dislocations from one extreme of the keyboard to the other, and in the contrasts of the keyboard registers he sounds as vehement and revolutionary to our ears today as Domenico Scarlatti and Soler.

Juan Cabanilles, 1644–1712, organist at Valencia cathedral, in brilliance is comparable to Araujo and also to Soler, with whom he shares a fondness for batallas, pasacalles, toccatas, folías, versos and pasos and a spirited originality in the variation. At the same time mysticism still pervades his creative sense and with Father Bruna he may be said to manifest some of the last spiritual expression from the great Spanish period.

Among many church musicians, Luis de Aranda of Seville was an outstanding example of those who impressed the worth of the native school through France, from Narbonne, Nîmes and Montpellier to Paris and the court of Louis XIII.

The Portuguese Manuel Rodriguez de Coelho, organist to Philip III and master of his Lisbon court, published a work there in 1620, *Flores de Música para instrumentos de Tecla y Harpa*. Here again we find a Spanish technique modified but enriched by the strong, vehement Portuguese nature, though still spiritually absorbed, and possibly extended by the touch and contact of the Anglo-Netherlands school. The word *Flores* may here signify floreos, glosses.

Catalan individuality continued at the Montserrat Escolanía whose Fray Juan Jarques, 1582–1658, succeeded Victoria at the Descalzas Reales; nothing of his work is now known. Fray Juan Romana (d. 1687) was known for purely instrumental music such as Toccatas for spinet and Gallardas for chirimías. More fortunately, the works of Juan Cererols, 1618–1676, have survived and have been published by P. David Pujol in the series *Mestres de l'Escolanía de Montserrat 1500–1800*; these contain psalms, antiphons, masses—one 'de batalla' for 12 parts in 3 choirs with basso continuo—tonos, romances, villancicos for 8 voices. Known as El Compositor, he was accorded the exceptional honour of 'perpetual performance' of a responso on his anniversary. Juan Pablo Pujol, *c*. 1570–1626, was chapel master at Tarrazona, Saragossa and Barcelona cathedrals and known for his sweetness and deep religious sense allied to great *ingenio*, or inventiveness, in the variation. The

Valencian Juan Bautista Cómes, 1568–1643, directed Valencia cathedral's music chapel; his many compositions were published in 1888. All this flourishing complexity may be appreciated as a remarkable background for the vitality and range of Antonio Soler's first years at Montserrat. The Escorial to which he transferred also had its innovators, who were drawn there from many parts of Spain. F. Pedro de Huéscar (d. 1631) was its first chapel master. The Segovian Manuel de León (d. 1632) used unprepared dissonance and the Navarrese F. Pedro de Tafalla (d. 1660) exploited chromaticism. However, little organ music of the 17th century appears to have been preserved here.

The redoubtable Fray Juan Bermudo of Écija followed the uncompromising and disquieting Bartolomé Ramos de Pareja, who demonstrated about 1480 to the theorist disciples of Arezzo in Bologna that it was necessary to tune the scale in equal temperament, the way Spanish instrumentalists had tuned their strings for generations, since they knew it was their business to trust their ears. In his book, *Declaración de instrumentos musicales* printed in Osuna 1549, Fray Bermudo made the same popular method of tuning the basis of his directions for tuning the bandurria, in the same way as the vihuela. 'I wish to say that from one fret to another there should be a semitone.' Thus he taught students to seek unisons and tune by them, as countless teachers had done before him throughout Spain. His book was acclaimed by Morales. A lesser work, *Arte tripharia*, also printed in Osuna, in 1550, was written to satisfy a lady who, on entering a convent, required to know in as short a time as possible how to sing the holy office and also to play (*tañer*) for the same exercise. In this three-part treatise, plainchant, canto de órgano (polyphony) and organ-playing, he recommends for the manochord works by the brothers Silvestre of Granada, Bernardino Figueroa—of the royal chapel there—Antonio de Cabezón and Morales, among others. Fray Bermudo practised what he preached, for he was both a good composer and organist.

Among theorists of the 16th century who include Bizcargui, Tapia Numantino, the blind abbot Francisco Salinas holds a unique place because of his anthology of popular melodies current in his time, collected and preserved to prove his argument in *De Musica libri septem* (Salamanca, 1577). He began at this university as a student of classics and became its professor of music, after living in Rome. Organist to the viceroy of Naples, the Duke of Alba, in 1558, he was made abbot there of San Pancracio at Rocca Galegna; he was thus nicely balanced in experience when illustrating his classical dissection of the musical art into its rational and irrational components with those naturally spontaneous little Spanish songs, selected with evident connoisseurship, which pertain to all—and yet to none—of those categories he pro-

pounds. All these writers cite Boethius and St Augustine among their authorities and carry their concepts into the next century, for there seems to have been continuous interest in this side of musical thought, particularly in Montano's *Arte de Música theorica y practica*, which when enlarged by later editors continued to be reprinted well into the 18th. A *Tratado de Glosas* (Rome, 1553) by Diego Ortiz, chapel master to Naples' viceregal court, is a pioneer work on thorough bass.

CHAPTER IV

Music and the Spanish Drama

The liturgical 'representaciones' in their early forms celebrated days in the Christian calendar as was the practice in western centres with the adoration of the Cross, the Three Marys; of these Vich and Ripoll each had a version in Catalonia probably at about the same time when Ripoll, towards the end of the 10th century set the lyric scene of the Reyes Magos in song, and it is a drama (*auto*) on this theme in the Spanish language dated about the end of the 12th century which is the earliest known.

Among such pieces—which further include the appearance at Emmaus, the scenes of the Holy Innocents, the feast of St Stephen and the 'mystery' of Elche commemorating the Virgin's death, from the Marian cycle—it is the *Canto de la Sibila* which appears to have been the most ancient dramatic representation in Spain. Anglés shows that the previous belief that it originated in France cannot be upheld, and that it first appeared in Castile during the 9th century, passing then to Ripoll in the 10th and northwards into France and on to Limoges. It was certainly widespread and developed from monodic forms through the 14th down to the 15th century into the polyphonic, in Seville, Toledo, Madrid, Gandía and Barcelona. The version of Toledo is dramatic compared with the lyrical simplicity of the Catalan version. The revival as given in Mallorca shows the mounting onto a platform of boy-angel-minstrels bearing great wax tapers followed by the appearance within a cloud of incense of the veiled boy sibyl flashing his shining sword aloft as he intones from the pulpit in a high-pitched voice the Eriytrean prophecy of the second coming of the Redeemer and the Day of Judgment. His veil symbolises Augustine's picture of pre-Christian times, well known from his day, of the Jewish people unwilling to see the Truth, as the boy's woman's clothes represent the prophetess.

It was St Augustine who set the Latin version of *Judicii signum*, with which this sibyl's prophecy opens, at the heart of Book XVIII in *The*

Canto de la Sibila.

(llamado de Manacor)

Palma de Mallorca.

Responsión.

El jorn del ju _ di _ _ _ _ _ _ _ _ _ ci

par _ _ rà qui hau _ rà _____

fet ser _ vi _ _ _ ci

Estrofa I.

Je _ _ su _ crist rej _____

u _ ni _ ver _ sal _____

homo i ver Déu e _ ter _ nal del

cel vin _ drà per a jut _ jar _____

i a ca _ _ _ _ da un lo just

da _ rà. _____

City of God where he recounts those prophecies through the ages of Christ's coming. His connections with the early Spanish church gave him a special place in its services as his mass in the Antiphoner of León and Mozarabic sacramentarios prove. As we have seen, he was associated with the Passion of the Spanish martyr St Vincent, having preached the sermon after its commemoration in Africa; he was, too, the most vehement enemy of that Arianism which later infected the Visigothic church, and through Orosius and his contemporaries his contact with Spaniards was closely personal.

The so-called 'Mystery' of Elche, one of a great many autos given in Spain between the 12th and 15th centuries commemorates the Virgin's death in the Marian cycle for the Feast of Assumption. As Cotarelo y Mori observed: 'Elche entered in Christian hands at the end of the 13th century, when there were no longer "mysteries" in Spain, if ever there had been, which is doubtful.'

Its text is in Lemosin, or Catalan, and like the music has undergone much alteration. The music dating from 1639, in Pedrell's version, includes several polyphonic pieces by Valencia's chapel master, Juan Ginés Pérez, a Ribera, who may have been the composer of works preserved in Toledo cathedral, and in the service of the papal chapel, 1506–1523, and Luis Vich, organist and chapel master in Elche since 1562. One of the numbers, however, is sung to music by the troubadour Raimbaut de Vaqueiras from his composition to the verse Quant vey. This suggests that the recitative or narrational colouring was assisted by the use of monodic melody which gave an air of antiquity's authority to the scene, to which the polyphonic choirs offered a more contemporary commentary by contrast in some cases. The melismatic plaint of Ay trista vida corporal! . . . Triste de mi! contains phrases familiar in fragmented shapes to those who trace the ever-changing variants of Spanish traditional songs.

It was Gil Vicente, *c.* 1465–1537, a resourceful playwright, master of characterisation and a writer of lyrics equalling Shakespeare's in their fleeting beauty and wayward rhythms for which he himself composed music, who most consistently explored the renaissance dream in musical-dramatic form. He wrote for the Portuguese court, which was graced by two Spanish queens in his lifetime, and drew on the language, types and ballads of both peoples. Music is worked into the textures of his mythological pieces in a manner which shows his appreciation of Renaissance potential, and it is possible that in those which celebrate royal marriages, such as *The Courts of Jupiter* on the marriage of Princess Beatriz to the Duke of Savoy in 1521, he staged a precedent which influenced such dynastic occasions so long as these continued, chiefly through those musical splendours which adorned his allegorical scenes and the court finales. These may be appreciated now as revivals of the classical *epithalamia*. *The Forge of Love* was performed at Evora in 1524 to celebrate the betrothal of João III to Charles V's sister Catherine and *The Ship of Love* was composed to welcome her arrival in 1527. Charles V's wedding to the Portuguese Princess Isabel in 1526 was greeted by *The Temple of Apollo*, as their betrothal had probably been by *Dom Duardos*, since though it was apparently written in 1522— though this is not certain and the date of 1524 is accepted by some critics —it was played for the wedding celebration. This neo-epithalamian pattern first revived by poets, was continued for the wedding of Charles V's niece in 1545 by d'Arco's *Galatea* and a French eclogue for Charles IX's marriage of 1570, to be followed by French monarchs between 1650 and 1690, and for Louis XV and Louis XVI. The most splendid of all probably was the staging of Cesti's *Il pome d'oro* in Vienna for the emperor Leopold I's marriage to Margarita of Spain in 1667. In Spain the custom was maintained as in Portugal till the end of the 18th c., after which the Napoleonic invaders broke the mould of this as of many other peninsular traditions. Musically, Gil Vicente went even beyond the lavishness of his other pieces in Dom Duardos for a romantic scene in the royal gardens of Constantinople, where the Prince disguised as a gardener woos the princess Flerida in a scene wholly filled with song and instrumental interlude, during which the action is suspended so that their mutual passion may be expressed through the sensitively chosen music which fills the air. Vicente greatly expands Encina's contrasting use of rustic airs with classical form and matches characters of every kind and condition with song.

At the opening of the 17th century musicians were employed for the Spanish stage to provide background music with tambourines, timbrels and guitars to which the company danced and sang in the interludes, the guitar being also required for song accompaniment. From 1608 there were already twelve royal, that is, licensed, companies who travelled round the country. The two Madrid groups were assigned to the Príncipe and the Cruz playhouses (*corrales*), these being named after those inns in which they were situated, and it was here that operas and zarzuelas in generations to come were to vie with one another.

In 1615 both comedies and tragedies opened with music and these *cuatros de empezar* in madrigal style kept their place as changes in the entertainment's order came and went. Important pieces were composed for this opening scene in which traditionally four of the company dressed in fine costumes set the atmosphere for the spectacle. Its prestige increased when the *loa* was suppressed and supplanted by a *jácara* whose place the baile or entremés of song with dancing usually then took over, for the substitution of the baile for the traditional loa which had served to introduce the cast meant that the cuatro de empezar's dignity was emphasised by contrast, since the jácara was not only light in tone, but acquired picaresque associations. The entremés, however, had its own importance of concerted appeal as dancers evolved patterns of chains, links, paseos, cruzados. Thus musicians found scope for a variety of forms of which they were already masters. Their travelling predecessors had played back-stage and it was the Toledan Navarro who 'brought forth the music which before had been sung behind the scene, into the public theatre', a promotion for the performers which, Cervantes, characteristically sympathetic, signalised in introducing his own Comedias. The dramatists indeed welcomed the musicians with open hearts and scripts filled with directions for musical intervention.

Cervantes' humanising of his characters yields precious evidence of the musician's life of his time. In *El Rufiano Viudo* the musicians are asked why they enter without guitars and explain that they are still in the barber's shop. The barber, always a good fellow in Cervantes' scenes and willing 'to gleek upon occasion', soon brings the instruments and the players perform 'de improviso' first 'this *romance*, after which they play the *gallarda* and after this dance, having made a *mudanza*, they proceed with the *romance* . . . after which they play the *canario*'. Sometimes he gives the texts of songs in full, his 'own inventions'; more rarely, he leaves the musicians to fill in with an appropriate ditty, or indicates by allusion some popular air which accords with his text. At one place, he writes: 'Let them sing what they will.' In a wedding scene, he directs: 'With music and torches aflame, guitars and voices and great rejoicing, singing the songs I shall name.' *El Rufián Dichoso* ends with an apotheosis of music; 'a glory, or at least an angel'. Cervantes was well acquainted with the limitations of stage resources, as this direction suggests.

On more formal occasions he orders the use of chirimías and flautas, usually flautas tristes—the wind instruments he seemed to like to hear 'lexos'—in the distance. In *Pedro de Urdemalas*, he calls for 'sounds within of every kind of music, and bagpipes of Zamora'. Later the gypsy dancers perform 'when the tambourine sounds'; the *comissario de las danças* has curious things to say about them and Cervantes himself ventures to add that one can dance 'like a mule'. Elsewhere the musicians perform 'mil zarabandas, mil zambapalos, mil chaconas, mil pesame dello, y mil folías'. The *zambapalo* was a grotesque dance from the West Indies.

Years of captivity in Morocco familiarised Cervantes with the Hispano-Muslim tradition over the water and in such plays as *Los baños de Argel* and *La gran sultana* he suspends the action for whole scenes together as Gil Vicente did before him while the music's waves of sound seem to float over the tides to Gibraltar, bearing the longing of captive Christians for the golden light of Andalusia, while in these African gardens Moorish atambores, flautas tristes, the guitar and rabel add to the animation of 'Li, li, li, que gran morisma allá corre . . .'

In the *Retablo de las maravillas* he puts in a friendly word in defence of the poor musician when the showman pleads that he may be allowed to remain on stage and not be relegated behind the repostero as was the old fashion. Sometimes he even gives the final moral of the piece to the musician. In the *Juez de los divorcios*, it is these performers who justly wind up with: 'Más vale el peor concierto que no el divorcio mejor'— 'the worst consort is worth more than the best divorce'.

Lope de Vega, however, sometimes brackets musicians with lackeys, as adjuncts to be hired and thrown aside; but he is exact in the use of dances old and new, and a vast amount of detail about music-making of his time is to be gathered from his plays. His own lyrical intensity is so fervent in its continual spate that it produces the movement of music, and the impatience of his characters is well-compared to the tuning up of instruments:

> *Que a un inquieto corazón*
> *Oír templar un instrumento*
> *Es darle mayor tormento*
> *Y doblálle la pasión.*

La Selva sin amor, which gives him the honour of being the first author of Spanish opera, however bears the subtitle 'Égloga pastoril que se cantó a su Magestad en fiestas a su salud' suggesting that he had Encina's experiment perhaps in mind when attacking his own. To pass from the glittering opulence of Lope's world into the regions of Calderón de la Barca's reflective genius is to leave the heat of the sun and the dazzle of action for a realm of starlight over which music rises like a pallid moon searching out the vague horizons of the soul. Calderón is a Spanish Prospero probing the mystery of the abstract. He peoples his island with Calibans, Ariels and with sweet sounds—sounds which hover through the air in shapeless imagery of dreams and memories from the unconscious. With him, the lights in the theatre are darkened—'oscurécese el teatro, que será de peñascos, con el foro de marina', he commands with the wand of imagination. It seems that as the vitality of his early characters cools down in the crucible of his labyrinthine mind he is driven more and more to rely upon such devices as scenic intricacies and the sibylline chant of unseen choirs. Indeed the words *confusión* and *memoria* could be used as cues for music in his later dramas. Often music is used as the guiding voice of conscience in the shape of a *coro subterráneo*; the Prince of Fez is converted by the Virgin and *música oculta* sung mysteriously from within a cloud. He is prone to use choirs in antiphonal style in his secular plays as well as in the sacramental autos. In *El mayor encanto Amor*, Circe's followers off one side of the stage sing 'Amor! Amor!' whilst off stage on the other side Ulysses' Greeks cry 'Guerra! Guerra!'. Music and love win the day, but not the final scene. In *El Mágico prodigioso* choirs of exaltation chant again off stage 'Amor! Amor!'. Peculiarly significant of a mind which wishes to lose itself in the infinite abstraction of things is Calderón's remark: 'Buena la música fuera si no tuviera músicos'— 'how good music would be if there were no musicians'. The humanism of Cervantes and the metaphysics of Calderón epitomise the spirit of their generations when compared in their musical sensibilities.

Although the gravitational pull of Calderón's planetary system is obvious in some of Agustín Moreto's plays, his famous comedies, and those the most faultless, carry us easily towards the 18th century and into an age which was to refine rather than to enrich. The heroic days were passing and Moreto's fine sensibility was among the first to catch the new tone. His use of music is deliberate. He weaves it delicately into the texture of his significant scenes, giving them a melting beauty and casting an iridescent enchantment over the moods of gallantry. He pricks the heart and pleases the imagination, though he scarcely ever wounds the soul. Even the prick he is quick to soothe with the balm of sound. He shows especial care to surround his heroines with music. In *El desdén con el desdén* Diana makes her appearance to the sound of singing. When she finds that her own weapon of disdain is being turned against her, she is amusingly sure of her power to bring the obstinate duke to heel by her own singing and playing. A less famous play *Lo que puede la aprehensión* in one edition is given the sub-title *La fuerza del oído*, the power of hearing, for its theme is of a man in love with the voice of a woman he has never seen. To deceive the eyes with the ears is how Moreto expresses this idea in another play; and again a character muses:

> *Me han vuelto los ojos a los oídos,*
> *Norte vocal, sed mi guia*

'My eyes have gone to my ears; vocal lodestar, be my guide!' This play concerned with the attraction of the human voice and the deception by which one sense will seek to maintain its ascendancy over another would make an admirable opera in the Spanish style, as Iriarte depicts it:

> *en que el discurso hablado*
> *ya con frecuentes arias se interpola,*
> *y ya con duo, coro y recitado . . .*

Moreto's theme of *San Gil de Portugal* is the tempting of a holy man by means of sensuous music. From the moment the musicians begin to play he is stirred by misgivings, but cannot resist the temptation to listen. He succumbs, and abducts the woman from whom immediately before he had persuaded her lover to separate. Elsewhere, with a craftsman's economy, Moreto uses the reverse pattern of this material in *La adúltera penitente*—where the man of weak conscience hesitates on the steps leading to Teodora's room when he hears music such as Calderón was wont to employ. Moreto rarely neglects the aid of musicians. He can even turn the accident of plot upon the fact that one of a group of serenaders cannot run away because his harp is too cumbersome to permit his escape with the others. Tirso de Molina's plays found musical settings in Mozart's *Don Giovanni* and *Cosí fan tutte*.

Though Lope's enormous appetite for life in all its aspects fed on themes of the past, he was alert to novelty and seized upon the operatic concept in writing the 'Égloga' *La selva sin amor* which 'was represented sung before their Majesties and highnesses, a new thing in Spain' —1629; it deserved the prompt publication of the text the following year, 'though the least in it are my verses' he adds. Unfortunately, though Lope generously praised many musicians, he omitted this composer's name, so that we can only surmise who wrote the music for this setting with a view of the Casa del Campo and the royal palace with a perspective of a sea wherein some fish swam about according to the impulse of the waves; there were a number of musicians more than competent to write songs for Venus, Amor, Silvio, Jacinto, Filis, Flora, Manzanares and the chorus of Loves. Another royal couple besides Philip III and his queen attended its production, for her sister María had recently married the King of Hungary, and in this epithalamian style they were being feted at this time by the Spanish court. Among those capable of gracing this score with music to match its fluent text was Carlos Patiño whose Cuatro de Empezar Cantar las gracias de Flora / quiere Amor y no se atreve, shows his ability to enhance a situation which exactly parallels Lope's theme and its personages. Born in La Mancha, he was a prolific composer and having served as royal chaplain to the convent of the Encarnación succeeded Mateo Romero, the 'Capitán', as director of the Royal Chapel in 1633, where he remained for a quarter of a century, dying in 1683.

Calderón approached this innovation with more deliberate consideration of its potential translation to Spanish tastes. His *El Jardin de Falerina* of 1648 for Philip IV's wedding to Mariana de Austria, his niece, was filled with *coros* and *danzas*. In 1659 and 1660 he wrote texts for two operas, the first, *La púrpura de la rosa*, for the wedding of the Infanta Maria Teresa to Louis XIV, being a one act piece in which both companies of the Madrid theatres took part. That he recognised the occasion as a foreign challenge is shown in the lines:

> *Ha de ser*
> *toda música que intenta*
> *introducir este estilo*
> *porque otras naciones vean*
> *competidos sus primores . . .*

When 'la Tristeza' points out the risk of enraging the impatient Spanish temper by the slowing down of the dramatic pace which operatic forms entailed:

> *No miras cuanto se arriesga*
> *en que cólera española*
> *sufra toda una comedia*
> *cantada?*

'el Vulgo' replies that it is only a little piece and suggests that blame for any error should be placed on the inventor.

From the text we know that it was sung in recitativo style alternating with solos, duets, quartets and chorus to an orchestra, with martial trumpets, dances and scenic complexities such as delighted audiences of the time. Again, the music is unknown and its composer also, though there is little doubt that this was Juan Hidalgo.

On 5th December 1660 Calderón's second opera was staged at the Buen Retiro; this was *Celos aun del aire matan*, called a 'fiesta grande cantada', in three acts, with music by Juan Hidalgo, whose score of the first act was discovered in this century by José Subirá in the Alba collection. This again is a mythological theme and includes Diana, Procris, Floreta, Mejera, Alecto, Thesifone, Zéfalo, Eróstrato, Clarín, Rústico, a chorus of nymphs and one of men, according to a reprint of 1663, which curiously omits the name of Aura whose lament occupies a significant part in the score; nor does the modern edition explain this discrepancy. Within the Italian mode of recitativo and aria the composer maintains a Spanish colouring in melodies of a rustic kind and in some Spanish rhythms; the recitative is flexible, conforming to Spanish requirements of close links with the words, the accentuation being generally faithful to them. It is curious to find the lament of Aura recurring and then referred to in later parts of the pastoral opera as if its motive were constantly in the dramatist's mind, in spite of the absence of the name Aura from the cast. Since her complaint recalls the theme of Arianna's lament, Monteverdi's most impassioned recitativo and aria, it is not irrelevant to suspect that this may have been in the Spanish author's mind. The scene where Aura is bound to a tree-trunk and calls vainly on the gods to save her recalls Arianna's classic plight as the Spanish aria mourns 'Ay, infeliz de aquella que hizo verdad a ver quien de amor muera!' in a parallel association with Monteverdi's form of short aria with comparatively lengthy recitative. Thus, it may have been in Calderón's mind to insert a Spanish parallel into this pastoral tale of the nymph who forswears her vow to Diana to shun human love. It is notable that the work opens with this scene of Aura's preparation for death by Diana's javelin. Aura does not figure in the cast list of 1663, it has been pointed out above; neither does Ana; this second omission makes Scene VIII more curious still because of its passage, sung by Rústico in explaining the plot's situation—'Por que a Aura acusaron, de cuyo enojo resultó que Doña Ana la atase a un tronco'. Did Calderón have a mental association in thus connecting Aura—a nymph—with Ana and the famous Arianna of Monteverdi's *Arianna* of 1608 of which the arioso 'Lasciatemi morire' alone survives? Aura refers to 'mi tragedia' in Scene II, though finally she is saved by Love, thus turning aside from the tragic fate of Monteverdi's creation. Taken together with the repeated motif of Aura's Lament on being bound to the tree-trunk, there seems evidence to suggest that Calderón here attempted a Spanish equivalent to the famous Italian composer's surviving recitative and aria, grafting it on to the pastoral eclogue, as may be appreciated in the manner by which the Spanish traditional type of rustic air mingles with a gallant first attempt at the novel Italian declamatory form which the composer boldly attacks, achieving an accurate word accentuation of the Spanish, as a native heir of Spanish chant might be expected to do.

Calderón's choice of Diana as the goddess in chief of this plot may or may not have been prompted by recollection of that first opera produced in Italy, Peri's *La Dafne*, in Florence 1597; its music is lost, but Calderón was familiar with the sylvan world in all its metamorphoses whether Spanish or Italian and probably with such eclogues as the Neapolitan Sannazzaro's of Diana's nymph *Salix* and those other pastoral poems in which nymphs are transformed into birds, trees and flowers, as Aura in Scene XIV is translated into the air, borne aloft on an eagle's back.

He would undoubtedly have approved the spiritually-conceived interpretation of the first surviving opera, *La rappresentazione di anima e di corpo* by Cavaliere (d. 1602), for with its combination of the old morality plays of Corpus Christi and contemporary staging with music, his own subsequent autos sacramentales are in agreement.

Contemporary accounts describe Juan Hidalgo (*c.* 1600–1685) as an outstanding harpist and musician of the royal chapel, inventor of a clavi-harp and an eminent musician and composer, 'of perfect taste, de tonos divinos y humanos'. Other accounts suggest that he was a modest man, and remained so amid the great esteem in which he was held. He entered the royal chapel in 1634 and his death was greatly mourned. His place in music history is assured by his music for Calderón's opera.

The name 'fiesta cantada' was given to these productions till the end of the 17th century, as when Charles II's birthday in 1692 was celebrated with *Amor, Industria y Poder*. The first opera performed in Spain, however, was Lully's *Armide*, in 1693; the advent of the Bourbons to the Spanish throne was not far away. In 1698 a fiesta de ópera was played before Charles and in 1700 an ópera cantada, so that the word only then had taken root; Calderón after his experiments had turned his meditative genius to the *zarzuela*, the first of which was *El Jardin de Falerina* 1648, as his introductory loa to *El laurel de Apolo* reminded his audience.

The first piece to bear the title of zarzuela, *El golfo de las Sirenas*, 1657, presents a one-act mythology, this time about Ulysses, Scylla and Charybdis; again the music is lost, though the singing parts were taken by leaders of the Madrid companies and it pleased so well that it was repeated shortly after at the Buen Retiro palace. *El laurel de Apolo* described by Calderón as 'zarzuela en dos jornadas' was produced here in the following year. The music to which subsequent 17th-century zarzuelas were set is almost wholly unknown, though Juan Hidalgo collaborated in *Los celos hacen estrellas*. It is supposed that José Marín wrote for J. B. Diamante's texts and, more certain, that he wrote music for *Venir el Amor al Mundo* by Melchor Fernández de León as for Antonio de Zamora's *Veneno es de amor la envidia*; thus the zarzuela in its early stages was a dignified entertainment, though the mythological figures would descend from their marble pedestals, as it were, to sing a native rustic air and even the seguidillas, which would explain the use of guitars among the stringed violin family and harps with trumpeters, buglers and drums, even with castanets. Since Monteverdi's development of dramatic style drew on instrumental chords in arpeggio to emphasise the characters' emotional states by supporting their airs, it is indeed interesting to find the famous Dr Amat's *Guitar Guide* of 1586 stressing this instrument's capacity to *tañer rasgando todos los puntos naturales y bemolados con estilo maravilloso*, with the additional fifth string now in established use. Spaniards had this Monteverdian style already at hand in the rasgueado style of the guitar's broken arpeggio technique and the diferencia declined before this means of expressing that native choler and impatience to which the ingenious doctor humorously refers, as well as its passions.

The zarzuela took its name from the royal residence, first used as a hunting-lodge, in which entertainments were held as occasion or bad weather suggested; the word zarzuela referred to the *zarzas* or bramble-bushes which grew on the site a short distance out of the capital.

A possible contact with Italian operatic events was the presence in Madrid of the nuncio Julio Rospiglioso (later pope Clement IX) from 1646 to 1653; he had already written the text for *Il falcone o Chi soffre speri* produced in the Barberini palace theatre in 1637, as an example of what might be achieved in tragic Christian drama, with music by Mazzocchi and Marazzoli, and this, like the Spanish, included popular types and dialect differentiations. On his return to Italy he immediately produced a comedy *Dal mal il bene* with music by Marazzoli and Abatini, and this work, recognisably influenced by his Spanish sojourn, is said to have affected the course of opera buffa in its early years. Romain Rolland's surprise on reading this pope's musical comedy might have been somewhat less had he taken into account that earlier production before a papal nuncio in Brussels of Gil Vicente's *Jubileu de Amor* in 1531, in honour of the birth of the future King Manoel, which in spite of and perhaps because of its satire meeting disapproval, made Romans notice that the peninsula even then was creating comedy with music.

Of the other outstanding musicians of this time, little is known about Juan de Navas except that he wrote tonadas y solos humanos—secular songs—and one act of the zarzuela *Apolo y Dafne* in collaboration with Durón. Appreciated for his native grace and spontaneity he was still living about 1700. In contrast to these conformable stylists, José Marín, born 1619, had a restless life, disrupted by violence. In 1644 he was tenor of the royal convent of the Encarnación's chapel—'the best in Madrid'. Then in 1656 he was involved in the assault, robbery and murder of a man, and was tortured with others accused of the crime; he was unfrocked and imprisoned in a high tower in so small a room that it was said he could entertain himself there with the sweet voice he had like a captive bird in a cage. Exiled for ten years, he went on a pilgrimage, repented and thenceforward led an exemplary life, was restored to the ecclesiastical fold and died 17th March 1699 at the age of 80, respected by everyone and known in Spain and abroad for his ability both as a composer and player on divers instruments. He wrote tonos, tonadas, solos, duos humanos and a tonada a solo dedicated to the Holy Sacrament. His fine Corazón que en prisión, a tonada for voice with guitar, seems to allude to his own prison experience, and he had an unusual affinity with the theatre writers in composing soliloquies, which in Calderón's generation was an adaptable art much in request. In a seemingly nonchalant way he could toss off snatches of clowns' ditties in the Shakespearean manner.

Sebastian Durón, born in Brihuega, was organist to the Royal

Chapel from 1691 and then chapel master and rector of the choir school, but inclined more to secular than sacred music and to a degree of temperament whose fieriness showed in the lively movements, syncopated rhythms and profane popular allusions in his church scores. Feijóo, who rather unjustly blamed him solely for introducing the violin to excess in the church services, was nearer the mark in saying that at times he would vary the effects of the singing six or eight times, according to the variations of the text; and that although this needed great ability, which he had, it was very ill applied, meaning that the church was not the proper place for it, as others, including Charles II, said, though more mildly than the critical Feijóo. In the War of Succession, however, Durón remained loyal to the old royal family and on the Bourbon entry was arrested and expelled to France where he died. His operas include *La guerra de los gigantes*; *Salir el amor al mundo*; his zarzuelas, *Selva encantada de amor*; *Las nuevas armas de amor*; *Apolo y Dafne*. He used seguidillas and their kind in these works. Lamenting his separation from Spain, he sought for his funeral to be commemorated there, though he was compelled to lie in France. Judging by his will, he had become very well off, and after providing for his sister, a nun, and his brother, a priest, he left a considerable residue for the adorning and perfection of the chapel and retable of Nuestra Señora de la Zarza, 'la Casa de la Virgen Santíssima de la Zarza . . . que en la Parroquial de dichavilla (Brihuega) mandó colocar . . .[1] The lengthy details and precise orders set out show that in Bayonne he had given much thought to this desire, suggesting that perhaps Our Lady of the Brambles, situated in his native Brihuega, not far from Madrid itself, was linked in his thoughts to the success opened to his muse by that novel form of which he was a genial master, the Zarzuela, and may have listened to his prayers.

Other musicians wrote music for Calderón's autos sacramentales, the first of which was written about 1634 to be followed in increasing numbers till his death in 1681. Cristóbal Galán, chapel master of the Descalzas Reales, composed music for the period of 1664, as for *A María el corazón*; *La inmunidad del sagrado o Nuestra Señora de Loreto*, and again, in 1671—after four years' suspension of performances

---

[1] In the chapel of the Holy Virgin of la Zarza, which in the parish of the said town (Brihuega) he ordered to be placed.
An old anonymous song for Christmas night has this verse for the shepherds:

> Ardía la zarza
> Y no se quemaba;
> La Virgen María,
> Doncella y preñada.

comparing the Virgin to the bramble which though afire was not burned.

following Philip IV's death—wrote the score for two more autos. In 1675 Gregorio de la Rosa was paid for setting *entremeses* or *sainetes*— which were played at the same function, to offer both genres as was the custom, sacred and profane. The musician's fees increased as the musical participation was expanded. In 1664 Galán had received 500 reales, and the same in 1671; Maestro Fray Juan Romero received 1,100 reales and Manuel de León Marchante 800 for the sainetes for the later pieces. In the first volume of his autos, 1677, Calderón regrets that these pieces lack the music and settings so important to the representation. Working until his death in 1681, he had finished *El cordero de Isaías* and was about to conclude *La Divina Filotea* when death suddenly seized him, 25th May. They were performed a few weeks later with music by Manuel de Navas, who was paid 1,000 reales, and another 1,000 reales went to Melchor de León for his conclusion to *La Divina Filotea* and his music for the two sainetes. After this, the autos slowly declined until Charles III finally extinguished their last flickerings among the many changes he instituted.

The Jesuit plays followed a similar course, though their cultivation spread across the world, both east and west. They, too, were aided by the music and splendid decor Calderón had prized. The Colegio de Sevilla saw the production of characteristic works of this kind in which solo airs contrasted with those elaborate choral stretches for which this tradition was famed; the most elaborate example was for the reception of Philip III on his peninsular journeyings after his accession, and such events were organised to grace royal celebrations continually before the expulsion of this Order in 1767, as instance, the reception at Elvas for the newly wed Princess Maria Ana Victoria, daughter of Philip V and Isabel Farnese, to the Portuguese Crown Prince José, upon the double marriage between this pair and Barbara de Braganza to the Spanish Crown Prince Ferdinand. Antonio da Costa tells of the great congregations which attended these tragicomedies with music sitting in absorbed silence in spite of their length, which at this time sometimes extended to two or three days; his comparisons here are not favourable to Italian noise and uninhibited manners as he describes opera performances there.

The smaller genre of secular entremeses cantados were given a helping hand by some of Spain's most brilliant literary men; Tirso de Molina, Hurtado de Mendoza, Moreto, Quevedo—the collaboration of this last satirist may be seen as equal to the participation of say, Dean Swift, in musical diversions—for irony and intellectually conceived satire were chief parts in their success. The tradition continued in the librettos by José de Cañizares and Torres Villarroel of the 18th century.

Dances of the century suggest costumbrismo as an increasing means of adding local colour and exotic spices to the regional bailes and courtly set patterns, the exoticisms including the Ye-Ye, Paracumbé, and Hu-Hu Indians. Vicente began this with negro patter and Lope followed with refrains alluding to Panama and the tamborito panameño in *La dama boba*.

In the background of social life, church music provided a constant factor. Gabriel Diaz Besson, chapel master of the Encarnación convent and later of the Descalzas Reales, wrote music that was apostrophised as 'celestial'. Diego Pontac, also highly esteemed, probably still holds the record for general post changes. Beginning as *seis* at 9 years old at Saragossa, at 16 he held the position of musician to the Hospital Real there; in quick succession he was appointed to Salamanca cathedral and Granada, the Madrid Encarnación convent, Santiago de Compostela, 1644; 1649 saw him back at Saragossa and now master to the cathedral. Within a year, however, he was off to Valencia in a similar post till 1653, then to Madrid as teniente of the Royal Chapel, like Besson before him—and this perhaps was the goal he had had in mind during his non-stop career, for it was in Madrid that he finally came to rest and died. Much of his work, like that of his contemporaries, was burned in the Palace fire, 1734.

Sebastian López de Velasco, of Segovia, in 1628 published his Masses, Motets, Salmos, Magnificats and so on. He was notable for expressiveness and grandiose style. Juan del Vado, organist of the Royal Chapel, is known for his Masses and the baroque daring of his technique in the canon. He translated verse by the Englishman, 'John Oven'. Two monks, Fray Dionisio and Fray Juan—the two Romeros—wrote villancicos besides music for Calderón's autos, though the music of Fray Juan for this is lost; Cristóbal Galán, associated, too, with Calderón, as has been seen, composed villancicos, also. The *Cancionero Sablonera* is analogous to the *Cancionero Musical de Palacio* in its collection of contemporary songs, copied by one of Philip III's musicians who, as he tells in a plea for a pension, worked by day and night by order of the Maestro Capitán for the king's entertainment and was a player of the vihuela de arco; all he begged for was 10 ducats yearly, being poor and necessitous after punctual service during 23 years. This memorial is dated 1622. He declared he had sorted out and copied the best tonos for 2, 3, and 4 voices then heard at the court and that he had done so because of the king's great love of music. Most of these tonos are by the Maestro Capitán, a total of 78: twenty-two by Mateo Romero himself, eighteen by Juan Blas de Castro, friend and music-setter to Lope de Vega; Gabriel Diaz de Besson and Alvaro de los Ríos, eight each; a Pujol—or Juan Pablo—seven; the Portuguese Manuel Machado, four; Miguel de Arizo, two; Palomares, Juan Torres, Juan

Bono, Diego Gómez, one; two anonymous, one of these the Seguidillas en eco, attributed to Machado or Romero. There are forty-two
romances, after which canciones influenced by the madrigal, and some
canciones in villancico form follow in numerical importance. Sablonera does not forget to give examples of endechas, folías and seguidillas
to exhibit the strongly marked popular taste of the reign. These have
been transcribed and published by Jesús Aroca, Madrid, 1918. Not so
accessible is the manuscript in the Biblioteca Nacional de Madrid entitled *Romances y letras a tres voces*, whose 135 pieces, mostly anonymous,
await thorough investigation. More voluminous still, the same library's
Tonos humanos a cuatro voces, dated 1655, contains about 226 examples,
also anonymous for the most part, but including some well-known
musicians, such as Francisco Navarro, Carlos Patiño, Mateo Romero,
Nicolas Borly. The Portuguese figure in this—it may be partly because of the Spanish occupation of their country between 1580–1640
when artists from Lisbon found favour at court—Manuel Machado of
Lisbon was a member of Philip III's chapel; Antonio de Viera figures
here and Padre Manuel Correa who excelled in tonos both humano and
divino and was chapel master to Saragossa cathedral at his death in
1653. Examples of his music appear in Pedrell's *Teatro Lírico Español
anterior al siglo XIX*.

The MS. *Tonos Castellanos*, Biblioteca Medinaceli, contain fifty
anonymous pieces and some honoured names. Juan Blas de Castro, the
distinguished contemporary of the Flemish Mateo Romero (alias
Maestro Capitán, by birth Rosmarín, a Fleming), born *c.* 1560, became
blind and retired for the last twenty years of his life; he was probably a
chamber singer and vihuelist as well as composer and served the Duke
of Alba *c.* 1594 and Philip III in 1605. The eulogies of Lope and Tirso
secure his fame although his works, preserved by Philip IV's orders,
were lost in the Palace fire. Pedro de Palomares is mentioned with him
in *El peregrino en su patria* by Lope as in the words 'Gracia tuvo del
cielo Palomares . . . en cinco cuerdos'—'Grace was given from heaven
to Palomares . . . on five strings'; Lope also praised Juan de Palomares
the composer in *La Dorotea* as a distinguished competitor of the famous
Juan Blas de Castro. Much later, Juan Serqueira or Cerqueiro was outstanding in the last years of the 17th century; in 1710 he was first
musician in the Madrid theatre company of José Prado.

Much is lost of the vast quantity of music written before 1734, but
much remains to be revealed. It was through the works of those already mentioned and many others, such as Miguel Ambiela, Diego
Casseda, Jerónimo de la Torre, Francisco Monjo, Miguel Martí
Valenciano, José de Torres, Martínez Bravo, Manuel de Villaflor and
their descendants of the next generation that Spanish musicians were

able to maintain a solid front in face of those Italian invaders enjoying the subsidies and overriding patronage of their operas under Bourbon rule.

The Flemish chapel enjoyed an Indian summer under the leadership of Philippe Rogier (1560–1596) who came to Madrid as a boy singer in Philip II's reign and grew up to be its most able composer and chapel master, founding a school of Flemish musicians which flourished under the direction of Matthieu Rosmarin (b. Liège, 1575–1647), and famous in Spain as Matheo Romero, 'El Maestro Capitán'—that is, captain or leader of the Flemish group. Rosmarin maintained this Flemish tradition alive in Spain during Philip III's reign and well into Philip IV's, keeping his ascendancy over this monarch after his retirement in 1634 as royal chapel master—which service had included his supervision of both Flemish and Spanish chapels—after forty-eight years in Spain. However, the personnel of the Flemish group had slowly dwindled, for in Philip III's days and onwards the members were drawn from Spanish musicians. Under Carlos Patiño, who succeeded Rosmarin and had had to contend with his predecessor's overweening interference, the Flemish chapel was finally merged with the 'capilla española' in 1637. The title of 'capilla flamenca' disappeared and the salaries of musicians from this time forward are listed as 'Gajes de la Capilla Real del Rey Nuestro Señor' and 'Gajes de las personas que sirven en la Real Capilla del Rey Nuestro Señor'. The Flemish contrapuntal influence in Spain survived into the 18th century; in exchange, Spanish styles and forms such as the villancico affected those Netherlanders still resident at court where El Maestro Capitán led the rest in cultivating not only the romance but also the folía and seguidillas.

CHAPTER V

Music under Bourbon Rule

The reign of a French-born king Philip V, 1701–1746, and his Savoyard and Parmesan wives is musically documented by scores from the
royal library now in the Biblioteca Nacional. There are printed French
works such as cantatas by Clérambault, arias by Lully and Philidor,
minuets, gavottes, passepieds, branles, courantes, melodies with basso
continuo. The Italian operas, however, are in manuscript; though some
famous names such as Alessandro Scarlatti are included in this repertory,
it is mostly of pieces by long-forgotten composers. The Spanish works,
also in manuscript for the most part, are mainly tonos and tonadas
though Durón's *Tonada humana* bears the privileged mark of Madrid's
Imprenta de Música. The duchy of Alba's archives show the continuity
of this house's discriminating patronage and are an indispensable adjunct to music of the period.

The growing secularisation of customs is described by Feijóo's essay
of 1726, *La Música en los templos*. This attacks the looseness with which
the flood-tides of theatrical entertainments are allowed to seep into the
church; canarios and jigs, scarcely masked, are added to the services
and abuses reach a point where some music performed there is set
down as 'grave'. 'What is this? In the temple should not all music be
grave? . . . So it is that one hears the organ playing the same minuet
heard last night at the party (*sarao*). This means, of course, that as one
listens one is only thinking of the lady with whom one danced it a few
hours ago.' Lamenting the alteration in Spanish musical taste, now given
over to frivolities, he blames the Italians 'who have made us slaves to
their tastes with the false flattery of assurance that music has made such
"advances" in our time'. Though he had been mistaken in blaming
Durón entirely for the abuse of violin-playing in church, he rightly
singles out composers like Literes (*c.* 1680–1755) who have kept their
heads and continue to write honest religious music: his arguments were
sufficiently acute to influence Pope Benedict XIV's reforming bull of

1745. There is no doubt that Madrid was being seduced by the sounds of what Feijóo called that 'música de tararira'.

Spanish musicians were justified in believing that their cultivation of the native zarzuela had taken root in the previous century and needed only nourishment to blossom in the eighteenth, but this was frustrated by the constant arrival of Italians on whom money and prerogatives were lavished, even the privilege of occupying those theatres whose stages Spaniards had a municipal right to tread. It was some time before a modus vivendi was established and Spaniards were forced to observe it since, in spite of several rebuffs, Italian opera eventually became a habit in the capital; however they never forgot this break in the eighteenth century in the evolution of their own musical expression.

Spanish competence was shown by the court performance of Antonio Literes' zarzuela *Acis y Galatea*, 1709, and also his *Jupiter y Danae* which includes a cuatro, tonadas, recitados, airosos, estribillos, coplas, an ocho with violins, and a ceremonial dance 'to a solemn text'. His style shows Handelian vigour based on sound contrapuntal form and his melody expands confidently when the action demands. That he was in touch with Italian novelties is seen in his 'ópera armónica al estilo italiano' *Los Elementos*, with parts for el Aire, Agua, Fuego, Tierra, Tiempo and Aurora with an orchestra of violins, cello, vihuelas and figured bass. José Nebra (d. 1768) was, like Literes, an organist of the royal chapel, similarly distinguished for religious and stage composition; he wrote twenty operas, psalms, villancicos and a Miserere.

The invasion began with a company of Italian farce-players, called *trufaldines*, after a comedian's name. Having played before Philip V at the Buen Retiro they founded a corral in the Alcalá and then obtained permission to organise a theatre on the site where the Caños del Peral theatre was later to be built, to be followed eventually by the Teatro Real. Here more serious fare was directed by Francisco Bartoli, and comedies alternated with serious opera. With the arrival of Anibal Scotti, the Parmesan minister who ousted Alberoni the patron of these players, Spaniards were faced by more ambitious rivals, for with Isabel Farnese's support, the Italian operas were given with extravagant splendour, while municipal theatres were left with rents unpaid by foreigners who made use of them at their own convenience. Nevertheless, some natives profited by what they saw, for example Manuel Ferreira whose *El mayor triunfo de la mayor guerra* contained 38 arias and showed what Spaniards could do. In 1721 the able Cañizares reminded Madrid that they could provide librettists also with his *Jupiter y Anfitrion* and for this Jaime Facco, a notable violinist recently arrived from Lisbon, wrote a score whose success secured him a life-appointment at court.

Farinelli's peculiar situation vis-à-vis Philip V, soothing his melancholic stupors with ravishing airs as David did for Saul, but singing only a handful of arias year after year into the royal ears alone, appeared a degrading affront to Spanish national pride, though he was an amiable, cultured fellow and used his influence to promote some national talents with generous discrimination. It was the competition of less legendary creatures, Francesco Coradini, Juan Bautista Mele and Francesco Corselli, with which Spanish composers had to deal. Coradini, called from the viceroy's court of Valencia to direct the royal chapel in 1730, wrote many operas, opening with *Con amor no hay libertad*—'melodrama harmónica al estilo de Italia'. In his series of comedies in Calderón's style and zarzuelas of similar origin, Cañizares supplied texts with Spanish words; the combination of Coradini's Italian style and native themes, such as *El asombro de Jerez* and *Juana la Rabicortona* proved irresistible to Madrileños. As a result, the Parmesan Francesco Corselli arrived to present his first work *La cautela en la amistad y robo de las sabinas* in 1735, and was soon promoted from secondary maestro to director of the royal chapel. He, too, was an amiable person and won esteem, though some members of the royal chapel said he neglected his duties there for stage productions. It was in the Buen Retiro theatre, enlarged in 1738, that Corselli's operas were sumptuously staged; *Alessandro nell 'Indie*, 1738; *Farnace*, 1739; *Achille in Sciro*, 1744, and others. Outstanding among Neapolitan musicians at court was Juan Bautista Mele who also won applause in the public theatre.

After the accession of Ferdinand VI and Queen Barbara of Braganza in 1746 Mele set Metastasio's *Angelica e Medoro* for her name-day, 4th December 1748, and the same poet's *Armida placata* for the marriage of Ferdinand's sister in 1750 to the heir of Savoy which was made 'to assure the tranquillity of Italy'; this opera was one of the most brilliant functions of the period; the dowager Isabel Farnese appeared and Farinelli, the director of its lavish setting, was made Knight of the Military Order of Calatrava. Mele returned to Italy in 1752.

These three Italians, Coradini, Corselli and Mele, directed the palace orchestra from the harpsichord; the players included 16 violins, 4 violas, 4 cellos, 4 double-basses, 5 oboes, 2 trumpets, 2 clarines, 2 bassoons and 2 kettle-drums. When required, players from the Guardias Española y Valona—Walloons—were added. At this time Nebra figured with Herrando and Misón and these, three of the most notable Spanish musicians of their time, played in the orchestra.

Another Neapolitan, Nicolo Conforto, replaced Mele, and arrived heralded by successes which included a serenata *Las Modas* to words by Pico della Mirandola in 1754. His first Madrid opera, *La ninfa smarrita*, staged at Aranjuez on 30th May 1756 for the king's name-day, is lost; this same year he wrote *Nitteti* 'at the request of his friend Farinelli' to Farinelli's old friend Metastasio's verse. For the next year he set the same poet's *Adriano in Siria* and finally *La Forza del genio o sia Il Pastor guerriero*, again staged at Aranjuez for the king's birthday. It was here that Ferdinand and Barbara were free from the dominating will of his stepmother and enjoyed a few idyllic hours among nightingales both natural and musical during these years which saw the completion of Herrera's designs. Though accounts of the luxury of these operatic settings have become part of European legend, there were continental judges who made comparisons not always in accordance with this scene of painted illusions. Sir Benjamin Keene, minister at court here after years in Lisbon, a friend of Dr Burney and as sound a judge musically, wrote from Madrid about the Lisbon preparations for the opening of the São Carlos opera house there: 'You outdo all mankind. We I fear must *baisser pavillon* before you. We will not throw our money out of the window; you seem neither to mind windows nor doors into the bargain.'

The triple direction of the palace orchestra at the Buen Retiro was latterly shared by Conforto with Nebra and Rabasa, so that natives were now finding their proper place and the orchestral sections were led as before by the violinist Herrando and the flautist Misón.

Nebra's 'dramas en música', a term synonymous with opera, were composed to texts by Cañizares, José Bustamente and Antonio Zamora and produced at the municipal houses; in these enterprises Diego Lana and the Neapolitan Duni were associated, and these city promotions made it possible to recoup some earlier losses incurred during the first Italian incursions. Mateo de la Roca, and Juan Sisi Mestres also joined forces in these more satisfactory developments as foreign rivalry stimulated national pride and local talents found stimulus in the innovations. Their pieces were billed as Dramas harmónicas, melodramas harmónicas, melodramas escénicos and dramas para música. Their titles suggest an older tradition of the classic Spanish drama, as in *El ser noble es obrar bien*; *Por amor y lealtad*; *Amor, constancia y mujer*; *La cautela en la amistad*; *Cumplir con amor y honor*; *Más gloria es triunfar de si*. Singers, too, showed their ability to equal Italian prime donne, and with Spanish texts to these foreign operas even all-feminine casts proved their capacity.

The violinist Herrando wrote one of the earliest violin treatises in Spain, 1756. Six of his sonatas for the five-stringed violin were written for Farinelli and later deposited at the Bologna Liceo. He wrote twelve sonatas and twelve toccatas for violin and bass, twelve trios for two violins and bass, *c.* 1751 and a *Libro de diferentes lecciones para la viola*, which includes violin lessons also. His *Arte de tocar el violin* antecedes by a year the *Obra harmónica en seis sonatas de Cámara de violín y bajo solo* of 1757 written by Francisco Manalt, who was also a musician of the royal chapel.

The municipal theatres would match the palace festivals with such events as the opening of the new Príncipe in place of the old house in June 1745 and for which Cañizares and Nébra—the most distinguished author and composer of this period—produced the 'gran zarzuela' *Cautelas contra cautelas y el rapto de Ganimedes* whose success more than justified the hopes raised by earlier works such as *Santa Francisca Romana*, 1724, and a religious piece for Christmas in 1729 *Música discreta y santa; Santa Matilda*; from the accounts of these we learn that Nebra received only about a third of Cañizares' fee. Their collaboration was felicitous in whatever they touched; *De los encantos de amor, la música es el mayor* proved one of their most resounding zarzuelas when produced in the Principe in 1725, though Nebra wrote only the first part of *La venerable sor María de Jesús de Agreda*, which was performed in 1725, a busy year for him. Evidently he was not only prolific but versatile.

Queen Barbara died on 20th August 1758, a year after her music master Domenico Scarlatti, and Nebra wrote her requiem for 8 voices, flute and strings. Did the famous flautist Luis Misón (b. Barcelona *c.* 1725, d. Madrid 1766) play the flute for this? It would seem a fitting farewell to those halcyon seasons shared by monarchs and musicians that Nebra should have composed this part for his colleague to express the last instrumental piece written in her honour. A year later, 10th August 1759, Ferdinand followed her, having succumbed to that deepening shadow of his life, chronic melancholia. Nebra lived on till 11th July 1768, thus outlasting those who had been his rivals. He may possibly be seen as flexing his sinews musically against those Italians in *Adriano en Siria, o Más gloria es triunfar de si* of 1737 and *Alejandro en Siria* his 'drama harmónica' which was represented as one of those determined efforts by Spanish musicians to close their ranks after the domination of Italians at the new Caños theatre in 1738 with operas by Hasse.

In Barcelona during this half century Caldara's *Il piu bel nome* saluted the brief reign of the Austrian pretender, Don Carlos 'III', Caldara coming from Venice to conduct on this politically defiant demonstration. Astorga's *Dafne* followed in 1709. Despite this association, Astorga's cantatas were to become favourite scores in the chambers of Philip V's and Isabel Farnese's daughter as the Princess

Maria Ana Victoria tells her mother in a letter from the Lisbon court.

Among the many Italians who thronged Madrid in this century, Neapolitans held a special place. They were part of the Spanish realms and so part of the greater Hispanic family in many ways; artists holding privileged positions came and went, equally at home in either court. This traffic was by no means one-sided. Neapolitans were familiar with the fine Spanish sculpture by Ordóñez, Diego de Siloe in their churches, and painters of the stature of Ribera were made welcome to such an extent that this robust colourist of the naturalist style spoke for other Spaniards when he said in 1625 that he did not return to Spain because at Naples he was at ease, admired and well paid, while in Spain he would be honoured the first year and forgotten the next. Many Neapolitan musicians of subsequent years would admit that similar advantages were now open to them when they arrived in Spain, usually upon invitation.

Domenico Scarlatti (1685–1757) went to Lisbon in 1721 to teach the Infanta María Bárbara de Braganza, remaining there until 1728, except for a return to Naples in 1725. In 1729, his royal pupil invited him to join her in Madrid, where she was now married to Ferdinand, heir to the throne; he was appointed palace harpsichordist and remained there until his death on 23rd July 1757. It was here that he wrote the greater number of the *Esercizi* and sonatas numbering over 500, which notably anticipate that first movement sonata form which was to shape European symphonic structure, and also, by his incorporation of popular features in Spanish musical idiom into his own brilliant inventions, became the classic keyboard composer to whom the modern line of Spanish musicians, Albéniz, Granados, Falla, Halffter and Rodrigo refer. He crowded these developments into the later years of his court service with an incessant productiveness that still evokes amazement, and it is equally remarkable that he wrote now entirely in the miniature genre.

An event of the reign which has not been linked with these phenomena was the official presentation to Barbara of Braganza of a copy of the *Cantigas de Santa Maria* made for her by the skilled paleographer Palomares at the instigation of the savant, Father Burriel. This would not be without interest to a musical descendant of those Braganzas whose music library was famous throughout Europe, and whose king, John IV, was author of a *Defence of Modern Music*; and the daughter of John V, who sent promising musicians to study in Rome and maintained a magnificent chapel, would hardly put such a presentation aside without examining it—she was a cultured lady who had collected a choice library of both music and literature. The use of the Portuguese-

Galician language would be of interest to her, as would the dedication of its music to the Virgin. Such French examples of musical form would be no less interesting to King Ferdinand himself, as Bourbon representative in Spain.

The form evolved by Scarlatti in these years concurs with the strophe and estribillo structure of the rondel and virolai as used in the Cantigas. In the virolai, the strophe's second line repeats the tonada of the estribillo and after the strophe the estribillo is repeated. In the rondel the estribillo reappears fragmentarily in the strophe, and this occurs in Alfonso X's chosen examples. Scarlatti's manner of cutting into the second part of his structure by the initial motif as a means of contrasting development initiated the first movement sonata form with which he is credited, and this is strikingly used in the later sonatas. These in fact tend to make use of the opening material in subsequent portions, as Kirkpatrick points out. Similarly the two halves of his sonata form often evolve by contrast, as in the Cantigas estribillos are more dynamic than the narrative strophes, and the gaiety of the former are emphasised in a way similar to Scarlatti's use of the recognisably quickening beat of popular refrain types. There are numerous formally serious examples in his sonatas, too, which might refer to those hymns which appear after groups of 9 Cantigas, as in his organ-like pieces K. 287, 288, 328, 255 and 254.

Instrumental effects which parallel those depicted in the Cantigas' miniatures are striking, and consistently used in the sonatas. The castanet and drum percussive effects are often remarked; they are featured in the miniatures. The old Galician bagpipe of Alfonso's time is as capable as any contemporary kind of producing the pedal drones to which the effects of Sonata K.513's Christmas pastorale are usually attributed. The concerted brilliance suggestive of village bands of wind, tambourines, drums, guitar, fiddles, is also seen in the miniatures, their rustic quality being stressed with gusto by the artist. In this sense of the archaic depicted as ingenuously rustic, Scarlatti's 'easy' sonatas create a corresponding picture of the primitive in sound, for the Cantigas are nothing if not ingenuous in their attractiveness. The instruments and players are paired throughout in the miniatures with very few exceptions; Scarlatti developed this form of pairing. He even distinguishes between the whirr of wooden castanets, the timbre of cymbals in percussion, and the dry bones rattle of the nakkers all so exactly drawn in miniature. Nor must his quaintly formal use of bells be forgotten, since the Cantigas are graphically demonstrated as playable on sets of these; listen to Sonata L.205, L.278, L.279 for this colouring. With strings in unison, L.201, and strings in concert, L.200, the parallels with Alfonso's minstrel string players as with those in Compostela's cathedral are copiously obvious. More significant still are those full illustrations of the many plucked keyboard instruments, ancestors of the harpsichord, psaltery, canón, medio canón, with broad-sweeping lengths of closely assembled strings capable of producing those thick, reverberant textures of which Scarlatti himself was a nonpareil master. His rich textures are often the result of doublings, both intricate and deliberately archaic in effect. Such doublings are evoked again and again in the miniature pictures of musicians playing together in close pairs. Again and again, also, his massively collected colouring and emphatic long-drawn, sustained forte climaxes suggest the duos of wind-players on albogues, horns, trumpets, flutes, with deep blasts depicting as being blown upon chirimías, shawms, and symphonia with heavy bass drones all to be seen in the miniatures. The dance-forms, too, of which he gives so many instances are utilised by Alfonso X, if seldom in the pictures. Many such tunes have altered relatively little in their essential rhythms and patterns, so that though he may have adopted contemporary airs, they were as likely as not of old descent. The use of the French rondo in several pieces has puzzled many listeners; their parallel with the French rondons in Alfonso's time may be more appreciatively enjoyed now. The contrasting thickness and thinness of his textures as developed in various series of sonatas may refer to the many ranging distinctions of the instruments in the miniatures. More fundamental in relation possibly is the basic simplicity of harmonic structure on which Scarlatti was content to depend; the trio of tonic, dominant and subdominant usually sufficed, and the cadential usage is formalistic in general. More suggestive even is his manner of frequently evading conclusive harmonic resolutions, by withdrawing from what in his day was expected as a formal resolution into a pallid unison. This, too, may have resulted from exploration of the music of the Cantigas period, so that avoidance of definite resolutions may have been his best means of entering into the spirit of the early 14th century modal ambiguities as he read it in these examples. It must be remembered that he had a life-long interest in old church music and counterpoint.

Scarlatti's G major Sonata, K.284 has drone basses and a simplified rondo form, suggesting the archaic form of the Cantigas and rustic dance derivation also. See also K.351 and K.265 for rondo form.

The systematic pairing of sonatas frequently includes pairs of the same keyboard range or similar instrumental characteristics of the same tonal schemes, again paralleling the illustrations of players and their instruments paired in the miniatures. The single instrumentalist in these pictures is exceptional, the most noteworthy being a keyboard performer of an ancestor to the harpsichord.

The vocal sense of line in some sonatas—e.g. K.308—developed with simplicity and restraint against a sparse accompaniment has been compared to Farinelli's essential quality of singing in later years; it may also be compared to the pure melodies of Alfonso X's essentially monodic art and to their relatively archaic instrumental setting.

In 1752 he was asked to score two hymns written for an ancestor of the king's major-domo, the Duke of Alba, of 1569. In his letter to this nobleman Scarlatti explains that he has had difficulty in deciphering the abbreviated Gothic style. No doubt he would have problems also in deciphering the music of Alfonso's Cantigas in the facsimile officially presented to Queen Barbara. He also wrote a four-part mass which was copied into a choir book of the Royal Chapel in 1754; this book also contains a mass by Victoria, and compositions by Literes and José Torres, also organists of the chapel. Here he shows that he could write in the 16th century manner; indeed, his Roman *Stabat Mater* is in ten parts a capella. These commissions in Madrid suggest that he was co-opted very thoroughly into the inner privileged circle of official musicians to the monarchs. The writing and compiling of the series of sonatas was an enormous labour, and explains why Scarlatti was not conspicuous at court functions. The Queen's manuscript of the series of 496 works is decorated with gold and coloured inks and embellished with the royal arms of Spain and Portugal; this collection has the splendid decorated dignity of a dynastic document, as have the Cantigas. Another set is minus these decorations and contains 463 pieces; a third has only 349. The absence of a manuscript set belonging to Scarlatti himself, suggests that this was an official document he was directed to produce for the royal household; the fact that three sets were made, parallels the number made, apparently, of Alfonso's *Cantigas*. It is thus interesting to note that Scarlatti's early sonatas are not copied into the Queen's collection.

The famous frontispiece for the *Esercizi* made by Amiconi could now be interpreted possibly as indicating that Queen Barbara—idealised in this allegorical scene—received the inspiration from the winged messenger who puts a music album beside her towards which she stretches out an arm while with the other she lays a hand on the drawn lines of another music album still to be written upon. It was designed for Scarlatti's *Esercizi* in 1738. The plan may have been in mind by then.

In 1738 Scarlatti was knighted by Queen Barbara's father, John V of Portugal, to whom the publication is dedicated. The lavish flattery addressed to this monarch does not obscure the emotional terms in which the composer expresses his appreciation of his royal pupil's musicianship which she 'now commands so knowingly and so masterfully'. 'Gratitude, united with the sweet flattery of such an honest Pride, compels me to give public Witness of it in print . . . But what expression of Thanks shall I find for the immortal Honour vouchsafed me by your Royal Command to follow this incomparable Princess. The Glory of her Perfections, of Royal Lineage and Sovereign Education, redounds to that of the Great Monarch Her Father. But your humble servant participates in it through that Mastery of Song, of Playing and of Composition, with which, surprising the wondering Observation of the most excellent Masters, she makes the Delights of Princes and of Monarchs.'

The preface to the *Esercizi* is also revealing: 'Reader, Whether you be Dilettante or Professor, in these Compositions do not expect any profound Learning, but rather an ingenious Jesting with Art, to accommodate you to the Mastery of the Harpsichord. Neither Considerations of Interest, nor Visions of Ambition, but only Obedience moved me to publish them. Perhaps they will be agreeable to you; then all the more gladly will I obey other Commands to please you in an easier and more varied Style. Show yourself then more human than critical, and thereby increase your own Delight.' Evidently the *Esercizi* were already intended as forerunners to other Commands to come. In these pieces the transformed Domenico reveals unflagging good humour and joie de vivre, revelling in his newly-discovered vein of inventive ingenuity. Did not Alfonso X in his own introduction to the Cantigas insist that these songs must always be gay—for are they not in praise of the Virgin? 'Rose of beauty and semblance, flower of joy and pleasure,' as the monarch apostrophised her. This was the 'gay science', and the Queen had found her jongleur.

Indeed, as the wife of Ferdinand V in the 15th century was entertained by her masters of the vihuela, so the wife of Ferdinand VI in the 18th found solace in these inimitable ingenuities of her own personal musician, and both left a testament for future generations to share their collaborative joys.

The examples of Portuguese themes and rhythms in K.238 and K.239 emphasise the dynastic aspect of the collection as a whole in relation to Queen Barbara of Braganza's family. The observance of the customs surrounding these royal marriages was strictly kept. For the wedding of Ferdinand VI's sister into the house of Savoy, which produced the most splendid musical celebration of this reign and Farinelli's knighthood—reference was made not only to the wedding of Ferdinand's mother, a Savoyard, but also to the wedding of Philip II's daughter Catalina and the protocol was debated between the courts of Madrid and Turin with close study of Spanish royal archives. It has already been pointed out that the traditions of the royal chapel in Ferdinand and Isabella's reign were referred back to the days of Reccared, the Visigothic monarch.

The Queen's library contained numerous volumes of history and well-chosen annals. In direct connection with Alfonso X's influence on the reign was that consultation of his book of laws, *Las Siete Partidas*, when consultations were held on the plan to form a Junta de Gobierno during the king's illness, and also of the parallel plan of Cardinal Cisneros to form a Junta de Gobierno during the reign of Ferdinand and Isabella's daughter, Juana, during the minority of Charles V.

Finally, in this introductory comparison, since reference has been made to Queen Bárbara's composition of a *Salve Regina*, Scarlatti's last work, the *Salve Regina* for soprano and strings, is doubly memorable. In this we may hear his own personal contribution to the translation into modern terms of the medieval king's *loores* in praise of the Virgin undertaken for Scarlatti's royal pupil, Bárbara of Braganza, consort of the Bourbon king Ferdinand VI of Spain. As deeply rooted in Europe as the Cantigas themselves were the origins of Scarlatti's novel and decisive effects upon the evolution of modern music. His *Salve Regina* was in a deep sense also a musician's *Nunc dimittis*.

The arrival of Charles III from Naples, 9th December 1759, brought abrupt changes to musical life. Farinelli was dismissed with his acquired wealth and returned to Italy where his charming villa near Bologna was visited by international connoisseurs until he died in 1782, soon after his dearest friend the poet Metastasio. Though Charles' wife Maria Amalia of Saxony was musical she died within a year of their coming to Spain and he shunned entertainments associated with the diversions of his melancholic predecessors. The Italian operatists then decided to cultivate the opera buffa, possibly hoping that this Neapolitan style would please him. It did not, and opera enthusiasts were obliged to confine themselves to performances in private palaces where pieces by Manuel Pla, José Mir de Llussa and the still lively Conforto were occasionally given. During Aranda's term of office some productions were put on at the Sitios Reales—the royal seats—of French tragedy and comedy and Italian shows, chiefly of dancing and light singing, and when these ended the municipality thought it necessary for Madrid's prestige to promote opera and reopened the Caños del Peral, with Italians as before. Functions, however, were 'de tarde', late afternoon matinées, so as not to prejudice the Spanish companies at the Príncipe and Cruz. Men and women were now allowed to sit together, so long as the women were unveiled and their faces visible, though it was not until 1797 that seats were put into the pit, or patio, of the Caños theatre, as a result of which audiences became comparatively sedate and possibly less restless. When these efforts closed in 1777, the Italians at last retreated to their home-land and for ten years no opera was organised by Italians in Madrid. Spaniards, nevertheless, showed their ability to sing Neapolitan classics as in Paisiello's *La Frasquetana* in 1782, in Italian, in 1783 *Los visionarios* and *La italiana en Londres*, and in 1786 Pergolesi's *La serva padrona*. The famous Caramba, Maria Antonia Fernández Vallejo, like other idols of the time, showed her capacity to sing the highly adorned Italian arias as well as those Andalusian scenas for which she was adored. La Tirana was famous as an actress, and not as a singer.

It was only during the king's last illness that an Italian company returned to the Caños del Peral, and from that time Madrid scarcely ever lacked an opera season. At this same time the Spaniards put on Paisiello's *El Barbero de Sevilla*, made into a zarzuela with recitatives in Spanish and this success at the Príncipe was imitated by the Cruz and Caños. The theatres were closed on the death of Charles III.

Barcelona had produced opera independently, especially during the brief period of the Austrian pretender's stay when Caldara and Astorga were staged. Catalan composers now had a prompt hearing, with José Durán's *Temistocle* in 1762 and Terradellas' *Sesostri*, in 1774. Still supporting native talents, this city produced Fernando Sor's *Il Telemacco nell' Isola di Calipso*—a youthful work of his 18th year, and *La princesa filósofa o sea El desdén con el desdén*, a setting of Moreto's musically conceived comedy by the Catalan organist Carlos Baguer, 'Carlet' as he was called—both of these in 1798. Both Domingo Terradellas and Sor found fame abroad, including London.

The accession of Charles IV in 1788 was greeted with a Spanish chef d'oeuvre, *Una cosa rara*, by the Valencian Vicente Martín y Soler (b. 1754, d. St Petersburg, 1806). After writing Italian operas in the 1770s, he left Italy for Vienna in 1785 where Lorenzo da Ponte provided him with libretti for his more successful pieces, *Una cosa rara* and *L'arbore di Diana*. In 1788 he succeeded Sarti as conductor to Catherine II of Russia, visiting London 1794–1795 to produce two more pieces with da Ponte, but returning to Russia where he died, having set three operas to texts by the empress. In spite of this imperial collaboration, it was Mozart's passing quotation in the last act of *Don Giovanni* of a tune from *Una cosa rara* which secured lasting fame for him. *Una cosa rara*, nonetheless, contains some good melodies, fluent in the Italian style and also communicating much of that bounding exuberance associated with the Valencian popular vein.

There may be more meaning in Mozart's passing allusion than has been suspected, for Martín y Soler's leading male character in *Una cosa rara* is also a Don Giovanni in name and a Don Juan in intent, though the village beauty he tries to seduce is less pliable than Zerlina. Mozart's next quotation is from Sarti's *Fra i due litiganti*, which, linked as it is to the passage from *Una cosa rara* may show that Mozart here had in mind the fact that he and Martín y Soler were competitors for public approval in presenting rival settings of *Don Giovanni* on the stage. The third quotation is from the triumphal twist to his own successful martial air in *The Marriage of Figaro*. The air Mozart quotes from *Una cosa rara*, 'O quanto un si bel giubilo', is an outburst of jubilation not in keeping with the approaching doom of Don Giovanni's last scene, but seems to release a gay exuberance appropriate to the knowledge of his own immeasurable supremacy in his own score of *Don Giovanni* now being confidently presented to the world—a superiority already apparent to those who had heard it in rehearsal. The quotation from *Una cosa rara* certainly reminds the listener of that rivalry in which it had seemed, for the time being, that Martín y Soler had scored over *The Marriage of Figaro*. Mozart does not quote 'Consola la pena', the Spaniard's aria whose carefully contrived chromaticism most nearly recalls Mozart's own. This interpretation reached by considering all three quotations together—and shall we not do so?—offers a more coherent and realistic picture of the contemporary operatic situation in which composers battled in rivalry, as well as one more example of Mozart's ingenuity and wit.

The hunting scene, like others of its kind in 18th-century opera, may have been calculated to please those kings, and especially those in the peninsula, much given to the chase, since such rural meets were to be seen in *El filósofo aldeano* by Galuppi and Gassmann's *Los Cazadores*, which were made over into zarzuelas. For the marriage of Charles III's sister, Maria Ana Victoria to Barbara of Braganza's brother, José, a comedia 'en música' *Las Amazonas de España*, was given in 1728 in allusion to the fact that like her brother Charles she was a fine shot and fast rider to hounds.

Charles IV and his brother Prince Gabriel remained attached to string music, the king being an assiduous violinist in chamber works. He amassed a very extensive collection of works by some 120 composers; the Bach family, Boccherini, Corelli, Dittersdorf (*Trois Simphonies Exprimant Trois Métamorphoses d'Ovide*), Dussek, Fux, Geminiani, Giardini, Gossec, Guenin, Haendel, Haydn (Josef and Michael) Hoffmann, Jomelli, Kreutzer, Lombardini, Manalt, Mozart (Cuartetos, quintetos, oberturas y sinfonías, published by Arteria), Nardini, Paisiello, Piccini, Pleyel, Romberg, Sacchini, Salomin, Shield, Stamitz (Antonio, Carlos and J. Giovanni), Teixador, Wranizky, Zanetti. Beethoven features with *Grand Quintetto per due Violini, due Viole e Violoncello*, dal Signor Luigi van Beethoven Opera 1 (A Vienna, presso . . . the publisher's name is erased). Boccherini is only partly represented by his chamber music, one set of *Sei Trio per Violino, Viola e Violoncello obligato* composti per S.A.R. il Signor Infante Don Luigi di Spagnia dal Signor Luigi Boccherini Di Lucca, Virtuoso di Camera della Prolata S.A.R. Op. 14 (Paris, La Chevardiere).[1] The king's music-master, Brunetti, however, figures with 63 quintets, 6 sextets, 14 'new' symphonies—having already produced 18—49 sonatas for violin and cello and 18 trios for two violins and cello. With such a continual out-pouring of musical exercises and offerings for his pupil, the monarch's hurry is understandable when we re-read Goya's letter to Zapater, describing how when he called on Charles IV, the king, having saluted him and asked after his son, began at once to play his violin.

Spanish composers after Herrando—including Francisco Manalt who became a leader among them—now found more prosperity with the rapid increase of string playing during this part of the century. Those attached to the king's circle found publishers abroad, Manuel Canales's *Six quartets* being printed in London, as were Nicholas Ximénez's *Seis solos para violin*, while Antonio Ximénez published *Tres Sonatas para violin y bajo* in Paris about 1780.

Luigi Boccherini found a patron in Prince Luis, uncle of Charles IV, when he arrived in Spain, 1768–1769, and on Prince Luis' death in 1785 was appointed to Frederick William II of Prussia as chamber composer until this monarch's death in 1797. On his return to Madrid, his poor health and the domestic troubles of his last years were not alleviated by royal favours, for Charles IV had formed an early attachment of loyalty to the prolific violinist, Gaetano Brunetti, pupil of Nardini, who had become his music tutor while Charles was still a prince, and Boc-cherini, a cellist, did not obtain the position to which his genius en-titled him. Like Domenico Scarlatti, he imbibed the Spanish idiom, as may be heard in the quintets *Músicas nocturnas en Madrid* and his guitar arrangements, especially 'El fandango que tocaba a la guitarra el padre Basilio', the *Ballet español* of 1774, and in those minuets having un-mistakable overtones of the contemporary seguidillas. *Músicas noc-turnas de Madrid* include recollections of the religious songs of the Rosario, street tunes, dances, guitar chord sequences, and a Tempo di Marcia based on the military Retreat.

Boccherini died in Madrid, 1805; Brunetti in 1808, the year of Charles IV's abdication and the beginning of the War of Independence.

Charles IV's consort, María Luisa of Parma, unlike the previous Parmesan queen Isabel Farnese, became identified with Spanish popular music from her first entrance into Madrid as a bride in her early teens in 1765. She was entertained with various zarzuelas and among the tonadillas escénicas there was one written for her, *La Parmesana y las*

---

[1] Revised lists include scores by Boccherini placed in the Palace after Charles IV's death—among them six divertimenti, 24 quartets, 27 quintets and a *Simphonie Périodique* in D minor.

Majas, a tonadilla a cuatro with music by Esteve, in which a Parmesan girl follows the princess to Spain which she has been told is a fine country, and when the flower-girl and vegetable seller learn that she has come to court with 'la Luisa' whom they now regard as 'our Princess' they shower her with fruits, flowers and vegetables, including 'los ajos'—the typical garlic. During María Luisa's years in Madrid, the royal library was to acquire about 500 tonadillas, of which copies were made for the palace. She took lessons on the guitar from that 'padre Basilio' whose fandango Boccherini immortalised, but not—so it seems—until she was older, for we learn that Godoy studied with him also. This Cistercian monk, Miguel García by birth, also kindled the interest of Charles IV in the guitar, but the monarch remained faithful to his first musical preferences. Padre Basilio, also an organist, strengthened the punteado technique and style, being himself an able contrapuntalist, and his innovations were to bear fruit in the generation of Sor and Aguado; his guitar pieces, both solos and duos, abundantly prove his passionate *afición*. María Luisa's tastes are also recorded in a volume entitled *Seguidillas a solo para diversion de la Sma. Sa. Princesa de Asturias*, and consisting of pieces extracted from tonadillas in fashion about 1780. She also performed on the Basque tambour, for which a Guide was written.

Prince Gabriel, Charles IV's younger brother, became a devoted pupil of Padre Antonio Soler and from childhood kept guitars, violins and a little clavichord beside his wooden toy soldiers and miniature pistol. It was in his Casita de Arriba at the Escorial that he studied the compositions Soler wrote for him. Soler's polemical *Llave de la modulación y antigüedades de la música* (Madrid, 1762) is not only a key to modulation as he proposed, but also possibly to his own approach to composition. José de Nebra observed that it had never occurred to him that fixed rules could be found for such strange modulations as Soler propounded: 'I had always lived in the belief that it was practice, good taste and the power of the ear which produced them.' Other theorists were less polite in criticising Soler's system for giving fixed rules to his extreme cases of modulation. His genesis of modulation is couched in what is a familiar scholastic manner. 'From the sound is born monody, and from monody comes melody. From melody comes harmony, and from this, modulation.' He refers to Boethius as his authority, but behind Boethius lies the more distant philosophy of Aristotle, who taught that the object of the ear is sound and the repercussion of air, and that the world is composed according to musical proportion, thus associating music and theology with mathematics, since both have needs of the arts of counting and measuring in their spheres.

Soler (b. Olot, 1729, d. Escorial, 1783) maintained the line of

Spanish medieval theorists like Ramos de Pareja. He may have been influenced by the *Libro de propietatibus rerum en romance* of which a revised edition, printed in Toledo, 1529, was well known. This work refers to Aristotle's teaching on the power of music to move the heart in sweet melodies, to fire combatants in battle and so on, also to Isidore's statements on music and those instruments of his time as given in his texts. Soler's categorisations of sounds and his measuring of the minutiae of intervals even to the point of exactitude attempted by his invention of a machine he called the 'Afinador o Templante', place him in the systematic world of Aristotle in practical experiment. Creatively, he dedicated his powers to the re-working in modern terms of the whole line of keyboard forms from Cabezón down to Domenico Scarlatti, to whom he submitted himself as a student in his search of knowledge, so that he left nothing untouched or unsounded within his field. The exhaustive method of his search as he contrasted the uninterruptedly contemplative tiento—'intento' he calls it—with the chattering toccata, the genteel minuet with the furious batallas, the severely intellectual fugue with the unpremeditated artlessness of folk song, the boisterous dance with the gravity of funeral marches, so that each is treated strictly according to its kind, bespeaks a theological-philosophical approach to composition never perhaps before so practically demonstrated, with the austerity of one who combined a formidable technique with the earnestness of a purely spiritual being, but one who, with all these attributes, would never have created this magnificent torrent of sound had he not been gifted with an extraordinary musical faculty.

His sense of the traditional part played by church musicians in Spanish life is seen in his villancicos for church festivals, including the Nativity, some of whose titles show an adaptability to human circumstance comparable to Alfonso X's Cantigas, as in *Un sacristán y un monago, Predicador y astrológo, Un monaguillo y un papa, Un cojo y un ciego, Un simple y un porfiado, Tutti li mundi, Dos peregrinos, Dos sacristanes*, and so on. Like his contemporaries, he also wrote pieces for the theatre, sententiously suitable as in *Afectos de odio y amor, El defensor de su agravio*, loas for the auto *Las Ordenes militares*, and *La Junta de médicos*.

His liturgical music written for the Escorial monastery includes many masses, Lamentations, Misereres, responses, offertories, Beatus vir, Pange lingua, Ave Marias, vespers, offices for the dead, for la Purísima, hymns to St Jerome and St Lawrence, patron saints of the Escorial's foundation. Results of his service in both monasteries are evident in his use of the Rondon, or round dance, of which the Llibre Vermell of Montserrat contains notable examples—and his work for two organs, which the Escorial's instrumental provisions made feasible, entitled *Seis conciertos de dos órganos obligados.* His best known compositions are the *Seis quintetos* con violines, viola, violoncello y órgano o clave obligado and the *Sonatas* for harpsichord, about 130 in number, to which more may yet be added after further search. 99 have appeared in a six-volume collection authoritatively edited by P. Samuel Rubio of the Escorial, up to 1962, thus making the greater part of these works now accessible to the wide public they deserve; further publications are in preparation by the Unión Musical Española, Madrid. In these, Soler's adherence to Spanish tradition may be traced, he himself explaining that he had as a boy of thirteen learnt the art of composing tonos from the twenty-four organ works by José Elías and had never considered himself an innovator in this kind. Elías was a disciple of Cabanillas. By this age, Antonio Soler was already a seasoned player, having entered the Escolanía of Montserrat at six, moving to the Escorial in 1753. He was wholly dedicated to his office. When summoned to La Granja, where Prince Gabriel took lessons from him, he would take his pens and papers so as not to lose any moments of leisure there. He was always happiest when working in his cell.

This tradition continued into the 19th century with Mateo Albéniz (d. 1831) and Mateo Ferrer (1783–1864) with whom the form of the sonata, as created by Domenico Scarlatti, actively survived until the birth of Isaac Albéniz. Albéniz and his contemporaries, Granados, Falla, Turina, and the younger generation headed by Ernesto Halffter, took Scarlatti as their keyboard master of line; a younger generation still, led by Rudolfo Halffter in his early *Sonatas del Escorial*, Joaquín Rodrigo and his followers, found an elder guide and mentor in Antonio Soler and through them, a still younger group, now looking beyond Falla's early period, find a convergence between the latter's *Concerto* and *Retablo de Maeso Pedro* and Soler's austerely spiritual creativity. It is possible that in these years of scientific preoccupation into whose abstract orbit musicians have moved, following their old colleagues, the painters, Soler's Aristotelian approach has renewed meaning for that research into the potential of sound per se which attracts many composers nowadays, and noticeably in Spain.

The tonadilla began to develop an independent tradition from about 1751. Led by Misón, a cluster of musicians created a minor theatrical genre which not only reflected contemporary local tastes with typical conciseness in the one-act form, but pointed a way for the modern one-act zarzuela's expansion on similar lines. These composers include Antonio Guerrero, José and Antonio Palomino, Manuel Pla, Pedro Aranaz, Juan Marcolini, José Castel, Ventura Galván, Pablo Esteve, Antonio Rosales, Jacinto Valledor, Pablo del Moral, Mariano Bustos, and Blas de Laserna. It reached its height between 1771 and 1790, and even in its decline during the first thirty years of the 19th century it occasionally reflects its times. The genre produced about two thousand examples. An idea of the tonadilla escénicas's extension may be seen in its crystallised forms of 1791 as laid down in the conditions for an open competition organised under the advice of Jovellanos and held in that year. For the three prizes the classifications were: one, for the best tonadilla lasting twelve minutes as a maximum, for one performer; two, for the best tonadilla lasting a quarter of an hour, as the maximum, for two players; and three, the best tonadilla lasting twenty to twenty-two minutes, as a maximum, for four performers. Traditional usage in the old theatres largely determined its form, the interludes and entremeses, the cuatros de empezar, the fin de fiesta, the regional dances and contemporary songs; the themes, too, had many continuing links with Spanish comedy.

It was Don Ramón de la Cruz, 1731–1794, experienced adaptor of Italian operas to native taste, who re-created the old sainete in 475 ways before exhausting the variations offered by ingrained customs and fickle vogue, the professions, labours, foibles, passions and graces of Madrileños and their country visitors. It was a happy circumstance which enabled musicians to draw simultaneously on those same conditions for many themes and popular rhythms. Their orchestras ranged from the ubiquitous guitar and reliable bass viol to the oboes, trumpets, first and second violins, cello and bass of Luis Misón's *Los ciegos* of 1758, a piece containing both Jota and Seguidillas; and the oboes, clarín de eco for an echo song reminiscent of classical zarzuelas, first and second violins, cello and bass for *Los signos del año* by Pablo Esteve, *c.* 1785. Blas de Laserna's *El trueque de los amantes*, a tonadilla a cuatro of about 1785, however, is content to obtain its effects with two guitars and the four voices, as might be expected from this musician who judged the Madrileño moods with the warmth of his castizo nature.

It is significant that a castizo tone of fine quality was consciously implanted by the collaboration of Don Ramón de la Cruz with the royal chapel music master, Antonio Rodríguez de Hita, in *Las segadoras de Vallecas* in the 1770s. This piece appears to aim at an atmosphere of the popular genre no less than that of Goya's delicately luminous canvases for the national tapestry factory. An aura of aesthetic consummation hovering over a popular genre also envelops Pablo Esteve's *Los jardineros de Aranjuez* and is then again assumed by those previous collaborators in *Las labradoras de Murcia*. Its influence was to infiltrate the finer composers' choice of themes for two hundred years and it has not yet lost its pervasive attraction.

The career of Manuel García (b. Seville, 1775, d. Paris, 1832) spans a period of tentative change in Spanish musical life. He began as a chorister in Seville cathedral and as a tonadilla singer appeared on the Madrid stage in *El majo y la maja* in 1798; in 1799 he sang in the Holy Week oratorio at the Cruz and then in Paisiello's *Nina*. With the so-called Reform of the Theatres enforced, in which some Spanish classic works were prohibited and replaced by translated modern French pieces, there was a trend towards French operetta. The Council of Reform collapsed in 1802, however, and García, having been excluded by these misguided zealots, returned from Málaga where he had been singing, and on 16th September 1802, appeared in his own one-act operetta, *El seductor arrepentido*, a reduction of a French larmoyante drama. He then produced various pieces of a similar kind, alternating with Cimarosa, and supported by the best performers of the day, and soon created his own stage image in solo airs such as the seguidillas in which he accompanied himself on the guitar; it is for this costumbrist stylisation that he is still remembered. *El luto fingido* of 1803 is a zar-zuela in one act containing seven numbers, supposed to be by his hand. In 1805, his popular opera *El criado fingido*, featuring the famous polo 'Cuerpo bueno', established his reputation, though not his finances; this polo was partly declaimed, partly accompanied by the orchestra, and partly accompanied by himself on the guitar. *El tesoro fingido*, adapted from Méhul, and his own *El poeta calculista* followed imprison-ment for refusing to fill a contract with the Cruz, and the latter piece contains the celebrated polo of the Contrabandista. Another 'solo' scene, *El prisionero por amor* re-set a text previously used by Pablo de Moral, and García makes a monologue of it, shifting emphasis from orchestral predominance to the character whose chief scene is again one where the hero accompanies himself on his Crummles-like handy guitar. It opens with a sinfonia and includes several interludes. There are several dances, contradanza, minuet, minuet afandangado and ale-mana, cited by the prisoner as he imitates their steps during moments of relief from the pressures of captivity. The same topic appears in *El cautiverio aparente*, the instruments for which include a fairly full orchestral range for the genre, strings, wind and timbales, tamboril and pandereta, these last for the fiesta in which there is an attempted abduc-tion by disguised Algerian corsairs.

The last work given by García in Madrid was to grace the historic occasion of Godoy's being appointed Admiral in January 1807 and for the last time he was seen in Spain accompanying himself on the guitar in an adaptation of a French text *Los ripios del maestro Adán*. Owing to what was only a trivial point in the translation of a verse, García sup-posed himself to be less cordially received than he deserved and shortly after this gala event he became, or pretended to seem, ill and left the country.

In Paris he continued these alternating currents of operetta and castizo 'unipersonal' songwriting—as he called these solo 'scenas'—the latter, like others of their kind now appearing in Spain, having been influenced by Rousseau's melologue, which had a vogue among Spaniards. His tours of America with his daughters, the swan-necked, fragile Malibran and the robust Pauline Viardot resulted in a dramatic but realistic confrontation with bandits such as he had impersonated on the Spanish stage and he was robbed of his New World gains. However, he finally enjoyed the height of that fame to which he had always aspired through his connection with Rossini and the part he played in the production of *Il barbiere di Siviglia* where at last these alternating aspirations of operatic internationalism and Spanish unipersonal costumbrismo were fused.

Some of the semi-anonymous patriotic songs of the Peninsular War include approving lines on English redcoats, but Fernando Sor's ardour for the French expressed in several of his songs during Joseph Bonaparte's rule in Spain made him so unpopular that he was accused of being a drinker, bigamist and, worst of all, a bad guitarrist. Like Manuel García, he did not return to Spain when once he reached Paris. Born in Barcelona in 1778, his studies began in the Escolanía of Montserrat and his early opera *Telemaco* was produced in his native city before he was twenty. His promotion to the captaincy in the French army brought him little luck until he settled in Paris where his guitar playing and composing were admired. He then became a travelling musician. London produced his opera *La Feria de Esmirna* and a ballet *El señor generoso* in 1822; in 1825 his ballet *Cendrillon* was staged in Paris. In St Petersburg in 1825 he wrote a funeral march for the Czar Alexander I and a ballet *Hercules y Onfalia* for his successor, Nicholas I. With his return to Paris the tides turned against him and both French and English theatres were reluctant to produce his pieces. By concentrating on the guitar from 1828 onwards, however, he wrote those works which guitarists play by heart today and his *Gran Método de Guitarra* became a classic guide. From the letter accompanying an overture *Hercules* to Ferdinand VII we learn that the Pope had decorated him for a hymn to the Holy Cross, that kings of several countries had honoured his 'débil talento' and that he desired now to win the same acceptance in his own country, to which he owed the first elements of the 'Ciencia Harmónica'. The overture is fully scored for wind and strings and at the foot of the first sheet appears this advice: 'Aucun instrument ne peut être suprimé sans nuire essentiellement à l'effet.' It may have consoled Sor to recall in his last years of exile that his *Canción patriota* of 1820 had been an effective instrument in Spain when sung by Ferdinand VII's enemies; but it is not impossible that

Ferdinand, who had an ear for his country's popular song, may have heard of it, for there is no sign that this work for 'gran orquesta' was taken any notice of. Sor died in Paris, 1839. Dionisio Aguado, 1784–1849, author of an *Escuela de guitarra*, which was printed posthumously, became Sor's close friend when he too left Spain for Paris, and played with him in a duet Sor wrote for them, *Los dos amigos*—The two friends.

From Castellón, Francisco Tárrega (1854–1909) became the leader of Spanish guitarrists, who learned from him that the instrument was amenable to a variety of new uses, partly as a result of his piano studies and transcriptions from pianoforte works; programmes of guitar-music seem incomplete without an example of his music, the *Tremolo*, for instance, evoking the last vibrations of the romantic mood as it was felt in Spain. His two pupils, Emilio Pujol and Miguel Llobet (d. 1938) maintained his quality of creative interpretation, Pujol as a scholarly editor, and Llobet as Falla's chosen interpreter for the *Homenaje a Debussy*, distinctively suited to this by his impeccably classic style and uncompromising purity of tradition.

The 19th century brought a Bourbon to the throne who shared the tastes of his people. Ferdinand VII, who reigned from 1808 to 1833, though some intervening years were wasted in durance at Valençay under Napoleonic surveillance, saw in the subjects who welcomed him on his return to Spain those he thought he could trust since they had fought to keep his crown for him. His enthusiasms for bull-fighting and the verbenas were castizo; his familiarity with Spanish songs was ready enough to bring one to mind when occasion required a more or less graceful quotation. With an illusion in love which perhaps compensated for his absolutist monarchical disillusionment with liberalising politicians, Ferdinand wrote a love-letter to his fourth wife-to-be a week before she was to join him in matrimony on her arrival from Naples. In this he confesses his passion, not with an operatic quotation, but with the refrain of a popular seguidilla, 'Anda, salero, salerito del alma, Como te quiero!' Like his subjects, this Bourbon Ferdinand never forgot the refrain, being as much a traditionalist in music as in all else.

Popular song played an essential role in this half-century of change. Through invasion and the horrors of war, Carlist division and guerrilla surprises, it was the semi-anonymous singers who preserved the thread of patriotism; and as war receded and bandits survived, the legend of smugglers and contraband settled into a genre which lingered almost into the 20th-century repertory. The desire to create a national zarzuela dramatic and musically lyrical enough to satisfy a local public and yet purged of Italianisms sufficiently to gain recognition abroad in its own right persisted, often supported temporarily by extended songs suited for the stage, sometimes reminiscent of tonadillas, often applying Ramón de la Cruz' or García's costumbrismo to contemporary incidents. In these the music could be entirely Spanish, and when extension called for explanatory soliloquy between airs, the declamatory manner was in order and satisfied the audience that it was natural enough, provided it was short. In these examples *melologue*, which on the first impact of Rousseau's example had been a raging furore and therefore short-lived, was adopted as a useful expedient, even when Rousseau's orchestra was reduced to those faithful servants of the Spanish theatre, a pair of guitars, with perhaps a lone surviving bass fiddle. Out of all this there crystallised a sense of what was castizo in the zarzuela and this, as its most perspicacious creators in the 19th century were to perceive, prominently included those enthusiasms dear to Ferdinand and his people, song, bull-fights and the summer nights' verbena.

Sebastián Iradier (1809–1865) is linked traditionally to Bizet's *Carmen* on account of his bull-fighter's songs and habaneras, as Manuel García is associated with it by his smuggler's airs. Iradier, however, is the more subtle artist of the two. He mobilises outworn forms with that pliable rhythmic permissiveness to be heard in Cuba and the Caribbean regions during the years he travelled there. His habanera, *La Paloma*, has outlived the two empires it served emotionally to unite, that of Napoleon III in Paris and Maximilian in Mexico; its later echoes were not happy ones to the bereaved consorts, proud Eugenia and the distraught Carlota. *La Paloma*, nevertheless, keeps a deeper significance throughout South America, for it was one of many melodies by which wanderers in the backlands sent messages on wings of song to loved ones left behind—as their words reveal, by swallows usually, or by blue-birds tokening faithful affection, whatever the distance or however long the separation. The cover of a mid-century album of Iradier's songs depicts a girl at her open window listening to the swallows who have sought her out to bring their message. It is through this common experience of the immigrant that Spanish nostalgia, the añoranza, and Portuguese saudades, or longing, have become fused in a new emotive potential. Many fine examples of this type have emerged from the backlands of Argentina, Brazil, Chile and Mexico. Through salon imitations it has taken root as a concert genre, with a pedigree as long as the *lieder* of Schubert, Schumann, Brahms and Strauss, but from a stock independent of theirs.

With the translation into Spanish of foreign operatic texts native singers were more advantageously placed and in 1821 the municipal theatres organised companies both of national and Italian opera; nevertheless, the impact of Rossini, especially his *Barbero de Sevilla*, was over-whelming and ensured the continuance of foreign influence despite the talent of Ramón Carnicer, who judiciously used Spanish themes such as *El convidado de piedra*, 1822, and *Cristóforo Colon*, 1821, in his half-dozen pieces; he shows taste in his choice of verse for his solo songs, even in those meant only for an ephemeral season. His appointment as first professor of composition to the newly founded Real Conservatorio de Música was merited, though the appointment of an Italian tenor as director was not acceptable. Queen Maria Cristina, who founded the Conservatorio, was of course blamed for this, in spite of the fact that one of its aims was to ensure that Spanish singers should be trained to compete on equal terms with the Italians. This situation continued during the infancy of Isabel II under her mother's regency after Ferdinand's death in 1833. In 1849 the impulsive Isabel, inexperienced but enthusiastic, organised a little theatre in the royal palace in which the young Emilio Arrieta produced two operas: the first, a medieval Italianate theme *Ildegonda*, presented for the queen's birthday, 10th October 1849; the second, *La Conquista de Granada*, 1850, had the advantage of being a patriotic theme with music more conformable to national pride. This enterprise proved a costly affair and the little theatre languished thenceforward.

However, by this time there had emerged a group of musicians able to promote Spanish opera on a wider basis and these included Eslava, Barbieri, Gaztambide, Salas. Barcelona also took a lead by establishing a Liceo Filarmónico Dramático from which eventually emerged the famous Liceo theatre. Though born in the same year, 1823, Emilio Arrieta and Francisco Asenjo Barbieri differed much in character. When the palace theatre he had assiduously helped to promote ceased to function Arrieta promptly took his score of the proposed next production, *Pergolese*, to the zarzuela theatres whose future now looked bright, and one of its numbers was transformed into the fishermen's chorus with which his greatest success, *Marina*, opened. Barbieri, modest assistant in those palace ventures, sought to create a national zarzuela which should rediscover its castizo spirit in the past, and more than any other man of his generation he showed Spaniards how to do this by his own successes. He next went on to organise the city's concert system and then to reveal their musical treasures lying untouched in collections such as the *Cancionero Musical de Palacio*. A pupil of Pedro Albéniz, who had been a late link with Domenico Scarlatti's school and piano teacher at the Conservatorio, Barbieri's composition studies were pursued with Carnicer. Brought up within hearing of those Italian operas staged in the Cruz where his grandfather was an official, he was by turns a clarinettist in a military band, chorus master, and zarzuela producer at a relatively early age, and versatile enough to sing the part of Don Basilio in *The Barber of Seville* in an emergency. His true path was indicated by the success of *Jugar con fuego*, 1851, his second zarzuela, which was not so Italianate as his first, *Gloria y Peluca*, of the previous year.

So the zarzuela's second phase began with the reforming musicians harking back to the classic period initiated by Calderón and prompting themselves by referring to the fertile though minor tonadilla genre. Gaztambide's *La mensajera* and *Catalina*, Oudrid's *Buenas noches, señor don Simón* and *El postillón de la Rioja*, Arrieta's *Dómino Azul* and *Marina* followed within five years and their activity was rewarded by the banker Rivas' financing of the Zarzuela theatre.

In 1864 Barbieri brought forth his crystallisation of the castizo, *Pan y toros*, and in 1874 *El barberillo de Lavapiés*. Both were in direct harmony with Madrileño tradition as visualised by Goya and drawn with reference to Scarlatti's linear humour. In 1866 he founded the Sociedad de Conciertos de Madrid and for the first time Spaniards heard a Beethoven symphony—the A major—in its entirety, and in the next year, the *Pastoral* and the C minor.

Felipe Pedrell, born in 1841, entered the lists with combative articles in 1867 and 1872 which led to his challenge to the nation—*Por nuestra música*—in 1891, the theme of which so impressed Albéniz, Granados, Falla and Turina when they came to take counsel with him. He sought the root of musical revival in popular music and folk song, as Barbieri found it in the culture of the capital where all sections of the race had mingled for centuries. These newer composers drew the best from both. Though sometimes known as the Don Quixote of Spanish music, Pedrell may more justly be called the Moses of his people, for he lived to see a younger generation entering the land he promised and in fact bequeathed to them the tables of the Law with those volumes of the *Hispaniae Schola Musica Sacra*, whose revelation of native musical grandeur outlasts any effects his own trilogy *Los Pirineos* might have achieved by performance even immediately upon its completion in 1890–1891. His four volume *Cancionero musical popular* has inestimable value for those seeking entry to the inexhaustible treasure-house of Spain's musical vitality and had a lasting influence on those who came after him.

Traces of the old exchanges between church and theatre musicians still survived in the 19th century though now scrutinised by more critical minds. Benito Feijóo's strictures on the theatricalisation of religious music had sounded a warning that was justified.

The plight of religious music in the 19th century is illustrated by the life of Hilarión Eslava, 1807–1878. Of modest parentage, he was a choirboy at Pamplona cathedral at nine, receiving the appointment as chapel master in Burgo de Osma in 1828. Not satisfied with the isolation in which he found himself here, he sought and won the coveted post at Seville where his reputation was quickly established. He wrote masses for organ and small orchestra, bailetes for the choirboys' famous dance of the *seises* and 'unos misereres' including the celebrated miserere which became, and long remained, a focal point for Seville's Holy Week commemorations. This work reveals the extent to which Italian theatricality had penetrated by degrees the previously austere church music of Spain. Obviously Benito Feijóo had not underestimated the alterations inflicted on services by the Italian 'tararira' exaggerations and the intrusion of instrumental interludes into the mass itself by excessive violinistic histrionics. Fairly recently, Cardinal Segura thought fit to have the performance of this 'celebrated miserere' set aside because of its lack of liturgical severity. Eslava corrected himself later and some lines in his *Breve memoria histórica* echo Feijóo's criticisms. At the same time, he insisted on music's right to the sincere expression of genuine emotion and placed this privilege above the conventions of correct but empty forms. Eslava was one of those who felt the pinch of those reforms which befell church music midway, and even earlier in the century, but his composing of stage pieces—in conformity with that old Spanish custom by which he might have relieved his penury—was disapproved of by the cathedral chapter, though successful elsewhere.

The closing of convents, monasteries and chapels all over Spain had effects probably most familiarly known to musicians from the accounts by George Sand of the atmosphere of desolation Chopin and she encountered in the deserted monastery of Valldemosa in Mallorca. It was from Mendizábal, the minister responsible for the edict of *desamortización*, that she had learned of the circumstances and decided to make that famous journey of which she wrote overheated descriptions, though the atmosphere of the deserted cloisters chilled the more genuinely impressionable Chopin to the marrow. If this disappropriation of 1835 struck at conventual life, the concordat of 1851 dealt a blow at the churches' musical existence, restricting the chapels to one maestro, one organist, a tenor and the choirboys though conceding to the metropolitan chapels one contralto also; it was insisted further that the maestro and organist should be clerics. Chapel masters now received less than a pittance and the situation of parish organists was worse, for these received no more than four reales a day, even in the most frequented churches.

It was the labour of restitution effected by Eslava, Pedrell, Olmedo in collecting the works of the great Spanish past, partly in response to the Benedictine studies at Solesmes that roused nation-wide interest, and with the organisation in Bilbao 1896 of a congress devoted to the revival, followed by the coming together of the fine Basque choirs, the apparent degeneration was halted and renewed vigour soon animated church music and its composers.

Juan Crisóstomo de Arriaga was born in Bilbao 1806, within a year of Boccherini's death. In the fine sensibility and idyllic purity of his musical perception he is the Garcilaso among Spanish composers, sharing also the fate of that poet who died young and was mourned by all who knew him. Juan Crisóstomo was already composing at the age of nine and at twelve wrote an overture for small orchestra. At fourteen, his opera *Los eslavos felices* astonished the Basque public and at sixteen he was in Paris, where wonder at his unforced gifts grew as his music showed him to be possessed of genius equally felicitous in string quartets, overtures, a symphony, a dramatic escena, *Erminia*, and *Agar*, a biblical representation. He was not yet twenty when he died there in January, 1826. In modern Spain his music is regarded as a supreme expression of native genius. When the National Quartet left Spain at the end of the Civil War to give the first concerts of Spanish musicians abroad after those years of isolation, the opening programmes were dedicated to his three string quartets, and Lisbon audiences to whom these concerts were given first, recognised this choice as fitting to the renascent spirit.

The quality of string playing manifest in Arriaga's own performance continued at a high level. Jesús de Monasterio, 1836–1903, although continental success awaited him, chose to stay at home, directing the new Conservatorio and producing pupils of the calibre of Enrique Fernández Arbós, the electric, generous conductor-to-be, whose place in history is assured by his dynamic projection of Albéniz, Falla, Turina in the early stages of their creative lives. Succeeded by Antonio Bordas, these men taught those younger violinists, some of whom then went on to the Belgian schools, links with which are firm to this day.

Pablo (christened Martín Melitón) de Sarasate y Navascués (b. Pamplona, 1844—d. Biarritz, 1908), was the finest violin virtuoso of Spain. Though a pupil of Alard in Paris, he was castizo born in style, an imperturbable master of technique, reducing rehearsals to a minimum, never sacrificing crystalline purity of tone for extraneous effect, never seeking to force sounds from his instrument foreign to its nature, but by the acuteness of his ear and the sensitive agility of his hands drawing qualities from the strings that made the listener suppose their like had never been heard before. There were no Paganini-like legends about compacts with the devil in accounting for Sarasate's fluid velocity and sparkling resilient rhythms; he played like an angel.

His repertory was enormous and composers were happy to write music for him. Saint-Saens wrote his Concierto in A major for Don Pablo; Eduardo Lalo, the Concerto in F and Sinfonía española; Max Bruch, his Second Concerto.

His own pieces include Canciones rusas, Melodías romanas, Aires bohemios, Barcarola veneciana, Aires escoceses. His rustic Navarrese humour sounds its notes in *La caza* and *El canto del ruiseñor*, but he keeps his unfailing sense of proportion in the perennially refreshing Spanish pieces; though nearly half—ten—are Andalusian he takes care to show the Jota's versatility by writing four, and the Basque Dúo Navarra with the Zortzicos, Miramar and De Iparraguirre. This last had a special place in Don Pablo's memory, for Iparraguirre was that Basque bard who roamed the mountains Sarasate described when telling tales of Basque guerrilla wars, stimulating the patriotism of the people with his sons, one of which, the zortzico *Guernicaco Arbola* became the Basque nationalist hymn. José María de Iparraguirre (1820–1881) in exile for fighting in the first of these Carlist wars, travelled nearly as far as Sarasate himself, but as a solitary singer of his own songs with his own guitar. In 1853 he was pardoned and returned to settle in Madrid, but later died in his native province where the people put up a statue to his memory.

The summer festivals of music organised by Sarasate in his native Pamplona, 1878, became increasingly important and attracted music-lovers through the years as the local nucleus for the help of whose charities the idea was first prompted was joined by orchestral elements, choirs and nationally-known composers. Don Pablo never allowed any tour or tempting contract to interfere with his direction of this annual festivity, and himself performed on these occasions. This Navarrese festival of San Fermín is a forerunner of Pablo Casals' Catalan season at Prades.

It was a pupil of Arrieta, the Italianate romanticist, who became leader of the next generation in the theatre. Tomás Bretón (1850–1923) based his first distinctive success, *Los amantes de Teruel* on Hartzenbusch's affecting drama, but this was not staged at the Teatro Real until 1889, when it appeared in Italian. It was then heard in Vienna, Prague and in Barcelona when it ran for thirty-nine consecutive nights. He repaid this compliment with *Garin*, the Catalan score of which had also to be done into Italian and then the Liceo mounted it in 1892. He next found himself involved with a libretto by Ricardo de la Vega in 1893, originally meant for Ruperto Chapí, a rival in success. The producers at the Apolo, quarrelling with the latter, hurried Bretón on with the work and he wrote the score of *La Verbena de la Paloma* in nineteen days. With it, the sainete—for such it was—triumphed anew.

135

No other Spanish piece ever knew such popularity; every available theatre staged it. In South America it was to be heard simultaneously with the Madrid run. In Buenos Aires it was sung in five theatres at the same time and four times of an evening in some of them. It is still to be heard and enjoyed as a period classic of the castizo taste. The delineation of its lower middle class types and customs led on to a deeper realism in *La Dolores* and here Bretón showed his capacity to create that national opera's emotional power on which he prided himself, more especially in scenes where the drama rose to climax. This had a success equal to *La Verbena de la Paloma* in 1895 and reached Prague and Milan. In its approach to verismo *La Dolores* is not necessarily in debt to Arrieta's school, which drew on earlier Italian lines, for in this piece the Spanish dramatic tradition is making its way to musical expression through Bretón's enlarged skill. None of his later works repeat this vigorous handling of Feliu y Codina's text which Bretón himself arranged. In date it follows closely on *Cavalleria rusticana*, 1890 and *Pagliacci*, 1892.

Unlike Bretón, Ruperto Chapí, 1851–1909, let his reins on Pegasus hang fairly loose. Born in Alicante, he arrived in Madrid in 1867 when Barbieri's Sociedad de Conciertos was altering the public's range of outlook. His first opera, *La Hija de Jeftá*, sent from Rome where with Bretón he was enjoying an academic grant, was staged at the Teatro Real in 1875, with Tamberlik as its starring tenor; his *Roger de Flor* appeared here also. *La Revoltosa* remains in the zarzuela repertory and airs from other scores such as *Las hijas del Zebedeo* are still to be listened to as typical expressions of the theatre in later 19th-century Madrid. Musical expression of romanticism in Zorrilla's style took shape in *fantasías moriscas* and evocations of the Alhambra both in Bretón's and Chapí's instrumental offerings. Chapí also essayed the chamber form from 1893 to 1897 and revised his labours in the early years of the new century. Don Ruperto's appeal relies on his natural ease in the re-creation of popular material, as his Basque friend, the ardent Gaztambide, appreciated, and his name remains associated with a certain style, an essence of the period's natural grace—so that when evoking its music younger composers are apt to refer colloquially to that 'estilo chapiano'. The light dexterity of his orchestration is castizo in the finer tradition of the zarzuela line. *La Revoltosa* includes a popular Guajiras whose rhythm he directs in the printed score to be accented in three-four, though marked as customarily in six-eight. Since the Guajiras from the New World was well known in Spain at this time, it is possible that he hoped the score would find a public beyond Spain, as its character deserved. Chapí has a rhythmic mastery beyond most of his fellows and makes effective play with it. His zarzuela *El Rey que rabió* of 1891 has a mazurka de los Segadores sung by Rosa in the corn-fields to the swathing sounds of the chorus' scythes with their *ras, ras, ras, ras* as these reapers wonder what she and her segador are doing in the depths of the nodding shocks of corn. Its period charm is even now recalled by Madrid connoisseurs when another chorus scene in the harvest-fields of La Mancha is evoked by a more modern piece *La Rosa de Azafrán* by Jacinto Guerrero of 1930. Chapí called *El Rey que rabió* an 'ópera cómica'.

The género chico in its late 19th-century cultivation by Federico Chueca and Joaquín Valverde drew efforts away from the levels of zarzuela grande reached by Barbieri, Arrieta, Gaztambide and Oudrid, but the pieces which followed Chueca's *La canción de Lola* in 1880, *La Gran Vía*, 1886 and *El año pasado por agua*—with Valverde—which ran for more than three years from 1889, show a genuinely Madrileño vein. Fernández Caballero's *Chateau Margaux* has satirical touches and his well-characterised *La Viejecita* of 1897 and the next year's success *Gigantes y Cabezudos* made a lasting place for themselves beside *La Verbena de la Paloma, La Revoltosa* and Chueca's *Agua, azucarillos y aguardiente*. Chueca and Valverde rely on contrasting effects when working together, as when after a prelude and introduction the scene opens with lively Sevillanas and caleseras, followed by Pasacalle, Barcarola, Pasodoble and finale of Act I. The next act's prelude leads to a tango flamenco, Panaderos a zapateado, Polka de los ingleses, Danza de los negritos, Canción del ciego, Marcha de la Constitución, and Jota with finale. Chapí's *Las Hijas del Zebedeo* contains more sentimental pastiche. There is a vals de las modistas, a duet for soprano and baritone and a dance trio to end Act I. The next act's prelude leads to a Pasacalle and duet for the old couple, Carceleras for the soprano and finale. Luisa's Carceleras are lively and still to be heard.

Old and tried themes mingle with newer attractions. In *Chateau Margaux* Caballero mingles the Malagueña, Gallegada, Javeras and Panaderos with valses for the heroine Angelita whose 'No sé qué siento' leads rather surprisingly to her acclaim of Bordeaux wines as contributing to joy; here some allusion to Verdi's *Traviata* may be suspected. *Las Niñas Desenvueltas* by Jerónimo Jiménez, a Juguete Comico-lírico, brings back to the stage an adventurous heroine of traditional drama, now a Mataora clad in feminine version of bull-fighter's ceremonial dress. The *Barber of Seville* was brought up to date in a one-act zarzuela by Nieto y Giménez. Its new version of the music-lesson scene is a Polacca for the customary aria, significantly revealing its old relationship to the Seguidillas. The quick dialogue recalls Rossini's patter and the instrumental manner is reminiscent of his also. The tiple, or soprano, demonstrates what a Spanish leading lady is now expected to display in the way of accentuated repetitions of high Bs, descending chromaticisms over an octave and a half, trills, roulades, triplets ad infinitum, and finally rapturous scaling the heights of C sharp, while the orchestra once more reminds us, in case we might have overlooked it, of the likeness between Polacca and the Seguidillas. Chueca uses the Polka in its more popular style in the Polka del Fotógrafo scene of *El Bateo*, another sainete, which is used here in traditional sense, implying a costumbrist atmosphere brought up to date in the satirising of people's naive reactions to the novel ceremonial of having their likenesses taken by machine.

On the whole, these Spanish musicians working for the theatre produced their best work in response to a challenging text. Chapí, for instance, slackens in verve when setting trifles like *Disparate*, cómico lírico, the point of which is not sharp enough to evoke amusing caricature. Bretón's *Los amantes de Teruel* genuinely rises to an occasion with Isabel's Romanza 'Mi vida fue quimera', according to the means of his time. It is his *Verbena de la Paloma* which shows what could be achieved within the castizo range of costumbrismo approached with modest circumspection but exact focus. On this hot summer night of a Madrid verbena, the salon music of the mazurka is contrasted with the Soleá of Andalusia and the colonial-styled habanera. There is buffa characterisation in the older men, a love affair with a chispa of independent spirit on the girl's side resulting in the plot's later confusion. The elder men's romanticising regrets allow for a relaxed comic quality with elements of mild caricature—recalling Goldoni's amiable observation—in don Hilarion and don Sebastian, likewise. Their opening scene is entitled Parlante y Escena. Julian's air is popular but touched with classic lyricism and leads on to the Chulapos' and Chulapas' version of the Seguidillas. This is followed by the old gentlemen discussing, not diet now, but the young ladies' various charms. The Soleá and its Cantadora give a more intensely passionate note, being sung 'muy abierto y vibrante', intentionally contrasted with the more self-conscious manner of the Madrileños, and under cover of its exotic excitement the comedy's action develops. Another costumbrist interlude is introduced with a Nocturno for Sereno and Guardias. Hilarion encounters the barrio's chulapas and invites then to drink liquors which stir everyone up to dance the mazurka, with period formality, notwithstanding. More sinister incidents arise sustained by the music and eventually the apothecary don Hilarion is beaten by Julian and denounced as *truhan*— a term unsuited for genteel ears in this innocent barrio; the local Susana is confirmed as chaste, despite the attempts of her elders, and bewitching, as the would-be Lothario admits.

Albéniz presses out the juicy flavour of this and Barbieri's zarzuelas in that most infectious gaiety of *Lavapiés* in his *Iberia* and leaves these scenes of his youth with undisguised nostalgia.

Admirers of Amadeo Vives, 1871–1932, were at first disconcerted when he turned to this minor genre after having shown talent in more formal musical spheres, but eventually he proved his capacity to raise its standards in *Doña Francisquita* and *Maruxa* by which audience perception of this lighter form's potential was quickened, as was needed if the zarzuela was to make new progress in the 20th century. His *Canciones epigramáticas* remain as evidence of his lyrical sensitivity to fine verse, a constant characteristic of Spanish composers from generation to generation. This suggests that it was now the writers' turn again to supply musicians in the theatres with the quality of libretto they often lacked.

It was the serious efforts of Albéniz, Granados, Falla and Turina to create zarzuelas and operas that carried the past struggle into contemporary Spanish consciousness. Their immediate successors have produced numerous examples to show that native opera remains a major consideration. Federico Moreno Torroba (b. 1891) made a vigorous contribution to the zarzuela with the personal colouring of his earlier orchestral work *Cuadros Castellanos* and that delicacy expressed in his *Sonatina* for guitar, as *Luisa Fernanda*, *La mesonera de Tordesillas* and *La Chulapona* prove. Pablo Sorozábal (b. 1897) in *Katiuska* and *La del manojo de rosas* turned Basque potency once again to the popular theatre. Toldrá's *El giravol del Maig*, *Lola la piconera* by Conrado del Campo, *La cabeza del dragón* by Lamote de Grignon, *Soledad* by Juan Manén, *La Lola se va a los puertos* by Angel Barrios, *El gato con botas* by Xavier Montsalvatge, *El mozo que casó con una mujer brava* by Carlos Suriñach all prove that musicians have added their contribution to this constantly revitalised collaboration with the theatre.

The part played by some scores of the género chico in the evolution of more serious music is sometimes overlooked. A forgotten one-act Juguete Cómico lírico, *El Cuerno de oro*, text by Merino y Navarro, music by G. Matos, in spite of its brevity has possibly had effects on no less a piece than Falla's *Three-Cornered Hat* (*Tricorne*). The popular Andalusian theme associated with the corregidor, or alcalde-mayor, is treated so as to underline its equivocal suggestion, Falla's scoring being amusingly clever in its use of muted undertones for the wind instruments, closely following *El Cuerno de oro*'s instrumentation. More than this, there is a bird in a cage in *El Cuerno de oro* whose flutteringly brief notes are imitated by the Flautín:

These notes come to mind during the ballet's opening scene when the miller's caged bird—a parrot in the original tale—has to be coaxed into chirping the time of day—two o'clock in the afternoon. It is not impossible that Falla on this occasion was a snapper-up of unconsidered trifles and that he read this score among many others during the years when he was himself looking about for material for his early five zarzuelas.

CHAPTER VI

Spanish Popular Music

'Fortunate is the country which jealously preserves this natural flower . . .' No one who has heard the anonymous songs of Spain would dispute these words by Debussy, though some might question the phrase which follows them: '. . . preserving them from the classico-administrative', since it is partly due to local collecting by church organists in times gone by that so much regional music has survived uncontaminated; their orthodox training enabled them to recognise the modes and scales from which these songs derived and thus to conserve them integrally according to original local practice. So reliable indeed has much of this evidence proved that Falla, Granados and even Albéniz used such specimens in re-creating the native idiom through their own compositions.

A neglected collection, *Alegrías y Tristezas de Murcia* by Julian Calvo, organist of Murcia cathedral, is a notable example of this valuable kind of labour, known until very recently only to pioneer musicians seeking to make a revivified 'música española con vistas a Europa'. The collection was compiled in 1857, so Calvo tells, adding that it was only the prompting of illustrious maestros which encouraged him to print the work in 1877. He begins his examples by dedicating to his mother's

memory a *Cantinela* 'used by mothers to put their children to sleep' and to this Morisco melody he gives the tempo 'lánguido'; in a footnote he reveals that this cantinela comes from the times of the Arabs and is a

141

species of song used at mulberry-leaf picking-time for the feeding of the silk-worms, adding that those melodies which we qualify as Arab, are, from observations made, attributed to various 'argelinos y algunos moros de Orán en sus cantos a solo o con acompañamiento de Marabba'. This transferance of Muslim field-songs to cradle-tunes is to be found elsewhere in Murcia, in Valencia and also in Extremadura; such first musical impressions on the infant ear have been incalculably effective in securing a native love for exotic scales unchanging down the centuries.

His examples of the *aguinaldos* sung by the peasants and the blind include some of great antiquity 'whose melodies are purely of Murcian origins'. Some are accompanied by guitarras, guitarriquío Bandurrias or with 'Timples, cembalos muy pequeños, sonajas y panderas'; he gives an upper treble line to one which he describes as 'Efecto de la Bandurria'. Example 6 is sung in the Huerta y Campo—those traditional market-gardens—of Murcia. 'They are called "de ánimas" because the cofradías—the brotherhoods—of this title sally out singing these songs when collecting alms for the culto from the neighbouring communities.' The verse describes the Three Kings from the East arriving at the stable-door. This may well be a survival of medieval usage. His note to the *Paño* records that this song dates from the 17th century, according to very illustrious persons versed in the history of Murcia. He gives, too, a variant of this famous air with a guitar accompaniment, entitling it 'Décimas Glosadas Llamadas Vulgarmente El Paño'. His placing of the syllables in relation to the notes and their accentuation is illuminatingly different at some points from the customary interpretation nowadays. He also gives four verses in full as used in his day.

Among *Malagueñas* he gives one sung by the youths of the Huerta when courting, and adds that the boys and youths who go round cleaning the streets in the morning sing this without the accompaniments of guitarras, guitarriquios or timples bandurrias and violins used the night before, thus giving a morning's echo of the serenading. The next pair of malagueñas are marked 'muy animado y marcado' in contrast to the languorous motions of the Andalusian song, though the second is ornamented by a flourish extending over two octaves, less one tone, and this is, of course, a cadential emphasis. He observes that the malagueñas in Murcia, as in Andalusia, the vito and rondeña are based on the fourth tone of the plainchant and furthermore affirms that the tones on which these melodies are based come from Greece, while the melodies are the work of Murcian and Andalusian Arabs, being adorned according to the taste of the local people.

He then proceeds to the *Parranda*, the castizo Murcian music. The first of these—of the Huerta and countryside—pertains to the set called *del Uno*. Detailing the accentuation of the words 'a bailar han salido los cuatro *soles*', he explains that some performers 'sing the last note of each line so softly and "abandonada" that very often it seems as if they do not sing it at all'. This is valuable information as is the note given to the three verses included; the dance of the parrandas previously given is stressed in particular by the men with strongly marked movements of the feet on the ground. The verse runs:

> *De bajo de la hoya del verde limón*
> *hay un amante dando quejas a su amor*
> *y se las daba de modo que a las piedras las quebrantaba.*

So accordingly these dancers demonstrate the desire to show their passionate love by stamping upon the stones as if to break them. Another set of parrandas given he describes as 'danced with much gravity and languor moving the feet only a very little'. Its recurrent accompaniment staccato sempre—has an unusual interest, for Granados opens the first of his *Danzas Españolas* with this characteristic accompaniment as its theme. When writing *María del Carmen* the composer spent some time in the Murcian huerta and his parrandas are happily developed in this, the most popular of his stage works. Calvo is of opinion that 'the parrandas date from the epoch of the Arabs in Murcia' adding that their light modulations are called *falsos*.

Calvo's example of the Parrandas murcianas—number 12 in his musical series—is now known everywhere in Falla's *Seven Songs*. Unlike some later editors who made use of his pages, he gives a triplet on the first accented note of the second and fourth phrases of the song, as well as the common triplet flourish before the final note of the melody. Since this gives brilliance and speed it is possible that its continuous use on the second and fourth phrases gave Falla a hint for his triple rhythmic pattern throughout the piano part and he follows Calvo's insistence on the importance of an additional phrase at the song's conclusion which is carefully set out thus by this scrupulous cathedral organist: 'se cantan tres o nueve coplas y cuando se va a terminar desde el calderón al Retal'—here he sets down two bars of accompaniment on the key chord of G and then states 'D.C. dos veces más con las siguientes coplas' the phrase BB/BCA/B being sung on the G chord five times. Falla ends his version with an additional phrase as a coda on the G major chord for cadence.

José Inzenga in *Ecos de España* gives Las Torrás as the origin of his example of this air, but his setting ignores Calvo's advice, unlike Falla, and constrains this ebullient song and dance to the last traces of early 19th-century salon dance with its ceremonial curtseying. Possibly it was this constraint of superimposed rhythmic rigidity and its impoverished harmonic retrogression that Falla had in mind when he once explained to me with an expressive gesture towards the window that he meant to set this song free to fly out of its cage and through the open window.

Calvo gives four examples of the huertanos songs in the field, those for when they pick the mulberry-leaves for the silkworms, those for their farm labours with mules and cattle, and those for harrowing and threshing. To his examples of the mulberry-cultivating songs he adds: 'These four songs are completely ad libitum in their rhythm, for to subject them to bar-lines destroys their character completely; the entry of each verse until the high notes are reached is often accelerated a little.'

Illustrating various local flourishes to end a song, Calvo adds *A ju—ju*! as a cry 'peculiar to the youths of our huerta, and they also give vent to it in their diversions . . . to convey messages to their sweethearts, and to insult one another'. It is of course still widespread in Spain and when parties are dispersing late at night still takes on a challenging pitch as young men go their ways to their several villages or barrios.

His Seguidillas Antiguas del Jo y Ja is followed by Antonio Martínez in an excellent *Antología Musical de Cantos populares Españoles* (1930) though, again, Calvo's closer recording has particular interest in that chromaticism on a rising group of four semi-quavers where the modern compilers offer merely a repeated G followed by repeated Cs instead of Calvo's A.A.B natural, C followed on the next beat by B flat in bar 11 of the melody, which, in the context of his other murcian tunes, is authentic. His accompaniment, too, here as elsewhere, is consistently true to the air and that popular instinctive modulation fitting to the old scale on which its structure was first based.

His account of local customs associated with the *Aurora* throws light also on this nationwide cult of the Virgin in which men and women take part in elaborate choral celebrations. The Salve in double chorus has been popularly known as La Aurora from time immemorial, and the services are held in the Rosario chapel. Those who form the chorus are known as cuadrillos; in the first there are four singers; in the second as many as wish to participate, providing they are members of the brotherhood, that is, the cofradia. The illustrations include an old traditional flourish before the final note. 'This Salve is accompanied by a bell which weighs twenty onzas and serves to mark the rhythm and the tuning, being played by the chief among them.' This custom is not always kept up nowadays, to judge by church festivals in many places where the bells ring out in discord with the anthem and organ preludio, not only out of key but out of time also. Once there were as many cuadrillos as there were parishes, but now, Calvo explains, there survive only those of Ríos el menor, San Pedro, Diega Ríos en el barrio, La

Merced and la Huerta. The choir sings in close thirds; the soloists, however, are trusted to sing their parts ad libitum, interspersing many adornments, in which they display their agility 'de la garganta' and their taste; the bell is not sounded during the coplas, but in the choral pauses, when one or two campanazos are given to indicate the points of rest to be observed.

The Aurora, as its name implies and as its texts reveal, is sung at dawn. 'En el cielo se reza el rosario todas las mañanas al amanecer Y Santiago lleva el estandarte, San Miguel la guia la cruz . . .' The chorus enters with its flourish of thirds on Y Santiago, befitting the praise of Spain's national saint.

In Solo 2 increasingly florid passages are given both to soloists and chorus, suitably illustrating the words on gathering these fragrant flowers which today Mary sows against the power of Lucifer. Next, the first choir, always in thirds, sing *pppp* with long vocalised passages of 17 and 22 notes, and then accompanied by the bells sing muy ritmado *Estas flores*. The leader of one cuadrillo confessed that he found special pleasure in introducing now and then some variation in the adornments with the object of differing from the rest. Among these singers the varying Auroras are given names such as Carnal, la Salerosa, La Pausada, la Aranada and the celebrated Chamberga, so called because of its length, since it lasted half an hour, the others being so distinguished according to certain words in the text, the tempo or the contrapuntal effect, possibly. Local fancy referred to the part-singing superimposition of one voice rising above the other as 'making the chimney'.

'We have already indicated that this custom of singing the Aurora is very ancient and perhaps dates from the end of the 15th century or beginnings of the sixteenth; the foundation of the archicofradia del Rosario dates from the epoch of the conquest of Murcia by King Jaime of Aragon. The church of this archicofradia possesses an organ in very good order and contains two panels with the following inscriptions; that on the left, "This organ is the property of the archicofradia, bought in Toledo for 400 pesos, in the year 1593"; the panel on the right, "Geronimo Balses, organ Builder". Bearing in mind the date of this instrument and that in that same epoch there were rosarios in four parts, violins, chirimías and bajones, and furthermore that the popular songs are more ancient than instrumental music it is logical that—as tradition affirms—the custom of singing the aurora dates from the epoch cited above.'

Inzenga's example follows Calvo's, but gives only the basic air and no detail. Calvo notes that the final phrase usually ends in the major. His Aurora gives a high G in the second phrase—Inzenga merely repeats the first; moreover, Calvo in this phrase drops to C sharp, A sharp after the third repeated D, where Inzenga merely repeats the first phrase; the latter's broken phrases are less expressive. The texts also differ significantly. Inzenga gives 'por una ventana arrojar'; Calvo's first line prudently avoids misunderstanding of the verb arrojar—to throw oneself out—in this context, and writes 'Un devoto por ir al rosario por una ventana se quiso bajar'—in which he was probably more correct in using the verb *bajar*—to descend.

From *Alegrías y Tristezas de Murcia* it is easily learned that this old Moorish kingdom was in musical contact with Andalusia, Valencia and Aragon. Inzenga, in his Murcian album, gives an air which he vaguely entitles Canción. This is 'Dos soles son los ojos de mi morena', one of the loveliest in southern and south-eastern Spain. Its modulatory descent shows it to be of malagueña form, as its smouldering languor also suggests and it is probably this languid vein which masks the relation of its rising opening phrase to the Seguidillas' customary commencement; its text, too, may be linked to the famous Seguidillas manchegas, to which the Seguidillas murcianas are also related. It seems thus to be a perfect hybrid bloom grown on Murcian soil, part malagueña murciana, part Seguidillas, in which the muy animado movement of the latter has slowed down to the Malagueñan pulsation of the true south.

Of Inzenga's three albums—Murcian, Valencian and Galician popular music—the chief virtue is the prominence given to rural instrumentalists of the last two regions, whose astonishing virtuosity, with gaita, dulzaina, and the drumming tamboril, deserve their place with the guitar, and its close companion here, the bandurria.

In *Canciones y Danzas de Onteniente y Bélgida* (1950) Manuel Palau gives examples of those cross-currents which give Valencia its fascinating variety of florid curves not always held in by Catalan restraints, of heat and its containment, of Neapolitan relaxation, perhaps, and Aragonese athletic vigour. As in Calvo's collection there are cançons de bressol—cradle songs—whose chromaticisms, murmured rather than melodically enunciated, flattened thirds, and slurring modulations from major to minor suggest that, as in Murcia, the Moorish field song was adapted to home use; the simplifications here sometimes suggest an adaptation of an older, subtler air. One example of the cradle song shades from major to minor, while the canço de batre to which it may relate, moves chromatically in an opposite direction harmonically; thus the first tends towards relaxation, the second towards action. Textual phrases, such as likening the child to the Flor del taronger, with all its poetic allusions, added to these unforgettable melodic twists and turns are influences capable of rearing a child having precocious awareness of the beauty of its heritage in popular music and verse also.

The Jota, as musical emblem of Aragon, has spread throughout Spain and into parts of Portugal. Outside the peninsula it has become the most familiar of native forms because of the frequent use of its virile rhythm and brilliant instrumental interludes by 19th-century European composers. Its ubiquity however has not entirely obscured those other manifestations of the rich Aragonese tradition which have remained intact alongside the treasures of the Corona de Aragon testifying to the splendours and enlightened musical tastes of the Aragonese court.

Angelo Mingote's *Cancionero de la Provincia de Zaragoza* (1945) is a useful compendium in which the proportion of the Jota to the Aragonese musical whole is fairly kept among albadas, auroras, bailes, danzas, gozos, cánticos sacro-profanos, villancicos, tonadas, and cantes de navidad. This last group shows the collective instinct for fine skill at church festivals, though in the profane series the guitar vibrates in the background. The albadas, serenades, first musical offerings to the bride on her wedding morning, and the Auroras, as in Murcia a century ago, still hymning the Virgin in rudimentary thirds and controlled flourishes, show their contacts, south and west. Aragonese dances are supported by that variety of instrumental colour and exuberantly florid outbursts to be expected in the land of the Jota. Related to the Castilian family as many of these traditional pieces are, there are also survivals of Moorish ancestors, as, for instance, a *Romance llamado Moro*, from Sástago (28, page 14). Dulzainas, tamborils, gaiteros, fiddlers share the virtuosity of village guitarrists along the lower banks of the Ebro, while in its higher reaches of Alto Aragón more archaic remains are found of dances with swords and sticks, survivals of fertility and seasonal ceremonials once more widespread.

Pride of place is reserved for a 'Villancico con tema de Jota aragonesa en honor de Santa María del Pilar en su venida en carne mortal a Zaragoza a Doce Voces divididas en tres coros (El tercero con bajoncillos y Bayon), de Dr José Ruiz Samaniego, Maestro de Capilla del Pilar año de 1666. Versión exacta del original, en notación moderna, de Gregorio Arciniego Pb. 1940.' The Jota theme is of 16 bars given in the treble and the conjunto instrumental consists of tiple alto, tenor, bajoncillo, bayón grande, arpa y órgano. The harp accompanies the first choir and the organ all three. This work shows the 17th-century church style at its apogee, vigorous, assured as leader in a free association of church and people in this apotheosis of the Virgin's visitation expressed in the native Jota, splendidly adorned musically in keeping with the magnificent robes of the state's Santa María del Pilar in the cathedral.

Antonio Martínez' *Antología* of Spanish and Portuguese popular music devotes the Aragonese section to Jotas with the exception of a marriage alborada from Alto Aragón which has a beautiful text. 'Mañana por la mañana levántate tempranito y verás en tu ventana de hierbabuena un ramito. A la una canta el gallo; a las dos el ruiseñor; a las tres la tortolita, y a las cuatro canto yo.' This is in moderato time. (The despedida—the envoi, or farewell—is allegro; La despedida les damos, la despedida les doy, que dan los labradores con el pañuelo en la mano quédanse con Dios, señores.) The Salute is in 3/4, the Despedida allegro in 2/4. The sense of form as in an embryonic suite is widespread.

The Jota, basically in 3/4 time with alternating four bars of tonic and dominant, penetrated Navarre, where it met the prevailing Basque elements—the Basques have not noticeably fertilised other regions. In Valencia the Jota has been assimilated with melodies from Castile and Andalusia. The jota alicantina, such as 'Visenteta, filha mea', has its own chord progression in the accompaniment; the jota valenciana, 'Valencianita del alma', is traditional; the famous Jota del Carrer has unusual idiosyncratic progression; the type known as El U y el dos—or dotze—recalls the extension found in Murcia and is more varied in its progression than normal, passing through E major, C major, F major, C major, G major. Ties to Catalonia are closer in 'Castellito de hermosura'. The jota can be seen spreading across the Castilian meseta and into northern Portugal by way of Leon, and more strongly, through Salamanca; among the northern Portuguese it is known as the Gota, so this title also has a guttural sound.

In his search for Arabic correspondences to the Jota in *La Música de la Jota aragonesa* (Madrid, 1928) Julian Ribera, the Spanish Arabist, amasses a vast quantity of material and many examples, schematising their structures as aids to identifying their predecessors. He finds the word *jota* in a music book from Avila from the end of the 17th or beginning of the 18th century and identifies it with the Arabic word *xatha*, for sota or bailar, and in the 17th century the Galician *choutera* for song; some argue, however that this could relate to a French root. It is, however, identified with Aragon first, then with Navarre, Valencia, Alicante and Murcia southwards, and on the west side of Castile south-west into Extremadura though he does not say so; thus there is an appearance of convergence into, or out of, Andalusia and this might support Ribera's case. At its most typical it is accompanied by an elaborate preluding and interluding by a band of virtuosi guitarists, into which others of the guitar family are co-opted and with which the bandurria has had a long association. Thus the most orchestrally elaborate of Spanish popular music types may be reasonably compared with the legendary groups of Moorish bands playing at party gatherings and in palaces.

Ribera finds three main types and says that the aragonesa pura has the peculiarly consistent detail of a flattened note, B flat, as in the example given, and that this occurs in some malagueñas and even sevillanas. It is clear at this point that he seeks to make contact with flamenco tradition. We have seen in Murcia, and in Valencia, and will see again in Extremadura, that this flattened note is constant in the mulberry-harvesting tunes and songs deriving probably from these, and that this cropping was associated with the morisco workers.

As for the relation between bands of Moorish virtuosi and the jota accompanists, it may be said that though the variation form, which the Arabs practised, is predominant in the longer interludes, it is the very simple base of alternating dominant and tonic major chords which make this continuous variational skill possible. The date of the jota in honour of the Virgin of Zaragoza, 1666, is not, after all, very much later than the last expulsion of moriscos from the country.

Ribera also finds the jota related to the Andalusian soleá gitana, claimed to be one of the earliest canto jondo types, with which he says it shares more than one likeness, and goes on to deduce that it is an andaluz melody in disguise which was introduced into Aragon. Further, he suggests a relationship to what he calls Andalusian jotas called after cities and belonging to the fandango group; that is, granadinas, malagueñas, rondeñas, sevillanas, and we might add, murcianas. On this point of contact Tomás Bretón agrees, observing that the jota was a consequence of the fandango and that it is only a matter of introducing the jota not with the major but a minor instrumental passage, for the Andalusian atmosphere to be established. Regionalists like the Basques seek to link the fandango vasco to the jota; Chavarri thinks the jota salmantina appears to resemble the Castilian fandango.

Basically, two types emerge; (a) begins on ré, rises gradually to the tonic, then descends to mi in the first phrase: its second phrase beginning on mi rises to ré and ends on fa, and both phrases repeat, alternating one with the other—in conformity, naturally, with the alternating base. This combination of alternating final notes on mi and fa has remained the classic jota aragonesa. Those jotas having a B flat followed by B natural are 'older', Ribera says. Some malagueñas and some sevillanas have it in the second phrase; it is to be found in field songs in parts of the south-east and south-west. The second type (b) have alternating phrases sol/Doh la/si sol/la fa/re re/si sol/lah fah/sol mi/repeat.

He classifies as a third type the specimen called La rabalera whose alternating phrases rise to fa and mi; but these are rare today. It lends itself to florid work in descending to the final note; its second phrase though Ribera does not say so, works the flourishes upon la, sol, fa, mi the Andalusian cadential fall. This jota was given to him by Eduardo

Torner, a conscientious collector and analyst, so it is curious that this Andalusian link has been missed. The first type, more virile, has been preserved intact. The second and third have lent themselves to other forms and the second especially is very familiar and popular among guitarist accompanists, in their zealous enjoyment of the variation form which they share with audiences everywhere. More about the jota will be found in the section on Andalusia, pp. 161–172.

In contrast to the regions centralised within the range of Castilian speech, both Basque and Catalan music are affected by linguistic differences. Lemosí has insinuated its charm on poets and musicians alike wherever it made its way over the Catalan borders from Languedoc and a lyrical impulse is noticeable along the Mediterranean sea-coast down to Valencia. Within the Aragonese kingdom Catalans have profited by its extension over the Balearic Islands and across to Naples. From these legacies they have inherited a sense of proportion and discretion which contains the lyricism within those bounds that distinguish the folk songs and modern melodies alike. This lyricism has a fresh spontaneity that seems to spring from an emotional response to the natural beauty of their surroundings and that sense of being nicely balanced between northern and southern cultures which makes them a privileged people.

A modest but very adequate collection of songs by Francisco Alió (1854–1908) remains a reliable introduction despite more recent large-scale publication of the *Cançoner popular de Catalunya* in a series beginning in 1926. A volume of dance-lore, edited by Francisco Pujol and Juan Amades, appeared in 1936, bringing up to date those labours which have gathered momentum in many works since Francisco Pelayo Briz brought out *Cançons de la terra* in 1866–1867. Felipe Pedrell's *Cancionero Musical Popular Español* (1920), while including a number of Catalan airs was concerned to prove how strongly popular music in general has influenced the whole musical history of Spain.

Alió opens with the cradle-song Que li darém, which runs as a deep current through Catalan song and has inspired some of its best Christmas villancicos; its inversion may be heard in Portugal, as a lively dance in quicker tempo and played by the gaita. These light melodies are older than they seem; an example, 'Una cansoneta nova', shares its end-phrases with a renaissance part song in the *Cancioneiro Horténsia*, a song book discovered in Elvas in recent years.

Mallorca echoes the mainland forms but with archaic insistencies of its own—as the Azores echoes the Portuguese—in which religious observances have a share. It is possible to note an unexpected correspondence here with the well-known Asturian chant in praise of Santa Maria and her star 'Que a los Asturianos guía' of an ancient Mallorcan tonada—de S'Etsecaiada—'Jo estic damunt d'un cimal'—again it is the final phrase which echoes the other. The islands equal the Catalan lyricism in Na Catalineta; A la vorera de mar and Vou Varirau; the last phrase of this third air paraphrases that of the Catalan cradle-song 'Qui li darém'.

Some tonadas are of considerable antiquity e.g. the Tonada de Sa Ximbomba—Vaig passar per un canyar- and Tonada de'scuir oliva—M'agrada escuir oliva—and similar field-songs. Their age is perhaps comparable to those twisting boughs of the venerable olive-trees under whose shade such tonadas are heard at harvest time. Such antiquity of culture reminds us that whereas the Azores were first populated only in medieval times, Balearic culture goes back to pre-history. Mallorca is nearer to the mainland than the Azores and has other ties with Spain besides Catalan. An example of this may be found in the well-known Bolero de Palma, which, it may here be suggested, is uncommonly like the Bolero del Déjame in Ocón's collection of Andalusian music—the origin of which, he says, is unknown.

The Sardana with its cobla of eleven instruments as evolved in the 19th century by José—Pep—Ventura, gives new impulse to Catalan taste for the round dance, which in earlier forms was performed by medieval pilgrims to Montserrat monastery and associated with the *goigs* or *gozos* of the Virgin, the older forms of which are preserved in the 14th-century *Llibre vermell* there, though the sardana's alternating six-eight and three-four rhythm is said to derive from the traditional contrapas. The singular charm of this open-air pastime which may be joined at any stage by any who wish, owes much to its melody which is given out not by the higher-pitched tiples, but by the tenora, a trait supposedly brought in from Perpignan, and an effect cherished in old France. Catalans cherish the thought that their round dance was brought to them first by the Greeks and in song have hallowed the earth 'de la plana d'Ampurdá' as home of the first arrival of this custom to a people who, as a poet said, 'advance, giving their hands' which is a characteristic gesture of the sardana.

Catalan composers are conscious of their traditional responsibilities, writing sardanas, burnishing the nativity villancico forms, setting unassuming songs to Catalan verse, and constantly renewing their indigenous qualities of artistic sensibility and moderation.

The effect of the Basque language on Basque music tends to create a system of one note per syllable in the older pattern, and the charm of these songs lives in the simplicity which such habits express. Many are settings of moralistic sentiment and are somewhat repetitiously shaped when compared to the more expansive melodies of neighbouring regions like La Montaña and Aragon. Nonetheless they are capable of expressing the sincere feeling of communal experience and the strength of an uncompromising people, tenacious of their traditions. Their dances, too, are perhaps athletically rather than aesthetically enjoyed as in other parts of the peninsula, their geometrically organised patterns being less obscured by the personal allure of more southerly dancers.

The 5 by 8 rhythm of the zortzico is exceptional among Basque customary regularities and there have been sceptics—in neighbouring provinces, it must be said—who deny that the Basques created this form and show that, for instance, there is a 5 by 8 rueda well enough known in Burgos and Soria. One of the most distinguished church musicians, composer and historian, Federico Olmeda, chapel-master of las Descalzas Reales de Madrid, in his *Folklore de Castilla o Cancionero popular de Burgos* (1903) supported the Castilian case with well-chosen examples from his vast collection and reasonable argument, to which Telesforo de Aranzadi replied in 1910 in 'A propósito de algunos 5/8 Lapones y Castellanos' in what he called *Buscapié de Zortzicos y Ruedas.* From these and many studies by Francisco Gascue several reputations have been built up by amateur folk-lorists who lack any disciplined knowledge and life-long intimacy not only with the Basque milieu but also with the music of those neighbours closest to them. A few basic facts may be summarised here. In the zortzico the unequal rhythm applies to every bar and is due to that jump with pirouette to right and a simple jump, followed by a jump with pirouette to the left and a simple jump; this can scarcely be called unequal as a dance figuration. Irregular rhythm also belongs to the ezpata-dantzaris which alternates 3/4 with 6/8, very common in Spain, as in the petenera, though with this the sword-dance of the Basques has nothing in common in its character otherwise.

Much more complicated is the measure of the aurresku with its 3/4 2/4 //; 3/4 2/4 3/4 3/4 2/4: // repeating these bars four times, with a similar modulation of the first with the fourth, the second with the third. By-passing the zealous Dr Aranzadi's detour through Laplandic addiction to the 5/8 rhythm with its references to Fétis and the Finns, which is concluded by the admission that he does not remember from whence he copied the last of his Finnish songs, we learn now as he settles down to discuss Olmeda's evidence that the 5/8 ruedas of Castile, and especially in Soria, are circular dances—as the name implies—composed of paired men and women who make the whole turn of the circle, dancing and marching; various classes of rhythmic organisation are used of the 2/4 and 3/4/, but the most characteristic and ancient are 5/8/. This bar is not symmetrical; its strong beats are the first and fourth, the weak, the second, third, and fifth.

To Olmeda's examples of the instrumental line to the rueda, pito and tamboril, gaita ordinaria and gaita gallega, the Basque defender turns to the Bordon-dantza or St John's Eve dance in which the regularity of the zortzico, he says, rises to its apogee, for besides being totally in 5/8, each strophe consists invariably of 8 bars. The Ezpatadantza is more complicated, having three strophes of 12 bars, with local variants.

Accepting the evidence of the genuinely 5/8 rhythm in Castile, though not identifiable with the zortzico, Aranzadi asks whether there is also a sword-dance there, for though he had seen bailes con palillos—sticks—the sword-dance he never saw, though a colleague in León obliged him with a fine example of the danza de espadas leonesa, which is a member of that basic 3/4 strongly tonic melodic line known also in Britain. He quotes Olmeda's examples of the Castilian sword-dances, in the series he gives beginning with a Valencian in 2/4 followed by some stick-dances, the fifth of which, 'arcos en 3/8' he admits as having a certain similarity, though remote, with the Yriyarena of the Basques, then lists six sword-dances in 2/4 first and then in 6/8; the seventh example is a canastillo in 3/8, and the eighth is a jota. But though admitting Olmeda's discovery of the 5/8 rhythm in Castile and being the first to publish the Castilian sword-dance, he does not accept this as admission that the 5/8 there pertains to any form other than the rueda. Comparing Basque sword-dances with Castilian he discerns nothing more than a light reminiscence, and the reminiscence is so remote that nothing may be deduced about any melodic affiliation between them.

Characteristically Basque, he then shifts the argument to Basque nomenclature. In the neighbourhood of Bilbao they sing what they call the purrusalda and this is used for the arin-arin; Olmeda heard this sung in Villanasur de Oca by an old man of 86, who had learned it when a child; today, Aranzadi says, many villages of Burgos call this song by its Bilbao name, doubtless transported to Burgos by miners returning thither. Of the agudillo number 12, he quotes the collector's remark that it is popular in the Asturias, as is number 15, the trébole; but does not connect this with the miners of that region—as he might—being content to quote Olmeda's comment that prudence should be used in attributing songs to any one district. But he admits further on with regard to the purrusalda that the manner of dancing it in Bilbao for the arin-arin is almost identical with that described by Olmeda for the agudo—al agudo, a lo ligero and many other names—in which they are seen *triscando* the fingers to produce what is here called the *pito*, the women with her eyes always looking downwards, the pairs in some villages changing position *canciacá cancialló*. Also, Olmeda tells us, he adds, that some rondas finish many times with what used to be de rigueur everywhere in Castile to round off these dances, the i ju ju, aturuxo, relincho o relinchido, as mentioned by Calvo. Typically, Dr Aranzadi, with what is apparently the last word, adds 'Also the nere gurdi-ardatza is sung in 2/4 in Basque and the gui gui va una carreta in 3/4 in Castilian, with different melody and words, and there is no reason why this should be objected to . . .'

Nevertheless, Aranzadi returns with strong circumstantial evidence to reinforce his defence. First, the 5/8 rueda, or round dance, is to be found in Burgos and Soria, not in distant Salamanca, Avila, Segovia etc. and here it must be pointed out in the history of Burgos and Soria that the reign of Sancho Abarca of Navarre extended to Nájera, Yanguas, sierra de Oncala, Alto de la Cúcula or Brújula, Valvaneda, Urbión, Vicierca, Peña Negra, río Razón, sierra Calcana, valle Gazala, Garray (Numancia) y Agreda, and also that the counts of Haro were lords of Vizcaya, and that the Basque influence is to be seen in the names of places pertaining to Haro and Santo Domingo de la Calzada. The list of Basque names and names alluding to Basques such as Viz-caínos, Bascones, Bascondillos, Bascuñana and so on becomes over-whelming, but then to these he determinedly adds that in the province of Palencia there are also three places named Bascones, 'el de Ebro, el de Ojeda y el de Valdivia'.

He then asks a question which is worth repeating. Having heard women sing Bein batian Loyolan in 3/8 with a melody distinct from its 5/8 rhythm, he asks whether women show more preference for the 3/8 over the 5/8 because in its primitive form the 5/8 rhythm was purely a danza varoníl sin letra, that is, a masculine dance without words? Refraining from discussing which are the older specimens and which are derivations (since, as he repeats, some things evolve faster in one country than in another) he rounds off this exposition of Basque virility as expressed in the native dance by the acceptable dictum that bordon-dantza, jorrai-dantza, brokel-dantza, ezpata-danza, etc. have nothing to be ashamed of before those *ruedas con chirola burgalesas y sorianas*. The *chirola* is Basque for pitero, the fifer who accompanies himself on his drum, and the word *pitero* is sometimes used to describe the man of straw, whose word is not worth much, or even for 'a musician of no account'. Thus its use here in argument may exemplify robust Basque humour in its allusion to Basque confrontation with the chirolas of Burgos and Soria. Typical Basque instruments in this group are the *silbote*, large flute, and the *txistu*, or little flute.

The Basques' sense of communal emotion is expressed in their native hymn—Guernicaco arbola—not an ancient song, for it is a zortzico written by the bard Iparraguirre, with which this centralising spirit has identified itself, but entwined now about their holy tree of the song's verses. To hear their choirs, from Bilbao, San Sebastian, Vitoria, Tolosa or Pamplona, performing the works of Spanish mystical composers in three-day festivals is to know the supreme musical experience Spain can offer today.

The vigour and uncompromising robustness of the zortcico harmonic progressions as well as the virility of its 5/8 rhythm has found its way to the New World where it has taken root in the pampas of the Argentine Gauchos, a community which relied on its nomadic way of life before the ranging herds were fenced in to farm ranches where nomadic cattle-men also found their roaming instincts corralled. Examples of the zortcico by Pedro Albéniz and Antonio Peña y Goñi show a striking resemblance to types included in the Cancionero Cuyano and others of the South American past.

A great contrast awaits the musician travelling from Basque territory into the province of Santander, the region of La Montaña. If the Basque women shifted from the masculine emphasis of the 5/8 zortcico to the 3/8 because of its softened appeal, the rounded melodious Santander songs like those of the neighbouring Asturias, accompany verses which in many instances present a feminine point of view, and this becomes more accentuated in the remoter region of Galicia, famous since medieval times for its cantigas de amigo in which the girls left behind sigh for their lovers in absence; this nostalgia, the añoranza, lingers musically like mists over remote valleys and inaccessible mountainsides.

When F. Nemesio Otaño subtitled his settings of Montañesa airs *Melodías populares recogidas y comentadas en forma de 'Lied'*, his purpose was to show them as worthy to be heard beside 19th-century European classics. He did not exaggerate; their natural beauty of pure melodic line, poised and graceful, may indeed be compared with Schubert's nature-songs.

'Donde vas' comes from the remote region of Potes, and Otaño's arrangement of an accompaniment here may be meant to remind the listener that liturgical elements are deeply rooted in this northern territory. 'Son las onze y no has venido' has the authentic plaint of the subdued añoranza. 'Ya no va la niña' soars upwards with a phrase that may be heard over the hill-side to the sound of sheep-bells or a passing goat-herd: with poetic assonance its verses deepen the añoranza in successive pictures of the forsaken girl's plight as she absents herself from the fountain, from the dance and then from everyone she knows with a shifting emphasis to which other Santander tunes may be compared. 'Como quieres que te quiera' is a miner's song to his sweetheart hastening to a quickened expression of devotion in words of endearment to be heard all across this northern country, la mi morena, la resalada, whose thrice repeated cadence is the most familiar of all Montañesa endings. 'Maria, si vas al prado' more light-heartedly warns the girl to lock the gate as she goes out to the fields because of the cinnamon-coloured dog who is waiting to find his way in if she forgets. Again, it is a well-pitched melody calculated to carry the whole air from one hill-side to another; it is on the slopes of these northern valleys that such songs are to be heard during the day's outdoor labour, hay-making, sheep-tending.

Some of these songs, however, have travelled much further. Fragments drift like thistledown along the banks of the Douro having found a way inland, so that like Aguas do rio . . . they reach into Portugal taking new phrases from the river's banks before its stream is navigable to other traffic. The best-known of Santander songs is a harvester's song: 'Segaba yo aquella tarde y ella atropaba la yierba, y estaba más colorada, morena y salada que en su sazón las cerezas.' This flawless melody, complete with estribillo, may be recognised in less exuberant floridity in Portugal, still in the major key and with the same slow tempo to suit the lifting of heavy harvest loads of hay or corn. Further south, however, in Portuguese Extremadura, this same Montañesa air has been translated into the minor, though still describing harvesters' work in its text, and with the same emphasis on a deliberate tempo; references to Serpa and Moura show how far south it has travelled and this the cadence confirms, since it now falls on the Andalusian la-sol-fa-mi pattern, which in fact becomes the basic harmony of the entire song. Similar *gruppetti* adorn the air throughout as in Santander; its further history may be gleaned further on.

Another Santander song has been a traveller, too. This is a slow song 'Si a adorarte, ay Petruca', but this has a shifting chromaticism more often associated with the south. In Extremadura it has been used as a ronda, to which the Santander text's last words 'Ay que no te vea' are fitting to the serenader's farewell in the ronda. Another Santander air, this time lamenting the sweetheart's absence 'La vi llorando'—the farewell is short, the absence long—has also gone southwards. The opening and closing words, 'La vi llorando', are also to be heard in Extremadura but the words do not fit the melody here so well as the Santander tune; however, given that chromaticism, is seems likely that the air has travelled northwards, so that the two-way traffic by seasonal field-workers may have to be taken into account.

Moving into Asturias, home of the ancient round dance, *danza prima*, rural echoes of these Montañesa melodies are to be heard, as in 'En toda la Quintana no hay quien baile'—a lament for the death of a shepherdess mourned by the whole valley. Here one begins to understand a Spanish church musician's complaint that strictly regional collecting should pause and begin to relate the thousands of locally known specimens with those in other provinces, because these songs were often more widely sung over the borders than locally realised. This is certainly true of Castile and its Castilian-speaking people, from which in this aspect both Basques and Catalans may be considered apart. A summer's music teaching in these northern regions among *colonias,* as they are called, of children brought up from the great inland heat to the mountain resorts and sea-beaches from Santander as far west as Gijón and to the first of those rías which mark the beginnings of soft-aired Galicia and its meandering estuaries, proved the truth of this criticism, for most of these boys and girls were already familiar with great quantities of words and music from northern as from central Spain, Asturias, León, Salamanca, Avila and so on, to Toro and Zamora and even Extremadura. As the opening bars of most Asturian airs were played on the piano some would leap into vocal response; the air was always confidently given, and even when the words faltered, there was usually one who could fill in the gap till they could follow on again; it was usually the boys who remembered the words best, though when we attempted part-singing it was most often the girls who held their parts, and were especially addicted to descant. Among these Asturian songs, 'En Oviedo no me caso' was one of the few they did not know. 'A la mar fui por naranjas' was sung without hitch always— not surprising, since it is known even in Extremadura. 'Caballo que a treinta pasos' was among the most vociferously enjoyed, for its text as for its lively tune, and this shared in popularity with 'Déxame subir al carro, carretera de Avilés'; 'A mi me gusta lo blanco' and 'Has de saber que yo gasto buen zapato y buena media'—all these favourites with the boys who claimed their own right to sing the chorus of the latter: 'Que soy melitar, melitar, melitar . . . y te olvido por un real.' 'Si me quieres que te quiero, si me amas te amo', with its refrain from St John's Eve: 'A coger el trébole la noche de San Juan', led to their own local songs and dances in honour of midsummer and its saint with which these evening hours usually ended in this summer season.

Some young Zamoranos wrote down for me verses I did not know for 'Dicen que tus manos pican para mi son como rosas', and also for 'Si se va la paloma ella volverá', versions which I was to hear again in the south-west. There was one lad of twelve who surprised us all by reciting twelve verses of the old fragment 'Quien dirá que no es una la rueda de la fortuna?' though he would not sing it. Generally, it was the strongly rhythmic songs which were best known to them; slower airs they knew so long as the time was strongly accented as in 'La barca marinera', whose rising utterance of passion 'No, no puedo olvidar porque yo tengo amor' they sang with an emotional quality in their treble voices surprising in those of pre-adolescent years. A San Vicente hymn and older airs of more solemn kind such as 'Válgame, señor San Pedro' were not so popular with them, though they were obviously acquainted with the old modes of the plainchant from which such prayers to the saints had sprung. They taught me to dance the jota and the baile a lo alto and the song 'Dicen que larga ausencia causa el olvido' which accompanies the old dance as still performed in León and across the Portuguese frontier in a slightly different guise.

When summer ended and the last *colonia* went its way back to the southern meseta villages their train lurched out of the railway station to their shrill singing of what had become a favourite song—possibly because of its cinnamon-coloured dog waiting to get into the farmyard if the gate was left open—'Mari-i-i-ia si vas al prado'—white handkerchiefs waving, waving, as they were off to the old junction of Medina del Campo, where, so they said, the oldest engine in the world would be waiting to take them on the last couple of hours to their journey's end.

The great festival of St Iago in July at Santiago de Compostela brings the popular music that high honour which is its due, for as Feijóo properly wrote—and Goya illustrated—it is on the man and woman that racial continuity and all its expression depend. When all the solemnity has been celebrated, from the swinging of the bota-fumeiro, the high mass of choirs and organ, the homage and symbolic gifts from the Armed Forces to their Patron Saint and soldier, all of which, though beginning early, take the full morning hours to bring to a climax, then, when elsewhere the event would be concluded with the blessing and organ despedida, there is a sudden hush in the packed cathedral and all heads turn expectantly towards the great open doors through which the sound of the gaitero is heard, thinly at first, as from a distance. A tremor of excitement runs through the congregation, growing almost uncontrolled as the gaitero enters playing in those two giant figures of Adam and Eve who begin to turn and return as they approach the altar to dance and bow before the Lord and St Iago. At this point, one sees nuns whose faces have been downcast and invisible throughout the service—now moved irresistibly by the vibrations of the gaita—suddenly scrambling up to stand on the pew-seats to get a glimpse of this popular culmination of the national day, and being steadied as they peer on tiptoe by the supporting hands of the soldiers.

The *gaita* (bagpipe) still in use in many parts of Spain, is most persistently associated with Galicia and it is this instrument's drone on which the most characteristic Galician music is based as the muiñeiras express this people's humour, for this is a land of humour as well as of the wailing 'Ai la la' with its many variants. The moodiness of celtic strains is heard not only in these but in the setting of some songs against a background of dark clouds passing across the moon's face, which is uncommon in Spain and more familiar in those fados de Coimbra of student life which there are sung to the guitar. The blind fiddler is still to be seen on the roads going from village to village with his stock of ballads to be sung by his boy who goes about cap in hand, when the programme is ended; like their Portuguese neighbours these musicians are ready with a new twist to an old air for sudden catastrophe, as when a fishing boat is overturned on a wild night and nearly the entire male population of a fishing-hamlet may be lost. I have heard such a ballad within three days after a disaster being sung and played by a trio—master-minded versifier, blind fiddler and boy—thirty miles from the coast where a village was in mourning; how many times this dirge-like narrative had been chanted by the boy and commented on by the fiddler's sharply scraped lament before it reached this spot proved hard to calculate, but its style of performance corroborated medieval illustrations.

The brisk airs with which Galician municipal musicians *de oficio* turn out shortly after dawn to greet visitors to Compostela during the July week of St Iago have a vigorous cheerfulness characteristic of the gaita's skirling and fixed bass. Accompanied by drums they make a deafening noise and as elsewhere during festivities can be heard near and far continually exciting their patrons to song and dance and feast. All over the north-west may be heard the exhortation of *Vinde nenas* and *Berdusido, chamate jardin de frores* would warm any cool heads to join in with them. These instrumentalists are virtuosi with phenomenal breathing capacity as their flourishes and thematic variations show. The most deeply-expressed airs are those like Alto Pino, Ai Airiños, and it may be a sign of ancient art that on their fixed base of the gaita the Galicians have produced such a variety of melodies capable of conveying a whole range of moods from humour both broad and shrewd to the most affecting melancholy. Pedrell's *Cancionero* offers a well-chosen selection of the 'Ai la la'. Inzenga in his album of Galician music records fine examples of the gaitero's musicianship, though in his generalised *Ecos de España* the melodies are presented with barely adequate piano support.

León, from which the early laws and political organisation emerged in the first stages of the reconquest, gives musical proof of the primitive Christian sub-structures underlying songs taken southwards as people gradually ventured to settle in the territories patrolled by the military Orders. Many songs are adjusted to the hexachord, as to the tritone scale and many airs avoid the dissonance on the 7th degree. Fragmented romances and villancicos show that memories here are retentive not only of the well-known Gerinelda, Delgadina and so on but also of many lesser-known ballads. Like the Asturians, they have songs to express añoranza and the temperaments of those who accept that greatness of historical events once touched them and now has passed them by. 'Desde la mi ventana te he visto arando'—from my window I have watched you ploughing—suggests that this temperament can create with poetic fantasy as an onlooker of events, not as direct participant, even in daily village occurrences. It has extended into Zamora and even to Toro.

Although León commonly contrasts major and minor modes in northern patterns, the southern la, sol, fa, mi persists in a shadowy undertone beneath more obvious melodic turns, as in 'Al lado de mi cabaña' with its continually falling cadential imitation, though only once is the Andalusian design openly stated. The ronda also may employ it allusively, as in a farewell phrase, on the dominant, with la, sol but followed by F sharp. 'El Zorongo' however plays with this Andalusian pattern all through its air. Of the well known 'Baile a lo Alto' familiar examples are in minor and major, yet it would be difficult to insist that one is more characteristic than the other, for anyone who has sat out a Leonese fiesta knows that in merry-making, dancing and singing, their repertory of variants seems inexhaustible, whether when performing bailes de dulzaina, or exchanging tonadas de ronda, romances, coplas or emulating one another in their local variant of jota or fandango. One of León's more unusual airs will be given later since evidently it has known southern influences, if it is not Andalusian in origin.

The rich folk-lore of Salamanca has inspired a classic work, *Folklore Salmantino* by F. Dámaso Ledesma (Madrid, 1907), in which four hundred examples are classified in seven sections. The first includes tonadas of an unspecified kind, some being of a jota type and some of Asturian character. The second includes charradas, fandangos—some of these related to the jota and charradas with rhythms associated with castañets and panderetas. The third contains field-songs; aradas, muelas, acarreo de mieses and siega. The fourth includes marriage songs, villancicos. The fifth, music associated with religious festivities, hymns to the Virgin and the saints. The sixth contains romances generally common to other regions, though some are here adapted to the music of charradas, fandangos, tonadas; and the last, instrumental forms like the gaita salmantino, the dulzaina, tamboril, la caja panarandinoa, and details of the typical boleros de Sequeros.

In 1943, since Salamanca had by no means revealed all its treasures in Ledesma's work, the Pbro Sánchez Fraile published a *Nuevo Cancionero*.

Salmantinos in rural areas enjoy the contrasts of major and minor familiar in León, as in Pastorcito que te vas; Levantaivos, Tia Imilia, where, however, la, sol, fa, mi is the basic cadence, as in other innumerable melodies. Canciones de cuna here are evolved with fine taste, a Nativity offering with guitarras y almireses a ro-ro for the Child, alternating major with minor; another ends with the Andalusian cadential fall; la, sol, fa, mi. Evidently, in Salamanca as elsewhere, it is the rural inhabitants and the women who continue the Moorish echos. Other survivals give signs of keen aural distinction; romances such as el Conde Lino are of the finest quality of rhythm, accent and melodic form consonant with the text.

They have a predilection for the 3/4 lively Allegro song and the dance; the acceptance of the jota in the province agrees with this taste. Examples like 'En casa del Tío Vicente' are very numerous. The Charrada Baile may be in the form of a jota on occasion but it takes on a light Salmantino gaiety and such dancing themes are embroidered with subtle florid passages veiling the phrases with a gossamer skill like the lace with which the handsome Salmantina women adorn themselves en gala. Their Canción Castellana has the air of grace and nobility of the Santander melodic line. 'Como vives en alto', 3/4 allegro moderato, for both its text and its music is not easily forgotten by those who have heard it. A very beautiful finish is given here to a song deservedly widespread in Spain, of which in a slightly altered version Joaquín Rodrigo has made an enchanting setting—the song is of a bird which flies down to drink of the fountain—'Una paloma blanca como la nieve.' Birds and their songs have an unusually prominent place in this people's repertory.

The musical treasure-house of the Castilian-speaking family with its melodic inter-marriages and continuous graftings of stock extends into the south-western region where Extremadura lies. Almost unclaimed riches have lain here, not in local neglect, but in a lack of wider recognition which they most certainly deserve. Restitution has been made much later than in other regions, in the pioneering work of M. García Matos, *Lírica popular de la Alta Extremadura*, containing 436 unpublished musical documents; this was unfortunately delayed in publication owing to the Civil War and thus only appeared after yet another carefully collected two-volume, *Cancionero popular de Extremadura*, by D. Bonifacio Gil García, a folklorist from Logroño who came to pursue his enquiries in the south-west. This work was printed in 1931, and a second edition was produced thirty years later.

García Matos in a valuable introduction details the scales and modes on which the people of this region have built up their means of musical expression. He gives as a base for the music on the rural estates and among field-workers the scale of mi, fa, sol, sol sharp, la—a semibreve indicating the half-way pause—si, do re, mi and of modal airs of this arabic type he has collected 'an infinity', he explains. This basic structure, as has been seen, is found in Murcia and in the adjacent lower part of Valencia. As a more exact definition of this arabic modal type he gives mi, fa, sol sharp, la. This gama, he points out, constitutes the rule in Andalusia and in its cante jondo and flamenco, and he quotes Eduardo Torner here as rightly insisting that mi is in fact the tonic, and not the dominant as it would be if, as some mistakenly hold, the tonality was based in the minor of la; it is on mi that the cadences repose, and as we have seen in those other regions where this scale was in use, and towards which they tend, anticipating it by various musical means, such as hesitation, pause, ornamentation, and of course accent and half-way contrast of the dominant in parallel. The gama given here indicates the familiar Andalusian la, sol, fa, mi with the incidence of chromatic third, which lends the charm of anbiguity and suspense, holding the melody's tonality in question until the end, the chromatic suspension increasing the tension by its contrast and unexpected interruption to the fall.

Such subtle suspensions still haunt the field-labours of the Extremaduran people and make the long day's work seem shorter to those whose ears are fascinated by endless re-patternings of the past. The Arabic chromaticism, though in use in olive-gathering to this day, is not so persistent as in the mulberry-picking centuries, for the Moorish art of silk-making has died out and olive-pickers are not the traditionalists they once were, though they are faithful to the cadence, as country people usually are. However, the *esquileos*—shearing songs—show the Arabic scale in use as in 'De San Juan a San Pedro: Van cinco díah; Cinco mil son lah penah Tuyas y mías', implying that between the lovers' meeting on St John's Eve and their meeting five days hence is an eternity, or inferno, of waiting. Though these editors do not say so, these canciones de faena have contacts far beyond their own estates bordering on Andalusia and southern Portugal, Gil García's volume I gives Allí arriba hay un pinar, muy hermoso y florido, que lo han querido cortar, y no se han atrevido. This is practically identical with the second part of the Santander harvest song Cuatro pinos tiene tu pinar y yo te los cuido; cuatro majos los quieren cortar y no se han atrevido. Comparing both settings, the Extremaduran seems textually contrived in its added detailing of 'muy hermoso y florido' compared to the northern, which keeps faithfully to the incident; the southern version is musically unadorned, and the editor says; 'Se canta actualmente en la romería de Santa Lucía en Cáceres.' Another song of faena, from Badajoz, has a clear parallel also to the Santander song in the grupetti which adorn both half-phrase and end-phrase in each section of the melody. Like that, it is muy lento, in the major key and in 3/4. This is given as 'De acarreo'—a carrier's song. It is entitled 'Dolores', and the text goes: 'Aay Dolores! Aay, Dolores! Con que te lavas la cara cara, si siempre te huele a flores? Aay Dolores! Aay Dolores!'

There is a striking similarity—also unremarked—in these words to the famous villancico by Luis Narváez 'Con que me lavaré, la tez de la mi cara; que vivo mal peinada. Lavánse las casadas con agua de limones, lávome yo cuitada con penas y dolores, con penas y dolores; mi gran blancura y tez yo tengo ya gastada, Con que la lavaré . . . que vivo mal peinada.' The Extremadura carrier's song is rustic, but in both the emphasis lies on the word Dolores and in the allusion to the woman's complexion. The Santander song explicitly compliments the girl's face, bright with the bloom of a cherry; thus, in all three the text is in praise of a beauty's complexion. Furthermore, the version in the minor of this Santander song which appears in the Portuguese Alemtejo, this time based throughout on the Andalusian gama, also tells of the lovers harvesting in the fields, with the same deliberate tempo and in 3/4. The Portuguese text again alludes to the girl's complexion, though here it is she who asks him to lend her his hat since there is no shade to be had in the sky: 'Alemtejo não tem sombra, Ai! se não é que vem do ceu; O amor da minha vida, Ai! empreste me o teu chapeu.'

A remarkably florid muleteer's song of León *A esa mula delantera* is so chromatically allusive to the Arabic scale that it is logical to compare it with another Extremeño air *De acarreo*—to which, among several other variants of this *Esta noche ha yovido*, and especially an example on page 62 it seems close; this, too, runs over the compass of an octave in the first phrase and in the second meanders down via chromaticisms on C sharp and C natural to the ornamental turnover preparing for repose on the tonic mi; both refer to the team of mules, the northern one with pride in esa mula delantera pues ella sola arranca el coche. The extremeño however reaches above the octave to the minor second. Another carrier's song, from Cáceres, again with Andalusian cadence and pretty ornamental grupetti, is also used for the ronda, these groups being insistently on the cadential la sol fa mi throughout. Opening phrases directly soaring up an octave are not uncommon here and it is with this manner that the Leonese *A esa mula delantera* begins and repeats.

It is here in quiet Extremadura that elder men recall their fathers' chanting in the fields before starting the day's work, the overseer or farmer calling for a blessing on the labour, the peasants responding, and the benediction and thanks returned for the work safely completed at sun-set giving both a biblical and patriarchal mood.

The prisoner's songs given in these collections are said to be as commonly used in the gaols, but the lines of one 'Yo no sé cuando eh de día, Yo no sé cuando e de noche' seem too artificially contrived for a popular origin and may be suspected as a fragment from a romance. This supposition is supported by another example in 'El prisionero y el pastor desgraciado', for it begins 'En Mayo y en Mayo era, Cuando lah fuerteh calores Cuando lah cebedah secas, Loh trigos en granaciones...' and this reveals contact with the great romance 'En mayo, fue de mayo'. At the same time, the skill of anonymous singers and versifiers at improvising on a fragmentarily remembered verse is not to be underestimated and in this province we are close to Huelva where some of the most fervid cantaores of Andalusian cante jondo have risen to fame; a prison is a likely hotbed for such brooding diversions, prompted by recollection of old romance ballads.

The Extremeños show a keen interest in strangers and the differences of travellers who pass their way, as many songs prove; they—and especially those of Badajoz—have come within the orbit of Seville since times impossible now to determine and the Extremeño has left his imprint on Cuba, Venezuela and Mexico, bringing back with him—when he is successful enough in seasonal or other labour there to return home—the punto de la Habana, and the guajira to add to his own rich cancionero which also contains now the son and pericón, which like him, have in this way returned to their native soil. Sr Gil García says that 'the punto cubano y punto guajiro, of structure very like "our guajira", are of Andalusian origin, so that this, together with the petenera, have been taken to Cuba by our ancestors'. With all these facets of its many-sided connections Extremadura has also preserved intact its own versions of romances, sacred airs, villancicos in honour of the saints and most of the surviving dances in the Peninsula, seguidillas, boleros, jotas, fandangos; the riband-plaiting male dance, las cintas, the quita y pon, the malandrín, son brincão and son llano o no brincão; they play the large bass guitar, the guitarrón; their gaita produces four fundamental tones. No wonder that when the shepherds of Soria leave with their flocks for Extremadura, as the old song says, the shepherd-girls weep when they are left behind to sing the lament 'Ya se van los pastores a Extremadura'.

Andalusian singers of flamenco and cante jondo admit that theirs is an anarchical style. They never perform with an orchestra, nor in choirs, nor in duets; they sing sitting down and their source of vocal power is concentrated in the tense, vibrating throat. Their songs are rarely narrative or descriptive but concerned with expressing the poet's mood with the maximum of emphasis, hence the frequency of depressed or of sharpened tone which interrupts the vocal line. The guitarrists contend that it is they who establish the atmospheric condition with what is a parallel to oriental preluding, those curtains of sound through which the cantaor abruptly breaks when rapprochement between musicians and listeners stirs, and they who rouse the mood of the song and sustain it with those modes and patternings with which they support the declamatory vocalisation. Certainly they exploit the guitar's portion of reciprocal allusive progressions peculiar to the laws governing each type of song with what is half a carefully considered repetition of hypnotic charm and half an exercise of resourceful wit quick to seize a vantage point for exhibitionist skill. As in the bull-ring, the aficionado plays a part in all this, for his making and breaking of reputations lies in the stimulus he gives or withholds from the performer, judging a performer's artistry by those moments when he brings forth that extra stroke of temperament—the plus ultra of individual inspiration—from the subconscious sphere in which the Andaluz creative spirit lives, according to the best authorities on this spirit of the 'duende'.

In spite of those facile exploitations which musicians like Falla deplored and which he sought to purge in that Concurso de Cante Jondo—held for Corpus Christi, be it noted, on the 13th and 14th of June, 1922 in Granada—a sense of antiquity still envelops both flamenco and cante jondo tradition and a firmly authoritative musical organisation lies beneath those variations of sevillanas, rondeñas, malagueñas, granadinas, soleares, murcianas, cartageneras, the polo, caña, siguiriyas and others.

The meaning of *cante jondo* is generally accepted in its obvious sense as song of the depths, but the word *flamenco* still pricks the over-ingenious aficionado into fantastic and sometimes nonsensical conjecture: in the context of the evidence from popular music that the Muslims in Spain have left imprints of their musical tastes in the peninsula, the proposal that the word flamenco derives from *fela-mengh*—Arabic for immigrant peasant—is unsupportable. Legend persists that the seguidilla was introduced into Spain by a certain berber who sang it in Córdoba after fleeing there from his own country. Banditry and piracy were exploited as fictional material by Christians and Muslims alike. Flamenco, in fact, is not confined to city forms and has rural counterparts. In connection with this tale, another legendary factor to be pondered is an emergence of the bandolero theme before the mid-19th-century revival of this musical tradition in the café-cantantes of Seville; it had tremendous popularity and the bandit's exploits against law and order were vociferously declaimed at the time Manuel García appeared to make it his own in those 'unipersonal' themes of the smuggler. The echoes of smugglers' songs and García's in particular in *Carmen*, draw a world public still today. Through such legends and neo-legends, however, the word 'flamenco' continues to recall the same groupings, as xatha for jota. Xatha, as jota, means dance, whereas *felamengh* has no known musical connection, though the urban haunts with which cante jondo was once associated might well have been places where fugitives gathered.

Etymologically, the word 'flamenco' refers to Flanders: musically, a qualification must be made to this, for though the Flemish were regarded by Spaniards as 'flamboyant' and it is this characteristic which is marked in 'flamenco' singing, neither cante jondo nor flamenco music have any polyphonic traces about them and it was Flemish polyphonic music which was performed in Spanish churches and at court during the time of the Spanish occupation of the Low Countries. More acceptable to some Spaniards is that the word refers to the style brought by gypsies from the Low Countries at that time. As Falla observed, primitive Andalusian cante jondo is grave, hieratic, of sober vocal modulation.

It was by study of its Andalusian enharmonic modulation that Falla came to evolve his own later system of composition, for he realised that such a system could engender new melodic series. His observations to those singers and guitarrists entering the Granada concurso of 1922 are illuminating. Preference would be given to those whose style was adjusted to the old practices of the classic cantaores, avoiding abusive flourishes and restoring to cante jondo that admirable sobriety which constituted one of its greatest beauties. For the same reason participants were told to take into account that all modernised songs would be eliminated however eminent the vocal qualities of the competitor. Equally, it was not to be forgotten that avoidance of all imitation of theatrical or concert style is an essential quality of pure Andalusian song and the aspirant must always bear in mind that he is a cantaor, not a singer. It should not dishearten a cantaor, or cantaora, to be accused of singing certain notes out of tune; such notes are not necessarily out of tune to the true connoisseur of Andalusian song. It should also be kept in mind that a wide vocal range, that is, a voice stretching over many notes, is not only unnecessary to cante jondo, but may be positively prejudicial to the pure style of this tradition.

The including of rural songs in the genre was a stream which kept the tradition fresh, giving it renewed vitality and musical impetus. Even the nana is included in the género chico of cante jondo, and this is understandable since this cradle-song drew on the old chromatically-inflected line in rural places where Muslims had worked in the fields, as in Murcia and Extremadura; it remains part of the tonal-harmonic

family, as Falla would say. He observed that although the melody of
the gypsies is rich in ornamental turns, these, as with primitive orient-
als, are used only at specific moments suggested by the text and the
emotion it conveyed, and they must furthermore be considered as
amplified vocal inflections rather than ornaments as such; and this is
the style of hieratic, semi-chanting in an undertone with which many
country people still pass the time of day when alone, walking and
working, especially in regions where oriental influences have lasted;
this may have included Byzantine infiltrations, too, for the ornaments
of the liturgical line are restricted to specific places in the text. Falla was
careful to include Byzantine survivals when discussing the question of
primitive Andalusian song.

The songs and their instrumental settings as known today are grouped
into *grandes* and *chicos*. In the grandes a distinction is made between
those which pertain to cante jondo and those which do not. Cante
jondo includes the caña and the polo with its pairs, the medio polo, the
martinetes, both natural and redoblado, debla, siguiriyas naturales or
carceleras, siguiriyas corridas, siguiriyas plañideras or playeras, machos
de siguiriyas, saetas (of two kinds, por siguiriyas and por martinetes)
tonas (two grandes and five chicas), javeras, livianas, soleá, soleares al
tercio and soleariyas.

To the chico group of cante jondo belong serranas, rondeñas, caleseras, cante de la trilla, las nanas, verdiales, malagueñas, granadinas,
peteneras, cante de las minas, tarantas, paño moruno, alboreas, fandango de la Peza, fandango de Lucena, temporeras and cante de los
campanilleros. Again, among songs belonging to the class grande,
whether jondo or not, some are regarded as distinctively gitanos, even
though there may be gitano dilutions in the others. Songs distinctively
gitano belong to the jondo; caña and polo, both with their macho,
martinetes, debla, siguiriyas corridas al cambio, playeras, machos de
siguiriyas, saetas por siguiriyas and saetas por martinetes, and as cante
gitano not pertaining to the grande group, but grande in themselves,
the tarantas, tientas, fandangos de la Peza and alboreas. From this it is
seen that the songs decidedly pertaining to the gitanos are very considerable in number, and have a style and character of their own.

Among the cantes chicos or livianas are listed: bulerías, tangos, caracoles, mirabras, alegrías, fandangos de Alonso y Rocieros, fandanguillo
de Almería, fandanguillos feria, sevillanas campiñeras y corraleras,
cante de jarria, romances volados, cante de Levante, and chuflas.

It becomes obvious that everything possible has been gathered from
Andalusian song and dance, whether cradle songs, threshing and
ploughing songs or broadsheet romances, and put to service in this
intensive and now sophisticated musical form.

The gathering together of these groups and their performers dates in modern times from the opening of a café cantante in the calle de los Lombardos in Seville, by Silverio Franconetti y Aguilar, born in Seville in 1831. It is an amusing coincidence that this adventurous entrepreneur was of Italian extraction and that he started his café in the street of the Lombards. Before this venture, so we are told, this kind of song had never left the countryside or the tavern. The varieties of some of the songs listed here, suggest as much. There are innocent rustic forms mingled with songs expressing smouldering individual resentments at fate, as when the miners and prisoners in labour gangs give vent to their sufferings. From this café cantante and its success, others soon sprang up and the singers grouped about them, and instrumentalists also, found it necessary and expedient to organise and reappraise their skills and, in short, to prepare themselves for the wider public acceptance which certainly lay ahead.

A chief arose among them, Francisco Díaz of Lucena in the province of Córdoba, who appeared before the public with such success that he abandoned his barber's trade and lived professionally by his playing; this sudden advance stimulated other guitarrists so that the group became a school culminating in our time with performers like Ramón Montoya and La Niña de los Peines. Descending from the miserable lot described by Cervantes and the tradition of music-making in the barber's shop where guitars hung on the walls for customers to strum at will, these anonymous artists found themselves heirs to a title, since the day they took it upon themselves as a body to grant the name of Don to the rarest and most flawless among them.

The greatest of all, for he attained comparative immortality, was Juan Breva; as poet-musician he reached classic stature. Though he died old, poor and blind, a fine verse epitaph 'Ni la fuente más risueña' ensures his place in music history. In 1884 he sang at Madrid's Príncipe Alfonso theatre, the café del Barquillo and the Imparcial. He sang before the king, who presented him with a tie-pin adorned with his initials and the royal crown, and although his last days were painful and penurious, it was found that twelve such royal testimonial tie-pins had been kept in his possessions, proof that he put artistic recognition above comfort. It was at this time and earlier that Eduardo Ocón made his transcriptions of these performances some of which he printed in his *Cantos españoles*, now very rare; his family with great kindness gave me their last copy from his stock, apart from those preserved as their private property.

Among cantaoras the life of Dolores 'La Parrala' recalls Carmen. Coming from Huelva, she quickly drew notice with her singing of the Malagueña—sign of vocal flexibility and volupté—and then established her ascendancy by learning other forms. She played with men's passions as she toyed with the songs she sang, it is said. Leaving the café-stage to marry she soon tired of her husband, and having ruined him, went off to Madrid, of which she tired also, and returned to Seville. She foretold her death to a fellow singer, Fernando el de Triana, as he was on his way to Alonso—home of the fandanguillo—and passed her house. Calling to him to come and hear her sing the last malagueña of her life, she added that on Monday when he returned, he would find her dead. And so it was, the legend tells. These neo-legends parallel some told of Muslim musicians in Andalusia.

It is agreed that the tradition at its most hieratic emerged in Córdoba —that great centre of culture in the west and seat of the caliphate which rivalled Baghdad. The Cordobese soleares are sung with more gravity and authority. The Fandango Cordobés likewise is serious and shows that the fandango, as distinct from the fandanguillo, pertains to the cante grande, and not to the cante chico. In Christian times the province has been the home of hermits and saintly recluses and this association remains, of a city spiritually aloof.

Though fallen into disuse, the caña is acknowledged as resembling the polo; indeed, to avoid the monotony rising from its being followed by the polo, the *medio polo* was introduced—hence the latter's name. The caña enters into song immediately, unlike many flamenco types in which the singer waits on the atmosphere to be created by the guitar 'buscando la entrada'. In this, however, it does not resemble the polo in Falla's *Siete Canciones*, which in some significant aspects apparently draws on Ocón's example.

The malagueña, though grouped neither in cante jondo nor gitano, merits its place in cante grande for its vocal line richly elaborated, the song for kings, it is called; it deserves the honour of representing not only the city but even the one-time kingdom of Arab rule. Its languorous rhythm and romantic expression contrast with the lively soleá, sevillanas and fandanguillo, though like them, it is associated with the generic fandango. It allows a singer to display coloratura warmth, for its ornamentation is determined by expressing the verses' emotion; but it demands controlled breathing, which the more ejaculatory types do not.

The soleá gives vent to the explosion of exaggerated disappointment with which the extrovert Andalusian expresses chagrin or spleen. Essentially ejaculatory, its older forms have much gravity and thus support the claim sometimes made that the soleá has developed from the more or less religious pregones, though whether exact parallels could be proved of old Spanish survival of these in Tunis is perhaps in need of more exact evidence than so far offered. There are pregones attached to regional religious ceremonies which could have contributed to its more ejaculatory style, as in the generic saeta. Its place in cante grande is now linked to the guitar, and both singer and player concentrate their forces within a narrow circle of musical expression; it is within this that traces are to be detected of that enharmonic modulation which to Falla was all-important in primitive Andalusian song. Temperamentally it is said to admit the llanto de venganza, the cry of revenge, of hate, or regret, but never the weak sigh of passive suffering. Considered to be the most expressive creation of Andalusian sentiment, it is attributed to Cordobese origins.

The seguidiya gitana is a venerable tree from which have sprung several ramifications. Most regions have had a type of seguidilla from early times, and perhaps it was in connection with this widespread culture that the legend of its being brought to Córdoba by a fugitive Berber in some way arose. Its satirical propensity is said to be an ancient characteristic. Playeras are seguidiyas in which the gorgeos of the truly flamenco style are replaced by the jipios desgarrados—heart-rending outbursts—of the gitanería. Here we may be close to distinguishing the difference between cante flamenco and cante jondo. It is said that when a cantaor tells his audience that he is in a mood to sing 'to lo hondo' he wishes them to call for siguiriyas gitanas. 'De lo más seco que hay' in this context are those machos de seguiriyas which are paired to the main coplas and accompanied 'a palo seco', without hand clapping and without guitar.

The martinete is most gypsy-like of all; its name derives from the hammers of the old blacksmiths' forges referred to in this group of cantes fragueros. In its association with the carceleros or prisoners' lamentations, it is never accompanied in its genuine form by guitar or by any instrument except a smith's tools or the palos secos. El martinete redoblao is less seco, more florid; the Debla, meaning goddess, is reputedly reserved mainly for ritualistic dances such as inciting to desire, and performances in which those opposites, life and death, appear like shadows on a cavern's walls.

No greater contrast to these could be heard than the seguidillas sevillanas, transformed from the prevailing minor modes of Andalusia by the use of the major key into extrovert radiance, though still adhering to a fixed and narrow series of harmonic cycles.

The fandango has suffered distortions in the course of its long existence but survived them. As the cantaor's first concern is to make the words of his song clear, so the guitarist's technical skill and taste lies in his articulation of the accompaniment. The fandango andaluz makes demands on both and is honoured with a high place in the género grande. The fandanguillo belongs to the chico. In rural scenes such as the romería the fandango is more primitive, the best-known being the Verdiales of Málaga and it is worth remarking that since it plays a large role in nativity rejoicings a rural origin or at least its adoption there is possible. Juan Breva performed a version of his own for the wine-harvest. In Córdoba it is more serious, in Almería especially good for dancing; in Granada it becomes la granaína chica, or media granaína, with a curiously keen effect on the high cadential dominant seventh, tuned, it might seem, to the sharp, dry air of the Sierra Nevada which blows that way, and contrasting with the warm expansiveness of Huelva's versions, where the fandanguillos especially are held by aficionados to be very lively and alert.

The exchange of rural and town types may be traced in the serrana, calesera, and trilleras, temporeras and without doubt many nanas have now been drawn into urban stylisations; Falla's example shows, and so do Ocón's and Pedrell's, that the Andalusian infant is familiarised with the old chromaticisms, modulations and rhythms before he himself can sing a note; some of the finest come from the region of Huelva. The serrana is steeped in the stirrings of nature—with bird songs as in Extremadura and Salamanca—and associated with Ronda and the Sierra de Morena, refuge of exiles and wandering vagabonds.

Among mining songs—and mining was done at both extremes of Andalusia, west and east—the cartageneras have first title, being placed in the género grande. Spreading from south-east its slow pace and melancholy air overstep the boundaries with Málaga and Murcia. This background of mining labour has given it a virile accent in parts of Almería and this reaches a climax in the tarantas. The lighter pace of these is said by some to derive from the tarantella, hence the name taranta, and is therefore considered Italianate, though a similarity to other songs to be heard in the south-east seems obvious enough, particularly when, as is usual, it is given the traditionally Andalusian accompaniment. Sung by El Cojo de Málaga for instance and more recent cantaores, it would pass as one of the género chico drawn from rural echoes of Andalusian tradition. If the ear detects a metallic emphasis and differentiation of timbres in Huelva's fandanguillos this may be because of mental associations with Huelva's ancient metallurgical connection, which brought traders from the other end of the Mediterranean. Certainly the variety of coppery tones of which the guitar is capable hereabouts recalls to the historically-minded at least that it was the southern miners who discovered the art of making bronze.

Ronda is the home of the rondeña's *coplas bravías* (wild verses), and the rondeñas malagueñas have peculiar fame for as a well-known version of these declares—'You do not know how to sing them unless you have fascination and wit'—based on the malagueña progression and much simplified in line they have the same slow rhythm; the punch lies often in the words, hence the term 'coplas bravías'.

Cádiz, surrounded on nearly all sides by the sea, knows less of that sense of barren poverty which the Andalusian soil at its most desolate provokes and which only the cities can forget. Conscious of the fame of its dancing-girls and poised on the low shore-line where the waters reflect the dazzlingly luminous air which bathes it, Cádiz' songs and dances move lightly with rippling undulations; this music is lithe and moves within the género chico class. Tangos and alegrías, the petenera, that equivocal air whose innuendo has insinuated itself to and fro over the Atlantic, El punto de Habana, the guijira—though having undergone sea changes, these are nevertheless still recognisable on their return, prodigal sons and daughters whose coming home ensures a cheerful celebration. The gravest, most dignified airs on their arrival at Cádiz have taken a new lightness of movement, even the venerable caña; the tangos have revivified into the tanguillos, the caracoles' inimitable airs take on new graces, and are as lively and humorous now as in the early days of the 19th century. Cádiz remains, in fact, the home of the Jaleo and its encouraging enthusiasm.

The saeta has attracted some ambitious historians who refer it to Edesa and Corinth, even to St Paul's approval of interjections from the faithful during divine service. At present it is assigned to cante jondo, whose aficionados differentiate between the saeta por siguiriya and por martinetes. As always, there are some who read a supranatural sense into a possible three-fold consummation of Syrian, synagogue and Arab almuédano chanting. There are parallels, also, so it has been said, in more modestly-conceived celebrations in rural centres as in an old ritual of Las purificadas enacted at Monroy and Santiago de Carbajo in Extremadura. There the faithful knock on the church door and on its being opened sing before the Virgin's statue and then set free two doves as messengers from God to Her; and while the birds flutter towards the light behind the image the primitive flute imitates their flight as the beat of the tamboril conveys that throbbing of the heart in a spiritual dialogue. There are Cofradías which still perform traditional mysteries dating from 1170. The saeta of Utrera is primitive also, though known as the saeta por siguiriyas and having probably shed some of its early customs. This region, it should be remembered, has from time immemorable moved in the Sevillan orbit.

A more generalised and consistent tradition than these is worth considering. In this same Extremaduran region, the venerable custom of Corpus Christi processions still opens with the statues of saints being brought out of the churches to be carried by the Cofradías; as they appear in the church portal the piper and drummer, having already paraded the streets performing the customary pasacalle in honour of the saint, strike up the alborada in greeting. San Sebastian has always had his special place among the martyrs and his own hymns—the alboradas—sung by members of the faithful, and like San Pablo, San Miguel and the rest, is treated musically with the type of musical offering played and sung for the Virgin also. One of the alboradas refers directly to the saetas, or arrows of his martyrdom:

> *Le amarraron a un troncu*
> *Y allí le dieron*
> *La muerte a saetazos*
> *Verdugos jueron.*

City Holy Week processions in which saetas are sung accompany the pasos with drums and bugles, and are thus instrumentally paralleled by the rural pipe and tabor.

The drumming of these pasacalles and alboradas also yields exceptional interest. In the pasacalles which escort a wedding-party to church there are rhythmic sequences which by their patterning designate the various members of the family; starting with a generalised—

for the company's entrance into church, the beating for the padrinos becomes more particularised:

When the novio is fetched, however, the rhythm picks up with greater accentuation and alternating patterns, as 4/8, 3/8; 4/8 3/8 3/8; 4/8 3/8 3/8; 4/8 3/8; 4/8 3/8 3/8; 4/8 3/8—a dotted crotchet here instead of quavers—3/8; 4/8 3/8; 4/8 3/8; 4/8 3/8; 4/8 2/8 3/8 2/8 3/8 finishing with three accented quavers and one more. The bride is escorted with alternations of 4/8 3/8; 4 times; half-way she is given a double 4/8 followed by 3/8 and then the 4/8 3/8 alternating again.

The bridegroom thus is given rhythmic patterns of sevens and tens, with a possible fourteen, or double seven, as a final flourish. The bride is given sevens, then possibly an eleven and back to the sevens. The interest of such examples lies in their comparisons with the rhythmic patterns given by Al-Farabī and Avicenna. Like their systems, these drum-beats are strongly accentuated.

But whence have descended the highly ornamented melodies played on the pipes over these drum-beats? Although as long ago as 1322 Valladolid authorities disapproved of Muslims taking part in the music of the Saints' Vigils, it is not surprising to find possible traces such as these rhythmic patterns in the pasacalle and alborada used in processions. Basically, the melodic patterns piped over them coincide with

Pasa-calle para cuando se va y se sale de misa.

Dicto: Celedonio Béjar, tamborilero de Casar de Palomero.

characteristics found in Mozarabic chants when Cardinal Cisneros organised the search of Mozarabic liturgy in those Toledan churches in which it had been permitted to continue. Although it has not yet been possible to compare *Cisneros Missal* of 1500 with its Visigothic forerunners, nevertheless, the solo chants exhibit characteristics similar to these instrumental pasacalles and alboradas as played in rural church processionals—Julian Calvo, for instance, calculates that the Rosarios in Murcia date back to the early 16th century. These characteristics include arabesques, short scale runs, gruppetti in threes, fours, fives and sixes repeated in varying juxtapositions, contrasting tessiture, diatonic tonality, rhythmic vitality and high pitch.

San Sebastian's martyrdom is enacted in alborás on 20th January each year in Piornal, of which he is Patron. The place of the martyr is taken by the *Jarrampla*, a man who has been saved from serious illness or accident by the saint's intervention. Donning a white costume adorned with galloon trimmings painted red, he goes to the church, where he

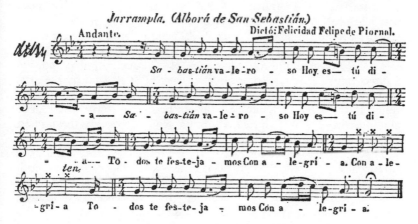

renews his devotion at mass before the priest while a chorus of young women sing the traditional hymns in praise of San Sebastian. Afterwards, the Jarrampla of the year goes about the streets, where amid great noise and excitement the children pelt him with all manner of objects. In the afternoon he goes before the saint's image playing the tamboril until the procession arrives at the church once more, where having deposited the saint before them they dance in his honour to the same music.

In Navaconcejo, however, where this ceremony is called the *Taraballo*, the year's martyr is stoned from windows and balconies with oranges and roast chestnuts; they do not dance to the saint here. The music of the Jarrampla's alborá lies in the five-note compass in a a b b form, the minor third alternating with the major in a a; the rhythm consists of two bars in 3/4 followed by one in 2/4. To this the Taraballo is related, though the melody here does not rise above a fourth till the last phrase which rises a semitone above the dominant to descend to the tonic.

These melodies are modal and simple in structure as befits the vocal technique of the devotees, but though different from the virtuoso instrumental pasacalles and alboradas, they also are evidently old. The verses in honour of St George, hereabouts, for example, refer to the persecution by Diocletian, and the martyrdom of St George in Capadocia and the vigil for San Roque and others evidently belong to a tradition whose age can scarcely be calculated, even if renovated.

San Sebastian's relics were preserved in Écija in the 7th century, according to an inscription, and in La Morera probably in Mozarabic times; in the second half of the 9th century there was a basilica dedicated to him in the serranía of Córdoba. His cult in Visigothic times was only local, apparently, but he is included in the *Antifonario emilianense* where his hymn 'Sollemne festum, plebs benigna promite' refers to the Arab oppression. Thus, his cult entered Spain in Visigothic years but was not generalised until the Mozarabic era. Though this may indicate a direct influence from Rome, it may have been effected by the 5th-century extension in Africa. Evidently, this activity was first concentrated in the south of Spain. His image became a constant favourite among painters and sculptors, inspiring what is possibly the highest expression of all native carving in Alonso Berruguete's *San Sebastián*.

Though several problems in Andalusian music have found solutions or partial resolutions, the central relationship of the variants of both groups in cante jondo and flamenco—grande and chico—remains obscure, while the puzzle of the naming of the various kinds of musical forms according to cities or provinces is still more enigmatic. In this connection some resemblances to Muslim customs suggest a means of clearing both basic puzzles of some obscurity if circumstantially. Farmer suggests that the name *nauba* given to a group of musicians probably originated from the circumstances that these musicians performed at certain specific periods of the day, or that they took turns in playing. In time the term nauba was transferred from performers to the performance, and the period-playing of the khalif's military band at the five hours of prayer being then called the nauba.

The *Kitāb al-aghānī*—or *Book of Songs* by Al-Isfahānī (d. 967)—describes the current type of vocal music as lighter—*qiṭ'a*—more in keeping with the taste of the period, but also describes the more serious pieces from the *qaṣā'id*. There were, then, two types of music in use, the lighter, *qiṭ'a*, and the graver, and this was the state of music when the components of musical performances known as the *nauba* combined a group whose music signified a set of organised variants within an office. From this developed a system whereby the khalif would bestow the honour of setting up a nauba upon his sub-chiefs and petty rulers; it became much sought after as a privilege and symbol denoting the delegation of authority to the local chieftain by the sultan. It has been observed that tradition refers to Córdoba as the original centre from which various kinds of the Andalusian musical style—grave, serious and

impressive—are derived, and it is a fact that those one-time petty kingdoms or states bore the names of those cities whose names now distinguish the varying forms still in use: Málaga, Granada, Seville, Ronda,
Murcia, and that this practice of associating newer types within the
family with places—such as Cartagena—has persisted. The word *nauba*
in northern Africa still signifies *vez o turno*, meaning 'in turn'. In 'La
nuba lo únicamente nuevo es la disposición orgánica del texto musical
. . .' Similarly, the difference between malagueñas, granadinas, sevillanas, rondeñas, murcianas, soleares—reputed as emanating from
Córdoba—lie in this organic disposition of their musical text, so that
each is recognised by the set rhythms and ordering of its tonal harmonies
'En este sentido los músicos del palacio se servían de esta voz para
indicar el turno de su actuación en la corte del soberano.' 'In this
sense the palace musicians made use of this type to indicate their turn
to perform in the sovereign's court.' Ribera says that the word *nuba*
passed from this generic meaning of the turn to signify the music that
each musician executed when his turn came to play, and that *nuba*
means the typical style of an unmistakable nature characteristic of
music peculiar to a region or to a composer. It was this localised singu-
larity to which Spanish Muslims gave this name. In such a context the
use of the term *qit'a* in association with the difference between a lighter
and more serious style—like the género chico and the género grande of
cante jondo—is worth notice. Taken together, it seems possible that
however much, or little, the musical content may have altered with the
passing of centuries, old concepts and old ways and patterns of thinking
persisted.

Of the *nubas* in Morocco, *La música hispano-musalmana en Marruecos*
(C.I.S. Madrid, 1950) gives a full account. The *nubas* of Tunis were
brought by emigrés from Valencia, those of Algiers from Córdoba, of
Fez from Seville, of Tetuan from Granada. 50,000 emigrated to the
Magrib after the reconquest of Seville in 1248; 200,000 to Granada and
Tunis from Valencia in 1238. From Seville, in 1248, under Ferdinand III,
there was another wave of departure. It was in the petty kingdoms of
the south that the medieval taifa kings became celebrated for the intensive musical culture displayed at their courts, vying with one another
to show their distinctive titles in such local centres of the art.

Possibly the jota might relate to this concept of the nauba as linked
to a subject city state within its regional province, since the jota Aragonesa is acknowledged as having its home in Aragon: in this aspect,
the differences of the jota murciana, jota valenciana and alicantina—
and even that jota of Almería of which Albéniz gives an unusual
version with turns in the minor—suggest the same regional concept at
work on musical organisation within this other group of Muslim

rulers. It will be remembered that Ribera analyses the jotas by schematising their structures, which obey a series of internal laws, as his investigations show. Historically, the *first* delegation of authority from Córdoba was given to the caliph's representative in Saragossa, capital of Aragon, which then became a kingdom, to be followed later by the taifa-kings of the south. It has already been pointed out that good Spanish judges are convinced that links between the jota and the Andalusian idiom exist beneath the exterior differentiations, as that, for instance, it suffices to prelude jota with an Andalusian minor mode of atmosphere for its southern ties to be noticeable; so affirmed Tomás Bretón.

A parallel system may be seen in the strictly organised corporation of poets whose office was to praise their ruler; the local songs extol their cities, as in Viva Sevilla! in the Sevillanas and Saragossa in the Jota aragonesa. Both systems originated in the East and were brought to the West. The palace poets' anthologies might be in four parts, one for the literati of Córdoba and the centre of the state; one for the same of Seville and the west; a third for those of Saragossa and the east; and one for distinguished visitors. Seville was next in importance to Córdoba for its reunions. Members of regional corporations would take a series of names to distinguish their group from another, as in Aleppo where members were named after birds, and a newcomer was given the name of 'nightingale'; this was in the 13th century. It will be remembered that Ziryab was given the name of 'blackbird' when he came to the west.[1] Since poets and musicians mingled at palace festivities, it is to be noted that among the year's celebrations, St John's fiesta was highly popular, as among Christians.

[1] Ziryab was named 'blackbird' because of his dark skin; this parallel suggests that the custom was widely used; and over a long period of time.

CHAPTER VII

'Spanish music with vistas towards Europe'

When Isaac Albéniz was born in Gerona on 29th May 1860, Spaniards had not yet heard a Beethoven symphony in its entirety, nor had Felipe Pedrell begun to publish those musical challenges which were to influence the course of Spanish music. As an infant Isaac possessed a rhythmic sensibility and acute perception of tone which precocious performances showed to be exceptional. On his first public appearance, aged four, dressed in Scottish costume in imitation of Prince Edward's sons at Balmoral, he played duets with his sister Clementina, aged seven, to which the delighted audience responded by pelting them with coloured celluloid balls which Isaac chased excitedly, forgetful of music, stage and applause. With a heavier ball Isaac broke a window in the Paris Conservatoire when he was six, postponing his entry and compelling his return to Spain, where he studied with Mendizábal and Ajero at the Madrid Conservatorio. Enthralled by immediate sensation he then developed a custom of surreptitiously setting off on infantile piano-playing tours through the provinces where he made his way by selling pages of improvisations on any given theme for three duros; these enabled him to buy seats for the local bull-fights of which he was also a precocious connoisseur. When threatened with prison in Cadiz if he did not return home, he hid in the steamboat *España* bound for Puerto Rico, expecting to pay his way by performing for the passengers, but instead found himself seized as a stowaway and landed at Buenos Aires, which happened to be the first port of call. Here he experienced his first sense of being at a loss, but only briefly, for he was soon heard playing in Argentine cafés. Such adventures led to travels further afield in Uruguay and Brazil and thence to the Caribbean and Cuba, where his father, a Customs official there, on reading in the newspaper that his son was about to give a concert, seized him afterwards, but observing that he not only had money in his pocket but had grown into a seasoned youth, decided to let him go his way, which was now to the United States. Here, Isaac's quicksilver genius was less appreciated and he took to music-hall tricks such as turning his back to the keyboard and playing in this position, with crossed hands into the bargain.

Behind these wanderings lay the almost mythical confrontation of an uninhibited innocence with a semi-anonymous treasure of sound which was his at a touch. The imprint on his ear of this uncontaminated music of the popular Hispanic tradition in the Old World and in Latin America, where stirrings of latitudinarian deviations were only then beginning to show, was instantaneous in effect and these precious first impressions never left him. He seemed to exist only to relive those sensations of pure delight communicated in the many pieces of his early maturity, and he lived only long enough to conjure them up once again and at last with that eternal farewell of evocation he called *Iberia*.

Returning to Europe, he found guidance through Count Morphy, editor of lutenists, and the Merry del Val family and, with a royal bursary secured by their intervention, was soon studying at the Brussels Conservatoire where he made the lifelong friendship of Arbós, then studying the violin; here they were both young enough still to wage endless strategic battles with toy soldiers in the intervals of practice. At eighteen he sought out Liszt in Budapest, and together they journeyed from Weimar to Rome. Liszt had travelled in Spain in 1844–1845, and knew that unexploited condition of Spanish popular musical life depicted with absolute fidelity in young Isaac's pages. The Hungarian, though moving in the Germanic circles of Schumann and Wagner, had managed to create his own climate by the side of theirs, and this Albéniz needed to do in Paris, where his own unique musical experience required a similar independence of expression if its opening success was to mature unspoilt. Dukas and Debussy, for instance, received Spanish newcomers with the pleasure of intelligent artists wholly masters of their own material and appreciative of these exotically original talents which, however, were still expressed in ingenuous manner. The Spaniards were sure of their instincts, but less trustful of organising their material as it merited. Albéniz, like Turina after him, chose to study at the Schola Cantorum where impressionism was to some extent deprecated and perhaps he found Debussy's manner at variance with his own clear-cut definition. Yet he was always Debussy's admirer, and handsomely paid his debt to French music by paying for the publication of Chausson's *Poème*. But for all the profusion of colour with which his *Iberia* is endowed, a colouring which was, after all, current already among his many Spanish painter friends, Albéniz here concentrated the resources of his last years on *La recherche du temps perdu*, and before he died was able to contemplate the full score of *Iberia* as *Le temps retrouvé*.

It was in Paris also that he wrote his stage works, *San Antonio de la Florida* and *Pepita Jiménez* which were successfully produced in Brussels at the Théâtre de la Monnaie in 1905; in these the casticismo of Barbieri's zarzuelas is profitably remembered, especially in *Pepita Jiménez*, the finer work of the two. As in earlier piano works, the malagueña here receives preferential treatment, as an interlude, and Córdoba is remembered, also with other native forms familiar in various of his suites. *San Antonio de la Florida*, a lighter piece, was praised in Madrid as successor to Bretón's *La Verbena de la Paloma* and later as precursor of Granados' *Goyescas*. It is most appropriately listened to as an extended tonadilla. *Pepita Jiménez* was staged in Barcelona, 1895, Prague, 1897 and at the Opéra Comique, Paris, 1923.

Compared to these, the English scores of *The Magic Opal*, *Henry Clifford* and *Merlin* scarcely belong to any consistent tradition. The first, produced in 1893, with text by Arthur Law, is a tale of brigands in modern Greece and was said to combine an accomplished melodic line with a genuine dramatic temperament in ensemble work. *Henry Clifford* and *Merlin* were written, not in London, like *The Magic Opal*, but in Paris where the first—an incipient Wagnerian treatment of a War of the Roses theme—would not be considered as an auspicious choice; nevertheless it won great success at Barcelona's Liceo in 1895, when the exuberant sonority of the orchestra was effective and the singers, though relegated to a secondary plane, were praised for being conceived in complete harmony with the whole creation. Albéniz here handled the orchestra as though it were an enormously sonorous pianoforte. *Merlin*'s scenes are placed on the steps of Old St Paul's and in the great hall of Tintagel, and afterwards against the evening light of a forest where King Arthur sleeps to a nocturnal theme which perhaps recalls Wagner's *Forest Murmurs*. Although the theme of Arthur and his knights is linked to a search for the Holy Grail and so to Montserrat in Spain, this scarcely gives licence for Viviana's dance in form like a polo, nor to her petenera, except as relief perhaps to Albéniz struggling with leit-motifs, for *Lohengrin* and *Parsifal* made a contribution to this opera, which was never produced in Albéniz' lifetime. However, it has been praised in Spain, by Mitjana, and was produced in Barcelona by that enterprising society, the Barcelona Fútbol Club Junior, in 1950.

Albéniz' reputation rests securely in the hands of those many pianists who find the Spain of earlier days in his *Chants d'Espagne*, *Danzas Españolas*, *Recuerdos de Viaje*, the two *Suites Espagnoles*, the *Oeuvres pour le piano*, *Piezas Características*, *España*, *Espagne-Souvenirs* and the apotheosis of his desire and pursuit of the whole in *Iberia*, which followed a growing sense of liberation in his orchestral pieces, *Rapsodia Catalonia*, *La Vega*, *Azulejos* and *Navarra*. The first set of Iberia (*Evocación*,

El puerto, El Corpus en Sevilla) appeared in 1906. The second and third, *Triana, Almería, Rondeña,* and *El Albaicín, El Polo* and *Lavapiés* in 1907 and 1908; *Málaga, Jerez, Eritaña,* in 1909. Within a few months Albéniz, who had been ill for some time, worsened and left Paris for Cambo, a melancholy place, but close to the Basque regions where he had many friends, and here he died. Debussy's *Iberia* came out in 1907, rather soon after the publication of Albéniz' first set in 1906.

A dual point of view not only deepens the emotional power of this final work but is inherent in its technique of combining, or comparing, one theme with another, the riches of personal self-identity with the artist. *Evocación* begins with a personal mood 'très doux et lointain' in which uncertainty in the minor key clouds the positive approach; a mingling of the Navarrese jota with an Andalusian fandanguillo suggests those two strains in Albéniz' blood which are not wholly resolved at the music's conclusion. The mood also recalls Cervantes' perplexity in having to compose a prologue for Don Quixote, also the late fruition of his genius. *El Puerto*'s swaying movement—the meneo— of water lapping about a boat recalls Isaac's embarkation as a boy in flight to the New World and its freer rhythmic currents. It contains some bold harmonies, and again two themes are entwined one with the other, a bulería and then a seguiríya gitana; the finale moving into the distance may illustrate the sailing from an Old World in search of the novelties waiting overseas. *Corpus Christi en Sevilla* is more than a Lisztian extravaganza of worldly exuberance and mysticism. Though it recalls Bizet's music and the march of military bands, it is the flattened drooping phrases of the saeta which express Andalusian religious instinct, being linked beyond the Arabic to that Byzantine ecstasy which Falla insisted was the origin of cante jondo. *Triana* affirms the major tonality of the seguidillas sevillanas in which this opulent city expresses its extrovert enjoyment of life; the contrast in a minor key is momentary; its march represents a bull-fight's opening ceremonial. *Almería* is musically the more curious piece. The tarantas are compared with the Almerían jota, and have the slower form of the old traditions, not that later tempo of the tarantas for which some link them to the gitano group. It is when the tarantas' pace quickens that Albéniz adds those *golpes*, or blows, associated with the miners' songs of this south-east region. The jota is affected here by the unusual downward minor inflection of its *giros*, or turns. Was he thinking of its text 'Ya me despido de ti' as taking his own farewell of the jota or associating it with the destitute life of miners and gypsies in the province? Falla in using this version for his Jota in the *Siete Canciones Españolas* gives it the customary major tonality. Albéniz' minor colour suggests an illustration of Bretón's theory that the jota belonged to Andalusia in origin. *Rondeña,*

182

VI. *Cantigas de Santa Maria*. Five groups of Musicians, redrawn from the Escorial MS for J. F. Riaño: *Early Spanish Music*

VII. Home of the Zarzuela

VIII. A Family Concert: sketch by Casanovas (late 18th Century)

alternating the rhythms of 6/8 and 3/4 in the style of the guajiras modulates from D major, passing to the sub-dominant and then to the dominant where it has a rendezvous with a malagueña, the voluptuous song of southern tradition whose cue to begin is always on the dominant chord, and thus illustrates that hybrid type of the malagueña rondeña. The languorous sentiment of the melody and the volatile irregularity of the guajira will obviously never form a lasting union and Albéniz in this amusing musical fantasy seems aware of the challenge behind the well-known coplas: 'Las malagueñas rondeñas, tú no sabes cantar, si no tienes sandunga y sal.' 'You will never be able to sing the malagueñas rondeñas unless you have grace and wit.'

El Albaicín leaves gaiety awhile to move inside the ritualist circle of cante gitano. The bulerías encroach on the copla's position of right here, but when it is heard, like the saeta in Corpus Christi it transports the listener to the eerie remoteness of Byzantine intonation; the circuit is made as in an incantation with a thin, keening tonelessness, punctured by jipios, or heartrent ejaculations, and accompanied by spare, colourless percussion according to ancient ways. After the second circuit, still hieratic but piercing in intensity, it is with great surprise that the ear recognises an A flat major conclusion as if it were a long-forgotten friend. El Polo, like the old caña, belongs to the cante grande class of cante gitano, and like the caña has its macho, or pair. It seems that Albéniz uses this idea of a type of song being matched by its pair in this culminating Suite Iberia, which, after all, is conceived with the aim of producing new fruits. Here the Polo's pair seems to be the Valse, which is treated to the luxurious abandon given by Ravel in his epitome, La Valse. Lavapiés commemorates Barbieri and, more closely, Bretón's La Verbena de la Paloma, in the scenes where the chulos and chulas dancing their vogueish Latin American numbers in Madrid still amuse, though now as a period piece of 1893. Albéniz had musical history on his side when he paired the Madrileño salon dances with the guajiras and habanera. Málaga does not again achieve that absolute purity of linear evocation of his earlier malagueñas. This Málaga is more involved with that Málaga cantaora as poets of the classical Arab-Andalusian world appraise the singer whose art is difficult though not austere. Concerned with her roulades and modulations to express amorous passion, she sings alone with the guitar tuned to that fountain set in an orange-grove where her admirers gather through Málaga's unceasing music-making nights. Jerez, in its oriental zambra, reaches back to the sonorous poetry of early Cordobese soleares and is reminiscent of Albéniz' own Córdoba of earlier times. Ravel extracted its linear essence—and the hints for its development—for the theme of that tour de force, his Bolero. Eritaña is the climax, an apotheosis of rhythm, the rhythm of extrovert sevillanas. In this way it may be paired with *Málaga*, epitome of melody, modulation and song. The dancers turn and return with a whirl of arms and flounces, but always towards the sunlight of the major tones, always anticipating that last fling on the upward rushing impetuosity of the perfect cadence on E flat. *Eritaña* is much more than a toccata in its uninterrupted sound; it is rhythm itself, the moto perpetuo of Spanish life. Those incessant seconds which strike some ears as superfluous as they bounce off Albéniz' chords here and in other pages of *Iberia*, are recorded in Ocón's *Polo*, in that example Falla was to use a little later.

Enrique Granados, born in Lérida in 1867, was a delicate child, cossetted at home in a circle of women. A lyrical impulse, natural rhapsodic talent and temperamental longing for vague horizons probably descended to him from his mother's stock; she was a Campiña and of Santander origin. Though it is sometimes said that a certain sensuality in his music—this should surely be translated as sensuousness—and rhythmic ebb and flow came from his Cuban father, it should be remembered that Cuba preserves many melodies of northern Spain testifying to its large Galician population, as also does Venezuela, so that his lyrical nature and flexible expressiveness are not necessarily lessened by links with Havana. Echoes of cadences from Montañesan songs are audible in his music. His last set of songs, *Canciones Amatorias*, contains in the opening to 'No lloréis ojuelos' an ornamented line identifiable with a harvest song which has travelled southwards and into Portugal. His fluctuating line elsewhere may be compared with the chromaticism and nostalgia of 'Ay Petruca' or 'La vi llorando'. 'Ya no va la niña' has an upward surging energy typical of Granados in buoyant mood, while the cadential line of 'Maria, si vas al prado' may be heard in piano works like the *Danzas españolas* when these are cast in northern forms. Like these songs, which, as Nemesio Otaño said, are comparable to the finest *lieder*, Granados' lyricism has an air of natural grace.

At sixteen he won first prize as pianist in a Barcelona academy as a pupil of J. B. Pujol, whose school produced the three best Catalan pianists of that generation, Malats, Vidiella and Granados. He played the Sonata in G minor by Schumann, a work likely to have encouraged his rhapsodic impulse and those energetic forces he could summon up at will. His studies with Pedrell in harmony at this time do not seem to have influenced him much, but Schumann certainly did. The apparent Schumannesque pianism of his smaller pieces, *Valses Poétiques*, *Bocetos*, *Escenas Románticas*, *Escenas Poéticas*, *Libro de Horas*, does not end with this miniature genre, as is widely supposed, nor is it exact to assume that the romantic traits of his work in general are to be shared vaguely among mixed influences from Chopin, the early Fauré, and even Weber and Gounod, as has been suggested. Schumann's guidance is paramount, threading his creative ideas with a consistency that shows in unexpected parallels. For instance, he wrote a guide to the art of pedalling, as did Schumann, and placed much emphasis on its use, as a modern piano rhapsodist must, training his own pupils in the minutiae of its proper application.

His two song cycles have themes remarkably like Schumann's. For the late *Canciones Amatorias* Granados searched the classic poets of Spain for personal love verses to set, so that they may be said in this respect to deserve the title of Spanish *Dichterliebe*. Their subtle grace, elaborately balanced, in the undulating rhythms of 'Mira que soy niña', 'Mañanica era', 'En vuestros verdes ojuelos', 'Descúbrase el pensamiento', the plaint of 'Llorad corazón, leading to that Montañesan reminiscence of melodic flow in 'No lloréis ojuelos' marked a deepening expression of sensibility which was immediately recognised when sung by María Barrientos, the Callas of her day. The earlier cycle, *Tonadillas*, also bears a Schumannesque imprint, since like *Frauenliebe und Leben* it moves from moods of light-hearted girlhood to a climax of passion and then to the shadows of desolation in which memory alone consoles. These cycles are so finely evocative of Spanish classical traditions that their Schumannesque conception has remained unobserved. Their impeccable line and discretion, their punteado counterpoint also, are disciplined by Granados' serious study of Domenico Scarlatti, of whose unpublished sonatas he edited no less than twenty-six; and it is to Scarlatti, as well as to Goya, that the *Tonadillas* are indebted for their castizo quality.

There is no doubt that his development of classical structures was retarded by the typhoid which prevented his entry to the Paris Conservatoire in 1887: nevertheless, his chamber music of the 1890s shows him struggling towards that aim expressed in statements like the following: 'In the 18th century our musical evolution suffered a parenthesis: it was like an accident which prevented us from continuing our march forward.' He goes on to attribute the renaissance of Spanish music in his time to Pedrell, 'from whom Albéniz, Falla and I received the nourishment of his precious counsel'. Granados in his own way followed that triple pact to write Spanish music 'con vistas a Europa'—not, however, with French guidance as in the case of Albéniz, Falla and Turina.

His chamber music series may be seen as studies towards this aim. The Piano Quintet of 1895 is in G minor, the key of Schumann's Sonata with which Granados won his first prize. This, and a Piano Trio in C major, were given at a Madrid concert. The Piano Quintet's first movement was encored as were the Scherzetto and Duetto of the Trio's four movements. The first work's opening movement was reported as being a mixture of a strong Schumannesque theme with a more timidly introduced Spanish second subject. Timidity passed with the succeeding movements which concluded in a presto molto in which appeared a Castilian rueda and some syncopation in style of a copla. Granados, Pablo Casals and Francés played in both works and were joined in the Quintet by Peralta and Cuenca. Between these works Granados performed some of his early piano pieces.

Supported by the experience gained in these efforts to give structural support to native themes, he emerged at the end of 1896 with the score of *María del Carmen* which was to bring him one of the greatest triumphs ever known in the Spanish theatre. First staged at the Comedia by its author Feliú y Codina on 14th February 1896, *María del Carmen* was promptly adapted as a libretto for Granados and after months of collaboration, which included a period of working together in the huertas of Murcia on Conde de Roche's estate, Granados let it be known on returning to Barcelona that he was anxious to hear the work in his orchestral score. Casals quickly responded by giving it a private audition in the old Principal theatre, though he had never conducted before. On 12th November 1898, its public début was made at the famous Circo Price in Madrid—recently closed—and Granados, now conducting, was recalled twelve times. Compared with Massenet, Bizet, Délibes, he reached that peak of national fame sought by so many; to win the hearts of the Spanish people in the theatre with a truly native theme is a triumph that nothing can erase. Significantly the press praised him for his union of 'la prosa y la música'. As Guerra y Alarcón wrote: 'It is more praiseworthy and patriotic to seek a subject for national opera in those works which reflect the popular customs of our regions than in those exotic types of foreign society and literature.' R. Blasco, in *La Correspondencia de España* asserted: 'In Granados we salute not only the hope, but the brilliant reality of our lyric art, which now has found in him one of the most robust pillars on which to raise the glorious edifice of Spanish opera . . . The religious majesty of the Auroras, the joyous thrumming of the Jota, the Parrandas, the Bolero, the Fandango and the virile coplas of the Murcian songs which palpitate in the verse are given brilliant local colour, inspired by the culminating phrases, and the principle motifs which describe a character, a passion, and in their union and totality give dramatic force to the situations.' The composer received a royal decoration for this work, in which he showed unusual skill and discretion in allowing the popular elements to express themselves naturally and then building up a more sustained musical force to hold those scenes of passion and emotion which emerged from the lives of the Murcian people. It may be supposed that he familiarised himself with Julian Calvo's *Alegrías y Tristezas de Murcia*, for evidence of this collection is to be heard in those numbers praised in the press.

After this achievement, his series of lyric scores, settings of the poet Apeles Mestres' classical aspirations, appear as digressions from the path of fame, for they occupied Granados from the opening of the century until the last years before his death. The mystery of this abrupt turning away from the native field in which he had proved his worth, to pursue the chimeras of *Gaziel, Petrarca, Picarol, Follet, Liliana,* has proved a baffling problem to Granados' friends and critics. On comparing their themes however with Schumann's works, again a consistent continuity of aim is revealed to widen Spanish musical style through the grafting of European experience such as Schumann had to offer. *Gaziel* is a Faustian theme; Schumann composed scenes from Goethe's *Faust* in his series for choirs and orchestra, with or without solo voices. *Picarol*, the clown in love with a noble lady, and *Follet*, a wandering poet similarly enamoured, recall works like Geibel's *Vom Pagen und der Konigstochter*; while *Liliana*, a version of Ondine and the sylph, belongs to the faery world of *Das Paradies und die Peri* of this author; all of these Schumann also set. *Petrarca*, a one-act poem and the enormous symphonic poem on *La Divina Commedia*, may derive from Lisztian ambitions to rouse the orchestra to larger-style works, but 1912 saw a Schumannesque miniature suite in *Elisenda* for piano and orchestra after yet another poem by Apeles Mestres, though Fauré's *Pelléas et Mélisande* has been suggested as an influence here. *Canto de las Estrellas* for piano, choirs and organ, nonetheless continues Schumann's choral concepts, and possibly the latter's *Requiem für Mignon* inflects *Nit del Mort* for orchestra since it is composed from Mestres' verse, as also is the rhapsodic *Elegia Eterna*, said to have been composed at a single sitting. His *Himno de los Muertos* (1897) precedes these.

In writing *Goyescas* Granados had in mind the 1898 celebrations in honour of Goya's birth a century and a half before, his own admiration for the painter being shown in a number of pen and ink sketches including the self-drawing as a majo. Musically, the *Goyescas* are linked to the *Tonadillas*, and their pianistic creation on Scarlatti's line of concentrated expressiveness might well be compared with Goya's etching. As evocations for the piano and in a series of episodes the *Goyescas* were first played in Barcelona in 1911 with the titles as follows: *Los requiebros, Coloquio en la reja, El fandango del candil, Quejas, o la maja y el ruiseñor, El amor y la muerte y Epilogo, Serenata del espectro*, to which was added *El Pelele*. Their connection with the *Tonadillas* was increased by the *Serenata del espectro*, for this, it may be noticed, echoes the idea of *El majo olvidado*, a song unjustifiably neglected since it is written for male voice and thus considered apart from the mezzo-soprano cycle.

In *Goyescas* the careful line-drawing of Scarlatti's period used in the *Tonadillas* is employed as a point of reference only, for Granados here draws on the piano's resources in the full spate of a virtuoso's plenitude, giving to Spanish music the ne plus ultra of romantic expression, and he uses throughout that traditional form of Spanish art, in modern times the most neglected, the *arabesque*. Each episode is treated according to this design and in the complex variation given to each one, Granados shows his mastery not only of the arabesque but of the *diferencia* of Spain. There is a clear allusion to Debussy's *Arabesques* in the first episode and moreover, Schumann—himself a master of this form as his Opus 18 *Arabesque* proves—is drawn into the working-out passages, not least in the *Pelele*. The interludes felicitously adopt various hints of procedure from both Scarlatti and Schumann as they draw the arabesques from their basic roots. Granados then directs their airy lightness to pervade the whole, unfolding like the tendrils of a vine, a vine of great antiquity but still capable of a profusion of shoots whose delicate tracery masks a constant search for a place in the sun. In the death scenes Granados' arabesques droop downward as he draws the revelation of this creative pattern to a close in an apotheosis from which the successors of Schumann, Chopin and Debussy may still find something to learn. In this last work, in his use of the Hispano-mauresque form, Granados made a unique contribution to the expressed aim of Albéniz, Falla and Turina to compose 'Spanish music with vistas towards Europe'.

This musical inspiration was necessarily overlaid in the operatic form with which he was persuaded to clothe his score and which he hurried through on the outbreak of war in 1914 and finally took to the New York Metropolitan theatre. Here, on 26th January 1916 he wrote to Amadeo Vives that at last he saw his dream realised, adding that he had many projects in mind. But on 15th March he and his wife were drowned when nearly home again, as the *Sussex*, crossing the English Channel, was torpedoed by a German submarine, a death both treacherous and ironic for a musician who so constantly sought to inject Teutonic imaginative craftsmanship into his country's art when, as he had long perceived, there was need of it. At the moment when he might have been saved—for the *Sussex*, though crippled, eventually made her way to port, Granados saw his wife, Amparo, mother of his six children, struggling in the water, and struck out to join her. *Amparo* means 'help, assistance'.

In a recent book, *Manuel de Falla* (Buenos Aires, 1961) Rodolfo Arizaga asks some basic questions about this composer and his music which have not yet been answered. Writing of Falla's asceticism and hermit-like existence, he asks: How is one to explain the fact that he has not left a single work of a religious nature? How can one explain the strange mystery of works like the *Noches* and *El Amor Brujo*, real enigmas in the life of one whose hidden character remains undeciphered? Does the artist echo the man in the purity of his actions and in his own manner release the violence of that intense temperament? Perhaps. Unable to give a direct answer Arizaga suggests that being Andalusian, Falla feels a love of death as a passionate reality of life and from that deduces the contrast between those pieces which betray sensuality and those expressing severe mysticism, adding that perhaps such pages are authentic promptings of his nature, to which, as an honest man who detested hypocrisy he refused to deny expression. Questions like these coming from Argentina, where Falla spent the last years of his life, require consideration in any discussion of his music today.

A hint of his own idealistic aim was published in *La Revue Musicale*, July, 1925, shortly before his *Concerto* was first performed. 'I believe in the beautiful utility of music from a social point of view. It is essential not to compose in an egoistic way, for oneself, but for others . . . Yes; to work for the public without making concessions: that is the problem. This, for me, is a constant preoccupation. It is necessary to be worthy of the ideal within oneself and to express it by pressing it forth as a substance to be extracted, sometimes with immense labour, with suffering . . . and then to hide the effort, as if it were a well balanced improvisation achieved with the simplest and safest means.' This confession of the pains he took to obscure his labours and their objective has remained an enigma after nearly half a century during which time his works have become familiar all over the western world.

Since Jaime Pahissa's *Vida y obra de Manuel de Falla* appeared in 1956, also in Buenos Aires, most critics repeat the fact that Falla first intended to take up a literary career, but Pahissa reveals that it was a conjunction of literary enthusiasm with musical inspiration that released his creative gift. It was when reading Rivas and then Mistral's poem, *Mireya*, that an intense desire to set them musically awoke in the boy's spirit. His critical writings, collected by Sopeña, illuminate this concern in several ways. While criticising Wagner's egoism and exaggerations, for instance, Falla praises his obedience to his texts, the fidelity of his songs and lyrical declamation to the expressive value of words and ideas; this he accounts among the major excellences of Wagner's art; rarely, Falla adds, did Wagner sacrifice the poem to the music and in this we have an example of probity worthy of notice, he concludes.

Defending Ravel's reputation, he insisted that shallow assessments of his nature were mistaken. 'Whoever has seen him in the supreme crises of life recognises the strength of his spirit: his honest, silent nature overflowed only at such times and in the creation of his music which was forged in that interior world which serves as refuge for the creative spirit against disturbing reality.' Such remarks throw light on Falla's own hermit-like existence and his ultimate refuge in the Argentine province of Córdoba.

Beginning with the youthful *Fantasia sobre 'Mireya' para quinteto*; violin, viola, violoncello, flute and piano, a number of Falla's works are settings of texts, libretti and poems. After *La Vida Breve*, 1904, with which the mature compositions open, he chose the texts himself,with very rare exceptions. The full list is as follows: *Cuatro piezas españolas* —Piano, 1907. *Trois Mélodies*—voice and piano, 1909. *Canciones españolas*—voice and piano, 1914. *El amor brujo*—Ballet in one act, 1915. *Noches en los jardines de España*—Symphonic impressions for piano and orchestra, 1916. *Fantasia bética*—Piano, 1918. *The Three-cornered Hat*—Ballet, 1919. *Homage to Debussy*—Guitar, 1919. *El retablo de Maese Pedro*—Obra para títeres, 1922. *Psyche*—voice with flute, harp, violin, viola y violoncello, 1924. *Concerto*—clave, flute, oboe, clarinet, violin y violoncello, 1926. *Soneto a Córdoba*—voice and harp, 1927. *Homages* for orchestra: Fanfare, a E. Fernández Arbós, 1933; A Claude Debussy, 1937; A Paul Dukas, 1936; Pedrelliana, 1938. *L'Atlántida*—Chorus and orchestra. *Balada de Mallorca*—Transcription for mixed choir of Chopin's F major Ballade (unpublished). *Música de Escena para Otelo de Shakespeare*, 1915 (lost). Music for *El Gran teatro del Mundo*, 1927.

Among these, two of his most important works, *Noches en los jardines de España* and *Concerto* appear to have no textual references. It will be suggested, however, that not only are they both composed to illustrate musically some famous poems but that each is linked with the other by this literary connection and that the use of a keyboard in each work is not incidental but bound to those poems to which their presence as leading instruments is due. Furthermore, that the subjects of these verses are of that kind to which Falla alludes most probably in that article published in *La Revue Musicale*, before the Concerto was first played, and that his explanation as to why the original inspiration is hidden relates to the import of the poet's message which he aims to offer to the audience in musical terms only as 'una bella utilidad de la música desde la punta de vista social'. Seen in relation to Falla's career as it developed they give a perspective of consistent integrity and of harmony between the man and his purpose. It is in keeping with his personal explanation in *La Revue Musicale* of 1925 that he should have hidden the traces of such poems, though two musicians, closely linked with him in Spain, interpreted verses by the same author, making their connections openly known in the usual way.

La Vida Breve, originally in one act, shows that after writing five unsuccessful zarzuelas Falla had almost entirely rid himself of those vocal clichés which had flawed most Spanish zarzuela-operas of the past century and it is thus his first mature work in line with those aims towards which he was striving. It was in the dance scene, however, that he found total freedom from the problems of textual fidelity according to high musical standards, and it was with his ballets, *El Amor Brujo* and *The Three-cornered Hat*, that he first decisively influenced his younger contemporaries and their immediate successors.

The *Cuatro Piezas Españolas* mark his meeting with Albéniz and that triple pact between them and Turina to write 'música española con vistas a Europa': in these piano pieces he was already abstracting qualities of character as the titles Aragonesa, Cubana, Montañesa, Andaluza and their Movimientos suggest, and as he wrote to Turina in verse when sending him this music 'no hay *de la musique ni plan ni même de iolis coins*'.

The *Trois Mélodies* search for another liberation, this time through setting the French language to music in Gautier's three poems, according to French modes of stylisation in vogue. Thus, the first, 'Les Colombes', is set with impressionistic resonance in the manner of Debussy; 'Chinoiserie' refers deferentially to Parisian competence in delineating oriental stylistics, while the third, 'Seguidille', gives his ironic approach open expression in mockery of French composers' *musique à l'espagnole*, the delicate point being reserved for the last line: Ola! Voilà! la véritable manola, the rhythm of which an average French musician would accentuate as if manola were equated with Voilà. Falla gives the correct Spanish accent for manóla, and that is all. It is humorous but courteously done.

The *Siete Canciones españolas* were arranged in response to a request from a Spanish singer making her début in Paris. His workmanship here adheres to the view expressed in an article for the *Revista de Música* in 1917: 'One must take one's inspiration directly from the people', and the vocal line and accentuation of popular singers is respected. Contrary to general belief some of the accompaniments are not his own but taken from collections of the 19th century; the opening page for 'El paño moruno' is taken directly from *Flores de España* by Hernández and the long introduction to the last, a polo, is taken from Ocón's authentically mid-19th-century setting. The *Seguidillas murcianas*, he explained to me, were set in order to free the song from the prison of past formality, adding, with a gesture towards the open window, 'like a bird from its cage'; probably the pattern in triplets is taken from Calvo's example. Possibly he had Inzenga's piano accompaniment in mind when saying this as it clamps this air and its rhythm within strict and rigid formulae. His ear for Byzantine survivals in Andalusian melody probably decided his choice of *Nana* with its echoes of both Dorian and Phrygian modes.

The ballet *El Amor Brujo* was written in 1915. Martínez Sierra suggested that he should write a song and dance number for Pastora Imperio and from this idea there emerged a one-act ballet about magic, exorcism and release. Pastora's mother was introduced to Falla and from her, it is said, he learned a great deal about gypsy lore and occult practices. Its first reception, in Madrid, 1915, though opening well because of the music, ended as a failure due to the distaste for its theme expressed by some writers and sections of the public, in spite of the fact that Falla's music emphasises the Christian triumph over magic by the ringing out of church bells at dawn with which the score concludes. It had two more performances when orchestrated as a suite, but again its reception was mixed. Falla then left to live in Granada and the suite languished until it was played abroad, and being revised then both textually and musically and at last presented as ballet in Paris, it has since that time always been successful. In view of Falla's last years of dedication to setting Verdaguer's *L'Atlántida*, which he never completed, it is curious that no reference seems to have been made to this theme of *El Amor Brujo* and the parallel event of the poet's life in which Verdaguer became over-involved in those psychopathic phenomena of 'possession' among his parishioners about which it was his duty as priest to take cognisance in case of extremity, but which unfortunately led him into error under the deceptions of two covetous women for whom his natural simplicity marked him out as an easy victim. His desire to alleviate and restore led to his taking a room where between the hours of eight and nine in the evening he would hold exorcistic exercises for those in need, afterwards writing down, as a psychologist might, the details of what had occurred. The glory of the first part of his life, crowned as Spain's great modern poet, was shattered by rumours that he had allowed parochial funds to be misused by these two women who furthered his exorcist enquiries for their own ends. Eventually, Verdaguer was restored to normality by the persistent efforts and many prayers of colleagues and friends and on his deathbed he appealed to Christ for help in his last verses expressing the desolation of a lacerated spirit; 'Cuan ne veja res . . .'

Falla's own sense of the supernatural was acute. Stravinsky says he was one of the most pious men he ever met but also one of the most superstitious. He was convinced that his life went in seven-year cycles and in Córdoba, Argentina, began to brood on what the cycle beginning with his 70th birthday might portend. He may have read portents in the deaths of Albéniz and Granados, for both died at the age of forty-nine.

The Three-cornered Hat, El Sombrero de tres picos, or *Tricorne*, in contrast, reveals Falla's delicate humour. Here he is again freed from close textual preoccupations and at ease in the 18th-century world of Domenico Scarlatti. The Spanish realistic tradition of Alarcón's story was suffused by reflections of the luminous delicacy of Goya's tapestry scenes, not excluding that example in the Prado of the grape-picking parallel to Alarcón's scene which is woven into his own score. In its pantomimic form—in which the ballet was first staged before Diaghilev was freed from war restrictions and able to mount it fully—it was staged in Madrid's Eslava theatre, April, 1917, within a few days of the Russian promoter's mounting of *The Good-humoured Ladies* in Rome, with Scarlatti's music. Falla's weaving of El Paño into the texture is witty, suggesting that underneath its light allusiveness by devious muted instrumental twists and turns, the moral of this tale is not forgotten.

He first thought of writing his three 'nocturnes', as he first called *Noches en los jardines de España*, for piano solo. Albéniz advised him to compose them on a larger scale, and eventually he did so. He occupied himself with this major work between 1909 and 1915 in Paris, and it was presented on 9th April 1916 in Madrid by the Orquesta Sinfónica conducted by Arbós. But he firmly resisted projects to turn the work into a ballet from Martínez Sierra and from Diaghilev who was persistent and only satisfied when Falla offered to prepare *The Three-cornered Hat* for him in its stead.

The poetic nature of *Las Noches* was immediately recognised. Writing in the *Imparcial*, M declared that these 'impressions' of Falla's are pages of sincerity in which with complete spontaneity the maestro portrays deep spiritual states, full of emotion and produced by the poetry, melancholy and perfumed, of Spanish gardens contemplated in the serene nights of Andalusia. Pahissa interprets the first movement as penetrating into the depths of man in his communal life: prayers, childhood songs, street-cries. Attempts to relate *Las Noches* to French poetry have not been successful, nor have parallels been suggested with any Spanish verse.

When Falla was rehearsing the work for a concert in Barcelona before the Civil War, he stopped the orchestra after a minute or two and suggested that it might be taken a little slower. 'Son nocturnos' he added. In the slight pause that followed, his sister, doña Maria del Carmen with whom I was sitting, leaned towards me and added, almost confidentially; 'del poeta americano' smiling and nodding in the direction of her brother and the orchestra. The music began again and no more was said. It was some time before I discovered that it was the three *Nocturnos* by the Nicaraguan poet Rubén Darío which were the key to this score.

Shortly before Falla left Spain to pursue his studies in Paris, Darío's *Cantos de Vida y Esperanza* were printed in Madrid, 1905, and with his other poems brought a new vitality to Spanish poetry, for this dynamic Nicaraguan, who spoke for the entire Latin American world, had assimilated the new rhythms and colour stirring in the verse of Baudelaire, Mallarmé and Verlaine, and adopted their novel dimensions into the Spanish tongue, altering the future course of Hispanic poets everywhere before Spanish traditionalists were aware of his experiments. He had in fact achieved for the language what Falla wanted to find for Spanish music. Both moved in the same artistic circles in Madrid and Paris for though Falla lived in withdrawn reserve, they had friends in common. Both left Paris in 1914 on the outbreak of war, Falla to settle again in Spain, Darío, already a sick man, to travel via Spain and New York, to die in Guatemala in February 1916. It was on 9th April that *Las Noches* were first performed in Madrid.

Darío's three *Nocturnos* are included in the series *Poema del Otoño* (Madrid, 1910) and linked to *Cantos de Vida y Esperanza* by verses in the latter entitled *Canción de Otoño en Primavera*. This is dedicated to Martínez Sierra, Falla's collaborator. *Las Noches* was to have been dedicated to Martínez Sierra, but owing to a coolness between them, the cause of which remains obscure, the work was dedicated to Ricardo Viñes, the pianist, who had been interested in the plan since its early stage. Most readers would agree with Octavio Paz, the Mexican philosopher-poet, that the *Nocturnos* are more deeply moving than any other verses by Darío in their meditations on death and the life he has lived, divided between great suffering and small daily cares, mingling pantheistic eroticism with painful memories of unfortunate mistakes and with a consciousness of ideas and feelings that have Christian roots, though lacking Christianity's eschatology. Oceanic metaphors surge in and out of Darío's lines and as Spanish poets see the conch shell as his emblem, filled with infinite rumour, so Octavio Paz singles out that comparison of his heart to a sponge saturated with the brine of the waves: in that climax reached by Falla which is often referred to as an echo of Debussy's *La Mer* it is possible that Darío's famous words are set. As Koechlin observed: 'Debussy sought nothing more than aspects of joyous light' and in comparing *La Mer* with his *Nocturnes*, adds: 'It is regrettable that the voice of human distress is never to be heard', which was a criticism made by many. Falla's *Nocturnos* communicate in Spanish tones a muffled anguish which is heard throughout the three movements.

Pahissa points out that foreign writers are mistaken in stating that the third Noche—*En los jardines de la Sierra de Córdoba*—describes a zambra gitana; that there is no description of a gypsy fiesta in the music nor any rhythm of the polo as has been imagined. To this may now be added that the *Sierra de Córdoba* is spiritually associated in Andalusian minds with its hermits' dwellings which seen from a distance appear to poets like the white doves of faith nestling in the green clarity of the serranía.

There is an analogy to the verse on the distant clavichord in the piano's subdued opening, which Falla when conducting would soften with a downward gesture of his hands and then extend his movements outward. There is the same focus on the distant (*lejano*) in Falla's title to the second Noche as in Darío's second Nocturno. Here the music evokes a distant fiesta as the poem describes the pain of distant recollections in a heart tired of far-away fiestas, too. The wakeful poet listens to the heart of the night punctuated by a distant carriage, a vague echo, the shutting of a door, a feeling that the echoes of the world's heart penetrate and move his own. Falla's second Noche closes with a similar evocation reminiscent of a throbbing beat. He said that the second theme of the second Noche is a consequence of the second clause of the first theme and that this new theme creates the theme of the third Noche. Darío's second poem repeats *lejanos recuerdos*—distant memories —the concept of distant music from the first poem. In Falla's third Noche there is the chiming of a clock in the night as in Darío's last line in the third poem. Both music and verse convey a muffled density of pain out of which rise sighs of grief at death's nearness, life's awareness of lost opportunities, presented with tremors of presentiment and the thud of suffocating heartbeats.

In the series *Poema del Otoño*, a poem, 'El Clavicordio de la Abuela' describes an 18th-century Marquesita playing ancient music, by Lully and Rameau, and singing verses of Ronsard on her grandmother's clavichord. She is so much in love with present life that she does not heed that the old instrument is not in tune with modern love and this season's roses. Darío exhorts us nonetheless to love and laugh for though life is short to enjoy April is what matters, and though the journey of men is accompanied by the bitter wind whose sinister name freezes, it is as well that the poor traveller should warm his spirit by the sound of love as played on the ancient keyboard. Evidence of Falla's thinking on the lines of this poem may be read in the *Revue Musicale*, February 1923, at the time he was composing the *Concerto para clavicembalo*, where he explains that when on the Alhambra's hill-side he asked Wanda Landowska to interpret ancient music for the company, in imagination he evoked the figure of Isabel of Parma in the 'Tocador de la Reina' playing the *Variaciones sobre el canto del Caballero* by Feliz Antonio de Cabezón. His own words show awareness of music's capacity to treat of time and space in dual unfolding of forms, which is Darío's theme in these verses. His words insist: We must not forget that music unfolds in time and space . . . nor that an internal relationship binds music's condition to them so that even when for instance the sounds depart from the tonal order of self-imposed limits it is only for a short excursion and with the intention of accentuating the tonal laws on returning to them again.

The *Concerto* was performed for the first time in Granada in 1926, and Fall insisted that it was neither neo-classical, nor an exercise in bi-tonality per se. It could be interpreted as an illustration, simultaneously in bi-tonal form and in the differentiation of time between the treble and bass parts, of these verses. Nor when compared to the poem is it an anachronism, as some have thought, that medieval Spain and the renaissance period are interpreted by an 18th-century instrument. The medieval Lento in this poetic context, may conjure up Darío's picture here of the medieval Inferno and Dies Irae, again comparing past and present, in the inferno of the Messina earthquake which suggested to men that hell is never far from human experience, and that its horrors are only to be mitigated by the misericordia of charity. When Falla himself performed this work, before beginning this second movement he bent his head, closed his eyes and folded his hands in sign of prayer. Thus, conceptually, the *Concerto*'s last movement may refer to further verses in Darío's *Poema del Otoño* which again exhort men to make the most of present loving and singing, since the birds' songs of springtime accompany us all the way if we listen to their voices and the poet's message they bring. Falla's spring song here is that 'De los álamos vengo madre', which admirably illustrates this poem.

The preceding work, *El retablo de Maese Pedro*, was received with a chorus of approval as the most appropriate theme for his gift. Choosing and arranging his own text from Cervantes' puppet-scene, Falla's care for the integrity of its words is impeccable. The choice of this scene, moreover, anticipates a weaving of times present and past into the structure as in the *Concerto* and it is possible now perhaps to find a key to Falla's pleasure when after the first performance of the *Concerto* a Belgian critic told Falla that the work had seemed to him like crystal, to which the composer answered that this remark satisfied him extraordinarily, for ever since *El retablo* he had tried to find instrumental combinations that would give the effect he sought of rich materials like crystal, metal, or other noble elements. In his poem *Un soneto a Cervantes* Darío writes: 'The christian and amorous knight speaks like a crystalline stream. Thus I admire and love him.'

Another correspondence with Rubén Darío may exist with his solo song, *Soneto a Córdoba*, for voice and harp.[1] Darío's well-known triple set of verses *Trébol* recount an exchange of courtesies between Góngora and Velázquez. The painter salutes Góngora with sonorous words, announcing the preluding hymn accompanied by lyres and chorus. As Pahissa observed, this song is set with noble declamation, sustained by robust, sonorous chords, rather in the style of the *Concerto*'s second movement. Here again, then, is a possible link with Darío's verse, with the parallel of harp to lyre, the noble declamation and a link once more with the *Concerto*. Falla's interest in the Spanish American poet sprung from early similarities in taste, for Darío also wrote on the theme of Mireya, which, in Mistral's verse setting, first stirred the composer as a boy to combine his two interests of literature and music. In sum, it seems possible that an uninterrupted period of years was dedicated to grafting Rubén Darío's own incorporation of the new French rhythms and resonances into the Spanish language, with music now to set beside the poet's art. It was indeed 'a beautiful utility', whose a-musical origin has been effaced in accordance with Falla's confessed principle and ideal purpose.

The *Fantasía Bética* (1919) appeared before the *Retablo* and *Concerto*. Since it is interwoven with allusions to Albéniz' themes and late technique, it might be interpreted as a homage to his memory on the tenth anniversary of his death in 1909. It was in the next year—1920—that Falla composed the *Homenaje a Debussy* in consequence of his death in 1918. It could have been the French tributes to Debussy which reminded the Spaniard of the tribute due to his own compatriot. This may be supported by his linking Albéniz and Debussy in the article he agreed to write for the *Revue Musicale*'s issue dedicated to Debussy's memory. Praising without stint the Frenchman's evocations of Spain, he makes a slight exception, couched with his customary exquisite courtesy, in the case of Debussy's *Iberia*, the thematic procedure of which differs from that taken in his other evocations and draws away from the true Spanish sentiment expressed elsewhere. Writing as he draws to a close of that carelessness with which Spanish composers had previously neglected those unusual harmonic phenomena inherent in the guitar and bandurria he observes that Claude Debussy had shown them how to make use of these. To this he adds: 'The consequences were immediate: it suffices to show this in the twelve admirable jewels that in the name of *Iberia* Isaac Albéniz bequeathed us.'

There are passages of native bitterness in the *Fantasía Bética*. Possibly it may be inferred that Falla made a quartet of requiems in memoriam of Albéniz, Debussy, Dukas and Pedrell. Neither of the two Spanish musicians found the consummation their genius deserved; the tide of

[1] On Góngora's poem.

change and opportunity in Spain had scarcely turned in their lifetimes. Vuillermoz wrote of Falla's tribute to Debussy that he brought a crown of carnations to the tombeau: the *Fantasía Bética* perhaps lays roses at the feet of Albéniz, for this music is not without thorns.

It was Falla's closest pupil, Ernesto Halffter (born 1905) who based his successful ballet *Sonatina* of 1927 on a poem by Rubén Darío of the same name. This was in the poet's lighter mood, a period piece of which he produced many examples in taking over the Old World's themes for New World observation. Halffter treats its incipient romanticism ironically, with dances for the shepherdess, gypsy and the young ladies, winding up with a vigorous finale. Pertaining thus to the arte de cámara, like those other works of this composer, such as *Sinfonietta* and the charming *Dos canciones* to texts by Rafael Alberti, *Sonatina* was staged in Paris, first at the Femina theatre and then at the Opéra Comique. Salvador Bacarisse, born 1898, pupil of Conrado del Campo, set a fine poem by Darío, *Heraldos*, for orchestra.

Falla's constant striving 'to work for the public without making concessions' but to be worthy of the ideal within his spirit and to express it, whatever the private effort involved, so that it appears finally as 'a well-balanced improvisation through the use of the simplest and surest of means' its conceptual source obscured and thus communicated to the world as a 'beautiful utility' from society's point of view, may now be appreciated as a constant factor in his creative life. It is a characteristic he shared with some of Spain's greatest artists—with Velázquez who set himself to the depicting of Francisco Sanches' philosophy expressed in *Quod nihil scitur* and then effaced his source, and with Goya, who similarly set himself, on becoming deaf, to communicate the salutary ideas of Feijóo, and again, like Falla, erased the conceptual approach so that art alone should express the whole experience.

In his music for Calderón's *El gran teatro del Mundo* commissioned for Salzburg by Max Reinhardt in 1927, Falla adhered to the dramatist's directions and to musical usage of the period, drawing on Pedrell's *Cancionero* for examples of the Cantiga, Berce and a Montañesan air, this last adapted to the scene of Death's announcement to Beauty of her fate; this association suggests that Falla—very properly—connected Montañesan songs with that feminine character which their lyricism of melody and verses often convey. His example of *Tantum ergo* is a free adaptation of Victoria's plainsong of Spanish origin in style, from Cantus II. Calderón directs here: 'Tocan chirimías cantando el Tantum ergo muchas veces', and Falla employs oboe, 3 clarinets, bassoon, 3 French horns, 3 trumpets, trombones, tuba and kettledrums. Though some might think them inappropriate for use in church drama, drums have been allowed to assist in various church events down to present times, as readers of these pages may have noticed. The theme phrase of the auto sacramental, 'Obrar bien que Dios es Dios', is sung five times, and derives from the Dresden Amen, on which the Prólogo, later to be known as *Fanfarre*, is also drawn. The solo singing is accompanied by modern guitar. This work was first performed in Spain for Cuenca's Holy Week, 1962, and at the Escorial in 1963.

It was about the time (1934) that he came to Barcelona to conduct the concert of his music that Falla's nervous tension began to appear, though noticeable only to his close associates at first. Doña Maria del Carmen believed that it was the shock of hearing gunmen sniping from the roofs of Granada's churches which precipitated his conviction that grave tragedy was about to fall upon Spain. In Barcelona, bombings at night were becoming more frequent and one morning there were unmistakeable signs that lorries had been throwing out heaps of sand in the streets to mop up the evidence of violence executed a few hours before.

Before Manuel de Falla and his sister left, she told me that they had visited many Catalan churches where his anguish at the growing lawlessness of unchecked evil was expressed by the manner in which he flung himself down before the crucifixes they sought. His conducting of this concert of his works which included the *Nights in the Gardens of Spain* is believed to have been his last public appearance in Spain.

Joaquín Turina (born Seville, 1882) was the son of a painter of Italian descent. His musical interest was first roused by an accordeon given to him by a family servant, his first known public appearance being as accompanist on this instrument to the girls' choir at the school he attended—the Santo Angel establishment described by Palacio Valdés in *La Hermana San Sulpicio*. Studying the piano, and very soon taking classes in harmony with the cathedral choir-master, he entered the orbit of the long-surviving baroque tradition as practised by Hilarión Eslava in his earlier years at Seville as may be seen in the score of that *Miserere*, which was regularly performed in Holy Week until recently put aside by Cardinal Segura as no longer suited to modern service.

Turina's early work. *Las coplas de la Pasión*, for chorus and orchestra, may thus be considered as a last expression of this flamboyant and dramatic Sevillan school. It, too, has been played annually in Seville, on 4th January. In his teens he practised his skill by arranging operatic scores for a small orchestra he organised locally, the performances of which were much enjoyed.

Urged by a friend to try his fortune in Madrid, for he was a modest youth, he took a score of his own to the capital and, although this was unaccepted, his foray into the Teatro Real brought him the advisers he needed and a friendship with Falla which lasted their lives. Here for the first time he heard symphonic scores played by full orchestras and foreign works which were almost as novel to Madrid audiences as they were to him. Of national music he heard Chapí's chamber scores, the castizo light operas of Barbieri and Bretón's *La Verbena de la Paloma*, but these did not offer foundations on which to build a style of his own. Like Falla, he worked at the piano with Tragó, perfecting his technique and range and then in May had the honour of writing music for the Quintero brothers' sainete, *Fea y con gracia*. Considering the popularity and gracia of the Quintero successes which established their Andalusian comedies as classics in their genre, this was proof of Spanish confidence in the twenty-three year old Joaquín Turina's future.

By the autumn of 1905 he was in Paris. But whereas Falla entered Debussy's circle, Turina took that narrow road of St Jacques to the Schola Cantorum, and here he found the solid training which he knew he lacked. After appearing as pianist in Brahms' and Franck's quintets he was ready by 29th April 1907 to present the first fruits of d'Indy's advice, thanks primarily to Albéniz' introduction, with *Poema de las estaciones*. By October his piano quintet was also ready for public hearing in the Salle d'Automne in a concert which included three of Albéniz' *Iberia* pieces. A meeting afterwards with Albéniz, and Falla also in the audience, resulted in a triple pact to write 'música española con vistas a Europa'. Turina's *Sonata española* for violin and piano, like the quintet, still steered an uncertain course between the Schola and Spanish-coloured *costumbrismo*, but his facility was obvious and his *Suite Sevillana* was promptly published by Eschig. Acclaimed on a brief visit to Seville, he returned to Paris to find his works now placed on concert programmes beside those of Debussy, Ravel, d'Indy and Schmitt. Like the sevillanas, he provided extrovert, affable relaxation and was always a popular figure as performer and conductor. There was serious endeavour behind the kindly smile, nonetheless, and on presenting *La Sonata romántica* for piano on 15th October 1909 in memory of Albéniz, he explained that here he sought to unite the vertical harmony of the Debussyites—the *Suite Sevillana* contained series of fifths, the counterpoint and form of d'Indy—with the feelings of the Spanish race. In 1913 he left the Schola with d'Indy's cordial endorsement of his assiduous attendance at classes, and Arbós welcomed him back to Spain with the first performance of *La Procesión del Rocío* by the Madrid Symphony Orchestra on 30th March. The programme—which included Beethoven's second symphony, Borodin's second, Bach's *Choral Variations*, Strauss' *Tod und Verklärung* and the *Ride of the Walküre*—gave the scintillating and generous Arbós ample scope to display the brilliance of his players; but it was Turina's work—his first fully orchestral composition—that had to be repeated. On 24th May Turina conducted it in the Salle Gaveau and the next season Arbós and his orchestra were summoned to give a Spanish programme in the Champs Elysées, under the patronage of Alfonso XIII. Pablo Casals played the Saint-Saens concerto, but otherwise the music was by Pérez Casas—conductor of the Madrid Philharmonic Orchestra—Conrado del Campo, Albéniz' *El puerto* and *Catalonia* orchestrated by Arbós, and *La Procesión del Rocío*.

Debussy wrote benignly: '*La Procesión del Rocío* is set out as a beautiful fresco. The frank contrasts of light and shade render listening easy in spite of the work's dimensions. Like Albéniz, J. Turina is strongly influenced by popular music and still hesitates in his development, finding it useful to make use of illustrious contemporary sources. One hopes J. Turina will pass them by and listen to more familiar voices.'

There were other 'contrasts' in Turina's style which were to accompany him for the rest of his life, but he took Debussy's advice to listen to more familiar voices as he settled in Seville when the 1914 war broke out, staying there permanently, marrying and entering on a typical Seville family life, which his *Recuerdos de mi rincón, Rueda de niños* probably depict. He conducted his setting of Martínez Sierra's *Navidad* at the Eslava theatre and knew that fame which in Spain is reserved for a command of the stage. He conducted Falla's *El Corregidor y la Molinera*, later to become famous as *The Three-cornered Hat* and then wrote music for *La adúltera penitente* by Moreto, the 17th-century dramatist, like himself of Italian descent, who achieved original situations and harmonious atmosphere with the use of musical themes woven into his drama.

In 1918 Diaghilev and his hordes penetrated Spain, and it is said that Turina's role was to make peace when misunderstandings arose. In 1920 Arbós conducted his *Sinfonía Sevillana* on 11th September with enormous success; in this work the grasp of those opposites which he had struggled to reconcile seemed within his reach; this work was broadcast in London in 1925. He essayed the theatre again with *Jardín de Oriente*, again to Martínez Sierra's words. The next year was marked by the success of his second *Trio* and the *Canto a Sevilla*. Casals' orchestra played the *Danzas fantásticas* and *Ritmos*, a choreographic fantasy; Havana received him with open arms and here he gave a serious account of his method of composing, lectured on musical history and contemporary Spanish music. But he did not teach at the Conservatorio Nacional until the days of the Republic. The Civil War surprised him in Madrid and here, for once, the concert appearance of this genial, greatly-liked man was hissed and booed. On the war's end, however, his *Fandanguillo*, played by Regino Sainz de la Maza, brought forth the old acclamations and the old rapport was renewed.

Of his chamber music, it is the first piano quartet that shows him searching to contribute to that triple pact, 'música española con vistas a Europa', here with the theme of the guitar strings treated in European manner; his use of 5/4 rhythm, of a zortzico, however, was even then thought outdated. *La Escena Andaluza*, a piano quartet with solo viola shows a maturing of aim; nonetheless Turina does not give up the expedient of ingenious variations on native rhythms such as muñeira, schottis, zortzico, jota and soleares, though the technical assimilation is noteworthy. Unlike Chapí, whose works had been inadequate to offer guidance, Turina acquired the necessary skills. Dramatic works on a large scale extended his powers overmuch; it was a pity he did not attempt more work in the Quintero vein, for he was a shrewd painter of Seville and Sanlúcar de Barrameda with a painter's knack of concentrated detail as in *El poema de una sanluqueña* and a love of portraiture, as in the *Mujeres españolas* where he is alone with his piano like an artist with his palette and canvas, and *La oración del torero*. In this piece for cuarteto de laúdes, first published for strings, and later orchestrated, the worn system of genre-painting is idealised, treated as a spiritual meditation. Beside these pictorially conceived compositions, there are many lesser works which show a similar visual conception; *Contes d'Espagne, ou Histoires en 7 tableaux* and its second series; *Jardins d' Andalousie*; *Verbena Madrileña*; *Silhouettes*; the *Souvenirs de l'ancienne Espagne* contain portraits of Don Juan and Carmen; *Feria de Abril*; *Noche de Sevilla* and *El Barrio de Santa Cruz*; *La Reja*. *Recuerdos de mi rincón* contains painter's sketches—el escultor, Amparo, la romántica gallega, el 'melitar melitar'; *Album de viaje* reveals *Retrato; Casino de Algeciras, Gibraltar, Paseo nocturno, Fiesta mora en Tánger*; there is the *Sonata pintoresca* of Sanlúcar de Barrameda; *En la torre del castillo*; *Siluetas de la Calzada*; *La playa*; *Los pescadores en Bajo de Guía*. The *Sinfonía Sevillana* is a *Panorama*. *Aparición del angel gigantesco* is one of several works probably derived from Goya. Perhaps the impasto of his work is most thickly applied in his *Rapsodia sinfónica* for piano and orchestra.

Conrado del Campo (1879–1953) counterweighs Andalusian-French predominance with Castilian emphasis on 19th-century German tradition in numerous string quartets and Straussian orchestral effects, in larger scores. From an orchestral string leader he developed into a vigorous, capable conductor and though his writing is at times over-charged and opaque his treatment of romantic and neo-classical themes, as in *Romeo and Juliet*, *Dante*, combined with a knowledgeable use of local colour as in *El Avapiés*, a three act opera, *Symphonie*

Madrilène with choirs, and also *El Final de D. Alvaro* have earned for him a substantial reputation. His settings of Becquer's *Caprices Romantiques* show that *Sturm und Drang* of which he became the leading Spanish exponent; and with distinguished competence, especially in quartet-writing, he has made a lasting contribution to Spanish musical evolution. The fruits of his labours have appeared in the achievements of his students, a school of composers whose influence affects several of Madrid's most valuable modern musicians.

Ernest Halffter (born 1905 in Madrid) very early showed talent as a student of the pianist Federico Ember and, after impressing critics with a quartet in 1923, became Falla's closest disciple, winning a national prize in 1925 with his *Sinfonietta*. In the ballet *Sonatina* (1928) a neo-Scarlattian clarity is also achieved and his settings of two poems of Rafael Alberti, *La corza blanca* and *La niña que se va al mar* were accepted as classics at first hearing. First among Falla's successors to follow his lead, Halffter led the rest in the modern ballet, in *Sonatina*, *Dulcinea* (1944) and *El cojo enamorado* (1951); the *Fantasía galaica* (1955) is regularly produced by world touring companies. It was because of his intimate identification with Falla's concepts and disciplined orchestral sense that he was chosen to reconstruct the fragments of *L'Atlántida*. Perhaps his *Muerte de Carmen* was prompted by Falla's other unrealised wish to express his admiration of Bizet's *Carmen* in such an aspect of the opera. Halffter's *Rapsodia Portuguesa*, resulting from many years' residence in Portugal, is an attractive evocation of its warm-hearted people and its orchestral colouring is in exuberant contrast to his neo-classical equilibrium of earlier days.

Rodolfo Halffter, born 1900, his brother, also one of Falla's chosen pupils, used to appear on the Madrid concert platform with him in the early thirties, also conducting and performing his own works. His ballet *Don Lindo de Almería*, arranged for orchestra, and his *Sonatas de El Escorial* for piano were repeatedly in demand. He works now in Mexico, where his ballet *Elena la traicionera* (1945), *Epitafios*, a choral work a capella (1954), his *Sonata No. 2* for piano (1951) and his violin concerto (1942) witness to the evolution of this finely integrated composer.

It was with a sonata for violin and piano in 1915 that Oscar Esplá (b. 1886) appeared as a composer in Madrid after study with Reger in Germany and Saint-Saens in Paris. A complex work in cyclic form, romantically treated, it is differentiated from others of this kind by its melodies taken from Alicantine song, not picturesquely enlarged but schematised on the scale he adapted from his province's popular music, this containing the minor 2nd, a diminished 4th and 5th and 6th and 7th minor. These were to be constant traits in his writing, as in the piano series, *Evocaciones, Ronda levantina* and *Cantos de vendimia* (1917), though it was with *Don Quijote velando las armas* (1925), *El contrabandista, La pájara pinta* and the poema escénico *Nochebuena del diablo* (1923) that his reputation was consolidated, leading to the abstract quality of *Sonata del Sur*. Of all these, it has been *Don Quijote velando las armas* which has made the most permanent mark, having first been played as a chamber suite under E. Halffter's direction and then, in amplified form, carried to decisive success by the power of Arbós and the Sinfónica of Madrid, 1927. His search for complexity and profusion of rich effects is contrary to Falla's school and it is the ballet, *El Contrabandista* (Paris, 1928), which relieves him from some of those problems inherent in the insistent deployment of the Alicantine scale, the ambiguity and episodic nature of which is less remarkable in minor forms. The ballet form gave him more room for intuition, less for schematisation. His *Canciones playeras* display these qualities without excess and *Pregón* and *El pescador sin dinero* enlighten and reward both singer and pianist. His efforts to create a regional contribution able to enter the national stream on equal terms ensures his place in Spanish musical history and has been sympathetically followed by others who have a similar purpose.

There is much attractive music in the south-east regions to be utilised in one way or another as Pérez Casas' *Suite Murciana* eloquently proves with a rhythmic energy and discriminating orchestration such as was to be expected from this classically distinguished conductor.

Jesús Guridi, born in the same year as Esplá, is also seriously conceptual though less cerebral. A pupil of d'Indy, he concentrated on Basque themes and by use of characteristic elements in its popular song raised the zarzuela to new heights with *Mirentxu* (1910); *Amaya* (1920); *El Caserui* (1921); *La meiga* (1928). A later period brought the *Diez melodías vascas* (1941); the *Cuarteto* (1946) and among other symphonic essays, the *Sinfonía Pirenaica* (1945). Emerging from local forms in his last years he produced an *Homenaje a Walt Disney* and here a tone of modernity is achieved by irony, or objectivity, replacing remnants of 19th-century romanticism. Guridi is not the only Spanish artist to have used this means of escape from tradition.

José María Usandizaga, also of the Schola Cantorum, died in 1912 at the age of 27; like Arriaga he flashed like a shooting-star across the Basque sky on a course so unerring that it seemed directed by unknown laws. *Mendi-Mendiyan, Las Golondrinas* and *La Llama* are his means of expressing dramatic passion in a natural verismo, entirely centred in its place and period.

Basque priests have long made contributions to Spanish musical history. Padre José Antonio of San Sebastian collected popular melodies together with the flora and fauna with whom they share the communion of nature. Padre Donastia, a prolific composer, took counsel in Paris in 1920 with Ravel and Roussel, producing *Les trois miracles de Sainte Cécilie, Le Noel de Greccio, La vie profonde de St François d'Assise,* and in 1937 his *Poema de la Pasión* for double choir, soloists and horn. In 1945 appeared *Canciones sefardíes, Tiento y Canción, Infantiles a cuatro manos* and *Misa de Requiem* for choir, organ and orchestra. Relaxation from these achievements may be heard in the 'goliardesca' *Venerabilis barba capucinorum* (1949) for four-part choir. *Infantiles* for four hands is not so infantile in purpose as may be supposed, for it is designed, among other things, to inculcate in a child curiosity about advanced musical explorations. In the period of his studies outside local horizons he composed a *Cuarteto para ondas Martenot,* presumably the first Spanish work for electronic instruments. He had the satisfaction of putting the last touches to his *Misa de Requiem* before he died in 1956.

Padre Nemesio Otaño (1888–1956) also actively collected melodic specimens of the Basque country and La Montaña, setting examples 'in the form of lied' for, as he said, the melodies here are as fine as any to be found in Europe. Basque musicians show a passion equal to Unamuno's and Pio Baroja's in the causes they espouse.

Catalans, like Basques, are preoccupied with the preservation of language and this gives importance to traditional forms concerned with musical texts. The Orfeo Catalá, like the great Basque choirs, is deeply rooted in popular sentiment which in this province is poured out with lyrical rather than dramatic force. The works of Antonio Nicolau (1858–1933) and Luis Millet (1867–1941) touch chords beyond normal soundings in the former's *La mort de l'escolà,* to Verdaguer's verse, *La Mare de Deu, El noi de la mare* and *Captant.* Luis Millet, pupil of Pedrell, co-founder with Amadeo Vives of the Orfeo, provides lyrical pages in *Muntanyas regalades*—an air whose original melody gave keen pleasure to Merimée—and the *Canigó,* recalling the more grandiose schemes of Pedrell's *Pirineos.* Intimate in feeling also are the evocations of Lamote de Grignon, whose oratorio *La Nit de Nadal* stirs up memories of the Christmas villancico celebrated with intensive musical preparation in Catalan churches in a glow of myriad candles.

Enrique Morera, pupil of Albéniz and Pedrell, contributed to this sense of renascence, not so much with his operas and chamber works, as with lively arrangements of folk songs and in particular with the sardana. Acclamation greeted his appearance in a Barcelona theatre one Sunday when folk-singing groups and sardana dancers had assembled from Tarragona, Valencia, Mallorca, and even Alicante for a celebration to which significance was given by the sight of numerous civil guards and police. When Morera's sardana, *La Santa Espina*—the performance of which had been forbidden owing to the autonomous undertones associated with it—was begun to open the day, it could not be heard in the uproar of cheering the composer and had to be started fourteen times before it could be heard in relative calm. Such was the background from which emerged some of Catalonia's most original composers of this century.

This was the largest musical assembly of a popular kind that I ever attended as a student in Spain. Pink and green announcements of a sardana festival, in which groups from Tarragona, Valencia and Alicante had been invited to take part together with their own coblas of instrumentalists, had been lying on park benches and café seats some days before. I was surprised to find the theatre crowded and the aisles fairly well lined with police and civil guards. The audience and the guards, however, were dressed in Sunday clothes; the latter wore very white gloves as well as their customary accoutrements and there was a brisk air of festive expectancy over all as the huge stage gradually filled with many groups of cobla musicians gathered about their local banners. It became clear that it was an occasion organised to demonstrate the solidarity of Catalan-speaking citizens and workers and this accounted for the roars of applause which greeted groups from a distance, since this signified that Catalan was used far beyond the boundaries of Catalonia itself. There were a number of artists, writers and musicians sitting in the pit and stalls as well as friends of Morera and other intellectuals in the lower boxes. There were no signs of political ferment, so far as an inexperienced young music student could see, and though I stayed till the end—it was several hours before all the various groups had finished their contributions—it seemed wholly given over to a cultural expression of a people who were convinced of their right to sing in their own language, just as the Basques did.

Nor did I hear anything resembling revolutionary threats in any musical assemblies organised along the northern coasts that summer. These were small, relatively, consisting of miners' choral groups, fisher folk and dock workers, mostly advertised locally in the same way on coloured hand-bills, either for Saturday night or Sunday late noon. I marvelled at the quality of Basque and Asturian male voices and admired the serious depths of their musical feeling, finding nothing but pure pleasure in these expressions of regional melodies. The revolutionary note only became audible during the first year or two of republican rule. In Andalusian towns, on the coast, though the methods of advertisement had not changed, the familiar green and pink hand-bills were still scattered on benches and cafés—perhaps in greater numbers, and left lying around the cheaper cafés longer than before—and now it was evident that the words were beginning to have more significance than the music. In Málaga, for instance, printed sheets were placed on the seats giving the texts of several songs which were sung to popular paso-doble airs used in the bull-ring accompanied by a small band. Sitting in the front of the small meeting-hall behind the docks, I was surprised when one of these singers stepped forward and, as it seemed, impro-vised a verse which plainly announced what they would do to the English when Spain had recovered Gibraltar. This caused a little amused embarrassment in my neighbourhood and two embarrassed civil guards approached me unobtrusively and suggested I should be well advised to leave. They kindly accompanied me not only out of the hall, but to the end of the side street and into the main road. Two or three weeks later churches nearby were set on fire. This song was in traditional form, estribillo, strophe, estribillo, though the refrain's words 'when we have broken the chains that bind us' recalled Rousseau's incitement to revolution.

Jaime Pahissa (b. Barcelona, 1880) was a prominent figure during the Republic, strongly identified with intertonal premises, or systems of 'pure dissonance'. These principles he took with him to America, where, however, in spite of his uncompromising theories he also published works reminiscent of his Catalan origin as in *Navidad* (Villancico); *Escenas Catalanas*; *Piezas Espirituales* and popular Catalan songs, in-cluding some with Catalan words; a *Nocturno* for violoncello and piano; a ballet, *Bodas en la Montaña*; *Marianela*, a three-act opera on a text by the Quintero brothers; two symphonies for strings; *Suite Intertonal*; these are some of his larger compositions. His *Vida y Obra de Manuel de Falla* (Buenos Aires) gives interesting glimpses of Falla in his retreat to the Argentine Córdoba, and related some of his own experiences and works in parallel to the maestro's, listing his own music on pages opposite to Falla's.

The generous talents of Eduardo Toldrá, a genuinely Catalan lyrical composer, produced many works including the one-act *El Giravolt de Maig*, 1933; *Seis Sonatas* for violin; the orchestral *Sardana*, *Vistas al mar*; *La maledicció del Comte l'Arnau* and many lovely songs whose well-chosen verse are fluently set with a natural sense of Catalan grace. His *Siete canciones populares catalanas* for mixed choir (1959) show what he might have achieved in later years had not the full responsi-bility of directing Catalan orchestral life fallen upon him, including the opera seasons at the Liceo, after earlier tasks as conductor of the Banda Municipal, the founding of the Cuarteto Renacimiento and much violin teaching. He was continually in demand for Spanish music festivals, at Granada, Santander, S'Agaró and latterly at Edinburgh,

Brussels and Besançon. His selfless dedication to these musical causes was exceptional, and has left both public taste and musical organisations immeasurably improved.

Federico Mompou's piano music alludes discreetly to the Gallic vein in Catalan taste. Intimate, restrained, he reveals luminous moments, exquisitely pointed against the background of his chosen gamme gris. *Suburbis* (1917); *Charmes* (1921); 10 *Preludios* (1927–1944); *Canciones y danzas* (1921–1953); *Impressions intimes* (1911–1914); *Trois Variations* and *Dialogues*; *Fêtes lointaines*—all show the continuous use of a cultivated simplicity drawing unobtrusively on the Catalan idiom. *Preludio gallego* (1960) reflects the not dissimilar colouring of Galician landscape and his versions of San Juan de la Cruz' *La música callada* and *Cantar del alma* withdraw to an extreme of meditative reserve. His songs with Catalan texts such as *L'hora grisa* and *Damunt de ti* are among the finest in Spain. By limiting the scope of his expression Mompou reverses the traditional poetic evocation of emotion recollected in tranquillity, offering instead his own experience of tranquillity remembered in musical emotivity.

Manuel Blancafort injected notes of mockery into the Catalan milieu with *Parc d'atraccions*; *La polka de l'equilibrista*'; *L'Orgue del Carrousel* and *American Souvenir* in the years 1918–1927. But despite his sympathy for Charles Chaplin as anti-hero, Blancafort attempted more serious works in *Quartet No. 1* (1948); *Concierto Ibérico* for piano and orchestra; *Preludio, aria y giga* (1944); *Cuarteto de Pedralbes* (1948) and *Sinfonía* (1950).

Juan Manén's expressive lyricism is chiefly given to many violin works with and without orchestra, and his *Concerto for Oboe* and *Interlude* from his stage work *Heros*, are frequently played also. His violin treatise remains a standard work in string players' libraries and his substantial reputation through Europe maintains his compositions in standard repertories in several countries.

Joaquín Rodrigo (b. Sagunto, 1902) received a national prize in 1925 for *Cinco Piezas Infantiles* for orchestra and went to Paris in 1927 where he worked with Dukas and quickly affirmed a personal style with works like *Zarabanda Lejana*, *Preludio al Gallo Mañanero* and *Per la Flor del Lliri blau* in the early 1930s. The *Concierto de Aranjuez* for guitar and orchestra (1938) appeared at a historic moment and is likely to remain a musical testament to the period marking the cessation of the civil war. Its well-balanced dialogue, articulate and penetratingly evocative, suggested to many that Rodrigo was in line of succession to Falla. However, he did not choose to follow the latter's course of abstaining from repetitions of form and went on to explore the concierto's Spanish potential in *Concierto Heroico* for piano and orchestra, *Concierto de Estío*, for violin and orchestra and *Concierto Galante* for cello. In 1948 he turned to his love of archaic themes and showed a discriminating choice of those most consonant to modern ears in *Ausencias de Dulcinea*. A finely acute intelligence and subtle distinction of timbre combined with this perception of sonorities to produce the polished *Suite Fantasía para un gentilhombre* in 1955 which discreetly enlarges the scope of Gaspar Sanz's early dances more than is generally appreciated; this now matches the *Concierto de Aranjuez* in wide and persistent popularity. The *Concierto-Serenata* for harp and orchestra, also of 1955, is originally conceived to display this instrument's use in Spanish music; the harp's appearances—first with a students' heterogeneous roving band which Rodrigo exploits with characteristic dissonances, then with a soliloquising interlude which includes some of his loveliest music in melancholy mood, and lastly in a series of stylised social *bailes*—show that what we have heard constitutes the life-story of a Spanish harp—the novelty of a biographical Concierto for this instrument.

It is in soliloquies that this composer's meditations are uninterruptedly communicated, as in the *Sonatas de Castilla*, which, with due respect to his many interpreters, no one else plays so well. Those slow examples, in form of the *tiento*, show him in direct line of thought with that tradition which still draws on Cabezón's spirit and at the same time is in accord with a younger generation's search for the absolute in more abstract consideration of sound. His literary sensibility, joined with a discriminating taste for Spanish musical stylistics, enables him to set great verse as 'Por mayo era por mayo', 'Cántico de la esposa', 'Coplas del pastor enamorado', and 'Aire y Donaire' with responsive creation. The same fine judgment serves his choice of folk-songs, and always with a grace unmistakably his own. This vein of poetic interpretation deepens with *Rosaliana*, a set of songs for the Galician poetess Rosalía de Castro's melodiously melancholy verse. Rodrigo does not believe in the 'progress' of the arts, but in their evolution and transformation; nor does he think there have been great changes in Spanish music, certainly not in the sense of classicism and neo-classicism. 'We have our casticismo and thus periods of neo-casticismo, but if we have had classical composers they are so few as scarcely to be counted. Our contribution to European music has remained one of personality.'

On the eve of Corpus Christi in the summer of 1971 he was in exceptionally relaxed mood, having on this day completed *Diez canciones sobre poemas de Antonio Machado*. His prolonged meditations on this poet's verse had proved an enriching experience, and a happy sense of a composer's fulfilment enveloped the small circle of musical colleagues drinking tea with him in his Madrid home on this doubly festive holiday. This series of songs follows Rodrigo's most recent works for the guitar; the *Sonata* of 1970 and an *Eulogio de la Guitarra* of 1971.

He continues to write in concerto style, as in the *Concierto Andaluz* for 4 guitars and orchestra, 1967, following the *Concierto Madrigal* for two guitars, 1966.

Among all the works given a first hearing in Barcelona during the 1930s it was the *Canciones y danzas de la isla de Mallorca* by Baltasar Samper (b. 1888) which gave keenest pleasure and most profound satisfaction. This orchestral composition translated Mallorca's finest themes into sparkling translucence vibrant with the intense light of this delectable isle; yet the intensity never spilled over the clear delineation of its form. So far as is known, this slight, serious figure, whose concert platform manner was extraordinarily like Gustav Holst's, did not continue to compose after settling in Mexico, where he dedicated himself to teaching.

Joaquín Nin Culmell (b. 1908) is closely identified with Spanish evolution, though working in California. *Concierto* for piano (1946) bears the hall-mark of Falla with whom he studied; *Diferencias sobre un tema de Gaspar Sanz* (1953) and *Seis variaciones sobre un tema de Luis Milán* for guitar (1954) led to the poem-ballet *Don Juan* of 1959, colourfully conceived and orchestrated with skill. He has expanded his father's well-known editing of Spanish popular and early music with his own arrangements such as *Doce canciones populares de Cataluña* (1957), *Tres tonadas mallorquinas, Canciones tradicionales cubanas* (1952), *Tres poemas de Gil Vicente*, felicitous in evoking this dramatist's lyrical originality, and music for García Lorca's *Yerma* (1956).

Roberto Gerhard, of Swiss parents, in spite of his early apprenticeship to Schoenbergian doctrines in the last years of the monarchy did not consistently conform to these after leaving Spain for England. Though a ballet, *Ariel* (1930), in which he had the distinctive aid of Juan Miró, brought success when orchestrated in 1936, a certain eclecticism already distinguishes him, as in the tentative post-Brahmsianisms of his early pieces written in Barcelona. On settling in England he took up various aspects of the Spanish idiom as in *Don Quixote* (1940), *Sinfonía homenaje a Pedrell* (1941), another ballet, *Alegrías* (1942), and *La dueña* (1947). With the war's conclusion he more definitely returned to the Germanic serialist fold with *Concierto* for violin and orchestra, *Sinfonia* (1953), *Concierto* para clavicembalo, strings and percussion (1956), *Nonet* for wind and accordeon (1957) and *Symphony No. 2* (1957) in which the conceptual syntheses pursued by numerous contemporaries are strictly adhered to. Latterly, he profitably deployed his by now very considerable technical skills towards French music, still methodically constructing his syntheses but utilising the more novel aesthetic compounds of Paris. To Spaniards he remains a musician lacking in essential rhythm and vital élan, and in spite of respect shown for his scholarly work in Catalonia before the Civil War, Spanish critics generally find his music frigid and marked by a 'certain aridity and expositional dryness which in its turn is converted into a uniformity of sound in which the composer's personality is diluted and consequently becomes irreconcilable'. More accurately, Gerhard should be assessed in the company of Swiss composers to whom he is linked by roots, such as Honegger and Martin. During pre-war days in Barcelona he was constantly preoccupied with Honegger's scores, for instance. In what was perhaps the first notice of his music printed in England, the present writer suggested that he seemed over-concerned with textures, tending towards a certain tightness even then; this is applicable to other composers of Swiss heritage, as is sometimes the tendency to eclecticism also.

Salvador Bacarisse (b. 1898 of French parentage), pupil of Conrado del Campo, showed impressionist qualities in early settings of Spanish verse and won the 1931 Premio Nacional with *Música Sinfónica*. He held this level in the polyphonic choral style of *Ojos claros y serenos* based on Cetina's poem, and showed full orchestral colour in setting *La Nave de Ulises* and *Heraldos* by Rubén Darío. In the 1950s he wrote a ballet, *La mujer, el toro, y el torero* and *Concertino* for guitar and orchestra (1952). *La Sangre de Antigone*, opera-oratorio (1950), shows him drawing still on classical themes, and is possibly influenced by Stravinsky, since his earlier *Tres marchas burlescas* already suggest this.

Julian Bautista's delicate effects of colour in *La flauta de jade* and *Preludio para un tibor japonés* also showed to advantage in his chamber music, in which he was del Campo's pupil. After removing to Argentina he wrote a *Fantasía española* for clarinet and orchestra (1945), *Sinfonía breve* (1956) and the choral *Romance del Rey D. Rodrigo* (1956). In the first festival of contemporary American music, Buenos Aires, his *Cuarteto* won a prize, thus repeating his early award of the Premio Nacional in Spain for his *Cuarteto No. 2*. His ballet *Juerga* was performed in Paris by Argentina's company not long after. He died in 1961. Also del Campo's pupil, Fernando Remarcha, with a Premio de Roma, worked in Italy with Malipiero: his piano quartet (1933), *Sonatina* for piano, the orchestral *Fiestas*, an oratorio *Vísperas* of the post-war years led up to the *Concierto* for guitar and orchestra (1955) and recently a *Rapsodia de Estella* won the Eduardo Ocón prize in Málaga (1960) for its original sonorities and thematic articulation.

Enrique Casal-Chapí (b. 1909) after writing for the Madrid theatre, left for America but later returned to Spain. Gustavo Durán (b. 1906) had much success with a ballet *El fandango del candil* produced by Argentina's company. Like Casal-Chapí he has also set Lope de Vega's verse and Rafael Alberti's highly popular modern poems.

With Gustavo Pittaluga's ballet of 1927—*La romería de los cornudos*—first performed 1930, castizo, dexterous and colourful, García Lorca's relations with the musical world were established and this composer's *Llanto por Federico García Lorca* (1944) impressed with the ingenuity with which the declamatory recitative and percussive use of two pianos are interjected into the whole. His earlier success in the ballet world, however, has drawn him more and more into that sphere as a master of the genre where his prestige is consistently maintained.

Federico Elizalde (b. 1890 in the Philippines) has also set works by Lorca for the stage, such as *Don Perlimplín* and *Títeres de la cachiporra*, but is best known for a violin concerto in the post-romantic style. José Maria Franco (b. Irun, 1894) also a pupil of Conrado del Campo, is well known for his moulding of regional themes in the Basque provinces. His *Concierto castellano para ondas Martenot*, 1957, is a Spanish experiment to bring electronic music into the Spanish orbit and thus follows up the first chamber experiments of Padre Donastia. Jesús Gay Bal, 1905, known for his scrupulous editions of early Spanish music wrote a *Concerto grosso* in Mexico (1951), and from here his reputation now extends through the New World.

It was in Mexico, too, that Adolfo Salazar wrote his many studies on such themes as a *Historia de la música en la sociedad europea*; *Conceptos fundamentales de la historia de la Música*; *La música en la antigua Grecia*; *Síntesis de la historia de la música*, *La música orquestal en el siglo xx*; *La danza y el ballet*; a work on J. S. Bach and the long-awaited *Historia de la música española*, published in Buenos Aires not long before his death in Mexico, 1958. Thus his transfer from Spain did not lessen his output, though in Madrid as a leading music critic he had been especially dedicated to the promotion of contemporary composition, insisting that Falla's way was the one for Spaniards to follow. His own music includes *Tres Preludios* for piano; *Tres Poemas de Verlaine*; *Paisajes* for orchestra; *Cuatro canciones* for vocal trio based on the Andalusian idiom which in its affinities with oriental modes led to his composition of *Arabia*, for piano quintet, and *Rubaiyat*, for string quartet. His books of this period include *El siglo romántico* (1936); *Sinfonía y ballet* (1929); *Música y músicos* (1928); *La música contemporánea en España* (1930); *La música actual en Europa y sus problemas* (1935) and *La música en el siglo XX* (1936).

Xavier Montsalvatge is one of those musicians who though well known in their early activities, achieve special recognition through a new and abrupt change of direction. In themselves *Cinco canciones negras* (1946) are witty and effective, though not necessarily unusual to those who know the Latin American music of the time, Cuban and Brazilian especially. In Spain, however, they appeared at a time—the year of Falla's death—when musicians, like other artists, were seeking for new contacts abroad to make up for their lost years during the Civil and European wars, and this sudden reminder that the world of 'hispanidad' offered such colourful vigour almost unknown in the peninsula brought Montsalvatge's name and his songs into the concert world throughout the country. (I myself received three manuscript copies from three different sources in the course of about ten weeks.) He did not abuse this privileged success: his *Cuarteto indiano* (1952), though evidently intended to consolidate this interest, uses the creole idiom with musical discretion and the interplay of the exotic is ingeniously contrived. In the same year his *Concierto breve* for piano and orchestra (1952) confirmed his reputation, which was further enlarged by *Partita* (1958), in which in spite of its classical suite-like movements (Fanfarria, Sarabanda, Intermezzo recitativo, and Finale) there was still an exotic aroma to be detected. His opera *El gato con botas* was concluded in 1947 and includes ballet scenes; however, the *Cant Espiritual*, a choral work on Maragall's poem (1958), is musically a more original work and considered a significant addition to the Orfeo Català's repertory.

Falla's death on 14th November 1946 coincided with the end of the war and was followed by groupings and regroupings among Spanish composers, the first of these being known as the Círculo Manuel de Falla. Its objective was to eschew propagandists who lacked the spiritual substance needed in these years of change, those who lacked horizon and a sense of social mission. Its members included Juan Comellas (b. 1913), José Cercós (1925), Alberto Blancafort (1928), José Casanoves (1924), Jorge Giró (1923) and Mestres Quadreny (1929). A sense of creative solidarity having been brought about by this grouping, the Círculo's functions were partly taken over by the formation of a Spanish section of Juventudes Musicales, which with greater means and the benefit of a world organisation—Jeunesse Musicale—set about the wider dissemination of ideas such as the Círculo's members in Barcelona had taken from Manuel de Falla.

Avant-garde groups then came to the fore in Madrid with the activity of a post-war generation including Juan Hidalgo (b. 1927), Cristóbal Halffter (1930), Luis de Pablo (1930), García Abril (1933), Narciso Bonet (1933), and a senior, Joaquin Homs (b. 1906), trying in their several ways to draw European experiments into the Spanish stream. Schoenberg, Varese, Stockhausen, Marchetti, Bo Nilsson, Eimert, Cage became guide-lining leaders among followers of the latest manifesto *Música abierta*, which might be seen as reiterating that triple pact of a previous generation to make 'música española con vistas a Europa', for the will to improve native composition still dominated. Critical caution was still forthcoming also, as in the words by D. Ridruejo: 'there is more water than thirst'; or, as another critic reminded them in Ortega y Gasset's observation: 'all that is lacking is the gift of ideas, of humanity'. Nevertheless, the vigour and purposefulness of these new generations is undeniable. This manifesto's text calls for 'Open music, active music, music of the immediate past, music of today and tomorrow'.

The senior member, Joaquín Homs, concentrating as Schoenberg did on sound rather than colour, was in line with the precepts of this school, as may be heard in his *Trio for Woodwind* (1954); *Quintet* (1955); *Three Inventions for Orchestra on a Theme by Webern* (1959); and *Music for Six Instruments* (1960).

From Bilbao, Luis de Pablo brought Basque determination to forge a new system of sound capable of interpreting the complex world of today. Starting in a between-wars manner with *Quartet* (1955), he broke with his past in *Sonata* (1959) and *Inventions No. 5 for Orchestra*; while latterly his *Progressus* for two pianos reaches out to spheres inhabited by Varese and Boulez. His place as a leader of new generations has been strengthened by *Radial op. 9* for 24 Instruments, *Glosa op. 10* for voice and four instruments; and *Libro para el Pianista op. 11*.

Mestres-Quadreny joined de Pablo in this rarified atmosphere, also suppressing his early works written before 1957, when his piano sonata set the tone for a chamber opera *El Ganxo* in 1958. *Epitáfios* for soprano, strings, harp and celesta followed in 1959, and in 1960 *Chamber Music No. 1* for flute, percussion, piano, violin and bass. *Invención móvil* (also 1960) for flute, clarinet and piano is an experiment in fortuity, in which the musical discourse is influenced by the many possibilities offered to the instrumentalists for a series of 'practically' infinite variations.

Juan Hidalgo very early showed a distinctive gift in his settings of Góngora and other poets whose difficult texts his fine sense of line etched with firm yet delicate assurance. He has recently embarked on another problematic translation in transferring John Cage's experiments to the Spanish idiom, as in *Aulaga*, *Caurga*, and a *Cuarteto* for strings in 1960. Like Quadreny, he invites performers to take part in an extended interpretation of the score bordering on creative response, if not responsibility.

Cristóbal Halffter's talent developed by way of chamber works such as Quartet (1955) and a religious series as in *Ave Maria* and *Panis Angelicus* (both of 1954), *Antifonía Pascual* and the *Misa Ducal* (1955–1956). Such themes and the religious forms chosen by other musicians also, lead some critics to suppose that a revival of church music is at hand; others see Stravinsky's influence at work as from the *Symphonie*

IX. Francisco Guerrero

X. Fernando Contreras

XI. Cristotfóbal Morales

XII. Isaac Albéniz, aged 17

XIII. Enrique Granados

XIV. Manuel de Falla

XV. Joaquín Rodrigo

des Psaumes, extending his already effective penetration of Spanish secular composition. It should be remembered, however, that P. Donastia was an active pioneer in the Círculo de Manuel de Falla and that his early experimental ideas in electronic music had been quickly taken up. In the *Misa Ducal* Halffter gives his choir a rhythmic-harmonic treatment without precedent in Spanish choral music and his choice of rhythmic irregularity in alternating combinations is comparable to Carl Orff's cantatas, though more intelligently complex than the latter. Donastia's influence may be working in this, also. The expectation aroused by this work was fulfilled by *Dos movimientos para timbal y orquesta de cuerda*, awarded a Unesco prize in 1956. Again rhythmic originality is evident and intelligently controlled speculation dynamically extends the strings' expressive means. *Jugando al toro* has proved a brilliant ballet whose stylised pasodoble recalls Walton's light irony and Copland's salty humour. The serialism in *Microformas*—perhaps already suggested in *Concertino* for strings (1956) and *Toccata* for piano—may partly owe its development to the arrival in Spain of music by Luigi Nono, Pierre Boulez and Stockhausen. Halffter's music for *Orestiada* in the production of Pemán's revision of the text, and with the prestigious decor of José Tamayo, has brought him recognition even among the most conservative of musical audiences, though this does not arise only from his impressive contribution to the nation's theatre. The character of his work is in keeping with the attractive complexity of his nature, and with Luis de Pablo he has emerged as the most decisive director of the course of Spanish music composition today.

The further progress of those who formed the Círculo de Manuel de Falla in Barcelona may be seen in Juan Comellas' early work, *Homenaje a Ravel* and *Sonatina* (1946) and his homenajes to Falla and Mompou. His ballet, *La Rambla* (1955) keeps a characteristic freshness of invention. José Cercós, throwing off Wagnerism, went on to seek new structural forms, reaching out past Schoenberg to Webern in *Variaciones perpendiculares sobre un tema de Webern* and a *Concierto para trece instrumentos sobre un tema de Mendelssohn*—treated in series. Alberto Blancafort's works, *Concertino de camara* and a *Sonata* for piano (1955) in their distilled essence of style contrast with Angel Cerdá's imaginative sense of colour in such pieces as *Divertimento* (1957) and the ballet *Chica y tiempos nuevos* (1957). More uncompromisingly, José Casanovas concentrates on the deploying of sound in the abstract and with string consorts chiefly, as in *Música para cuerdas* and *Sinfonía* (1957). Agustín Bertomeu shows links with Bartók in his quartet *Confluencia sobre do sostenido* (1971), confining his score within definitely formal boundaries.

* * *

Spaniards have long enjoyed the services of several orchestras equal to any in Europe. The Orquesta Sinfónica, the Orquesta Filarmónica, both of Madrid, and the two orchestras of Barcelona have been the mainstay of national concert life for many years under Fernández Arbós, Pérez Casas, Pablo Casals, Eduardo Toldrá; to these was added the Orquesta Nacional in 1940, directed by Pérez Casas and then by Ataúlfo Argenta. Scarcely less important has been the creation of such entities as the Orquesta Municipal de Barcelona, formed and fostered by Toldrá from 1944, the Orquesta Sinfónica de Bilbao under Rafael Frühbeck de Burgos and the Orquesta Municipal de Valencia under Lamote de Grignon. Madrid has had reason also to be proud of its chamber groupings, the Orquesta Clásica, the Orquesta de Cámara and the Orquesta de Arcos de Madrid. Barcelona again levels up to this activity with its chamber group Solistas de Barcelona and the highly appreciated orchestra of the Gran Teatro de Liceo. Enrique Jordá conducts regularly in America.

The traditional dynastic patterning of musical interest shows once more in the introduction of English scores during the reign of Alfonso XIII and Queen Ena Victoria. Arbós' orchestral programmes included many British names—such as Elgar, Bax, Scott, Delius, Holst and Vaughan Williams—whose works were chosen with the knowledge of one who had played and taught in London for many years. Arturo Saco del Valle, the royal chapel master, consistently included English works in the last seasons of the monarchy in the Clásica's Madrid series of concerts; Elgar's *Introduction and Allegro for strings*, Holst's *St Paul's Suite*, Vaughan Williams' *Greensleeves* were repeated at the final performance, and despite the anxieties of those last months, the Queen attended regularly; this attention to duty in the musical sphere should be added to that eulogy of her written by no less an author than Unamuno. Saco del Valle also introduced Elgar's music into the royal Chapel's service in response to a score sent to him by an English music student.

The world-known figure of Pablo Casals is inseparable from his cello. At home in Barcelona he was constantly seen with conductor's baton in his hand, giving memorable performances of Beethoven's Choral Symphony, when the Orfeo Català joined his orchestra, Strauss's *Sinfonia Domestica, Don Quixote, Verklärung*, and the *Don Juan* tone poem. Bach, Haydn and Brahms were staple fare. Casals, too, found room for British musicians, to the extent of punishing his finger-tips when preparing the cello concerto written for him by Donald Tovey, declaring to friends who ventured to expostulate with him when he emerged from his music-room at San Salvador ruefully holding up his hands as proof of his loyal labours, that the English did not appreciate this grand musician as the fine composer he was, and that he, Pau Casals, was going to prove them wrong at the coming Edinburgh concert when he was to give this work its première. It was his zeal for Granados' music which led to Casals' first experience as conductor, as has been mentioned already. It was for a Granados memorial evening in his own home that Pau Casals gathered his brothers' young children around his piano, leading the family in an early performance of his own Mass. Though now publicly known, the work was not at that time available, and only the closest friends of Granados were invited. Casals had begun to compose in early youth; a set of seven songs dates from 1895 to 1901; their natural melodic line and delicate harmonic sense show him already at ease in the spheres of Schumann and Fauré. Three are on texts by Apel-les Mestres, on whose poetry Granados relied; one by Jacint Verdaguer; one on Verlaine's 'En sourdine' and the last on Matthew Arnold's 'Absence'—in Catalan—and Gautier's 'Son Image'.

For many years diffident about the public performance of these works, he eventually became known as a composer for the cello with pieces like the *Sardana* for massed players of this instrument.

Known also all over the world, Andrés Segovia achieves for the guitar that quality of crystalline transparent brilliance which Falla sought for the orchestration of his *Retablo de Maese Pedro*. Beside him now stands Narciso Yepes, the opposite of his mythological namesake, lucid, objectively master of a finely articulate classic style; and Miguel Llobet, Emilio Pujol, Sainz de la Maza, virtuoso among virtuosi, and the seductive Renata Tarragó uphold that great tradition through the 20th century.

Casals' circle has long included Gaspar Cassadó whose temperamental warmth compassed both romantic Schumannesque moods and the impressionistic vibrations of French music. Younger cellists, conscious of their great predecessor are now appearing, among them Ruiz Casaux, Ricardo Boadella, José Trotta, Marçal Cervera, Ernesto Xancó. Violinist successors to Juan Manén and Eduardo Toldrá include Francisco Costa, Manuel Quiroga, Rafael Alós, Enrique Iniesta, Xavier Turull, Juan Palau, Agustin León-Ara—son-in-law of Joaquín Rodrigo —Enrique Caslas, José Sánchez, Eduardo Asiain.

Conchita Badía with a voice of 'malvasía' perpetuates Granados' lyrical intimacies of song, as Alicia Larrocha disseminates his pianism. Lola de Aragón ensures the true continuity in Madrid of many talents of past and present generations, her school of singing being justly praised as is her own singing. Victoria de los Angeles effortlessly reached those levels of international accomplishment immediately predicted by those who heard her early singing in Barcelona's theatres;

and Teresa Berganza, equally famous now internationally, does not allow foreign success to override her natural castizo quality; with these two singers and sharing their qualities of international and national style must rank many others, including Montserrat Caballé, Pilar Lorengar, Anna Ricci, Marimí de Pozo, Maria Rosa Barbany, to name only a few of what is a galaxy of lustrous talents.

After the legendary Ricardo Viñes (d. 1943), devoted servant at the piano to Albéniz, Falla, Turina, Gonzalo Soriano remains the faithful interpreter of Falla's expressed desires in his keyboard music. José Iturbi, also world-known as conductor, Leopoldo Querol, Luis Galve, Joaquín Achucarro, Ruiz Pipó, Pedro Vallribera, Rosa Sabater, Paquita Madriguera, Pilar Bayona and many other pianists, including Rafael Orozco, now a frequent performer in London since winning the Leeds Festival Prize, interpret between them the whole repertory, giving due precedence to Spanish works, classical, romantic and the experimentally new. Among the best of this keyboard company Nicanor Zabaleta is distinguished as one of the world's most excellent harpists of our time.

CHAPTER VIII

Spanish Music in Latin America

An occurrence which probably influenced early developments in Spanish American music appears to have been neglected by musicologists. In his *Historia de la Orden de San Jerónimo* Fray José de Sigüenza describes a petition by Jeronymite monks to be recalled from their mission in the New World where they were among the first to be entrusted with the care of the natives; they found their hermit way of life did not fit them to cope with the fortune-hunting adventurers who were roaming the new territories seeking whom they might despoil, and felt unable to protect and educate their charges as directed. They were eventually replaced by orders more experienced in dealing with worldly men, when Franciscans and the new Spanish order of Jesuits took over this task. In their institutions music was given a major part in education; workshops were set up for the making of instruments and many natives, and later negroes, proved naturally amenable to musical training and became gifted performers. Accounts of these organisations and their festivals give evidence of the rapid assimilation of the music brought from Spain and the skill these pupils showed in singing and dancing. As early as 1560 a group of five Indians were to be heard playing European music on their primitive flutes in Cuzco, where music hitherto had been confined to variations on the five-tone and three-tone scales. In this Inca eyrie of the Andes the cathedral already in 1553 possessed Morales' two books of masses printed in Rome, 1544. In 1559 Morales' music was chosen to celebrate the memory of Charles V in Mexico City, and the congregation dissolved in tears as they listened.

By 1539 Mexico city had a printing press which published over 230 volumes within a century. Its first book containing musical notation appeared in 1556 and its title shows how venerable were those ties which now bound the New World to the Old: *Ordinarium Sacri Heremitarum Sancti Augustini Episcopi & regularis observatio*, nunc denuo correctum, sicut non secundum more antiquo, ceremonie x siant, sed secundum choros altos. A *Manuale sacramentorum secundum usum ecclesie Mexicane* printed in 1560 was the second work containing music to be printed there: the British Museum has a copy of this. A *Graduale Dominicale* followed in 1576. By 1561 another press was licensed and yet another in 1563. An *Antiphonario* of 1589 has marginal notes, some of which give directions for the organ accompaniment. The last book in Gothic type and with music to appear in the 17th century was a volume of Holy Week music, the *Liber in quo quattuor passiones Christi Domini continentur*, 1604, compiled by the Franciscan Juan Navarro, *Gaditanus* (of Cadiz) choirmaster of Mexico City's cathedral.[1] After this time, the church music books were imported from Europe and though this alteration has puzzled musicologists, the change is comparable with building practice, for parts such as doors and window frames were now brought over also, for assembling on the sites. Historically, however, it must be seen as related to the Spanish crown monopoly over the printing of church graduals throughout the empire and so as part of the determination to guard the hegemony, spiritual and material, of Hapsburg control.

The *Psalmodia Christiana* by Sahagún, 1583, is of special interest, for it is said to mark the start of determined efforts to supplant native music with European. This suggests that there were natives sufficiently trained by now to perform the hymns translated by Sahagún into Mexican for them to sing: it was also at this time that the process by which native songs and dances were replaced by Christian examples was hastened. Thus, those minor forms approved in Augustine's *De Musica* were adapted to the new subjects' diversion. Only three years after Cortés captured Mexico City in 1519 a school for natives including musical training was set up at Texcoco by Fray Pedro de Gante. This was transferred to Mexico City in 1527 and here the Indians were taught to copy musical notation, to perform the chanting, make instruments and play them and to compose hymns and masses.

That American-born descendants of Spanish stock—*criollos*—or mixed Spanish and American race could acquire an education equal to that given in Spain is shown by the achievements of the most remarkable woman the New World has yet produced. The beautiful nun and writer (1651–1695) Sor Juana Iñés de la Cruz had a passionate love for intellectual beauty, for poetry and music, in addition to her convent-given learning in theology, philosophy, humanism, astronomy. She wrote an auto sacramental, *El Divino Narciso*, villancicos and, possibly, music for such performances, though nothing of this survives. Her collection of instruments was given up together with many of her books

---

[1] Not to be confused with Juan Navarro of Seville c. 1530–1580, composer of *Psalmi, Hymni ae Magnificat*, Rome 1590, continually and widely performed.

when it was suggested that she was becoming more attached to intellectual pursuits than religion approved and she died not long after nursing natives, during a plague to which she herself succumbed. She wrote a treatise on music she called *El Caracol*—the Shell—which is lost. Her outline of it is felicitously set down in one of her longer poems and this shows her familiarity with musical theory from Pythagoras onward. She speculates on whether the Enharmonic can be reduced to practice or if it must remain 'cognición intelectiva'; and whether the Cromático receives its name from the colouring of the keys or from the variety of added voices. She explains that since she believes that Harmony is not a circle but a spiral and by reason of its form returns upon itself, she called it *El Caracol* since this shell is similarly shaped and returns upon itself. Though writers have interpreted this reference to the shell's curvature as baroque symbolism, musically it is interesting to recall that the large marine shell was an important instrument to the Aztecs and it was from a study of this that Chávez deduced that these Mexicans understood and applied the natural phenomena of harmonics. Thus, Sor Juana's application of El Caracol to music may have been realistically as well as symbolically meant.

More significant, however, is its probable relation to St Augustine's discussion of a higher musical intelligence in Book I of *De Musica*. Here he points out the power of numbers to return to unity in the process of originating numerical series which will be infinite unless limited by some external means, and illustrates this connection with metre by the picture of a man beating time rhythmically, creating a sound of short duration followed by another sound of double that duration, while another man dances in conformity. From this, he suggests that even if we do not know it, we acknowledge that we enjoy rhythm. It is this idea which leads to his famous definition of music as knowing how to make controlled variations of sound correctly, which is to say, all movements whose variations are under correct control. As he shows that existence of rhythmic order is universal and thus is evidence for God's eternal law of unity it may be reasonably supposed that Sor Juana—known for her intellectual grasp of universal principles in art and thought as La Décima Musa—had Augustine's interpretation of music in mind when she herself compared Harmony to the shell's return upon its own form.[1] We may assume that when teaching her pupils she had also in mind his remarks about the ultimate pur-

---

[1] Referring to her book on music she writes:

En él, si mal no recuerdo
Me parece que decía,
Que es una línea espiral
No un círculo la Armonía.
Y por razón de su forma

poses of teaching the less highly endowed intelligences to sing and dance.

'Now if we normally think with closest attention about immaterial, changeless things, and if it happens that, at the time, we are performing temporal rhythm in one of the kinds of bodily movement which are ordinary and quite easy, such as walking or singing, we may never notice the rhythm, though it depends on our own activity . . . how much more, concentrated on the one God . . . shall we perceive, with joy, the rhythm by which we actuate our bodies with no unpeacefulness?' With such motives, native pupils were taught to sing and dance to Christian metres so that they might be brought into that higher rhythmic law of universal unity.

This musical training was set in motion throughout the New World and zealously recorded. It extended, for instance, to mission schools through the Antilles, where in 1697 F. Labat observed that the negroes were taught many dances such as the *minué*, *corrente*, the *paspie* and those like *branles* and round dances, in order that they should forget their own kind and yet be able to dance and leap as they desired. Fray José de Parras in 1750 found the same purpose at work in the instruction given by the Jesuit missions of Alto Paraná where the Indians learned with great facility. 'And I have seen those among them dance minuetes and contradanzas with grace equal to that to be seen in Madrid.' Thus those minor forms of dance and song were directly inculcated by the Church.

The European dance arrived in Spanish America immediately on the establishment of the viceregal authority and courts, with the Branle, the Gavota, the Volta—known to Queen Elizabeth—Gallard, Pavana, Corrente, Canario, Zarabanda, Chacona. These dance forms were so completely absorbed by all levels of society that they had become the people's folklore by the time succeeding waves of 'Minué', Paspie, Bourré, Giga and Contradanza arrived to be absorbed in their turn in widening country circles. With the fading of French influences through the passing of Bourbon strength, other European dances arrived, such as the Cuadrilla and Lancers, Polka, Mazurka and Chotis. Through association with these, the Minuet and Gavotte survived; the Argentines' rural Cielito, Pericón and Media Caña preserve remains of the contradanza and the same people, with the Chileans and Bolivians, preserve vestiges of the Minuet in the famous Cuándo. In these, the influence of the valse became overriding and the old grafting systems survive in those variants known as the 'Cueca valseada' in Chile during

Revuelta sobre sí misma
Le intitulé Caracol
Porque esa revuelta hacía.

the struggles for independence and in Argentina where the Polka grafted to the gaucho gato produced the 'gato polqueado'. The Habanera was only dislodged by the Tango, Fox-trot, Rumba, Ranchera, and of these both Tango and Ranchera retain very early hybrid European-American characters. The basic rhythm of the Habanera and the closely related Milonga, widely spread as far south as the River Plate regions, may be seen in the *Cancionero Musical de Palacio*, number 78 (Barbieri's edition), as Carlos Vega shows. This example has Italian words, however. Nevertheless its place in this Cancionero proves its high ancestry, and Spanish practice in the 15th and 16th centuries.

Viceregal balls set the entertainment pattern for colonial society. They opened with formal dances as performed in Madrid; with the Bourbons on the throne French styles were emphasised; then as time passed, these formalities attached to the evening's first hours gradually gave way to criollo dances set to livelier measures which still showed their links to older forms which graced previous functions. Harp and guitar were early used in consort with the violins. Stage productions as under royal patronage in Madrid were less frequent, though the viceroy's palace witnessed *Partenope*, the opera by Manuel Sumaya, in the 17th century and a music drama *El Rodrigo* by the same. Calderón's text of *La Púrpura de la Rosa* was heard at the viceregal court in Lima to celebrate Philip V's first year of accession in 1700: the music was by Tomás Torrejón de Velasco. Calderón's text had celebrated forty years earlier the marriage of Louis XIV to the Infanta Maria Teresa which brought about the Bourbon rule in Spain. When this piece was revived on 31st May 1970, however, the Madrid *ABC*'s critic asked whether the labour spent on its resuscitation had been worth while and then gave his own opinion: '*Sinceramente, no*'.

Though the Jesuits were withdrawn by Charles III's order, the rigorous training they had given survived, particularly in musical theory. In 1819, for instance, a Mexican musician, probably an organist, sent a questionnaire to the *Noticioso General* on some problems which he laid before other musicians for their solution. A group of these, calling themselves Los Sapientísimos Euterpianos, engaged in a long controversy about the points he had raised, such as the rhythmic interpretation of church chanting, the physical causes of the impressions made on the soul by music, and whether plainsong should be considered as a ground bass. This controversy is supposed to show the decadence of church music in the Mexican way of life; it suggests, however, that the old training had not yet disappeared from men's minds. Benito Feijóo is also still quoted, for example, when 'an indignant reader' of the *Diario de México* in 1806 referred other readers to his famous essay 'Music in the

Churches'. A mass of 1810, by the Mexican Aldana, conforms closely to Spanish church composition of the time.

The Church's situation in Argentina after the Jesuit expulsion is well documented in Francisco Curt Lange's *La Música Religiosa en el área de Rosario de Santa Fé y en el Convento San Carlos de San Lorenzo* (1956) during the period between 1770 and 1820 approximately. This convent was ceded to the Franciscans by Charles III and its inventories give details of their building a church on the estancia where the Jesuits had had a chapel. There is little evidence that the Franciscans took over many musical goods except possibly a volume of plainsong. The bells, however, were much appreciated. The newcomers bought three Missals in 1787, a Breviary in 1789 and built up their stock until they had a Requiem. A Misal Veneciano for bishops of 1692 and a work of 1689, a Missa Pontificalis, are supposed to have been brought by a Bishop of Córdoba (Argentina) when he was confined to San Carlos for involvement in an affair against the Junta of Buenos Aires. The inventory shows continuity of tradition. The 1804 list describes 'a fine little organ with four registers for 30 Sonatas', these being contained in three cylinders of 10 each, all good and new, without defect. What these Sonatas were is not known. In 1819 this organ was replaced by a costly organ from Buenos Aires. Added to its cost were the journey of the organ-builder, a gratuity, a mulatto organist, manucordio y *Arte de Clemente*, for the new mulatto organist to practise his keyboard skill, presumably. This mulatto cost 280 pesos. The mulatto youth evidently ran away, for his being brought back cost 44 pesos and 4 reales. The convent also owned a psaltery, which may have come from the Jesuits. The convent offered up masses for the soul of Charles III, then for the recovery of the towns of Buenos Aires and Montevideo, for the health of Ferdinand VII, for the general Peace, and lastly 'for those that are directly related with the struggles of Independence a Mass requested by General Belgrano', another in thanksgiving for the victorious arms at San Lorenzo and one for those killed in that battle. In the Disposition of 21st October 1813, there appears another, in thanksgiving for the combat of Salta. So was the making and remaking of history in the New World accompanied by music set in the moulds, modes and tones of the Old.

The part played by Indians and negroes in the performance of Jesuit plays in America seems to have been in singing and dancing roles and also as instrumentalists, their skill being frequently praised by travellers until the Jesuits left.

The tonadilla's arrival in Spanish America about 1770 gave added impetus to the small forms now inseparable from the new way of life. The sainete came with it and both found the loa and entremés already at home; Sor Juana wrote a loa in the 17th century Madrid style. Sainetes, however, quickly established a more popular place for themselves in the sainetes gauchescos, for Argentine customs and dances were beginning to supplant the Spanish tradition by the end of the 18th century. In Mexico many tonadillas were staged dealing with majo Goyescan themes, suggesting that in the capital cities viceregal manners still effectively influenced social taste; hybrid evolution was more noticeable in the dances. Though famed as the last tonadilla producer and for what he called his 'unipersonal' performance, Manuel García with his daughters came to display also the more novel genius of Rossini's operatic comedy, *The Barber of Seville* in 1827 and thus decisively opened a door for Italian opera with Bellini, Donizetti, Meyerbeer and then Verdi, whose Spanish plots gave him a special place of honour, as he had in Spain, throughout the 19th century.

The tonadilla reached to distant corners and continued for years to give rural people an easy means of expressing musical enjoyment; at the same time it created a taste for staging scenes of local life. The larger zarzuela did not enter so fully into criollo practice though Spanish companies came for tours: Joaquín Gaztambide's season of 1869 proved the most brilliant of these, but it was the staging of the lighter kind, such as Bretón's *La Verbena de la Paloma*, which roused and excited local audiences.

The romantic movement and the gathering momentum of criollo self-consciousness stirred up a need for serious self-expression. In Mexico the salon replaced the aristocratic privileged circles and although the dance still predominated, the piano became the instrument about which a search for more American musical expression centred through fantasias on operatic themes, romanzas, caprichos, nocturnos, serenatas, idylls, and *piezas exóticas*. Among these themes which exercised immature talents and young ladies' fingers, the military march was seriously cultivated, for local wars were not matters merely for reminiscence. These tentative groupings of the 19th century gradually produced greater capacity for organised art through the efforts of Felipe Larios, Tomás León, Melesio Morales, Julio Ituarte, Ricardo Castro, Felipe Villanueva, Ernesto Elorduy. Here was repeated that classic struggle, familiar in many countries, to establish native opera in competition with Italian, with attempts by Melesio Morales to stage his *Romeo y Julieta*, which were realised in 1863. His second piece, *Ildegonda*—the theme used by Emilio Arrieta for Isabel II's little royal theatre—failed to secure production when Tamberlick excused himself by telegram from appearing in it; Morales had to wait till 1891 to see his *Cleópatra* accepted and then rejected by the public. It was Aniceto Ortega's one act *Guatimotzín* (1871) which united Mexicans in enthusiasm for its native theme and the use of Mexican musical airs and rhythms. The aria of Guatemoc is introduced by strings in unison playing the notes of the tritonic scale—the chord of the major perfect. The March and *danza tlaxcalteca*, based on a theme still used for dancing in the Sierra de la Huasteca, were the pages most free from Italian style. Ortega here plied his orchestra with the characteristic timbres of popular native instrumentalists, with their strong metallic accent on the weak beats of the bar; their effect was increased by the contrary melodic play of the dance, the pizzicato effect which was the pride of popular harpists, the firmly distinguished colouring of strings, oboes, clarinets, flutes and bassoons, and the use of a Wagnerian germinating motive to warm the whole with a sense of national unity that was to find real consummation in the 20th century. As in Brazil, with Carlos Gomes' *Guaraní*, it was a native hero who really fired the audiences.

The *romance* arrived with the first explorers and settlers and survived in recognisable form—its variants have been collected through Mexico, Venezuela, Argentina, Chile and Uruguay. The troubadour manner also survived in these regions as through the 'puetas' of Chile and the payadores who travelled around the country accompanying themselves on the large guitar (*guitarrón*) and by wandering fiddlers celebrating local events, playing for 'wakes' and the *velorio del angelito* with its pathetically unconvincing dance about the child's bier, for since faith insisted that the innocent spirit flew straight to heaven, tears must be held back and joy simulated, so as not to dim the infant's glory. Romances such as *Delgadina*, *Estaba Catalina* and *Muerte de Elena* (whose version in Montevideo refers to Santa Irene, patron saint of Santarem, also honoured in Portugal and Galicia) survived to an astonishing extent. *A las doce de la noche* resembles the Asturian variant of *Entre San Pedro y San Juan*: this, like other examples of the *romance*, is also found in Mexico and the Caribbean regions.

Chile's geographical situation linked her in colonial times with viceregal society in Peru as also to the then unsophisticated cattle-breeders of Argentina; some music adopted in Chile came first from Lima and after being popular within her borders went on to Argentina, whence it returned with and without alterations from the River Plate to make the journey northwards again to Peru. The Chileans were famed for the spirited grace of their dancing, particularly in the cueca and cuando. The surviving Araucanian Indians were also known for their *perun* round dances, to which infants not yet able to walk were introduced in a form called *perunpichich en* by a dipping movement of each shoulder in turn—a characteristic motion of the adult dance. Some indigenous effects have been traced in ceremonial dances connected with church festivals such as the Fiesta de la Cruz de Mayo and the Fiesta de Andacollo of Christmastide; the latter opens with a marching dance resembling the colonial Resbalosa, followed by a dance of the Turbantes who are fantastically dressed with conical hats about three feet high and many-coloured ribbons hanging down the back; these groups wear white pantaloons, jacket and white shoes. A sword-bearer directs the movements of the two files of dancers who play tabors, tamboriles, pipes, guitars, accordeons, cymbals, triangles and cornets. At Chiloé, dances for the Fiesta de la Candelaria, Assumption, date from Jesuit times and Franciscan missions, and local variants display mingled strains of European and Araucanian styles.

Colonial dancing in Chile included the purely Spanish fandango, seguidillas, bolero tirana and zapateo, and the formal court series. For the frequent holiday seasons booths (*chinganas*) were set up in towns and villages, where people entertained their friends with non-stop dancing. Chile was 'covered' with chinganas, travellers reported. These booths, it may be observed here, served the same purpose as the *barracas* still in use at Seville's fair time. The old Chilean harp, indispensable in both formal and popular musical events, was small and triangular, and played by women. The fiddle of rustic type, the *rabel*, had from one to three strings. Santiago de Chile had 20 to 30 harps in the 18th century but only a few spinets; the first piano, made in Seville, arrived about 1792. The cathedral mustered eight instruments, including an organ, three singers and a chapel master. Wind instruments were unknown before 1814. It was due to an English naval deserter from the *Phoebe* in 1814, a clarinet player, that this instrument entered local musical life. A violin and a bass drum then known as a tambora, accompanied the Sacrament —though only at night—taken to the sick and dying. Attempts to found a more formal musical society in the 1820s were centred in a *Sociedad Filarmónica*, but its members, obsessed by what was called the 'furor pedestre' came only to dance, while the instrumentalists complained that they were treated worse than beasts of burden.

The delectable cuándo, a New World minuet with criollo impulses, had an allegro tacked on to give a stirring finale. The only rival to the cueca as the national dance, the cuándo may derive from an old Andalusian custom of taking cups of hot chocolate to newly married couples in bed on the morning after the wedding-night, for the best-known verse of this dance runs:

> *Cuándo, mi vida, cuándo?*
> *Cuándo será ese día*
> *De aquella feliz mañana*
> *Que nos llevan a los dos*
> *El chocolate a la cama?*

The cueca, also known all through Latin America, may owe its name to the fashion of the long Parisian pantaloon which innumerable sketches of the time show as worn by Chilean women and which they lifted up their skirts to show when dancing. The cueca was danced to many tunes. Another popular dance was the resbalosa, the music of one example being quoted by Carlos Vega in *Panorama de la Música Popular Argentina*, p. 309. Though he does not observe this, in fact it has a cadential phrase, Sol, Fah, Mi used in alternating lines which recalls the early 19th-century nightwatchmen's call to be heard all over Valparaiso, as they blew the notes of the 'All's well' on their piercing whistles.

An older contact with Spanish tradition may be seen in Vega's examples (page 201ff.) of a rare cadential phrase in the minor. This may relate to the time when the romances were glossed by countless vihuelistas and in particular to those whose music echoes the famous 'Vos me habéis muerto', whose cadential phrase is strongly recalled in Vega's section on the minor ending. The Spanish words too, have a mood of complaint connecting with some tristes of South America.

Many dances have only succumbed to age; these include the abuelito, sombrerito, verde, torito, maisito, palomita. Others, such as the nave, sapo, tras-tras, salchica, loro, survive as variants to the cueca, resbalosa, or cielito. The costillar, however, belongs to a more masculine humour as displayed by the robust ranching huasco. A bottle is placed in the middle of the room about which the dancers circle to the zapateado, closing in upon the bottle and even leaping over it. When it is hit, a forfeit is paid, and a new bottle bought. The music is traditional and said to be 'very old'.

The Argentine gaucho music is perhaps the most virile of the New World, probably owing much to the settlement of many Basques there. The Cancionero Cuyano and its Gato and Vidalita have a strongly marked cadence on the fourth step of the scale descending to the third. Their influence is still active on the estilo, criollo, bailecito, cielito, pericón, and though the valse has made obvious inroads on popular taste, the typical cross-rhythmic accents have not been effaced. In the Andean foothills Argentine music has taken account of the pentatonic melodies of the Huaino and Jujuy laments.

Italian immigrants have not affected the popular music as much as their numbers might seem to warrant; many Italians have identified themselves enthusiastically with the masculine gaucho culture and it is through some older composers of salon music that a long-drawn mellifluous line has become apparent as a trait of Italian lyricism, threading now into Argentine urban song. Argentine musical ties with Chile remain firm, though perhaps there are not so many Argentines nowadays so obsessed with the old 'furore pedestre' as to wish to return to the famed inn of El Parral only to dance once more the Chilean zamba associated with the great battle of Yungay whose victory fused all hearts in the cause of independence.

Uruguay shares the vidalita, which includes both pentatonic and tritonic melodies, with Argentina, as the vidala reached the latter from Chile. It was probably brought here by the armies of Echagüe; the soldiers under San Martín carried many dances from northern Argentina—such as the Sanjuriana and the cuándo—into Chile. The Uruguayan people have adopted the pericón as their own national dance, however, though the old church influence on the formation of popular tradition is missing from parts of their cancionero. The earlier absence of chapels in those regions of the extensive estancias in northern Uruguay obviously accounts for this gap, in contrast to Tucumán whose villancicos have been preserved.

Venezuela is rich in musical survivals which have become part of the country's daily and holiday life. In the interior Spanish elements have remained as vital influences, strongly entrenched, in spite of Negro effects spreading in from the Caribbean coast. The inland Indian contribution includes choral, heterophonic groups who sing different strands simultaneously, alternating with solo song and with primitive instruments such as the pan-pipes or siringas; their musical structure includes a four-note scale entirely free as to measure and rhythm, also the pentatonic scale with alternating rhythms such as 5/8 and 3/8.

The Negro share is much in evidence in the two Christian festivals of San Juan and San Benito, the first of which is especially widespread and connects with the feast of San Pedro, as in Spain. These saints are honoured with four types of tambor, one of whose rhythms, called the cinquillo cubano, is widely distributed. These celebrations also include alternating solo and chorus form, though this differs entirely from the primitive Indian traits. Both San Benito and San Juan are commemorated with polyrhythmical complexities. The vocal invocations are still called 'novenas' and are intoned before the image by the leader, after which the drumming is made by six tambores, or twelve or eighteen. The devout then dance in respectful homage. The band includes various drums, large, medium and small, and the long transverse flute plays short, high phrases during the whole time that these drummings are offered. This is very like those celebrations of saints recorded in Extremadura, many of the people from which went to this area of the Caribbean to work on the farmlands, as also did Galicians.

The rural workers' songs, too, may be paralleled with the Spanish tradition as in the cattle calls, milking, grinding of maize, harvest, clothes-washing, and sugar-cane milling songs. The cattle songs extend

229

all through the area and accompany the ranging cattle as in Spain. As in sheep treks of the Asturias and Galicia to Extremadura, it is usually the leader who goes ahead singing the music, which is taken up by the men behind with shouts and cries. Some of these melodies are brief ejaculatory phrases, others are complete melodic forms, recognisably referring to old modal scales. The long, placid lives of generations centred about the hacienda are expressed by the peon's mild milking songs, when the cow to be milked is called by name in the song, to which she answers with a lowing acknowledgment, coming peacefully to her place before the door.

The Rosario and Velorio remain the most important religious songs, still sung in parts, alternating chiefly in the Ave Maria and Padre Nuestro. Romances, salves, décimas are added to the Rosario in the region of Mérida; estribillos, salves and romances in Falcón. Harmonies and modulations resemble those set down by Julian Calvo in *Alegrías y Tristezas de Murcia*. These practices of constancy extend beyond the plains to the foothills of the Andes and reach down to the mountainous region of Carabobo. The airs are often sung in three parts, for descant and a simple counterpoint are added when the devout are skilled and of good memory.

The Maytime fulía songs are said to descend partly from the *folía*, a Portuguese dance from medieval days. For a performance of this kind Ferdinand and Isabella sent out invitations for the peoples of their realms—including moriscos—who could perform it to celebrate the marriage of their heirs. In Venezuela, the fulía has a fast, carnivalesque rhythm in which many performers join. In Barlovento these melodies exhibit not only Negro elements but the unmistakable old Andalusian cadential fall.

The galerón, still heard extensively on the coast, has reached Ciudad Bolívar and the principal places on the banks of the Orinoco. It has lost some of its ancient tunes but retains the accompanying progression of chords; in other areas the dance tradition is forgotten. Nevertheless, it harks back to an old instrumental line and a habit of using a fixed harmonic base to allow a corresponding compensation of great metric liberty. Instead of the strumming cuatro, it was once accompanied by the bandola, which in form and the number of its strings most nearly resembles the Arabic laúd. The cuatro's part when playing with mandoline and guitar is very strongly marked; the voice, too, opening on a high head note which is then quickly repeated, shares this atmospheric condition of Muslim Spain. The Spanish zapateado has changed only its name, apparently, and to estribillo, in Estado Sucre; a reason for this altered name may be partly related to the old Cuban practice of ending a song with a quick 6/8 rhythm like that of the zapateado in the

Spanish custom. Also found in the Venezuelan interior, it is now a favourite with accordeonists to whom the cuatro may give an accompaniment.

Christmas has its popular celebrations, which include the plaiting dance round a pole, or tree, which is also performed in May festivals. Other diversions are the death and revival of a bird, as in Europe. Christmas songs include the aguinaldo and this predominates in central Venezuela and has now spread beyond; with these are found the songs of Christmas Eve, villancicos and pasacalles in honour of the Virgin and the saints. Saetas survive with little change generally and are also sung between prayers for the dead as a farewell in music.

The gaita, however, is here a round dance, with men and women holding hands while the musicians play inside the circle. These are lively and the tunes vary greatly in rhythm. El Tamunangue, danced in honour of San Antonio though including pieces in its series which show a Negro influence—also includes pieces such as La Batalla which recalls the Basque espatadanza, or sword dance, and El Seis por Ocho which typifies the contradanza. The instrumentation for this series is also mixed, with guitars of four, five or six strings and variously tuned, maracas and tambor of cumaco type which is played by placing it on the ground upon its side; from it has come this serial dance's name, for this tambor is known as the tamunango. The galerón is included in this series of forms. The voices sing in thirds, mainly, but also in seconds, fourths, fifths and sixths, as also in the golpe which is sometimes accompanied by harp, but more often now by the maracas, and still by the old bandola and cuatro. The pasaje has local variants, but the harp accompanies them all, and has proved a repository of many European traditions; its repertory contains suites which even display rudimentary forms of the concerto, including cadenzas. The corrido, on the other hand, is a store of vocal memories parallel to the juglaresque tradition and it is in this form that many romances have been conserved, *Blanca Flor, El Conde Olinos, Las Señas del Marido*; to these have been added New World epics of these peoples' adventures during the Wars of Independence. The form maintains a medieval habit in a simple melody of modest proportions; the binary rhythm, however, has been loosened to include the ternary of the maracas and the cuatro, though the binary is basic. The harmony remains restricted. The Venezuelan polo keeps the Andalusian cadence, but it is now expanded to form the base of the entire melody, an expansion to be found also in the regions of northwest Spain where this cadence has been adopted. It maintains the Spanish air of intensity and is also used as a porfía—in a kind of counterpoint to the diverse themes introduced, so that the singers alternate line by line, competing for mastery in repartee, according to this ancient musical sport of the challenging desafío and porfía. Venezuela's influences extended to Argentina where such challenging scenes were part of a gaucho's life.

The transformation from habanera to bambuco was first made in Colombia and from the Cuban habanera the Venezuelan bambucos and their like were born. The Havanese romantic songs' descendants also passed over to Venezuela and there resemble the Brazilian modinhas which also include operatic effects. More recently the bambuco has been concocted into the merengue, which is a confection from various light dances such as the polka and the tango gaditano. Though it emerged first in Caracas, its name suggests contact with the Dominican republic which has a traditional piece with this title. It survives the recent outpourings of 'new' rhythmic combinations from Cuba and has gone on to experience a more settled existence in the Venezuelan interior, where, like many of its predecessors, it may enter into that rich repository of Venezuelan lore, which in the long run may prove to be even deeper than its oil deposits. The jorope is applied here to the old-style communal dancing; to go to a jorope is to take part in a country dance where old instruments provide traditional music. The name, nevertheless, has been appropriated by urban composers and given to a type of piece in three, four or more movements, though the people continue to christen some music 'jorope' for reasons only known to their instinctive associations with past memories. The harp with its long use in rural festivities continues to play a large part in these countryside junketings.

As has been said, the transformation from habanera to bambuco was made first in Colombia and there its instruments include the bandurria colombiana, guitar, flute and the bandolín andino. Colombian popular music shows much grace in the weaving of thematic material into the background of dance and song. Here, again, there is an early tradition of training, for music was taught in the mission schools at Bogotá early in the 17th century. This country has attracted and given birth to talented composers like José Dadey and Juan de Herrera and musical natures like Juan Velasco (d. 1859) who introduced the symphonies of Haydn, Mozart and Beethoven here. Henry Price, born in London, took his skill as organist and pianist to New York and then to Bogotá where he settled and founded the Sociedad Filarmónica. Colombia was among the first American countries to have regular visits by operatic companies and the first opera by a Colombian to be staged was Ponce de León's *Ester* in 1874. Sharing the common inheritance of the continent's popular music, Colombia's native elegance of style is characteristically displayed in the pasillo, bambuco and gabina torbellino.

The music of Paraguay's Guaranis has been seriously studied by Paraguayan scholars. The Jesuit mission schools here were among the most important in the New World and from their large estates their influence permeated all those countries lying in this more southerly region, acting as a powerful centralising force in general as well as on musical education.

Ecuador, like Peru and Bolivia, has a large Indian population whose music has been collected in d'Harcourt's *Le folklore musical de la région andine*. The common instruments among them are the rondador, pan-pipes, antara or sicu which, like the flute, are heard in groups playing the pentatonic melodies such as the Huainitos, Huainos and the Yaraví. The flute soloist generally accompanies himself on the tinya or tambor.

Criollo traditional dances and songs include the danzantes, pasillo, sanjuanito, zamba and amorfino and with the gaiety of these the Indian yaraví yields an extreme contrast, equally beautiful but hauntingly echoing an imprisoned emotion totally opposed to the extrovert pleasures of criollo self-assurance. Early Spanish music here has been diluted with Negro elements, as in the zamba and marinera. Peru also has the cachua and tondero.

The Bolivian Indians are of Aymará and Quechua race. Again, the music here is divided between two geographical spheres, the mountains where Indian music is practised almost entirely in isolation and the lowlands where Spanish styles prevail; thus the forms are divided between bailecito, tonada, zamba, cueca and the huaíno and yaraví. The Indians, however, have a shoe-tapping dance, the kaluyo, like the zapateo, related to the Chilian cueca. The estilo and triste resemble the Argentine forms.

In Cuba little has survived of recognisably Indian origin, but Spanish and Negro elements meet here as throughout the Caribbean. The country people use the Andalusian cadence and the zapateo is still their typical dance. The criollo picaresque dances are practically all in 6/8 rhythm; the guajiras and puntos end in the dominant; the punto is in the major key; the guajiras begin in the minor and end in the major whence the term 'to dance on your grave', it is said. The Cuban romantic song parallels the modinha in its sentimentality and heavy leaning on Italian operatic style. Early descriptions are preserved of bands playing violins, viola and clarinet, while Negroes played the vigüela and the legendary 'Mama of Habana' who gave birth in about 1598 to the *Son de Ma Teodora* in that binary colonial style surviving in the *son* of Mexico and all this Caribbean basin, acquiring new colour so that it superseded the danzón played by student type groups. It emerged from the island's eastern provinces with its Spanish origins still discernible despite the added percussion and exaggerated syncopation. To Spain were returned the bolero, polo, seguidillas, tiranas with complimentary adornments at the beginning of the 19th century, also the guajiras, punto and habanera with their characters rhythmically revivified, while the old Spanish pregón has survived only to develop into a commercially exploitable air. The tango congo has a habanera rhythm related to the contradanza; the rumba—often like the son though with a faster tempo—as a dance recalls the zapateo and still adheres to the early colonial binary form, while the movements of the congo here, as in Brazil, include the familiar slight lifting of the leg and the accentuating of the beat with a brusque movement of the body.

The Bongo y el tres, the calabazo, the güiro or dried squash, the bembe (or prayer) ñáñigos and Afro-Cuban toques de Santo are included in those incantatory rites to which percussion and drums give a basso continuo. These are exotic elements compared with the use of the traditional Spanish palos—or sticks—to be heard with percussive effects in choral groups about the streets. This exchange of the traditional patterns, which in Spain produce many rhythmic variants and have done so for hundreds of years, for a furiously cross-grained amalgam produced to arouse voodoo excitement shows the New Young World giving up one rattle for another.

The Cuban theatre mingles Galician and Negro characters as did the plays of Gil Vicente; the zarzuela holds its place alongside Italian opera, maintaining its unpretentious *costumbrismo* in dance and song. Ernesto Lecuona's zarzuela *María la O* remains costumbrist despite the romanza atmosphere. The sainete—still a one-act farce—though basically adhering to current topics has gradually developed a more serious dimension as in Grenet's *La Virgen Morena* which has had the longest run in Spain of any Cuban work. In 1935 *La camagüeyana*, another zarzuela by Grenet, was staged in Barcelona's Teatro Nuevo. Moisés Simons' *Toi se Moi* was staged in Paris, 1934. In opera Gaspar Villate's *Baltasar* was played in Havana, Madrid and Paris and this level was also attained by Sánchez de Fuentes, creator of *Doreya*, *La Dolorosa*, *El caminante* and *Yumuri*. Nicolas Guillén, fluent writer of verse and song, remains an unrivalled exponent of those hybrid influences still fermenting in the Afro-Cuban minor, though explosive, genre.

The silence of Cortés and his men 'upon a peak in Darien' was only momentary for by the time Shakespeare created Prospero's island, supposedly in the waters around central America, the whole area was 'peopled with strange sounds'. In Panama, Costa Rica, El Salvador, Guatemala, Honduras and Nicaragua, the earliest arrivals of Spanish music-making have been recorded in the names of instruments associated with Moorish centuries in Spain. The word *aduf* is used by Indians of Guatemala to designate a square drum; the Arabic term *atabal* also survives among them. The *rabel* for a three-stringed violin and *chirimía* for the wind are recognisable still though *zarabanda* has undergone a sea-change from the early formal dance to meaning an orchestra of harp, guitar, rabel and aduf, which, however, still maintain the earlier group connection. The Arabic-sounding word *almirez* survives as the name of a metallic mortar-pounding instrument in Panama.

Besides their use of the brass almirez, the Indians in Panama have a fondness for bronze bells which survive among their instruments.

The *punto* dance has made its way everywhere in these regions while the *mejorana*, similarly widespread, is also a five-stringed guitar. Best known to travellers are the varying forms of the ceremonial dance known in full as 'Historia de Moros y Cristianos', though its origins may be older than Moorish times in the Spanish peninsula and perhaps relate to the mumming and mock battles of solar festivals at midsummer and midwinter solstices, since these survived within the Christian calendar under the benign patronage of San Juan. More truly indigenous are the bird dances of the *zopilote* or buzzard and vulture, linked nowadays to the antics of politicians as birds of prey in Nicaragua, though the bull-dance under many names perhaps reached its most intense cultivation among Brazilians where its Spanish and Portuguese relationships have been authoritatively established. The Yucatan dance of the sacred *tapir* in the sphere of Mayan tradition, however, like the ritual *yaraví* of Inca antiquity, retains its air of remoteness, pertaining to sacrifice upon the altars of other gods preceding ours.

The emergence from Nicaragua of the universifying spirit of Rubén Darío who sang of and for the whole South American world gives musicians cause to expect the appearance among these central states of a composer similarly gifted to express that variety they share in equal intensity with larger entities in the continent; their recent agreement on economic unity may be a sign, as history shows, that spiritual harmony will eventually follow the material coming together.

From this profusion of latent musical riches individual American composers have taken what they would and made what they could. Obviously in the 19th-century nationalist expression of local forms was more or less a duty and in many cases a simple pleasure. Equality of opportunity in reaching creative standards according to European evolution was not possible. The larger cities, however, afforded scope for progressive performance beyond the reach of minor Latin American states. It was chiefly in Mexico and Argentina that talents strong enough to override past circumstances emerged to give shape to the material at hand; and among these are to be found composers of the 20th century representing within fifty years the various stages of evolution Europe had been over a century in organising. It was from the time of the Great War and the break in communication with the Old World that American musicians found their spiritual independence, a century after political emancipation.

It was with the return of Manuel Ponce (1886–1948) to Mexico that Mexican music found liberation. His European studies had convinced him that Mexico had a wealth of natural idiomatic musical matter of a kind the Old World had scarcely imagined. Although his *Chapultepec* and *Ferial* do not advance beyond the picturesquely colourful scenes of the kind Manuel de Falla called 'de jolis coins', his violin concerto of 1942 is marked by abstract purging of local impressionism. A similar progress marks José Rolón (b. 1883) and his piano concerto of 1942.

The last year of the old century saw the birth of composers who have changed the course of Mexico's music, Silvestre Revueltas (1899–1940) and Carlos Chávez in particular, who has lived long enough to realise a success unparalleled elsewhere in the New World. *Planos* (1934) for most critics remains the work in which Revueltas was best able to harness his richly endowed temperament and acute sensibility to instrumental timbres and dissonance. Even his earlier use of agglomerates rather than musically cohesive logic was superseded here by a controlled geniality which showed him ready now to work on a larger canvas than normal in Mexico, though his vitality was still most clearly expressed in minor forms.

Born in the same year, Hernández Moncada wrote a *Sinfonía en Do* (1942) which represents the steady evolution of a musician emerging from an uncomplicated use of local colouring to the point where excessively emotional chromaticism is put away and a conscious pursuit of logical structure takes precedence. In this work and the *Concerto* for piano and orchestra by Blas Galindo (b. 1910) a definite advance is made, beyond the efforts of Candelario Huízar (b. 1889) to force Indian material into symphonic conventions; the advance may be measured by comparing the latter's efforts of this sort with motifs of the Huichol Indians and Blas Galindo's evocations of this people among whom he was born. These explorations of different Mexican stocks have been followed up by Daniel Ayala (b. 1908) who specifically entered the Mayan field, while Salvador Contreras (b. 1912) was drawn into the sphere which Revueltas' early death left silent.

Carlos Chávez, emerging from this background and those varying endeavours to express the Mexican people's singular destiny which resulted sometimes in emphasising differences of race rather than their coordination because of the frequent incongruity between matter and musical form, has pressed on since boyhood with uninterrupted concentration towards the complete integration of Mexican potential, passing with direct rapidity through the several stages in Latin American evolution of an entire century. He has been compared with Stravinsky, as in *El nuevo fuego* (1921) and the ballet *Los cuatro soles* which show a Mexican idiom shaped into the spirit of *The Rite of Spring*. Engrossment with instrumental explorations in Stravinsky's manner is more violently expressed in *Xochipilli-Macuixochitl* (1940). The *Sinfonía India* (1935–1936) however, is concerned almost completely to realise a full coordination of native musical potential, as scattered across the whole country, into the main stream of modern composition. The *Sinfonía de Antígona* (1933) based on the idea of depicting a native classically tragic figure, is conceived as a dramatic overture whose clear polyphonic instrumentation compresses an intensity of experience unapproached by 17th-century Italian composers of classical heroics and which is less cerebral than Stravinsky's symphonic writing for wind consorts and when re-composing Greek themes also.

The *Third Symphony* (1951–1954) returns in spiral form to the thematic tensions of the first two and with permanently enlarged concerting of stylistic sonorities. A sense of relief from these earlier and unremitting preoccupations with the adequate expression of his creative forces emerges in the *Fourth Symphony*, especially in the last movement, Vivo non troppo, written in October 1953. The work was rapidly conceived and in its brevity makes fine play with many timbres of metallic novelty and a flexible consideration of wind cantabile. This period, probably the most fertile in Chávez' life, brought a commission from the US Library of Congress which resulted in the *Fifth Symphony*, first performed in December 1953 in Los Angeles under his direction, for string orchestra only.

In this work his chief characteristics, dissonant polyphonic writing, insistent rhythmic patterning, dramatic tenseness and brilliantly contrasted instrumental timbres, are deployed with exceptional assurance. The finale, Allegro con brio, however, finds spiritual relief in recollections of Bach's happy melodic serenity, though some listeners detect a continuance of Stravinsky's neo-classicism even here.

These works, read programmatically, may give the impression that Chávez is consistently concerned with the dilation of existing forms imported from Europe and their implanting in American soil with New World sophistication. In reality he has always maintained close contact with the smaller forms of Spanish American tradition and returned to them after each major effort, possibly for recuperation and certainly to regenerate his energy. That he was aware from the first of this inner continuous reaction is clear from some lines he wrote in 1942: 'In the sonatinas I was returning to some extent from the large forms and preoccupied with conciseness: I achieved in a short work the sensation of roundness and completion sought in the larger form.' Moreover, his larger works are often made up with short sections as in his first Indian ballet, *El fuego nuevo* (1921) which is a series of contrasting scenes. This 'new fire' is the spirit of *alegría* and it is nearly always this joy which captivates the listener in the short fast finales Chávez prefers for conclusion. This was followed by an accumulation of small pieces, again during the time when he was consolidating his style; every little piece emerges fresh and novel from his moulding hands. *Polígonos* is a suite of seven pieces, of very brief duration. So are the *Three guitar pieces*, eventually presented in 1954. The *Tres exágones* of 1923 are miniatures of strong but concise emotional power. The *Sonatinas* of 1924 are equally short. The violin and piano *Sonatina* is in one movement, divided in five finely balanced sections, and again expresses intense force. The *Sonatina* for piano is contained in four pages but is perfect in form; 'brief, compact, potent', as Paul Rosenfeld has said. The cello *Sonatina* is another miniature. *Energía*, first performed in Paris in 1931, yields sensational tension, its last and shortest movement being, as usual, the best. It was now clear that Chávez shunned the anecdotal as a means to dilate his music. Though there is an apparent return to large form in *Los Cuatro Soles*, this on examination proves to be made of short interludes and much contrasting alternation of moods which give rise to the points of tension; however, the uninterrupted excitement of the previous short works is not maintained throughout. A sense of vitality, generated within cellular fragments which are then used to dynamise the working-out passages becomes now a persisting habit and in later works constantly communicates essential creative force to them; in the same way, his orchestral percussiveness strikes sparks that provoke explosive oppositions among the instruments.

Caballos de Vapor, a symphonic ballet (1926–1927), strives to energise its larger scale by contrasting North and South American ways of life, but again its motive force is most intensely felt in the fragmentations. Here his use of Latin American folklore is exploited in depth and he creates electrifying juxtapositions of North American and Spanish American rhythms as he had already done with Indian motifs, which are also included here. However, the use of agglomerations begins to show as assisting the generation of dynamism in these many melodies and tunes. Nevertheless, in this work Chávez communicates a heightened sense of *alegría* unmatched in American music.

Again a return to lesser dimensions intervenes and from now onwards he resorts also to a return within the form itself at certain points as if seeking inner creative reassurances. Here he seems to hark back to Sor Juana's concept of harmony as moving in a spiral. A little piece of

1934 for violin and piano he actually named *Espiral*, which would have pleased her. The *Sonata for Four Horns* (1931) was only later enlarged to concerto form with orchestra. *Paisaje* consists of only 13 bars, but is as closely devised and pondered as any larger form. Thus the recourse to miniature conciseness became a significant and constant factor in Chávez' creative life and is to be accepted as natural to him.

His *Concerto* for four wind instruments is often compared to Falla's *Concerto*: more intimately related to Falla perhaps are Chávez' *Cuatro nocturnos* (1938–1939) settings of poems by Villaurrutia for soprano, contralto and orchestra, first performed in 1947, soon after Falla's death. These poems are surrealist whereas Darío's Nocturnos were created within the symbolist sphere; but this difference does not obscure the fact that Villaurrutia's second nocturno's last lines possibly refer to Darío's theme in the observation 'porque el sueño y la muerte nada tienen ya que decirse', 'for dreams and death have nothing now to say', and that Chávez, who gave a lecture on surrealism in 1944, gave this verse a setting alluding to the medieval organum.

Always at home in the percussive range since his first interpretations of the collective aboriginal idiom, it is not surprising that Chávez' *Toccata for Percussion Instruments* is ranked with Bartok's *Music for Two Pianos and Percussion*. It is unremittingly concise throughout its 15 minutes. The structure of *Toccata for Orchestra* (1947) consists basically of dance and song proportionately balanced on several planes in closely controlled manner. 1948 and 1949 find him again writing little piano pieces, including a *Chopiniana* for the Chopin centenary, conceived with some intention of paralleling Vila Lobos's *Bachianas brasileiras*; nevertheless Chopin's art is seen through a Mexican prism, and not relaxed in style as are Vila Lobos' variations on Bach.

The *Violin concerto* of 1945–1950 is concerned with variations on form, of the four movements whose order is inverted in repetition as in mirror reflection. Between the two Scherzo middle movements Chávez places a Cadenza which is the longest section of the whole work —seven minutes—and is a brilliant challenge to the soloist. Upon this original scheme Chávez has created a witty work in which joy and alegría prevail. It is worth noting the parallels here with the eight movements of El Tamunangue, that suite of dances with varied rhythms and melodies danced in honour of San Antonio in Venezuela, and the custom of including instrumental interludes for old instruments like the harp to display not only virtuosity but their memories of 18th-century classic style.[1] This concerto does not conceal some ironic

---

[1] In some Tamunangue suites the four central pieces are Negro dances, the two extremes being both of European extraction. Thus a rudimentary sense of mirror form is shown. It is the middle pieces which allow improvisations, as with Chávez' central Cadenza.

allusions to the valse which penetrated the Caribbean region, and indeed all Latin America, not least Caracas, with effect upon many older dances there. Chávez had many contacts in Caracas, where his third symphony won first prize in 1954, played by the Orquesta Sinfónica of Venezuela under his direction, and again in April 1957. The Scherzo's treatment here of the old habanera motif may be related in its ironic approach to that of the valse in the *violin concerto*.

From his early years Carlos Chávez studied Bach and his predecessors with singular dedication. He also demonstrated from boyhood his desire to draw the neglected Indian into the field of American creativity and to give his art the dignity and prominence it deserved. His experiments of this kind have been inadequately described as 'petrified'. To say that his technical coordination of these untried sources is more truly a process of stratification is not to be interpreted as denigratory. The state of Latin American culture is one of stratification and will remain so for many years as the varying stages of existence reveal themselves musically in turn. To artists as uncompromising as Carlos Chávez partial fusions occurring in privileged regions of the hemisphere remain the self-expression of the few and exceptionally fortunate. He has shown by his own unceasing labour that coordination of all the peoples in the South American continent is musically practicable. He has not minimised the obstacles in the way of this consummation and it is possible that his lifelong study of Bach's contrapuntal creation concurrently with his efforts to bring Indian material into linear harmony with the wealth of colonial themes reveals a sense that the coordination is only to be achieved by close, continuous harmony on horizontal planes in Bach's manner. This was the means constantly employed by musicians who forged the great contrapuntal traditions of Spain, and these composers are Carlos Chávez' ancestors.

Though highly gifted, the Cuban composers, Amadeo Roldán (1909–1939) and Alejandro Caturla (1906–1940) died too young to carry the Afro-Cuban rumba on to the plane of Ravel's evocation of the valse. In contrast, the more temperate zones of the River Plate give a naturalist tone to the work of musicians contemplating impressionistically the placid scenery of its farmland and rolling pampas. Fabini, in Uruguay, evokes the less glaring light of *La Isla de los ceibos*. Alberto Ginastera has often composed music that reflects a spirit rather similar to that of southern England or northern France, with the aesthetic of which Argentine literature has not infrequently identified itself, as have some Argentine painters who find tonal agreement with the English school of Turner and his various descendants both French and British. Julian Aguirre's *Huella y Gato* accentuates the virile nature of the men who roam the pampas, rather than the landscape itself. Soro's nationalism in Chile and Humberto Allende in works like *Tonadas* exhibit a natural desire to express their Pacific differences of outlook with a musical atmosphere beyond the scope of language's factual outlines which are common to all Spanish-speaking Americans. Adolfo Salazar suggests that Pedro Prado is a South American Vaughan Williams, for instance. The Colombian Guillermo Uribe he finds comparable to Ginastera in his invention of motifs that evoke popular idiom without exactly defined imitation.

The nationalistic exploration of local music in Peru was led by María Valle Riestra (1859–1925), who wrote operas on Incan subjects if not exactly on Incan motifs, as in *Ollanta*, 1901 and *Atahualpa*. Peruvian Indian material was more consistently explored by Daniel Robles (1871–1942) and Theodoro Valcárcel (1902–1942) in opera, ballet-opera and symphonic poems, and the Peruvian school now contains a number of active personalities extending their talents into a field which equals the Aztec in yielding material survivals of a previously great civilisation; these musicians include such varied figures as Pablo Chávez Aguilar, Carlos Sánchez Málaga, Roberto Carpio, Raoul de Verneuil, Carlos Valderrama, Alfonso de Silva, Rosa Mercedes de Morales, and in the contemporary world the resilient figure of Armando Guevara.

Juan Carlos Paz (b. 1897) in Argentina, however, submerged himself, not in tritonic and pentatonic scales, but in the twelve-note order of atonality, becoming the focal point of this school in southern latitudes; while Juan José Castro (b. 1895), also emancipated from the apron-strings of folklore, has thus found it possible to write in the symphonic dimension works whose national titles *Sinfonía argentina* and *Sinfonía de los campos* do not confine the music to a local atmosphere. There is a correspondence between this personal realisation that technical sophistication may be a Pandora's box as illustrated by Dukas' *Sorcerer's Apprentice* and the work in Chile by Domingo Santa Cruz and the Venezuelan Juan Lecuona. There are signs that other Latin American composers, some of whom have already been named, are inclined to re-echo that famous cry wrung in the 1920s from the genial Brazilian Heitor Vila Lobos when asked to align himself with the furore of Brazil's Semana Moderna: 'Não sou modernista! Não participei na Semana da Arte Moderna! Sou um artista livre!' 'I am not a modernist! I did not participate in the Week of Modern Art! I am a free artist!'

Vila Lobos, the leader of Portuguese-American music, sought to bring a new world synthesis into Brazilian music by harmonising Indian, colonial, classical Portuguese and European strains together, with varying success. More reflective and analytical, Chávez is able to balance more securely as wide a range of musical elements. Having heard indigenous music as a child his ears assimilated its idiom naturally, making it inevitably an essential element in his own creative demands of sound. There was nothing strange, therefore, in his early exercise of such Indian survivals as he found in conjunction with the mixed strains in criollo tradition. What he consciously strove for was to renew their potential in the syntheses their elements offered, in particular their rhythms, scales, and instruments.

The Spanish qualities in his nature, the tenacity, the refusal of useless complication or padding, the constant search for definition, the renovation of popular tradition by contemporary expression, have proved of incomparable aid in the enormous task he deliberately set himself to accomplish. Possibly the kind of Spanish musician he most resembles is Antonio Soler, austerely energetic, but fired with warm impetuosity, technically armed cap-á-pie and justly proud of the fact that each work, large or small, presents an achievement different from the rest. Falla could claim the same distinction had he wished. Chávez wrote that music is a social necessity; Falla confided to his notebooks that by effacing the original thought which lay behind his work this was obscured so that the music might serve in purely musical terms as a 'beautiful social utility'. Though there is a slight difference of meaning here, their purposes converge.

The original thought, that new musical systems might be created from harmonics, which occurred to Falla when seeking sounds of crystal purity to express the nature of Don Quixote, according—so it now seems—to the American poet, Rubén Darío, was also utilised by Chávez in his *Fifth Symphony*. He, however, had developed this from the harmonics produced by the great Aztec sea-shell which he believed the Aztecs understood and applied, adding, moreover, that not one of the Aztec instruments produces sounds outside this system of so-called natural harmonics. The use of their notes in this last symphony is made to evoke an unreal atmosphere of submerged dreaming, symbolising, it is said, the ringing of different church bells, and presenting one of the most notable experiences of contemporary music.[1] Falla and other Spanish composers would agree with Chávez' words that each composition should have its own particular form, according to its component parts, but that there are certain eternal values, like the parity and trinity of elements, and symmetry, which must always be present, in one way or another, though not obviously. They would also agree that the personal is also national and therefore the artist's personal work is by necessity national since the national is the centre of our experience which we absorb and which feeds our personality and capacity for *pure*

[1] It seems more likely, however, that these pages prove the active survival of Indian genius through this use of the Aztec harmonic system.

invention, as Chávez says, for this is fundamentally the meaning of the Spanish term *castizo*, when applied to Spanish art.

Like true Americans, Chávez defends his freedom of choice in style applying this to the over-systematisation of serial music; for, he argues, why should we deprive ourselves of tonality for ever, since it is a natural phenomenon and remains an immense fountain of expression? And besides, our own personal tendency to tonality cannot be stifled, for there is within us a physiological function, natural and congenital, which ensures our affinity with its physical resonance. Though we may be unaware of it we subconsciously expect and await the process of tonal functions. Here, the unmistakable voices of Spain's independent musical thinkers are heard, Pareja, Bermudo, Salinas, Numantino, Ortiz and many others, proclaiming the ascendancy and rightness of the ear's unfailing instinct in its definition of tone.

Later in life, Chávez refers again to form and with an almost mysterious exaltation of its communal significance, insisting that form and the essential foundations of matter are one and indivisible. He illustrates this by Beethoven's Ninth Symphony, the depths of which, he says, could only have arisen out of the composer's simultaneous conception of the form proper to this great work. Form is not, nor should be, a pattern. Here there is a return to the idea of music illustrating the origins of universal creation, as some following lines suggest also, when he says that music ought to be national in character but universal in its fundamental nature and in this way should reach the majority of people. Thus, as with Sor Juana's conception of the spiral movement of harmony, the leader of American music in our time returns to the thought of Augustine, who visualises the creation of music in conformity with the creation of the world, expressing in time the divine essence of eternity. Chávez' knowledge of *De Musica* is closer than some modern critics may have supposed, for in his composition called *Espiral*, recalling Sor Juana's treatise which refers to *De Musica*, he inserts a sporadic, but repeated rhythmic figure in 4/8 within the general 3/8 pattern, which thus follows Morales' probable illustration in his two Cantatas of *De Musica*'s final pages contrasting the rhythm of carnal perception with 'that vital movement agile with temporal intervals' and referring again to the power of numbers to create in series, from which Sor Juana's title *El Caracol* for Harmony is drawn in token of this continual returning upon its form which is the function of music's rhythm and harmony.

Chávez' own creation of this force finds its great expression in the passacaglia of his Sixth Symphony's last movement. Here the varied strands of sound in the New World are gathered into the measured flow of this form, whose name is Spanish in origin, partaking both of march and of dance, and having spiritual as well as communal festal meaning, and yet retaining the workmanship of the great musical scientists of the classic past. Its wonderful slow passages suggest ethical confirmation of true alegría such as Beethoven wrought out of Schiller's Ode to Joy, and Blake visualised in the Sons of Men rejoicing.

Chávez' meditation on form continues in *Fifty Years of Music in Mexico*. 'It is well known that in all epochs and places there has always existed a current of mutual influence between cultured and popular music; between that of Church and people during the first fifteen centuries of the Christian era; between the cultured forms sung and played in court and theatre which began to develop during the Renaissance, and again with the people; and finally, between this and instrumental music of the 17th century and all centuries since to this day.'

Coming then to the major preoccupation of his generation, the proper aims of sincerely conceived national music in Latin America, he insists that in itself national music is of little use; what matters is good music, and good music can only be written by good composers, masters of a superior talent, universal information and an experience constantly growing and enlarged. However isolated he may suppose himself to be, the true creative artist cannot escape the influence of his time and surroundings. Because of the elementality of popular forms of expression a country begins with these, and only with the passing of years and with the general cultural growth will it achieve forms of artistic superiority. It is towards this achievement that Carlos Chávez and his musical equals have laboured in America.

As an American, writing in 1952 on 'American art', he declares: 'I consider that Americans are direct heirs of western culture, as much as Europeans; it is not a question of preference, for one cannot renounce the inheritance, although one might wish to do so. They are owners and participants of the Greco-Roman tradition, as the Greco-Romans were of the old cultural foundations of the Orient. They are an American branch of western culture. Man is everywhere, he is owner of his little planet. The feeling of universality is not new in history . . . localism also has existed always, but with the limitations of fear, or poverty of spirit. For this reason, it has been an error to seek the originality of American art by way of nationalism inspired in localisms and limitation. No. The American is as universal as the rest.'

GLOSSARY

acarreo de mieses Melodies to accompany the transporting of crops.
aguinaldo Song of those who seek alms at Christmas.
alabado Motet praising the Eucharist or Virgin; workers' song in the
  fields before starting the day's work and on its conclusion; night-
  watchman's song at daybreak.
albogón Flute-like wind instrument with low compass.
albogue Double-piped wind instrument.
alborada Music at dawn, as on a saint's day or to honour a bride; both
  vocal and instrumental and performed in the open air.
añafil Long, straight trumpet.
arada Ploughing song.
arrorro, arrullos Cradle songs.
atabal Small drum.
aurora Religious song at daybreak.
axabebe Reed flute.

baile a lo alto Dance in 2/4 time on tonic and dominant, sometimes on
  fixed bass, widespread in Castile and northern Portugal under many
  names, e.g. *al agudo*; *a lo ligero*; *a la pandera*; *al pandero*, that is, accompanied by *pandereta*; *brincadillo*; *arriba*. Both song and refrain accompany the dance of men and women facing each other but keeping a
  certain distance.
bambuco Dance and its song popular in Colombia.
bandola Small four-stringed instrument resembling the *laúd* in appearance.
bandurria or *pandora* Six-stringed instrument of the mandoline type,
  its double strings being plucked with a *púa*. Much smaller than
  guitar. Used in the *rondalla aragonesa*.
barrio Section of a district. In *zarzuelas* or *tonadillas* often the background scene for the *bailes* and *verbenas*.

bolero Dance in 3/4, more deliberate in tempo than the *seguidillas*, and having a triplet on the first weak beat of the bar.

botafumeiro Incense swinger.

cachucha Ternary dance popular in Andalusia introduced in 19th-century stage pieces with variants such as the *boleras acachuchadas*.

caleseras Songs of the drivers of two-wheeled open light carriages, or *calesas*.

canario Old dance associated with the Canary islands, in 3/8 dotted time, danced by pairs making oblique passages across the floor, with arms interlaced overhead. Tempo slightly quicker than the *siciliana*.

cancionero Song-book; from *canción*, song.

cante jondo lit. 'song of the depths'. See section in Chapter VI.

cantilena A simple melody. In rural areas *cantinela* is sometimes used for the same.

castizo Of good stock, preserving its original purity.

caracol Andalusian song of light-hearted nature. Snail.

caramillo Small reed pipe or flute of very high pitch.

carcelera Popular Andalusian song lamenting the woes of imprisonment.

charrada Dance in 3/4 or 3/8 time of the *charros*—rural people of Salamanca province.

chirimía Wood-wind instrument resembling the shawms.

chufla Light jocular song.

chulapos, chulapas Lively boys and girls featured in *zarzuelas* and *tonadillas escénicas*.

cielito Argentine and Uruguayan dance popular throughout the River Plate area, taking its name from the refrain's repeated word *cielito* 'little heaven'—the couples hold hands.

cítara Small instrument plucked like the *bandurria* with the triangular *púa*.

cobla Group of musicians devoted to playing *sardanas* in Catalonia.

coplas Short verses commonly used in popular songs.

corregidor Magistrate, official exercising royal jurisdiction.

corrido *Romance* or *jácara*, usually accompanied by the guitar playing a *fandango* type of tune.

cossante Early medieval verse, probably derived from *consoante*, of parallelistic songs with a single-line refrain, and thus perhaps reminiscent of psalms such as 118 and 136. Their mood became like that of the *saudades*, lamenting the loved one in absence.

costumbrismo The depiction of customs and manners peculiar to a place or region.

danzón Cuban dance related to the *habanera*.
darbuca See *laúd*.
décimas Combination of ten eight-syllable lines.
diana Flourish of instruments; used sometimes in *zarzuelas* to open a scene.
duende Spirit said to haunt certain houses; fig. to be imaginatively excited (*tener uno duende*).
dulzaina Wind instrument resembling the *chirimía*.

endechas Laments.
españolado Foreigner who apes Spanish ways; music imitating Spanish styles and colour.
españoleta Old Spanish dance.
estribillo Refrain.
estudiantina Student festivity.
exabeba See *axabebe*.
exaquier One of the piano's oldest predecessors. Square-shaped like virginals.
ezpata-dantza Basque sword-dance.

fandango Old Spanish dance with strongly marked 3/4 rhythm; now-adays sometimes describing a noisy gathering; *fandanguillo*, a variant of fandango.
Flamenco See section on Andalusian popular music in Chapter VI.
flaviol Small reed pipe of high range.
folía Old dance for many persons, of Portuguese origin; also a Spanish solo dance with castanets; fig. light music of popular nature.
frottole Italian ballads, as in the *Cancionero Musical de Palacio*.

gaita Bagpipe, widely used in the west of Spain, Galicia and Portugal; its drone bass has influenced many melodies. Also the *gaita de ruedas*, or viola—*vielle*.
gato Dance of the *gauchos*—Argentine cattle hands.
goigs Joys, as in the Joys of the Virgin Mary.
guajira Popular Cuban song of mixed 3/8 and 3/4 measure, as also in Andalusia and Extremadura.
guajiro White rural worker in Cuba; introduced to the *zarzuela* in the 19th century.
guitarra See *vihuela*.

habanera Dance of Havana, spreading along the Caribbean coasts and down through Venezuela, Brazil to Uruguay and Argentina. Slow 2/4 time, with dotted first note.

huapango Mexican dance with complex rhythmic crossings.

huertano Inhabitant of the Murcian *huertas*—small holdings and gardens.

jabera, javera Popular Andalusian song in 3/8 time.

jácara Romance verses usually describing picaresque events. Sung and danced in the early Spanish popular theatre.

jarabe Its lively 6/8 footwork derives from the *zapateado* with mazurka accents added.

jarana Mexican dance, derived from the Spanish *jarana* meaning a noisy diversion of 'ordinary' people.

jota Dance in 3/4 time, four bars in the dominant key alternating with four in the tonic, and alternating with song in parallel phrases, usually in slower measure than the dance, pertaining to Aragon and Valencia. Most popular of all Spanish forms, it has produced many variants. See Chapter VI.

juerga Similar to *jarana*, more especially referring to popular Andalusian entertainment in which *cante jondo* and *flamenco* music are prominent.

juglar One who recited or sang the troubadours' ballads and lays and who danced or took part in public spectacles including games with juggling on occasion. See Chapter II.

karsi An introductory movement to each of the Muslim nauba's five movements. See Chapter II.

kharja Mozarabic song of two and four short lines, written in Castilian but with Arabic or Hebrew characters, and treating usually of love in absence.

laúd Spanish lute; known in its Arabic form as al'ud—also as *darbuca*, according to Ribera who derives darbuca from the Persian *darbat*, signifying duck's breast, in allusion to its shape.

loor Praise, or hymn, as in the *Cantigas de Santa María*, in honour of Our Lady.

malagueña See *rondeña*.

manocordio Vicente de Burgos in his *Libro de proprietatibus* (Toledo 1529) classes this keyboard instrument among those to be played— *por tocar*—like the *laúd* and psaltery; thus its strings were *martilladas*— struck or hammered.

marizápalo Ancient dance in 3/4 measure.

martinete Andalusian gypsy song unaccompanied by guitar.

matachín Masked dancing of grotesque figures in which wooden swords and bladders filled with air are used in blows and counter-strokes; in 6/8 time.

mejorana Dance, usually accompanied by two guitars, from Panama; the *mejoranera* guitar has five strings.

monocordio Very early string instrument used in 11th-century Catalonia for the teaching of singing. Its single string was used for measuring vibrations from Pythagoras' times.

moriscos Moors remaining in Spain after the reconquest. The archpriest Juan Ruiz mentions the *guitarra morisca* first, before the *alaut* and *guitarra ladina*—or Spanish form; the *rabel morisco* had two strings, but a sonorous belly.

muelas Songs to accompany the grinding of corn.

muiñeira Popular Galician dance in 6/8 time; *muiñho*—mill; *muñir*—to draw an assembly together; some opening words of *muiñeira* songs suggest this getting together of people.

nanas Cradle songs.

nauba, nuba Musical privilege granted by the caliph to his lesser chiefs but with fewer flourishes and drum-beats than his own which was the fivefold *nauba*. The kind and number of instruments was strictly ordered. Later, the *nauba*, or *nuba*, received special attention from composers, being cultivated in every mode, and in five movements, each of which had an introductory section, or *karsi*. See Chapters II and VI.

organillo Small mechanical (barrel) organ.

panaderos a zapateado Dance in 6/8 quick time with continuous heel-stamping.

pandereta tambourine or timbrel. Survived as *pandero morisco* from Moorish times as rustic percussion. *Pandero* is also a brisk Navarrese dance with leaps during which the dexterous youth, as in *estudiantinas*, may strike the instrument with hands, elbows, knees and feet. See *baile a lo alto*.

pandora See *bandurria*.

pasacalle Popular march used on secular occasions and also to celebrate saints' days; on going to church for weddings and other services. Also an ancient dance of slow 3/4 rhythm. The pipe and tabor are traditional instruments for the pasacalle to church. Derived from *pasa*—walk—and *calle*—street.

pericón Old dance for several pairs in ternary rhythm; cultivated particularly in the River Plate region and in Uruguay as a national dance. *pericón* is also a very large fan.

petenera Belongs now to the *canto flamenco* group, and is thought to have derived from the *zéjel*. The song consists of four lines of eight syllables each.

plañideras Women hired to sing laments at funerals.

polo This quick, tense air in 3/8 rhythm holds a high place in *cante jondo*, belonging to that group containing the *seguiriya gitana*, together with the *soleares* and *martinetes*. The guitar interludes demand crisp ornamentation and complex rhythmic technique as does the true vocal line and in spite of 19th-century theatrical stylisations the castizo *polo* preserves its character, as in Ocón's example and Falla's parallel, which fittingly concludes his *Siete canciones populares españolas*.

pregón, pregonero Street-cries, town-crier.

púa Triangular spike of tortoise-shell or horn used to pluck the *bandurria*.

punteado, puntear To play the guitar, or similar instrument, by striking each string with one finger. The punteado linear style is classically identified with the art of the *diferencia*—difference.

rabel Rustic three-string violin, still in use. Cited by Cervantes.

rasgueado, rasguear Close arpeggio, or broken chord technique, or chord strumming of the popular guitarist, striking several strings together with the finger tips.

rondalla A reunion of youths to go singing and playing about the streets at night; the *rondalla aragonesa* is famous for the number of its instruments of the guitar family, larger and smaller than the customary size in general use; these bands include the *bandurria*.

rondeña Song deriving from the *fandango*, pertaining to the *rondeños*, inhabitants of Ronda. Associated with the *malagueña* in the *rondeñas malagueñas*—of Malaga—both have a slower tempo than the *sevillanas*. All of these are in 3/4 tempo, *rondeñas* and *malagueñas* in the minor, *sevillanas* in the major.

ruedas Dances 'en corro'—in circles; many of these are pre-Islamic and are still danced in many parts of the peninsula; in Castile, some *ruedas castellanas* are similar to the Basque *aurresku*, in 5/8 time and thus to the *zortzico*.

salero Natural gift of personal attraction and wit.

sandunga A valse in parts of Latin America, still Spanish in style and with the style associated with the word *sandunga* in Spain as meaning gracefully attractive.

sarao Evening concert or dance.

sardana Catalan traditional circular dance in which any number may join and dance to a band, or *cobla*, of eleven instruments. See Chapter VI.

seguidillas seguir—to follow. Verses of four or seven lines. Highly popular dance and song in quick 3/4 tempo. *Seguidillas sevillanas* are in the major key, *seguidillas manchegas*—of La Mancha—in the minor; *seguidillas boleras* show the adaptable qualities of the generic form; *seguidillas murcianas* are in the major. In constant use in *zarzuelas* and ballets, the *seguidillas sevillanas* have the special function of lightening the atmosphere of the Andalusian musical idiom, since many Andalusian songs and dances are in the minor.

seise Seis—six. A dance by choir boys, six in number, who play castanets before the altar; still performed in Seville cathedral; once widespread in Spanish cathedral festal services.

serranillas Rustic love songs from the mountains, or *sierras*, usually in short metre.

siega *Canciones de siega*; field songs of the harvest seasons, sung by *segadores*, harvesters.

sinfonía Has had several names since medieval times, as *cinfonía, viola de ruedas*, or *gaita de ruedas, sambuca, symphonía*; the *symphonia* is cited in the poem of *Alexandre*, 13th century, as played by the *juglars*. The surviving instrument in Galicia is still played by wandering beggars turning the old wheel as more northern beggars in living memory still played the hurdy-gurdy.

soleá, soleares These Andalusian songs, as their name suggests, are verses on the pains of bereavement, betrayal and loneliness, the word *soleá* being used as an exclamatory refrain in many examples. The guitar part has become complex but maintains the ejaculatory style the word *soleá* or *soledad*, for solitary, demands. See Chapter VI, Andalusian section.

son Sound—agreeable sounding. The traditional *son brincao* and *son llano o no brincao* of Extremadura are in quick 3/4 time, the first allegro, the second vivo, with tabor-beats accompanying the *gaita* throughout. The older dance, the *son brincao*, has a movement known as the *brincado* related to primitive times in its short turning pattern about the same spot, taking one step forward and one back, ending two bars of this with a jump. Castanets are not used in the *son brincao*, but may be added in the *son llano o no brincao*. The *son* from Spain has been applied to numerous dances and songs in Mexico. The *bolero son* is in the old 2/4 rhythm, though in the Caribbean it has acquired local syncopations. The Afro-Cuban *son* has adopted the 3/4; the Guatemalan *son* has become a valse.

sonajas Pairs of metal clappers, or bells for jingling as in *sonajero*.

strambote, estrambote   Fig. extravaganza, oddity. Poetically, lines added to the end of a metrical combination, especially of the sonnet.

taifa   Small state in Muslim Spain whose chief was subject to the caliph; later, the *taifa* states became kingdoms as the controls from Córdoba weakened.

tambor de orden   This dance has been devised as a corrective to the *tamborita* in those more restrained movements which curb the extremely free figures now associated with the old tamborita of Panama.

tango   Having the same rhythmic pattern as the *habanera*, but quicker, 4/8 rather than 4/4, the first note of each bar being dotted. In Honduras, Indian name for a drum of hollowed tree-trunk.

thaqīl   One of the basic rhythmic schemes of Muslim music as in the following: *hazaj, ramal,* first and second *thaqīl,* the *makhurī,* described by some as similar to the first *thaqīl,* and by others as like the second *thaqīl.* See Chapter II

tono   Verses written to be sung, also the music for them, sacred and secular pieces: *tonada* has similar meaning. *Tonadilla* derives from *tonado* as a light song developing into a short theatrical piece in miniature for one or more performers and instruments. The *tonada* in America usually keeps the 2/4 rhythm of the older tradition.

trilla, canción de   Threshing song.

verbena   Popular fiesta with dancing held out of doors at night in the summer heat.

vidala, vidalita   Argentine song and dance, taking their names from the refrain's repeated word, as in 'vida mia, vidalita mia', as the *cielito* also does.

vihuela   Until the 12th century *vihuelas,* or *fideles,* were played with fingers or plectrum, at which time bowed instruments—*de arco*— appeared. At Santiago de Compostela a musician playing the guitar is sculptured *c.* 1188. In the 13th century the type of guitar known as *mandola* is called *quiterne moresque* in France. *Laúd, guitarra, rabe, vihuela* and the small rustic *guitarra serranista* are cited in the poem of Alfonso XI *c.* 1328. Then the archpriest Juan Ruiz cites the *guitarra morisca, guitarra ladina*—latin—*vihuela de péndola*—plucked—and the *vihuela con arco*—bowed. There then appeared an instrument partaking of *guitar* and *laúd,* later known as the *chitarra battente.*

About 1570, the guitar settled on five strings, la re sol si mi, ascending, and it was on this systematic adoption of the 5th string that it became generally known as the *guitarra española,* though the adjectival distinction disappeared later. Bermudo also records that the bandurria was a variant of the guitar and that the *laúd europeo* was becoming known as the *vihuela de Flandes* (Flanders).

The word *violero* for vihuela-player in the 13th century was, by the 16th, applied to vihuela-makers; the word *violão* has been kept in Portugal for the guitar, and also in Brazil. *Violeiro* is used for guitarist in both these countries. *Marabba* square flat-backed guitar.

villancico Rustic music with refrain, especially popular as nativity songs and by Juan del Eneina's time also adapted to the 'pastorale' style. In this dual role, it developed steadily in the 17th century and by the 18th, was appearing as cantata and oratorio.

villanesca An ancient little rustic song and the dance that goes with it.

virelai Medieval French song adopted in Spain and prominent in the *Cantigas de Santa María*. From *virelai*, a lay from Vire in Normandy.

zapateado Spanish solo dance in 3/4 quick rhythm with marked heel-stampings. From *zapato*—shoe.

zarzuela Spanish form of opera in which dialogue and song alternate. See Chapter IV.

zéjel Popular poetic composition of Muslim Spain, this form emerged from Cabra in Andalusia when a blind poet Muqaddam wrote verses whose refrain he created in the popular romance tongue and which spread through southern Spain and to Aragon, being sung by every-one when it was set to music; the *zéjel*'s popularity spread to north Africa and to Bagdad.

zorcico, zortzico Basque song and dance in 5/8 time. See Chapter VI, Basque section.

zorongo Old Andalusian dance with song in 3/8 time, patterned mainly on the cadential minor fall.

BIBLIOGRAPHY

This short book list supplements the works quoted in the text.

Alcocer Martínez, R., *La Corporación de los poetas en la España musulmana*. Tetuán 1940

Anglés, Mgr. Higinio, *El Códice de las Huelgas*. Barcelona 1931
— *La Música de las Cantigas de Santa María*. Barcelona 1943
— *Cancionero musical de Palacio*. Madrid 1941
— *La Música en la corte de Carlos V*. Barcelona 1944
— *La Música en la corte de los Reyes Católicos*. Barcelona 1947
— *Juan Vázquez; 'Recopilación de Sonetos y Villancicos a quatro y a cinco,'* Barcelona 1946

Aretz, Isabel, *El folklore musical argentino*, Buenos Aires 1952

Bal y Gay, Jesus, *Romances y villancicos españoles del siglo XVI*, Mexico 1939

Chase, Gilbert, *The Music of Spain*, New York 1941
— *Guide to Latin American Music*, Library of Congress, Washington 1943

Collet, Henri, *L'Essor de la Musique Espagnole au XXe. siècle*, Paris 1929

Croce, Benedetto, *La Spagna nella vita italiana durante la Rinascenza*, Bari 1949

Cruz, Sor Juana Inés de la, *Obras completas*, Mexico 1951

Daniel, Salvador, *Arab Music and musical instruments* (ed. Farmer), London 1914

Eximeno, Antonio, *Dell' origine e delle regole della musica*, Rome 1774

Farmer, Henry, *History of Arabian Music*, Luzac, London 1929

García Morillo, Roberto, *Carlos Chávez*, Mexico 1960

García Rodríguez, Carmen, *El Culto de los Santos en la España romana y visigoda*, Madrid 1966

Grenet, Emilio, *Popular Cuban Music*, Havana 1939

Hernández Azevedo, *Los cantares populares chilenos*, Santiago de Chile 1933

Joaquim, Manuel, *Cancioneiro musical e poético da Biblioteca Públia Hortênsia*, Coimbra 1940

Bibliography

Kastner, Santiago, *Música hispanica*, Lisbon 1936
— *Contribución al estudio de la música española y portuguesa*, Lisbon 1941
Kirkpatrick, Ralph, *Domenico Scarlatti*, Princeton 1953
López Chavarri, E., *Música popular*, Labor, Barcelona 1927
Mayer-Serra, Otto, *Panorama de la Música Mexicana*, Mexico 1941
Menéndez Pidal, R., *Poesía juglaresca y juglares*, Madrid 1924
Mitjana y Gordón, R., *Estudios sobre algunos músicos españoles del siglo XVI*, Madrid 1918
Pedrell, Felipe, *Cancionero musical popular español*, 4 vols, Valls 1918–22
— *Hispaniae schola música sacra*, 8 vols, Barcelona 1894–98
Penney, Clara, *List of Books printed 1601–1700 in the Library of The Hispanic Society of America*, New York 1938
Pereira Salas, E., *Historia de la música en Chile*, Santiago de Chile, 1957
Pinto Ferreira, J. A., *Correspondencia de D. João V e D. Barbara de Bragança, Rainha de Espana*, Coimbra 1945
Querol Gavaldá, Miguel, *Romances y letras a tres vozes*, Barcelona 1956
Ribera, Julián, *La Música árabe y su influencia en la española*, Madrid 1927
Ribeiro Sampayo, Mário de, *Os Manuscritos musicais da Biblioteca Geral da Universidade de Coimbra*, Coimbra 1941
Salazar, Adolfo, *La Música de España*, Buenos Aires 1953
Sopeña, Federico (ed.), *Manuel de Falla, Escritos sobre música y músicos*, Buenos Aires 1950
— *Memorias de músicos*, Madrid 1971
— *Joaquín Rodrigo*, Madrid 1946
Spell, Lota M., *The first Music Books printed in America*, Schirmer, N. Y. (s.d.)
— 'Music in the Cathedral of Mexico in the 16th century', *Hispanic American Historical Review*, Aug. 1946
Stevenson, Robert, *Spanish Music in the Age of Columbus*, The Hague 1960
— *Spanish Cathedral Music in the Golden Age*, University of California 1961
Subirá, José, *Historia de la música española e hispanoamericana*, Barcelona 1953
— *Celos aun del Aire matan*, Barcelona 1933
— *La tonadilla escénica*, 3 vols, Madrid 1928–30
— *Tonadillas teatrales inéditas*, Madrid 1932
Valdés Pereda, I., *Cancionero popular uruguayo*, Montevideo 1943
Vasconcellos, Joaquim de, *Os músicos portuguezes*, 2 vols, Oporto 1870
Vega, Carlos, *Panorama de la música popular argentina*, Buenos Aires 1944
— *Danzas y canciones argentinas*, Buenos Aires 1936
Vicente, Gil, *Copilaçam de todalas obras* (facsimile 1928), Lisbon 1562.

INDEX

A

'Abbadids of Seville, 29
'Abdu'l-Rahman I of Córdoba, 25; II, 25; III, 26
Aguado, Dionisio, 129
aguinaldos, 142
Aires Nunes, 41
'Alam, 21
Alarcón, Pedro de, 193
Albéniz, Isaac, 114, 125, 138, 141, 179f., 193, 197, 200
Albéniz, M., 125
Alberti, R., 198, 203, 211
alborada, alborá, 52, 148, 173, 175, 245
Aldana, 224
Alemtejo, 162
Alfonso V, of Aragon, 'the Magnanimous', 50, 51, 53
Alfonso X, of Castile, 'the Learned', 1, 38, 40, 41, 42, 48, 57, 115, 116, 117, 118, 119
Algeciras, 29
Alió, Francisco, 150
alleluia, 15, 44
Almería, 3, 36, 177
Amades, Juan, 150
Amat, Juan Carlos, 65, 102
Ambroa, Pedro de, 41
Amor Brujo (Falla), 191, 192
Ampurias, 4
Anchieta, Juan (Johannes), 54, 55, 57, 67
Andalusia, 161-172
Angeles, Victoria de los, 217
Anglés, Mgr. H., 9, 17, 45, 46, 47, 54, 59, 92
Antiphoner of León, 10, 14, 15, 20, 21, 141
antiphons, 7, 15, 22, 44
Aragon, 17, 32, 46, 49, 53, 58, 87, 147, 148
Aragon, Lola de, 217
Aranda, Luis, 89

Aranjuez, 112; Concierto de (Rodrigo) see *Concierto*
Aranzadi, Telesforo de, 152, 153, 154
Arbós, E. Fernández, 134, 193, 200, 201, 216
Argenta, Ataúlfo, 216
Argentina, 222f., 224, 240
Arianism, 7
Arizaga, R., 188
Aristotle, 123, 124
Arriaga, J. C., 134
Arrieta, Emilio, 131, 132
Astorga, 113
Asturias, 156, 157
Augustine, St., 2, 5, 8, 9, 10, 13, 18, 19, 71, 72, 79, 83, 84, 91, 92, 221
aurora, 144, 145
Auto de los Reyes Magos, 51
Avempace (ibn Bajja), 27, 30
Averroes (ibn Rushd), 27, 29
Avicenna (ibn Sina), 28, 33, 34, 174
Avignon, 46, 49
Avila, 77
Azores, 150, 151

B

Bacarisse, Salvador, 198, 211
Badía, Conchita, 217
Baena, Lope de, 57
bagpipes (*gaita*), 35, 46, 52, 59, 96, 115, 158
Baguer, Carlos, 120
ballades, 51
ballads (see *romances*), 7
Balteira, María Pérez, 41
Barbara of Braganza, queen of Ferdinand VI, 105, 111, 112, 113, 114, 115, 117, 118, 119
Barbieri, F. Asenjo, 131, 132
Barcelona, 15, 50, 113, 120, 131
Barrientos, María, 185
Barrios, Angel, 139
Bartolí, F., 110

Basilio, Pe., 122, 123
Basques, 54, 61, 123, 134, 151f., 204
Bautista, Julian, 211
Baveca, Juan, 41
Bécquer, Gustavo A., 203
Beethoven, 121, 132, 179
Berganza, Teresa, 218
Bermudo, Fr. J., 59, 61, 65, 72, 90
Bertomeu, Agustin, 215
Bizet, Georges, 130, 203
Blancafort, Alberto, 215
Blancafort, Manuel, 208
Boccherini, Luigi, 121, 122, 123
Boethius, 7, 8, 91, 123
Bolivia, 233
Bordas, Antonio, 134
Bretón, Tomás, 135, 136, 138, 149, 181, 183, 200, 225
Breva, Juan, 168, 171
Briz, F. B., 150
Brou, Dom L., 17
Bruch, Max, 135
Brunetti, G., 122
Buen Retiro, palace, Madrid, 100, 102, 110
Burgundy, 49
Byzantines, 3, 7, 14, 19, 21, 192

C

Cabanilles, Juan, 89
Cabezón, F. Antonio, 64, 65f., 77; Hernando, 67
Cádiz, 3, 172
Caldara, 113
Calderón de la Barca, P., 97f., 198, 223
Calvo, Julian, 141f., 174, 187, 192
Campo, Conrado del, 139, 198, 202, 203
Canales, Manuel, 122
Cancioneiro da Ajuda, 39
Cancioneiro Hortênsia Públia, 61 (note)
Cancionero de Baena, 51
Cancionero Musical de Palacio, 28, 51, 56f.
cantares de gesta, 38, 39
cante jondo, 162, 164, 165
cantigas de amigo, 34, 41, 42, 59
Cantigas de Santa Maria, 1, 38, 40, 41, 42, 48, 57, 114, 115, 116, 117, 118
carillons, 86
Carmen, 130, 166, 168, 203
Carnicer, Ramón, 131
Cartagena, 7

Carthaginians, 4
Casal-Chapí, E., 211
Casals, P., 135, 186, 201, 216
Casanovas, J., 215
Cassado, G., 217
castanets, 3, 37, 39
Castile, 153
Castro, Juan Blas de, 107
Castro, Juan Carlos, 241
Catalonia, 17, 37, 89, 150, 151, 205, 206
Cecilia, St, 20
Celts, 3
Celtiberians, 3
Cerdá, Angel, 215
Cererols, Juan, 89
Cervantes, 39, 96
Chapí, Ruperto, 135, 136, 137, 200
Charles V, Emperor, 65, 67, 68
Charles III, king, 119; IV, 120, 121, 122, 123
Chavarri, E. López, 147
Chávez, Carlos, 2, 236f., 242f.
Chile, 222, 226, 227
chirimías, 41
Chopin, 133, 185
Chueca, Federico, 137
Cistercians, 7, 44, 46, 52
clavicembalo, 52
Clavijo del Castillo, B., 88
Clement IX, Pope, 103
Cluny, 37, 52
cobla, 151
Codex, Martin, 42
Codex Calixtinus, 38, 43, 44; of Las Huelgas, 38, 44; of Liebana, 14
Coelho, Pe. M. Rodrigues, 89
Colombia, 232
Comellas, Juan, 215
Comes, J. B., 90
Compostela, see Santiago
Concierto de Aranjuez, (Rodrigo), 208, 209
Conforto, N., 111
Conservatory (Madrid), 131, 179, 201
Contreras, Fernando de, 68, 69
Coradini, F., 111
Córdoba, 24f., 87, 169
Córdoba, Argentina, 224
Cornago, Fr J., 50, 53, 57
Corpus Christi, 172
Corselli, F., 111
corrido, 231, 232
Correa de Araujo, F., 88
cossantes, 57

Costa, António da, 105
Costumbrismo, 105, 130
Cruz, Ramón de la, 126, 130
cuándo, 227
Cuba, 130, 164, 184, 232, 233, 234
cueca, 228
Cuzco, 219
cymbals, 37, 41

D

Damasus, St, 6
Dance of Death, 47
Darío, Rubén, 194f., 198, 211
Daza, Esteban, 64, 65
Debussy, 141, 180, 182, 188, 194, 197, 198, 201
De Consolatione Philosophiae (Boethius), 8
De Musica (St Augustine), 2, 18, 74, 76, 79, 80, 82, 83, 84, 85, 243
Descalzas Reales, Madrid, 106, 152
Diaghilev, 193, 207
Díaz, Francisco, 168
Diaz Besson, Gabriel, 106
diferencias, 62, 188
Dolores 'la Parrala', 168, 169
Donastia, Pe. J. A., 61, 205
drums, 30, 31, 37
'duende', 165
Dukas, 180, 197
Dunstable, 56
Durán, Gustavo, 211; José, 120
Durón, Sebastian, 103, 104, 109

E

eclogues, 56, 97, 99
églogas, see eclogues
Elche, mystery of, 92
Elizalde, Federico, 212
Encina, Juan del, 56, 57
Enríquez de Valderrábano, 64
entremés, 95, 96, 105
epics, 13
epithalamia, 12, 95
Escobar, Pedro de, 55
Escorial, 48, 85, 90, 124, 125
Eslava, H., 132, 133
espata-dantza (sword dance), 152
Espinel, Vicente, 62
Esplá, Oscar, 203
Esteban, Fernando, 48, 57
Esteve, Pablo, 126
estrambote, 56
estribillo, 60

Etheria Abbess, 6, 22
Etymologies (St Isidore), 8, 9
Eugenia, St, 20, 22
Eugenius III, metropolitan of Toledo, 10
Eulalia, St, 19
Extremadura, 161f.

F

Facco, Jaime, 110, 111
Fadl, 25
fado de Coimbra, 159
Falla, Manuel de, 2, 39, 114, 125, 129, 139, 140, 143, 144, 165, 166, 167, 182, 188f., 198, 199, 200, 201, 203
fandango, 35, 169, 170
Fantasía Bética (Falla), 197, 198
Al-Fārābī, 26, 27, 174
Farinelli (Carlo Broschi), 25, 111, 112
Farmer, H. G., 176
Feijóo, Pe. Benito, 104, 109, 132, 133, 232
Ferdinand III, V, 53, 54, 55; VI, 111, 113; VII, 128, 129
Fernández, Alejo, 72, 73
Fernández, Caballero, 137
Ferreira, Manuel, 110
flamenco, 165f.
Flecha, M., 64, 87
Flemish chapel, 67, 168
flutes, 27, 35, 41
France, 49, 51, 109, 151
Franconetti, S., 168
Frühbeck de Burgos, R., 216
Fuenllana, Miguel de, 64

G

Gabriel, Infante, 121, 122, 123
gaita, 35, 46, 59, 158
Galicians, 5, 34, 40, 41, 59, 115, 158
García, Manuel, 123, 126, 127, 128, 165, 166, 225
García Lorca, F., 210, 212
García Matos, M., 161, 162
gauchos, 155, 225, 228
género chico, 137, 139
Gil García, B., 161
Ginés Pérez, Luis, 94
Gerhard, Roberto, 210
Ginastera, Alberto, 240
Gómez Manrique, 33
Góngora, Luis de, 157
Goya, 122, 126, 132, 187, 193, 202
Goyescas (Granados), 187, 188

Granada, 29, 30, 31, 39, 192, 195, 196
Granados, Enrique, 114, 125, 141, 181, 184f., 217
Greek music, 4, 7, 26
Greeks, 4, 22
Gregorian chant, 55
Gregorius of Iliberris, 6, 34
Guadix, 21
guajiras, 136, 172, 183
Guerrero, Francisco, 64, 68, 73f.
Guerrero, Jacinto, 137
guitar, 35, 65, 95, 96, 122, 129, 226f.
Guridi, Jesús, 204
gypsies, 96, 166, 170

H

habaneras, 130, 232
Al-Hakam II, 26, 28, 31
Halffter, Cristóbal, 213, 214, 215; Ernesto, 114, 115, 198, 203; Rodolfo, 125, 203
ibn Ḥamdiṣ, 29, 30
harp, 12, 37, 65
Herrando, 112, 113
Hidalgo, Juan, 100, 101, 102
Hidalgo, Juan (b.1927), 213, 214
Hita, Juan Ruiz, Archpriest of, 33, 41, 42, 43
Holy Week, 173, 199
Homs, Joaquín, 214
Honegger, 211
hymns, 13, 40

I

Iberia (Albéniz), 181, 182, 197, 200
Iberians, 4
Ildefonso, St, 10, 18, 19, 20
d'Indy, V., 200
Infantas, Francisco de las, 87
Inzenga, José, 143, 145, 146, 159, 192
Ionic, 4
Iparaguirre, J. M., 135, 154
Iradier, Sebastian, 130
Iranzo, Miguel Lucas de, 51, 52
Isabella I, 55, 61; II, 131
Al-Isfāhāni, 26, 31, 176
Isidore of Seville, St, 2, 7, 8, 9, 10, 11, 13, 41, 42, 44
Italy, 50, 51, 100, 103, 108, 109, 110, 114, 120, 130, 225

J

jácara, 60, 95
jaleo, 172

Jarques, Juan, 89
Jesuits, 105, 224
Jiménez, Jerónimo, 137
John, St, the Baptist, 20
John II of Castile, 52
John I of Portugal, 52; III, 53; IV, 114
Jordá, Enrique, 216
jota, 126, 135, 147f., 177, 182
Jovellanos, 126
Juana Inés de la Cruz, Sor, 220f., 225, 243
juglares, 12, 32, 38
Julian, St, 4, 14

K

Kastner, S. M., 88
Katherine of Aragon, 56, 66
Keene, Sir Benjamin, 112
kharjas, 34
Khwarizmī, 28

L

Lalo, Edouard, 135
Lamote de Grignon, 139, 205, 216
Landowska, Wanda, 195
Lange, F. C., 224
Larrocha, Alicia de, 217
Laserna, Blas de, 125, 126
laúd, 25, 27, 61
Leander, St, 7, 10
Ledesma, Dámaso, 160
leila, 32
León, 10, 11, 14, 44, 151, 159f.
Liceo, Gran teatro del (Barcelona), 131, 135, 181, 207
Liszt, 180
Literes, António, 109, 110, 117
liturgy, 7, 14, 37, 174
Llibre Vermell, 38, 46, 151
Llobet, Miguel, 124, 129, 217
loa, 95
López de Velasco, Sebastian, 106
lute, 26, 34, 36, 61

M

Machado, Antonio, 209
Machaut, Guillaume de, 49, 51, 52, 53
madrigals, 60
Majorca, 150, 151
Málaga, 4, 29
malagueñas, 142, 168, 169
Malibran, 128
Manén, Juan, 139, 208
manochord, 62

Manoel I, king of Portugal, 32
Maragall, 213
María Ana Victoria, 105, 114, 121
María Luisa of Parma, 123
Marín, José, 103
Martial, 5
Martínez, Antonio, 144, 147
Martínez Sierra, G., 192, 194, 201
Martenot, 205
Martín y Soler, V., 120, 121
Matos, G., 139, 140
Mecca, 24
Medina, 24, 25
Mele, J. B., 111
melisma, 5, 15, 16, 17
melodramas, 112
melologue, 128
Menéndez Pidal, R., 13, 38
Mercury, 4
Mérida, 4, 5, 19, 20, 21, 22
Mestres, Apel-les, 187, 217
Mestres-Quadreny, 214
Metastasio, 111, 119
Mexico, 203, 212, 219, 220f.
Milan, Luis, 53, 62, 63
Millet, Luis, 205
Mingote, Angel, 147
Misón, Luis, 112, 113, 125, 126
Mithras, 4
Mitjana, R., 131
modes, 15, 18, 26, 35, 36
Mompou, Federico, 208
Monasterio, Jesús, 136
La Montaña, 155f., 184
Montano, A., 91
Monteverdi, 100, 101
Montsalvatge, Xavier, 139, 212, 213
Montserrat, 38, 46, 47, 48
Morales, Cristóbal de, 47, 63, 69, 70, 71, 219
Morales, Melesio, 225
Morera, Enrique, 205, 206
Moreto, Agustín, 98, 99, 105, 120, 201
moriscos, 32, 141
Morton, Robert, 58
motets, 45, 54, 72, 79
Mozarabic rite, 14, 17, 20, 37, 38, 174
Mozarabs, 14, 34
Mozart, 99, 120, 121
mudanza, 86
Mudarra, Alfonso, 63
Muqaddam of Cabra, 30, 33
Murcia, 141, 142, 143, 174

Al-Mu'tamid, 29
muwashah, 34

N

Naples, 46, 50, 88, 114, 119, 120, 156
Narváez, Luís, 103, 163
Naṣrids, of Granada, 30
Natalia, St, 20, 21
nauba (nuba), 30, 31, 176, 177, 249
Navarre, 135
Navarro, Juan (of Cádiz), 220
Navarro, Juan (of Seville), 220 (note)
Navas, Juan de, 103
Nebra, José, 110, 112, 113, 123
Negro dances, 106, 229, 233, 234
neums, 12, 13, 14, 17, 38
Nicaragua, 235
Nicolau, Antonio, 205
Nights in the Gardens of Spain (Falla), see *Noches*
Nin, J., 210
Nin Culmell, J., 210
Noches en los jardines de España (Falla), 190, 193, 194, 195, 199

O

Ocón, Eduardo, 151, 168, 191
Olmeda, Federico, 133, 152, 153
opera, 97, 99, 100, 101, 102, 104, 109f., 119, 131
orchestras, 216
Orfeo Catalá, 205, 213, 216
organ, 36, 53, 61, 67, 86, 87, 145
Orozco, Rafael, 218
Ortega, Aniceto, 225, 226
Ortíz, Diego, 91
Osius, bishop, 5
Otaño, Pe. F. N., 155, 184, 205
Oudrid, Cristóbal, 132, 137
'Oven', i.e. Owen, John, 106

P

Pablo, Luis de, 213, 214, 215
Pacian, bishop, 5
Pahissa, J., 189, 193, 195, 207
Palacio Valdés, A., 199
Palau, Manuel, 146
La Paloma, 130
Palomares, P., 107, 114
palos (sticks), 5, 58
Panama, 235
paño, 142, 193
pandore, 37

Paraguay, 233
parrandas, 142, 143
Patiño, Carlos, 99, 108
Paz, Octavio, 194
Paz J. C., 241
Pedrell, Felipe, 59, 61, 65, 107, 132, 133, 150, 159, 184, 185, 197, 198, 205
Peñalosa, Francisco de, 54, 55
Pereira, João Leite, 89
Pergolesi, 120
Philip II, 67, 82, 85, 86, 87; III, 82; IV, 108; V, 109, 111
Phocaeans, 4
Phoenicians, 3, 4
Pisador, Diego, 63
Pittaluga, Gustavo, 202
plantos, 12, 45
Plato, 8
playhouses, 95
Poblet, 87
polo, 127, 169, 184
polyphony, 48, 49, 52, 67, 77
Ponce, Manuel, 236
Pontac, Diego, 106
Ponte, L. de, 120
Portugal, 32, 34, 52, 114, 150, 203
Price, Henry, 232
Prudentius, 6, 19, 20, 22
psalms, 1, 7, 11, 22, 54, 59
psaltery, 21, 37, 39
Pujol, David, 89
Pujol, Emilio, 129, 217
Pujol, F., 150
Pujol, Juan, 89
Pythagoras, 8, 26, 34, 49, 51, 221

Q
Qalam, 25
Al-Qazwinī, 29
Que li darém?, 45, 150
Querol, Leopoldo, 218
Quintero, Alvarez, 200, 207
Quintilian, 5, 6, 8

R
rabab, 35, 37
Ramos de Pareja, B., 48, 49, 90, 124
Ravel, 183, 189, 205
rebec, 34, 37
Reinhardt, Max, 198
Retablo de las maravillas (Cervantes), 97
Retablo de Maese Pedro (Falla), 39, 196
Revueltas, Silvestre, 236
Riaño, J. F , 17

Ribera, Julian, 28, 31, 35, 148, 149, 161, 177
Ridruejo, D., 214
Rodrigo, Joaquín, 125, 208f.
Rodrigues, Johan, 45
Rodriguez de Hita, A., 126
Rolón, José, 236
Roman rite, 14
romances, 39, 56, 60, 61, 64, 226
Romans, 5
romerías, 33, 40
Romero, D. and J., 106
Ronda, 171
Rosmarin (or Romero), M., 167, 168
Rossini, 128, 130, 223
Rousseau, J.-J., 128, 130
ruedas, 152
ibn Rushd, see Averroes

S
Saco del Valle, A., 216
saeta, 172
Sahagún, 220
sainete, 105, 126, 135
Saint-Saens, 135, 203
Sainza de la Maza, R., 202, 217
Salamanca, 48, 50, 90, 160, 161
Salazar, Adolfo, 212
Salcedo, Martín de, 67
Salinas, Francisco, 35, 90
Samper, Baltasar, 210
Sanches, Francisco, 198
San Juan de la Cruz, 208
Santander, 155f.
Santiago de Compostela, 1, 23, 38, 41, 44, 49, 158
Santillana, Marqués de, 51, 57
Saragossa, 29, 87
Sarasate, 134, 135
sardana, 151, 206
Scarlatti, Alessandro, 109; Doménico, 89, 113f., 125, 185, 187, 188, 193
Schumann, 184, 187, 188
Sebastian, St, 175, 176
Segovia, Andrés, 217
seguidillas ('seguiriyas' etc), 107, 122, 123, 126, 144, 170, 182
Seven Spanish Songs (Falla), 143, 169, 182, 191
Seville, 10, 35, 41, 48, 68, 69, 74, 133, 168, 178, 199, 201
Shahrūd, 37
Al-Shaqandī, 29, 34
shells, 3

Index

Shilb, see Silves
Sibila, Canto de la, 92, 93, 94
Siete Partidas, 38, 119
Siete Canciones (Falla), see *Seven Spanish Songs*
Sigüenza, Fr. José de, 85, 86, 219
Silius Italicus, 5
Silos, 14
Silves, 29
ibn Sina, see Avicenna
Sociedad de Conciertos, 132, 136
soleá, 169
Soler, Antonio, 89, 90, 123, 124, 125
Sombrero de los tres Picos, see *Three-Cornered Hat*
Song of Songs, 6, 34
Sor, Fernando, 120, 128, 129
Soriano, Gonzalo, 218
Sorozábal, Pablo, 139
Spinoza, 2
Strabo, 3, 5
Sueves, 7
Sumaya, Manuel, 223
Suriñach, Carlos, 139

T

tabl (Sp. atabal), 30, 31
tarantas, 182
Tárrega, Francisco, 129
Tarragó, Renata, 217
Tartessos, 3
Three-Cornered Hat (Falla), 139, 191, 193
tiento, 62, 88, 124
Tirso, St, 21
toccata, 62
Toldrá, Eduardo, 139, 207, 216
Toledo, 7, 10, 19, 20, 21, 29, 38
tonadas, 151
tonadillas, 122, 123, 125, 126, 187, 188
Torner, Eduardo Martínez, 42, 150, 162
Torre, Francisco de la, 57, 58
Torroba, Federico Moreno, 139
trumpets, 4, 11, 41
Turina, Joaquín, 125, 199

U

'ud, 25, 34, 36
Uruguay, 226, 229
Usandizaga, J. M., 204

V

Vado, Juan del, 106

Valencia, 29, 32, 90, 120, 146
Valle Riestra, M., 241
Vásquez, Juan, 59, 60, 64
Vega, Carlos, 223, 228
Vega, Lope de, 97, 99
Venegas, Luis, 64, 66, 88
Venezuela, 229f.
Ventura, Pep, 151
La Verbena de la Paloma (Bretón), 135, 136, 138, 181, 183, 200, 225
Verdaguer, Jacinto, 192, 217
Viardot, Pauline, 128
Vicente de Córdoba, 15
Vicente, Gil, 33, 35, 94, 95, 103, 210
Vich, 38, 87, 92
Vich, Luis, 94
Victoria, Tomás Luis de, 47, 74, 77f., 117, 198
vidalitas, 229
vihuela, 39, 61, 62, 64, 252–3
Vila, P. A., 87, 88
Vila-Lobos, H., 241
villancicos, 56, 59, 60, 64
villanescas, 73
Viñes, Ricardo, 218
Vincent, St, 19, 94
Virgin Mary, 6, 18, 19, 40, 144, 172
virolai, 46, 49
Visigoths, 7, 10, 11
Vives, Amadeo, 139, 188, 205

W

Wagner, 180, 181, 189
Wellesz, Egon, 17

X

Ximénez, N., 122

Y

Yepes, Narciso, 217
Yradier, see Iradier

Z

Zabaleta, Nicanor, 218
zambra, 32
Zarzuela (theatre), 102, 103
zarzuela, 2, 102, 104, 110, 122, 127, 129, 137, 139
zéjel (zajal), 30, 33, 253
Ziryāb, 25, 178
zortzico, 152, 153, 155

WORLD P

Trend and Transformation